Comparative Constitutional Law Documents

COMPARATIVE CONSTITUTIONAL LAW DOCUMENTS

AALT WILLEM HERINGA AND SASCHA HARDT (EDS.)

Published, sold and distributed by Eleven International Publishing
P.O. Box 85576
2508 CG The Hague
The Netherlands
Tel.: +31 70 33 070 33
Fax: +31 70 33 070 30
e-mail: sales@elevenpub.nl
www.elevenpub.com

Sold and distributed in USA and Canada
Independent Publishers Group
814 N. Franklin Street
Chicago, IL 60610
USA
Order Placement: (800) 888-4741
Fax: (312) 337-5985
orders@ipgbook.com
www.ipgbook.com

Eleven International Publishing is an imprint of Boom uitgevers Den Haag.

ISBN 978-94-6236-930-6

© 2019 The authors | Eleven International Publishing

This publication is protected by international copyright law.
All rights reserved. No part of this publication may be reproduced, stored in a retrieval system, or transmitted in any form or by any means, electronic, mechanical, photocopying, recording or otherwise, without the prior permission of the publisher.

Printed in the Netherlands

Table of Contents

Preface — vii

United States — 1
1. Constitution of the United States of America of 17 September 1787 [including Amendments] — 1

France — 17
2. Declaration of the Rights of Man and the Citizen [Déclaration des Droits de l'Homme et du Citoyen] of 26 August 1789[section] — 17
3. Preamble to the Constitution of the IV. Republic of 27 October 1946 — 20
4. Constitution of the V. Republic of 4 October 1958 — 22
5. Electoral Code [Code Electoral] — 50

Germany — 55
6. Basic Law for the Federal Republic of Germany of 23 May 1949 — 57
7. Federal Elections Act [Bundeswahlgesetz] — 107

The Netherlands — 123
8. Charter for the Kingdom of the Netherlands [Statuut voor het Koninkrijk der Nederlanden] of 28 October 1954 — 125
9. Constitution for the Kingdom of the Netherlands [Grondwet voor het Koninkrijk der Nederlanden] of 24 August 1815 — 137
10. Elections Act [Kieswet] — 160

United Kingdom — 165
11. Bill of Rights 1689 — 167
12. Parliaments Act 1911/1949
13. Fixed-Term Parliaments Act 2011 — 173
14. Human Rights Act 1998
15. Constitutional Reform Act 2005 — 184
16. United Kingdom: Constitutional Reform and Governance Act 2010 — 187
17. Scotland Act 1998 — 195
18. Northern Ireland Act 1998 — 203
19. Government of Wales Act 2006 — 217
20. European Union (Withdrawal) Act 2018 — 235

TABLE OF CONTENTS

European Union
21	Treaty on European Union	263
22	Treaty on the Functioning of the European Union	287
23	Protocols to the EU Treaties	344
24	Charter of Fundamental Rights of the European Union	353

European Human Rights — **365**
25	European Convention for the Protection of Human Rights and Fundamental Freedoms	367
26	Protocols to the ECHR	371

Preface

The present book contains a selection of constitutional and fundamental legislative provisions from the Unites States, France, Germany, the Netherlands and the United Kingdom. Furthermore, it provides the full text of the European Convention on Human Rights, the Treaty on European Union and the Charter of Fundamental Rights of the European Union, as well as a selection of articles of the Treaty on the Functioning of the European Union.

This compilation helps students of comparative constitutional law to gain easy access to the relevant (constitutional) standards. It functions as the ideal companion to the textbook *Constitutions Compared* by Aalt Willem Heringa, 5th edition, Intersentia, 2019.

Evidently the American and British instruments, as well as the treaties, are reproduced in the original, authentic, English language, whereas most of the French, German and Dutch sources are rendered as new English translations under critical editorship. Only the French Declaration of the Rights of Man and the Citizen, and the Preamble to the Constitution of the Fourth Republic are reproduced in the much-quoted and widely accepted translation provided by the *Conseil Constitutionnel*. The translations remain true to content, style and syntax of the original. For easy reference, key legal terms and proper names are added in the original language as in-text citations between square brackets. Enactment formulas are always omitted, preambles are retained unless indicated otherwise.

Many of the documents herein contained may also be accessed in the 4 volumes of the *Maastricht Collection*, 6th edition, edited by Sascha Hardt & Nicole Kornet, Europa Law Publishing, 2019, ISBN 9789089522115 (specifically volume I: International/European Law, ISBN 9789089522153 and volume II: Comparative Public Law, ISBN 9789089522160).

Maastricht, June 2019.

The Editors
Sascha Hardt is Assistant Professor of Comparative Constitutional Law at Maastricht University.
Aalt Willem Heringa is Professor of Comparative Constitutional and Administrative Law at Maastricht University and Director of the Montesquieu Institute Maastricht.

United States

1   Constitution of the United States of America of 17 September 1787 [including Amendments]

Preamble
We the People of the United States, in Order to form a more perfect Union, establish Justice, insure domestic Tranquility, provide for the common defence, promote the general Welfare, and secure the Blessings of Liberty to ourselves and our Posterity, do ordain and establish this Constitution for the United States of America.

Article I.
Section 1. All legislative Powers herein granted shall be vested in a Congress of the United States, which shall consist of a Senate and House of Representatives.
Section 2. The House of Representatives shall be composed of Members chosen every second Year by the People of the several States, and the Electors in each State shall have the Qualifications requisite for Electors of the most numerous Branch of the State Legislature.
No Person shall be a Representative who shall not have attained to the Age of twenty five Years, and been seven Years a Citizen of the United States, and who shall not, when elected, be an Inhabitant of that State in which he shall be chosen.
Representatives and direct Taxes shall be apportioned among the several States which may be included within this Union, according to their respective Numbers, which shall be determined by adding to the whole Number of free Persons, including those bound to Service for a Term of Years, and excluding Indians not taxed, three fifths of all other Persons. The actual Enumeration shall be made within three Years after the first Meeting of the Congress of the United States, and within every subsequent Term of ten Years, in such Manner as they shall by Law direct. The Number of Representatives shall not exceed one for every thirty Thousand, but each State shall have at Least one Representative; and until such enumeration shall be made, the State of New Hampshire shall be entitled to chuse three, Massachusetts eight, Rhode-Island and Providence Plantations one, Connecticut five, New-York six, New Jersey four, Pennsylvania eight, Delaware one, Maryland six, Virginia ten, North Carolina five, South Carolina five, and Georgia three.
When vacancies happen in the Representation from any State, the Executive Authority thereof shall issue Writs of Election to fill such Vacancies.
The House of Representatives shall chuse their Speaker and other Officers; and shall have the sole Power of Impeachment.

Section 3. The Senate of the United States shall be composed of two Senators from each State, chosen by the Legislature thereof for six Years; and each Senator shall have one Vote.

Immediately after they shall be assembled in Consequence of the first Election, they shall be divided as equally as may be into three Classes. The Seats of the Senators of the first Class shall be vacated at the Expiration of the second Year, of the second Class at the Expiration of the fourth Year, and of the third Class at the Expiration of the sixth Year, so that one third may be chosen every second Year; and if Vacancies happen by Resignation, or otherwise, during the Recess of the Legislature of any State, the Executive thereof may make temporary Appointments until the next Meeting of the Legislature, which shall then fill such Vacancies.

No Person shall be a Senator who shall not have attained to the Age of thirty Years, and been nine Years a Citizen of the United States, and who shall not, when elected, be an Inhabitant of that State for which he shall be chosen.

The Vice President of the United States shall be President of the Senate, but shall have no Vote, unless they be equally divided.

The Senate shall chuse their other Officers, and also a President pro tempore, in the Absence of the Vice President, or when he shall exercise the Office of President of the United States.

The Senate shall have the sole Power to try all Impeachments. When sitting for that Purpose, they shall be on Oath or Affirmation. When the President of the United States is tried, the Chief Justice shall preside: And no Person shall be convicted without the Concurrence of two thirds of the Members present.

Judgment in Cases of Impeachment shall not extend further than to removal from Office, and disqualification to hold and enjoy any Office of honor, Trust or Profit under the United States: but the Party convicted shall nevertheless be liable and subject to Indictment, Trial, Judgment and Punishment, according to Law.

Section 4. The Times, Places and Manner of holding Elections for Senators and Representatives, shall be prescribed in each State by the Legislature thereof; but the Congress may at any time by Law make or alter such Regulations, except as to the Places of chusing Senators.

The Congress shall assemble at least once in every Year, and such Meeting shall be on the first Monday in December, unless they shall by Law appoint a different Day.

Section 5. Each House shall be the Judge of the Elections, Returns and Qualifications of its own Members, and a Majority of each shall constitute a Quorum to do Business; but a smaller Number may adjourn from day to day, and may be authorized to compel the Attendance of absent Members, in such Manner, and under such Penalties as each House may provide.

Each House may determine the Rules of its Proceedings, punish its Members for disorderly Behaviour, and, with the Concurrence of two thirds, expel a Member.

Each House shall keep a Journal of its Proceedings, and from time to time publish the same, excepting such Parts as may in their Judgment require Secrecy; and the Yeas and Nays of the Members of either House on any question shall, at the Desire of one fifth of those Present, be entered on the Journal.

Neither House, during the Session of Congress, shall, without the Consent of the other, adjourn for more than three days, nor to any other Place than that in which the two Houses shall be sitting.

Section 6. The Senators and Representatives shall receive a Compensation for their Services, to be ascertained by Law, and paid out of the Treasury of the United States. They shall in all Cases, except Treason, Felony and Breach of the Peace, be privileged from Arrest during their Attendance at the Session of their respective Houses, and in going to and returning from the same; and for any Speech or Debate in either House, they shall not be questioned in any other Place.

No Senator or Representative shall, during the Time for which he was elected, be appointed to any civil Office under the Authority of the United States, which shall have been created, or the Emoluments whereof shall have been encreased during such time; and no Person holding any Office under the United States, shall be a Member of either House during his Continuance in Office.

Section 7. All Bills for raising Revenue shall originate in the House of Representatives; but the Senate may propose or concur with Amendments as on other Bills.

Every Bill which shall have passed the House of Representatives and the Senate, shall, before it become a Law, be presented to the President of the United States: If he approve he shall sign it, but if not he shall return it, with his Objections to that House in which it shall have originated, who shall enter the Objections at large on their Journal, and proceed to reconsider it. If after such Reconsideration two thirds of that House shall agree to pass the Bill, it shall be sent, together with the Objections, to the other House, by which it shall likewise be reconsidered, and if approved by two thirds of that House, it shall become a Law. But in all such Cases the Votes of both Houses shall be determined by yeas and Nays, and the Names of the Persons voting for and against the Bill shall be entered on the Journal of each House respectively. If any Bill shall not be returned by the President within ten Days (Sundays excepted) after it shall have been presented to him, the Same shall be a Law, in like Manner as if he had signed it, unless the Congress by their Adjournment prevent its Return, in which Case it shall not be a Law.

Every Order, Resolution, or Vote to which the Concurrence of the Senate and House of Representatives may be necessary (except on a question of Adjournment) shall be presented to the President of the United States; and before the Same shall take Effect, shall be approved by him, or being disapproved by him, shall be repassed by two thirds of the Senate and House of Representatives, according to the Rules and Limitations prescribed in the Case of a Bill.

Section 8. The Congress shall have Power To lay and collect Taxes, Duties, Imposts and Excises, to pay the Debts and provide for the common Defence and general Welfare of the United States; but all Duties, Imposts and Excises shall be uniform throughout the United States;

To borrow Money on the credit of the United States;

To regulate Commerce with foreign Nations, and among the several States, and with the Indian Tribes;

To establish an uniform Rule of Naturalization, and uniform Laws on the subject of Bankruptcies throughout the United States;

To coin Money, regulate the Value thereof, and of foreign Coin, and fix the Standard of Weights and Measures;

To provide for the Punishment of counterfeiting the Securities and current Coin of the United States;

To establish Post Offices and post Roads;

To promote the Progress of Science and useful Arts, by securing for limited Times to Authors and Inventors the exclusive Right to their respective Writings and Discoveries;

To constitute Tribunals inferior to the supreme Court;

To define and punish Piracies and Felonies committed on the high Seas, and Offences against the Law of Nations;

To declare War, grant Letters of Marque and Reprisal, and make Rules concerning Captures on Land and Water;

To raise and support Armies, but no Appropriation of Money to that Use shall be for a longer Term than two Years;

To provide and maintain a Navy;

To make Rules for the Government and Regulation of the land and naval Forces;

To provide for calling forth the Militia to execute the Laws of the Union, suppress Insurrections and repel Invasions;

To provide for organizing, arming, and disciplining, the Militia, and for governing such Part of them as may be employed in the Service of the United States, reserving to the States respectively, the Appointment of the Officers, and the Authority of training the Militia according to the discipline prescribed by Congress;

To exercise exclusive Legislation in all Cases whatsoever, over such District (not exceeding ten Miles square) as may, by Cession of particular States, and the Acceptance of Congress, become the Seat of the Government of the United States, and to exercise like Authority over all Places purchased by the Consent of the Legislature of the State in which the Same shall be, for the Erection of Forts, Magazines, Arsenals, dock-Yards, and other needful Buildings;–And

To make all Laws which shall be necessary and proper for carrying into Execution the foregoing Powers, and all other Powers vested by this Constitution in the Government of the United States, or in any Department or Officer thereof.

Section 9. The Migration or Importation of such Persons as any of the States now existing shall think proper to admit, shall not be prohibited by the Congress prior to the Year one thousand eight hundred and eight, but a Tax or duty may be imposed on such Importation, not exceeding ten dollars for each Person.

The Privilege of the Writ of Habeas Corpus shall not be suspended, unless when in Cases of Rebellion or Invasion the public Safety may require it.

No Bill of Attainder or ex post facto Law shall be passed.

No Capitation, or other direct, Tax shall be laid, unless in Proportion to the Census or enumeration herein before directed to be taken.

No Tax or Duty shall be laid on Articles exported from any State.

No Preference shall be given by any Regulation of Commerce or Revenue to the Ports of one State over those of another; nor shall Vessels bound to, or from, one State, be obliged to enter, clear, or pay Duties in another.

No Money shall be drawn from the Treasury, but in Consequence of Appropriations made by Law; and a regular Statement and Account of the Receipts and Expenditures of all public Money shall be published from time to time.

No Title of Nobility shall be granted by the United States: And no Person holding any Office of Profit or Trust under them, shall, without the Consent of the Congress, accept of any present, Emolument, Office, or Title, of any kind whatever, from any King, Prince, or foreign State.

Section 10. No State shall enter into any Treaty, Alliance, or Confederation; grant Letters of Marque and Reprisal; coin Money; emit Bills of Credit; make any Thing but gold and silver Coin a Tender in Payment of Debts; pass any Bill of Attainder, ex post facto Law, or Law impairing the Obligation of Contracts, or grant any Title of Nobility.

No State shall, without the Consent of the Congress, lay any Imposts or Duties on Imports or Exports, except what may be absolutely necessary for executing it's inspection Laws: and the net Produce of all Duties and Imposts, laid by any State on Imports or Exports, shall be for the Use of the Treasury of the United States; and all such Laws shall be subject to the Revision and Controul of the Congress.

No State shall, without the Consent of Congress, lay any Duty of Tonnage, keep Troops, or Ships of War in time of Peace, enter into any Agreement or Compact with another State, or with a foreign Power, or engage in War, unless actually invaded, or in such imminent Danger as will not admit of delay.

Article II.

Section 1. The executive Power shall be vested in a President of the United States of America. He shall hold his Office during the Term of four Years, and, together with the Vice President, chosen for the same Term, be elected, as follows:

Each State shall appoint, in such Manner as the Legislature thereof may direct, a Number of Electors, equal to the whole Number of Senators and Representatives to which the

State may be entitled in the Congress: but no Senator or Representative, or Person holding an Office of Trust or Profit under the United States, shall be appointed an Elector.

The Electors shall meet in their respective States, and vote by Ballot for two Persons, of whom one at least shall not be an Inhabitant of the same State with themselves. And they shall make a List of all the Persons voted for, and of the Number of Votes for each; which List they shall sign and certify, and transmit sealed to the Seat of the Government of the United States, directed to the President of the Senate. The President of the Senate shall, in the Presence of the Senate and House of Representatives, open all the Certificates, and the Votes shall then be counted. The Person having the greatest Number of Votes shall be the President, if such Number be a Majority of the whole Number of Electors appointed; and if there be more than one who have such Majority, and have an equal Number of Votes, then the House of Representatives shall immediately chuse by Ballot one of them for President; and if no Person have a Majority, then from the five highest on the List the said House shall in like Manner chuse the President. But in chusing the President, the Votes shall be taken by States, the Representation from each State having one Vote; A quorum for this purpose shall consist of a Member or Members from two thirds of the States, and a Majority of all the States shall be necessary to a Choice. In every Case, after the Choice of the President, the Person having the greatest Number of Votes of the Electors shall be the Vice President. But if there should remain two or more who have equal Votes, the Senate shall chuse from them by Ballot the Vice President.

The Congress may determine the Time of chusing the Electors, and the Day on which they shall give their Votes; which Day shall be the same throughout the United States.

No Person except a natural born Citizen, or a Citizen of the United States, at the time of the Adoption of this Constitution, shall be eligible to the Office of President; neither shall any Person be eligible to that Office who shall not have attained to the Age of thirty five Years, and been fourteen Years a Resident within the United States.

In Case of the Removal of the President from Office, or of his Death, Resignation, or Inability to discharge the Powers and Duties of the said Office, the Same shall devolve on the Vice President, and the Congress may by Law provide for the Case of Removal, Death, Resignation or Inability, both of the President and Vice President, declaring what Officer shall then act as President, and such Officer shall act accordingly, until the Disability be removed, or a President shall be elected.

The President shall, at stated Times, receive for his Services, a Compensation, which shall neither be increased nor diminished during the Period for which he shall have been elected, and he shall not receive within that Period any other Emolument from the United States, or any of them.

Before he enter on the Execution of his Office, he shall take the following Oath or Affirmation:–"I do solemnly swear (or affirm) that I will faithfully execute the Office of President of the United States, and will to the best of my Ability, preserve, protect and defend the Constitution of the United States."

Section 2. The President shall be Commander in Chief of the Army and Navy of the United States, and of the Militia of the several States, when called into the actual Service of the United States; he may require the Opinion, in writing, of the principal Officer in each of the executive Departments, upon any Subject relating to the Duties of their respective Offices, and he shall have Power to grant Reprieves and Pardons for Offences against the United States, except in Cases of Impeachment.

He shall have Power, by and with the Advice and Consent of the Senate, to make Treaties, provided two thirds of the Senators present concur; and he shall nominate, and by and with the Advice and Consent of the Senate, shall appoint Ambassadors, other public Ministers and Consuls, Judges of the supreme Court, and all other Officers of the United States, whose Appointments are not herein otherwise provided for, and which shall be established by Law: but the Congress may by Law vest the Appointment of such inferior Officers, as they think proper, in the President alone, in the Courts of Law, or in the Heads of Departments.

The President shall have Power to fill up all Vacancies that may happen during the Recess of the Senate, by granting Commissions which shall expire at the End of their next Session.

Section 3. He shall from time to time give to the Congress Information of the State of the Union, and recommend to their Consideration such Measures as he shall judge necessary and expedient; he may, on extraordinary Occasions, convene both Houses, or either of them, and in Case of Disagreement between them, with Respect to the Time of Adjournment, he may adjourn them to such Time as he shall think proper; he shall receive Ambassadors and other public Ministers; he shall take Care that the Laws be faithfully executed, and shall Commission all the Officers of the United States.

Section 4. The President, Vice President and all civil Officers of the United States, shall be removed from Office on Impeachment for, and Conviction of, Treason, Bribery, or other high Crimes and Misdemeanors.

Article III.

Section 1. The judicial Power of the United States shall be vested in one supreme Court, and in such inferior Courts as the Congress may from time to time ordain and establish. The Judges, both of the supreme and inferior Courts, shall hold their Offices during good Behaviour, and shall, at stated Times, receive for their Services a Compensation, which shall not be diminished during their Continuance in Office.

Section 2. The judicial Power shall extend to all Cases, in Law and Equity, arising under this Constitution, the Laws of the United States, and Treaties made, or which shall be made, under their Authority;–to all Cases affecting Ambassadors, other public Ministers and Consuls;–to all Cases of admiralty and maritime Jurisdiction;–to Controversies to which the United States shall be a Party;–to Controversies between two or more States;–between a State and Citizens of another State;–between Citizens of different States;–between Citizens of the same State claiming Lands under Grants of different States, and between a State, or the Citizens thereof, and foreign States, Citizens or Subjects.

In all Cases affecting Ambassadors, other public Ministers and Consuls, and those in which a State shall be Party, the supreme Court shall have original Jurisdiction. In all the other Cases before mentioned, the supreme Court shall have appellate Jurisdiction, both as to Law and Fact, with such Exceptions, and under such Regulations as the Congress shall make.

The Trial of all Crimes, except in Cases of Impeachment, shall be by Jury; and such Trial shall be held in the State where the said Crimes shall have been committed; but when not committed within any State, the Trial shall be at such Place or Places as the Congress may by Law have directed.

Section 3. Treason against the United States, shall consist only in levying War against them, or in adhering to their Enemies, giving them Aid and Comfort. No Person shall be convicted of Treason unless on the Testimony of two Witnesses to the same overt Act, or on Confession in open Court.

The Congress shall have Power to declare the Punishment of Treason, but no Attainder of Treason shall work Corruption of Blood, or Forfeiture except during the Life of the Person attainted.

Article IV.
Section 1. Full Faith and Credit shall be given in each State to the public Acts, Records, and judicial Proceedings of every other State. And the Congress may by general Laws prescribe the Manner in which such Acts, Records and Proceedings shall be proved, and the Effect thereof.

Section 2. The Citizens of each State shall be entitled to all Privileges and Immunities of Citizens in the several States.

A Person charged in any State with Treason, Felony, or other Crime, who shall flee from Justice, and be found in another State, shall on Demand of the executive Authority of the State from which he fled, be delivered up, to be removed to the State having Jurisdiction of the Crime.

No Person held to Service or Labour in one State, under the Laws thereof, escaping into another, shall, in Consequence of any Law or Regulation therein, be discharged from such Service or Labour, but shall be delivered up on Claim of the Party to whom such Service or Labour may be due.

Section 3. New States may be admitted by the Congress into this Union; but no new State shall be formed or erected within the Jurisdiction of any other State; nor any State be formed by the Junction of two or more States, or Parts of States, without the Consent of the Legislatures of the States concerned as well as of the Congress.

The Congress shall have Power to dispose of and make all needful Rules and Regulations respecting the Territory or other Property belonging to the United States; and nothing in this Constitution shall be so construed as to Prejudice any Claims of the United States, or of any particular State.

Section 4. The United States shall guarantee to every State in this Union a Republican Form of Government, and shall protect each of them against Invasion; and on Application of the Legislature, or of the Executive (when the Legislature cannot be convened), against domestic Violence.

Article V.
The Congress, whenever two thirds of both Houses shall deem it necessary, shall propose Amendments to this Constitution, or, on the Application of the Legislatures of two thirds of the several States, shall call a Convention for proposing Amendments, which, in either Case, shall be valid to all Intents and Purposes, as Part of this Constitution, when ratified by the Legislatures of three fourths of the several States, or by Conventions in three fourths thereof, as the one or the other Mode of Ratification may be proposed by the Congress; Provided that no Amendment which may be made prior to the Year One thousand eight hundred and eight shall in any Manner affect the first and fourth Clauses in the Ninth Section of the first Article; and that no State, without its Consent, shall be deprived of its equal Suffrage in the Senate.

Article VI.
All Debts contracted and Engagements entered into, before the Adoption of this Constitution, shall be as valid against the United States under this Constitution, as under the Confederation.
This Constitution, and the Laws of the United States which shall be made in Pursuance thereof; and all Treaties made, or which shall be made, under the Authority of the United States, shall be the supreme Law of the Land; and the Judges in every State shall be bound thereby, any Thing in the Constitution or Laws of any State to the Contrary notwithstanding.
The Senators and Representatives before mentioned, and the Members of the several State Legislatures, and all executive and judicial Officers, both of the United States and of the several States, shall be bound by Oath or Affirmation, to support this Constitution; but no religious Test shall ever be required as a Qualification to any Office or public Trust under the United States.

Article VII.
The Ratification of the Conventions of nine States, shall be sufficient for the Establishment of this Constitution between the States so ratifying the Same.

Done in Convention by the Unanimous Consent of the States present the Seventeenth Day of September in the Year of our Lord one thousand seven hundred and Eighty seven and of the Independence of the United States of America the Twelfth. In Witness whereof We have hereunto subscribed our Names

[*The names and signatures are omitted.*]

Amendments to the US Constitution
[*The preamble to the Bill of Rights is omitted.*]

Amendment I. Congress shall make no law respecting an establishment of religion, or prohibiting the free exercise thereof; or abridging the freedom of speech, or of the press; or the right of the people peaceably to assemble, and to petition the Government for a redress of grievances.

Amendment II. A well regulated Militia, being necessary to the security of a free State, the right of the people to keep and bear Arms, shall not be infringed.

Amendment III. No Soldier shall, in time of peace be quartered in any house, without the consent of the Owner, nor in time of war, but in a manner to be prescribed by law.

Amendment IV. The right of the people to be secure in their persons, houses, papers, and effects, against unreasonable searches and seizures, shall not be violated, and no Warrants shall issue, but upon probable cause, supported by Oath or affirmation, and particularly describing the place to be searched, and the persons or things to be seized.

Amendment V. No person shall be held to answer for a capital, or otherwise infamous crime, unless on a presentment or indictment of a Grand Jury, except in cases arising in the land or naval forces, or in the Militia, when in actual service in time of War or public danger; nor shall any person be subject for the same offence to be twice put in jeopardy of life or limb; nor shall be compelled in any criminal case to be a witness against himself, nor be deprived of life, liberty, or property, without due process of law; nor shall private property be taken for public use, without just compensation.

Amendment VI. In all criminal prosecutions, the accused shall enjoy the right to a speedy and public trial, by an impartial jury of the State and district wherein the crime shall have been committed, which district shall have been previously ascertained by law, and to be informed of the nature and cause of the accusation; to be confronted with the witnesses against him; to have compulsory process for obtaining witnesses in his favor, and to have the Assistance of Counsel for his defence.

Amendment VII. In Suits at common law, where the value in controversy shall exceed twenty dollars, the right of trial by jury shall be preserved, and no fact tried by a jury, shall be otherwise re-examined in any Court of the United States, than according to the rules of the common law.

Amendment VIII. Excessive bail shall not be required, nor excessive fines imposed, nor cruel and unusual punishments inflicted.

Amendment IX. The enumeration in the Constitution, of certain rights, shall not be construed to deny or disparage others retained by the people.

Amendment X. The powers not delegated to the United States by the Constitution, nor prohibited by it to the States, are reserved to the States respectively, or to the people.

Amendment XI. The Judicial power of the United States shall not be construed to extend to any suit in law or equity, commenced or prosecuted against one of the United States by Citizens of another State, or by Citizens or Subjects of any Foreign State.

Amendment XII. The Electors shall meet in their respective states and vote by ballot for President and Vice-President, one of whom, at least, shall not be an inhabitant of the same state with themselves; they shall name in their ballots the person voted for as President, and in distinct ballots the person voted for as Vice-President, and they shall make distinct lists of all persons voted for as President, and of all persons voted for as Vice-President, and of the number of votes for each, which lists they shall sign and certify, and transmit sealed to the seat of the government of the United States, directed to the President of the Senate; – the President of the Senate shall, in the presence of the Senate and House of Representatives, open all the certificates and the votes shall then be counted; – The person having the greatest number of votes for President, shall be the President, if such number be a majority of the whole number of Electors appointed; and if no person have such majority, then from the persons having the highest numbers not exceeding three on the list of those voted for as President, the House of Representatives shall choose immediately, by ballot, the President. But in choosing the President, the votes shall be taken by states, the representation from each state having one vote; a quorum for this purpose shall consist of a member or members from two-thirds of the states, and a majority of all the states shall be necessary to a choice. And if the House of Representatives shall not choose a President whenever the right of choice shall devolve upon them, before the fourth day of March next following, then the Vice-President shall act as President, as in case of the death or other constitutional disability of the President. The person having the greatest number of votes as Vice-President, shall be the Vice-President, if such number be a majority of the whole number of Electors appointed, and if no person have a majority, then from the two highest numbers on the list, the Senate shall choose the Vice-President; a quorum for the purpose shall consist of two-thirds of the whole number of Senators, and a majority of the whole number shall be necessary to a choice. But no person constitutionally ineligible to the office of President shall be eligible to that of Vice-President of the United States.

Amendment XIII. Section 1. Neither slavery nor involuntary servitude, except as a punishment for crime whereof the party shall have been duly convicted, shall exist within the United States, or any place subject to their jurisdiction.
Section 2. Congress shall have power to enforce this article by appropriate legislation.

Amendment XIV. Section 1. All persons born or naturalized in the United States, and subject to the jurisdiction thereof, are citizens of the United States and of the State wherein they reside. No State shall make or enforce any law which shall abridge the privileges or immunities of citizens of the United States; nor shall any State deprive any person of life, liberty, or property, without due process of law; nor deny to any person within its jurisdiction the equal protection of the laws.
Section 2. Representatives shall be apportioned among the several States according to their respective numbers, counting the whole number of persons in each State, excluding Indians not taxed. But when the right to vote at any election for the choice of electors for President and Vice-President of the United States, Representatives in Congress, the Executive and Judicial officers of a State, or the members of the Legislature thereof, is denied to any of the male inhabitants of such State, being twenty-one years of age, and citizens of the United States, or in any way abridged, except for participation in rebellion, or other crime, the basis of representation therein shall be reduced in the proportion which the number of such male citizens shall bear to the whole number of male citizens twenty-one years of age in such State.
Section 3. No person shall be a Senator or Representative in Congress, or elector of President and Vice-President, or hold any office, civil or military, under the United States, or under any State, who, having previously taken an oath, as a member of Congress, or as an officer of the United States, or as a member of any State legislature, or as an executive or judicial officer of any State, to support the Constitution of the United States, shall have engaged in insurrection or rebellion against the same, or given aid or comfort to the enemies thereof. But Congress may by a vote of two-thirds of each House, remove such disability.
Section 4. The validity of the public debt of the United States, authorized by law, including debts incurred for payment of pensions and bounties for services in suppressing insurrection or rebellion, shall not be questioned. But neither the United States nor any State shall assume or pay any debt or obligation incurred in aid of insurrection or rebel-

lion against the United States, or any claim for the loss or emancipation of any slave; but all such debts, obligations and claims shall be held illegal and void.

Section 5. The Congress shall have the power to enforce, by appropriate legislation, the provisions of this article.

Amendment XV. Section 1. The right of citizens of the United States to vote shall not be denied or abridged by the United States or by any State on account of race, color, or previous condition of servitude–

Section 2. The Congress shall have the power to enforce this article by appropriate legislation.

Amendment XVI. The Congress shall have power to lay and collect taxes on incomes, from whatever source derived, without apportionment among the several States, and without regard to any census or enumeration.

Amendment XVII. The Senate of the United States shall be composed of two Senators from each State, elected by the people thereof, for six years; and each Senator shall have one vote. The electors in each State shall have the qualifications requisite for electors of the most numerous branch of the State legislatures.

When vacancies happen in the representation of any State in the Senate, the executive authority of such State shall issue writs of election to fill such vacancies: Provided, That the legislature of any State may empower the executive thereof to make temporary appointments until the people fill the vacancies by election as the legislature may direct.

This amendment shall not be so construed as to affect the election or term of any Senator chosen before it becomes valid as part of the Constitution.

Amendment XVIII. Section 1. After one year from the ratification of this article the manufacture, sale, or transportation of intoxicating liquors within, the importation thereof into, or the exportation thereof from the United States and all territory subject to the jurisdiction thereof for beverage purposes is hereby prohibited.

Section 2. The Congress and the several States shall have concurrent power to enforce this article by appropriate legislation.

Section 3. This article shall be inoperative unless it shall have been ratified as an amendment to the Constitution by the legislatures of the several States, as provided in the Constitution, within seven years from the date of the submission hereof to the States by the Congress.

Amendment XIX. The right of citizens of the United States to vote shall not be denied or abridged by the United States or by any State on account of sex.

Congress shall have power to enforce this article by appropriate legislation.

Amendment XX. Section 1. The terms of the President and the Vice President shall end at noon on the 20th day of January, and the terms of Senators and Representatives at noon on the 3d day of January, of the years in which such terms would have ended if this article had not been ratified; and the terms of their successors shall then begin.

Section 2. The Congress shall assemble at least once in every year, and such meeting shall begin at noon on the 3d day of January, unless they shall by law appoint a different day.

Section 3. If, at the time fixed for the beginning of the term of the President, the President elect shall have died, the Vice President elect shall become President. If a President shall not have been chosen before the time fixed for the beginning of his term, or if the President elect shall have failed to qualify, then the Vice President elect shall act as President until a President shall have qualified; and the Congress may by law provide for the case wherein neither a President elect nor a Vice President shall have qualified, declaring who shall then act as President, or the manner in which one who is to act shall be selected, and such person shall act accordingly until a President or Vice President shall have qualified.

Section 4. The Congress may by law provide for the case of the death of any of the persons from whom the House of Representatives may choose a President whenever the right of choice shall have devolved upon them, and for the case of the death of any of the persons from whom the Senate may choose a Vice President whenever the right of choice shall have devolved upon them.

Section 5. Sections 1 and 2 shall take effect on the 15th day of October following the ratification of this article.

Section 6. This article shall be inoperative unless it shall have been ratified as an amendment to the Constitution by the legislatures of three-fourths of the several States within seven years from the date of its submission.

Amendment XXI. Section 1. The eighteenth article of amendment to the Constitution of the United States is hereby repealed.

Section 2. The transportation or importation into any State, Territory, or Possession of the United States for delivery or use therein of intoxicating liquors, in violation of the laws thereof, is hereby prohibited.

Section 3. This article shall be inoperative unless it shall have been ratified as an amendment to the Constitution by conventions in the several States, as provided in the Constitution, within seven years from the date of the submission hereof to the States by the Congress.

Amendment XXII. Section 1. No person shall be elected to the office of the President more than twice, and no person who has held the office of President, or acted as President, for more than two years of a term to which some other person was elected President shall be elected to the office of President more than once. But this Article shall not apply to any person holding the office of President when this Article was proposed by

Congress, and shall not prevent any person who may be holding the office of President, or acting as President, during the term within which this Article becomes operative from holding the office of President or acting as President during the remainder of such term.

Section 2. This article shall be inoperative unless it shall have been ratified as an amendment to the Constitution by the legislatures of three-fourths of the several States within seven years from the date of its submission to the States by the Congress.

Amendment XXIII. Section 1. The District constituting the seat of Government of the United States shall appoint in such manner as Congress may direct:

A number of electors of President and Vice President equal to the whole number of Senators and Representatives in Congress to which the District would be entitled if it were a State, but in no event more than the least populous State; they shall be in addition to those appointed by the States, but they shall be considered, for the purposes of the election of President and Vice President, to be electors appointed by a State; and they shall meet in the District and perform such duties as provided by the twelfth article of amendment.

Section 2. The Congress shall have power to enforce this article by appropriate legislation.

Amendment XXIV. Section 1. The right of citizens of the United States to vote in any primary or other election for President or Vice President, for electors for President or Vice President, or for Senator or Representative in Congress, shall not be denied or abridged by the United States or any State by reason of failure to pay poll tax or other tax.

Section 2. The Congress shall have power to enforce this article by appropriate legislation.

Amendment XXV. Section 1. In case of the removal of the President from office or of his death or resignation, the Vice President shall become President.

Section 2. Whenever there is a vacancy in the office of the Vice President, the President shall nominate a Vice President who shall take office upon confirmation by a majority vote of both Houses of Congress.

Section 3. Whenever the President transmits to the President pro tempore of the Senate and the Speaker of the House of Representatives his written declaration that he is unable to discharge the powers and duties of his office, and until he transmits to them a written declaration to the contrary, such powers and duties shall be discharged by the Vice President as Acting President.

Section 4. Whenever the Vice President and a majority of either the principal officers of the executive departments or of such other body as Congress may by law provide, transmit to the President pro tempore of the Senate and the Speaker of the House of Representatives their written declaration that the President is unable to discharge the powers and duties of his office, the Vice President shall immediately assume the powers and duties of the office as Acting President.

Thereafter, when the President transmits to the President pro tempore of the Senate and the Speaker of the House of Representatives his written declaration that no inability exists, he shall resume the powers and duties of his office unless the Vice President and a majority of either the principal officers of the executive department or of such other body as Congress may by law provide, transmit within four days to the President pro tempore of the Senate and the Speaker of the House of Representatives their written declaration that the President is unable to discharge the powers and duties of his office. Thereupon Congress shall decide the issue, assembling within forty-eight hours for that purpose if not in session. If the Congress, within twenty-one days after receipt of the latter written declaration, or, if Congress is not in session, within twenty-one days after Congress is required to assemble, determines by two-thirds vote of both Houses that the President is unable to discharge the powers and duties of his office, the Vice President shall continue to discharge the same as Acting President; otherwise, the President shall resume the powers and duties of his office.

Amendment XXVI. Section 1. The right of citizens of the United States, who are eighteen years of age or older, to vote shall not be denied or abridged by the United States or by any State on account of age.
Section 2. The Congress shall have power to enforce this article by appropriate legislation.

Amendment XXVII. No law, varying the compensation for the services of the Senators and Representatives, shall take effect, until an election of representatives shall have intervened

France

2 DECLARATION OF THE RIGHTS OF MAN AND THE CITIZEN [DÉCLARATION DES DROITS DE L'HOMME ET DU CITOYEN] OF 26 AUGUST 1789[1]

The Representatives of the French People, organized in a National Assembly, considering that ignorance, neglect or contempt of the rights of man are the only causes of the public misfortunes and of Governments' corruption, have decided to expose, in a solemn Declaration, the natural, inalienable and sacred rights of man, so that this Declaration, constantly present to all members of the social body, continually reminds them of their rights and their duties; so that the acts of the legislative power and those of the executive power may be compared at any time with the aim of every political institution, and that they would be more respected; so that the grievances of citizens, founded henceforth on simple and incontestable principles, result in the preservation of the Constitution and in the happiness of all.

Therefore the National Assembly recognizes and proclaims, in the presence and under the auspices of the Supreme Being, the following rights of man and of the citizen:

First Article. Men are born and remain free and equal in rights. Social distinctions may be based only on the common good.

Article II. The aim of every political association is the conservation of the natural and imprescriptible rights of man. These rights are liberty, property, safety and resistance to oppression.

Article III. The principle of all Sovereignty resides essentially in the Nation. No body, no individual may exercise any authority that does not expressly emanate from it.

Article IV. Liberty consists of being able to do everything that does not harm anybody else: thus the exercise of the natural rights of every man has no boundaries except those that ensure to other Members of the Society the enjoyment of those same rights. Those boundaries may be defined only by Law.

---

1 Translation: Conseil Constitutionnel.

Article V. The Law does not have the right to forbid any action except those that are harmful to society. Nothing which is not forbidden by the Law may be barred, and no-one may be forced to do what it does not dictate.

Article VI. The Law is the expression of the general will. All Citizens have the right to contribute personally, or through their Representatives, to its formation. It must be the same for everybody, whether it protects or punishes. All citizens, being equal before it, are equally eligible to all public dignities, positions and employments, according to their capacities, without any distinction other than those of their virtues and their talents.

Article VII. No man may be accused, arrested or detained except in the cases determined by Law and in the forms that it has prescribed. Those who solicit, send, execute or let execute arbitrary orders must be punished; however every Citizen summoned or arrested pursuant to the Law must obey immediately: he makes himself guilty with his resistance.

Article VIII. The Law must establish only strictly and evidently necessary penalties, and no-one may be punished except pursuant to a Law established and promulgated prior to the crime, and lawfully applied.

Article IX. Every man being presumed innocent until he has been declared guilty, if it is deemed indispensable to arrest him, any harshness which is not necessary for the securing of his person must be severely repressed by Law.

Article X. No-one may be disquieted because of his opinions, even religious, provided that their manifestation does not disturb the public order established by Law.

Article XI. The free communication of thoughts and of opinions is one of the most precious rights of Man; every Citizen may therefore speak, write, print freely, save answering for the abuse of this freedom in the cases determined by the Law.

Article XII. The guarantee of the rights of Man and the Citizen requires a public force: such force is therefore established for the advantage of all and not for the specific utility of those who have been entrusted with it.

Article XIII. For the maintenance of the public force, and for the expenses of the administration, a common contribution is indispensable. It must be equally distributed among the citizens according to their means.

Article XIV. All Citizens have the right to ascertain, personally or through their Representatives, the necessity of the public contribution, to freely consent to it, to monitor its use and to determine its proportion, base, collection and duration.

Article XV. Society has the right to call every public Agent to account for the administration.

Article XVI. Any society in which the guarantee of Rights is not ensured and the separation of Powers is not determined, has no Constitution.

Article XVII. Property being an inviolable and sacred right, no-one may be deprived of it, except when public necessity, lawfully assessed, evidently requires it, and under the condition of a just and prior indemnity.

3   PREAMBLE TO THE CONSTITUTION OF THE IV. REPUBLIC OF 27 OCTOBER 1946[2]

§1. In the morrow of the victory achieved by the free peoples over the regimes that had sought to enslave and degrade humanity, the people of France proclaim anew that each human being, without distinction of race, religion or creed, possesses sacred and inalienable rights. They solemnly reaffirm the rights and freedoms of man and the citizen enshrined in the Declaration of Rights of 1789 and the fundamental principles acknowledged in the laws of the Republic.

§2. They further proclaim, as being especially necessary to our times, the political, economic and social principles enumerated below:

§3. The law guarantees women equal rights to those of men in all spheres.

§4. Any man persecuted in virtue of his actions in favour of liberty may claim the right of asylum upon the territories of the Republic.

§5. Each person has the duty to work and the right to employment. No person may suffer prejudice in his work or employment by virtue of his origins, opinions or beliefs.

§6. All men may defend their rights and interests through union action and may belong to the union of their choice.

§7. The right to strike shall be exercised within the framework of the laws governing it.

§8. All workers shall, through the intermediary of their representatives, participate in the collective determination of their conditions of work and in the management of the work place.

§9. All property and all enterprises that have or that may acquire the character of a public service or de facto monopoly shall become the property of society.

§10. The Nation shall provide the individual and the family with the conditions necessary to their development.

§11. It shall guarantee to all, notably to children, mothers and elderly workers, protection of their health, material security, rest and leisure. All people who, by virtue of their age,

---

[2] Translation: Conseil Constitutionnel.

physical or mental condition, or economic situation, are incapable of working, shall have to the right to receive suitable means of existence from society.

§12. The Nation proclaims the solidarity and equality of all French people in bearing the burden resulting from national calamities.

§13. The Nation guarantees equal access for children and adults to instruction, vocational training and culture. The provision of free, public and secular education at all levels is a duty of the State.

§14. The French Republic, faithful to its traditions, shall respect the rules of public international law. It shall undertake no war aimed at conquest, nor shall it ever employ force against the freedom of any people.

§15. Subject to reciprocity, France shall consent to the limitations upon its sovereignty necessary to the organisation and preservation of peace.

§16. France shall form with its overseas peoples a Union founded upon equal rights and duties, without distinction of race or religion.

§17. The French Union shall be composed of nations and peoples who agree to pool or coordinate their resources and their efforts in order to develop their respective civilisations, increase their well-being, and ensure their security.

§18. Faithful to its traditional mission, France desires to guide the peoples under its responsibility towards the freedom to administer themselves and to manage their own affairs democratically; eschewing all systems of colonisation founded upon arbitrary rule, it guarantees to all equal access to public office and the individual or collective exercise of the rights and freedoms proclaimed or confirmed herein.

4   Constitution of the V. Republic of 4 October 1958[3]

Preamble

The French people solemnly proclaim their attachment to human rights and the principles of national sovereignty as they are defined by the Declaration of 1789, confirmed and complemented by the Preamble to the Constitution of 1946, as well as to the rights and obligations as defined in the Charter on the Environment of 2004. By virtue of these principles and that of the self-determination of peoples, the Republic offers to the overseas territories that express the will to adhere to them, new institutions founded on the common ideal of liberty, equality and fraternity and conceived with a view to their democratic development.

Article 1. France is an indivisible, secular, democratic and social Republic. It ensures the equality of all citizens before the law, without distinction of origin, race or religion. It respects all beliefs. Its organization is decentralized.

Statute promotes equal access of women and men to elected offices and electoral functions as well as to professional and social positions.

Title I. On sovereignty

Article 2. The language of the Republic is French.
The national emblem is the tricolour flag of blue, white, red.
The national anthem is the Marseillaise.
The motto of the Republic is Liberty, Equality, Fraternity.
Its principle is: government of the people, by the people and for the people.

Article 3. National sovereignty belongs to the people, who exercise it through their representatives and by means of referendum.
No part of the population nor any individual may arrogate the exercise thereof.
Suffrage may be direct or indirect in accordance with the condition of the Constitution. It is always universal, equal and secret.
All French nationals of the age of majority and of both sexes, who enjoy their civil and political rights, have the right to vote, under the conditions provided by statute.

Article 4. Political parties and groups contribute to the expression of suffrage. They establish themselves and carry out their activity freely. They must respect the principles of national sovereignty and of democracy.

---

3   As last amended by constitutional statute 2008-724 of 23 July 2008. Translation by Philipp Kiiver, Sascha Hardt & Gisela Kristofertisch.

They contribute to the giving effect to the principle enshrined in the second paragraph of Article 1 under the conditions provided by statute.

Statute guarantees pluralist expressions of opinions and the fair participation of political parties and groups in the democratic life of the Nation.

Title II. The President of the Republic

Article 5. The President of the Republic sees that the Constitution is respected. He ensures, by his arbitration, the proper functioning of the public authorities as well as the continuity of the State.

He is the guarantor of national independence, territorial integrity and observance of treaties.

Article 6. The President of the Republic is elected for five years by direct universal suffrage.

No-one may serve more than two consecutive terms.

The details of the implementation of this Article are determined by an organic statute.

Article 7. The President of the Republic is elected by the absolute majority of votes cast. If this is not obtained in the fist round of elections, a second round is held on the fourteenth day thereafter. Only the two candidates may run who, after the withdrawal of candidates with more votes where applicable, find themselves having obtained the largest number of votes in the first round.

The elections are opened by a call of the Government.

The election of a new President takes place at least twenty days and, at most, thirty-five days before the expiry of the powers of the incumbent President.

In case of a vacancy of the Presidency of the Republic for whatever reason, or in case the President is prevented from exercising his functions as declared by the Constitutional Council [Conseil Constitutionnel] by absolute majority of its members upon request by the Government, the functions of the President of the Republic, with the exception of those provided by Articles 11 and 12 below, are provisionally exercised by the president of the Senate and, if he in turn is prevented from exercising his functions, by he Government.

In case of a vacancy or when the prevention from the exercise of functions is declared definitive by the Constitutional Council, a vote for an election of a new President takes place, except in cases of force majeure established by the Constitutional Council, at least twenty days and at most thirty-five days after the opening of the vacancy or the declaration of the definitive character of the prevention.

If within seven days prior to the deadline for the filing of candidacies, one of the persons who has publicly announced his decision to be a candidate less than thirty days before that date, dies or finds himself prevented from running, the Constitutional Council may decide to postpone the elections.

If before the first round one of the candidates dies or finds himself prevented from running, the Constitutional Council declares the postponement of the elections.

In the case of death or prevention of one of the two candidates with the largest number of votes in the first round before any withdrawals, the Constitutional Council declares that the election procedure must start entirely anew; the same applies in the case of death or prevention of one of the two remaining candidates for the second round.

In all cases, the Constitutional Council is seized under the conditions prescribed by the second paragraph of Article 61 below or under those provided for the running as a candidate by the organic statute stipulated by Article 6 above.

The Constitutional Council may extend the periods provided by the third and fifth paragraph as long as the vote does not take place any later than thirty-five days after the date of the decision of the Constitutional Council. If the application of the provisions of the present paragraph has as an effect that elections are postponed to a date after the expiry of the powers of the incumbent President, he remains in office until the proclamation of his successor.

Neither Articles 49 and 50 nor Article 89 of the Constitution may be applied during a vacancy of the Presidency of the Republic or during the period between the declaration of the definitive character of the prevention of the President of the Republic from exercising his functions and the election of his successor.

Article 8. The President of the Republic appoints the Prime Minister. He terminates the functions of the Prime Minister when the latter tenders the resignation of the Government.

On the proposal of the Prime Minister, he appoints the other members of the Government and terminates their functions.

Article 9. The President of the Republic presides over the Council of Ministers.

Article 10. The President of the Republic promulgates statutes within fifteen days following the transmission to the Government of the statute finally adopted.

He may, before the expiry of this period, ask Parliament to deliberate anew on the statute or certain provisions of it. Such new deliberation may not be refused.

Article 11. The President of the Republic, on proposal of the Government during sessions or on joint proposal of the two chambers, which are published in the Official Journal [Journal Officiel], may submit to a referendum any government bill [projet de loi] regarding the organization of public authorities, reforms relating to the economic, social or environmental policy of the nation and the public services which contribute to it, or proposing the authorization of the ratification of a treaty which, while not being contrary to the Constitution, would have an effect on the functioning of the institutions.

Where a referendum is organized on the proposal of the Government, it makes a declaration before each chamber, which is followed by a debate.

A referendum regarding a subject mentioned in the first paragraph may be organized on the initiative of one-fifth of the members of Parliament, supported by one-tenth of the voters registered in the electoral lists. Such initiative takes the form of a private member's bill and may not have as its subject the repeal of a statutory provision promulgated less than one year earlier.

The conditions of its submission and those under which the Constitutional Council controls the compliance with the provisions of the preceding paragraph are established by an organic statute.

If the private member's bill has not been considered by the two chambers within a period determined by organic statute, the President of the Republic submits it to referendum.

Where the private member's bill has not been adopted by the French people, no new proposal for referendum regarding the same subject may be submitted before the expiry of a period of two years following the date of the vote.

Where a referendum has resulted in the adoption of a government bill or private member's bill, the President of the Republic promulgates the statute within fifteen days following the proclamation of the results of the referendum.

Article 12. The President of the Republic may, after consultations with the Prime Minister and the presidents of the chambers, declare the dissolution of the National Assembly.

General elections take place at least twenty days and at the latest forty days after the dissolution.

The National Assembly reconvenes by operation of law on the second Thursday following its election. If this convention takes place outside the period envisaged for an ordinary session, a session is opened by operation of law for a period of fifteen days.

No new dissolution may take place during the year following these elections.

Article 13. The President of the Republic signs ordinances [ordonnances] and decrees [décrets] debated in the Council of Ministers.

He appoints civil servants and military personnel of the State.

The members of the Council of State [conseillers d'État], the grand chancellor of the Legion of Honour, the ambassadors and special envoys, the magistrates of the Court of Auditors [Cour des Comptes], the prefects, the representatives of the State in overseas entities governed by Article 74 and in New Caledonia, generals, the rectors of the academies and the directors of the central administration are appointed in the Council of Ministers.

An organic statute determines the other posts to be filled in the Council of Ministers as well as the conditions under which the power of the President of the Republic to make appointments may be delegated by him to be exercised in his name.

An organic statute determines the posts or functions, other than those mentioned in the third paragraph, for which, by reason of their importance to the guarantee of rights and freedoms or the economic and social life of the Nation, the power of appointment of the President of the Republic is exercised on public advice by the competent permanent committee of each chamber. The President of the Republic may not proceed with an appointment where the added negative votes in each committee represent at least three-fifths of votes cast in the two committees. Statute determines the competent permanent committees for the posts or functions concerned.

Article 14. The President of the Republic accredits ambassadors and special envoys to foreign states; foreign ambassadors and special envoys are accredited before him.

Article 15. The President of the Republic is the commander-in-chief of the armies. He presides over the supreme councils and committees of National Defence.

Article 16. Where the institutions of the Republic, the independence of the Nation, the integrity of its territory or the execution of its international commitments is jeopardized in a serious and immediate manner and the regular functioning of the constitutional public authorities is interrupted, the President of the Republic takes measures as the circumstances demand, after official consultation with the Prime Minister, the presidents of the chambers as well as the Constitutional Council.

He informs the Nation in an address.

These measures must be inspired by the will to ensure the constitutional public authorities, in the shortest of periods, of the means to accomplish their mission. The Constitutional Council is consulted regarding their subject.

The Parliament convenes by operation of law.

The National Assembly may not be dissolved during the exercise of exceptional powers. After thirty days of exercise of exceptional powers, the Constitutional Council may be seized by the president of the National Assembly, the president of the Senate, sixty deputies or sixty senators, with a view to examining whether the conditions provided in the first paragraph remain met. It decides within the shortest of periods by a public advice. It commences such examination by operation of law and decides under the same conditions after a period of sixty days of exercise of exceptional powers and at any further moment after that period.

Article 17. The President of the Republic has the right to grant pardons in individual cases.

Article 18. The President of the Republic communicates with the two chambers of the Parliament by addresses which he orders to be read out and which are not followed by any debate.
He may speak before Parliament assembled for that purpose in Congress. His statement may, in his absence, be followed by a debate which may not be the object of any vote. Outside sessions, the parliamentary chambers convene especially for that purpose.

Article 19. The acts of the President of the Republic other than those stipulated in Articles 8 (first paragraph), 11, 12, 16, 18, 54, 56 and 61 are countersigned by the Prime Minister and, where appropriate, the competent ministers.

Title III. The Government

Article 20. The Government determines and conducts the policy of the Nation.
It has at its disposal the administration and the armed forces.
It is responsible before the Parliament under the conditions and following the procedures stipulated in Articles 49 and 50.

Article 21. The Prime Minister directs the actions of the Government. He is responsible for the National Defence. He ensures the execution of statutes. Save for the provisions of Article 13, he exercises the power of regulation [pouvoir réglementaire] and appoints civilian and military personnel.
He may delegate some of his powers to the ministers.
He substitutes, where appropriate, the President of the Republic in the presidency over the councils and committees stipulated in Article 15.
He may, by way of exception, substitute him in the presidency over a Council of Ministers by virtue of an express delegation and for a fixed agenda.

Article 22. The acts of the Prime Minister are countersigned, where appropriate, by the ministers who are charged with the execution thereof.

Article 23. The functions of a member of the Government are incompatible with the exercise of any parliamentary mandate, any function of professional representation at national level and any public employment or any professional activity.
An organic statute determines the conditions under which a replacement of the holders of such mandates, functions or employments is provided for.
The replacement of members of the Parliament takes place in accordance with the provisions of Article 25.

Title IV. The Parliament

Article 24. The Parliament adopts statutes [loi]. It controls the action of the government. It evaluates public policies.
It comprises the National Assembly [Assemblée Nationale] and the Senate [Sénat].
The deputies of the National Assembly, whose number may not exceed five hundred seventy-seven, are elected by direct suffrage.
The Senate, the number of whose members may not exceed three hundred forty-eight, is elected by indirect suffrage. It ensures the representation of the territorial entities of the Republic.
The French established outside France are represented in the National Assembly and in the Senate.

Article 25. An organic statute determines the length of the powers of each chamber, the number of its members, their remuneration, the conditions of eligibility, the regime regarding disqualification and incompatibilities.
It equally determines the conditions under which the persons are elected who are called upon to ensure, in case of a vacancy of a seat, the replacement of deputies or senators until new general or partial elections of the chamber to which they belonged or their temporary replacement in case of the acceptance by them of governmental functions.
An independent commission, the composition and rules of organization and functioning of which are determined by statute, pronounces itself in a public advice on government proposals for texts and private member's bills for statutes delimiting the districts for the election of deputies or modifying the distribution of seats of deputies or senators.

Article 26. No member of Parliament may be prosecuted, investigated, arrested, detained or tried based on the opinions or votes expressed by him in the exercise of his functions.
No member of Parliament may be subject to an arrest or any other measure of a criminal or correctional nature depriving him of or restricting his liberty, except with the authorization of the Bureau of the chamber to which he belongs. Such authorization is not required in case of a crime or misdemeanour in flagrante or in case of a final conviction.
The detention, the measures depriving of or restricting liberty or the prosecution of a member of Parliament are suspended for the period of the session if the chamber to which he belongs so demands.
The affected chamber convenes by operation of law for supplementary meetings in order to allow, where appropriate, the application of the preceding paragraph.

Article 27. Any binding mandate is void. The right to vote of the members of Parliament is personal. An organic statute may authorize, by way of exception, the delegation of a vote. In such case, no-one may receive the delegation of more than one mandate.

Article 28. The Parliament convenes by operation of law in an ordinary session [session ordinaire] which starts on the first working day of October and ends on the last working day of June.

The number of meeting days [jours de séance] which each chamber may hold during an ordinary session may not exceed one hundred and twenty. The meeting weeks are determined by each chamber.

The Prime Minister, after consultations with the president of the chamber concerned, or the majority of the members of each chamber may decide on holding additional meeting days.

The meeting days and hours are determined by the rules of procedure [règlement] of each chamber.

Article 29. The Parliament convenes in an extraordinary session upon the demand of the Prime Minister or of the majority of the members composing the National Assembly, under a fixed agenda.

Where the extraordinary session is held upon the demand of the members of the National Assembly, a decree of closure intervenes as soon as the Parliament has exhausted the agenda for which it has been convened and, at the latest, twelve days from its convention. Only the Prime Minister may demand a new session before the expiry of the month that follows the decree of closure.

Article 30. Outside the cases where the Parliament convenes by operation of law, the extraordinary sessions are opened and closed by decree from the President of the Republic.

Article 31. The members of the Government have access to the two chambers. They are heard when they so demand.

They may be assisted by Government agents [commissaires].

Article 32. The president of the National Assembly is elected for the legislative term. The president of the Senate is elected after each partial elections.

Article 33. The meetings of the two chambers are public. The complete minutes of the debates are published in the Official Journal [Journal officiel].

Each chamber may meet in closed committee upon the demand of the Prime Minister or of a tenth of its members.

Title V. The relations between Parliament and the Government

Article 34. Statute determines the rules regarding:

- the civil rights and fundamental guarantees granted to citizens for the exercise of the civil liberties; the freedom, pluralism and independence of the media; the duties imposed on the person and property of citizens by the National Defence;
- the nationality, the status and capacity of persons, the matrimonial regime, inheritance and gifts;
- the determination of crimes and misdemeanours as well as the penalties applicable to them; criminal procedure; amnesty; the establishment of new court systems and the status of magistrates;
- the basis, rate and method of collection of taxes and charges of any nature; the regime for the issuing of currency.

Statute equally determines the rules regarding:
- the electoral system for the parliamentary chambers and local assemblies and the representative bodies for the French established outside France as well as the conditions for the exercise of elected offices and electoral functions for members of the deliberative assemblies of the territorial entities;
- the establishment of categories of public bodies;
- the fundamental guarantees granted to civil servants and members of the armed forces of the State;
- the nationalization of enterprises and the transfer of property of enterprises from the public to the private sector.

Statute determines the fundamental principles:
- of the general organization of the National Defence;
- of the self-administration of territorial entities, their competences and their revenue;
- of education;
- of the preservation of the environment;
- of the property system, real rights and civil and commercial obligations;
- of labour law, trade union law and social security law.

Financial statutes [lois de finances] determine the revenue and the expenditure of the State subject to the conditions and with the reservations provided for by an organic statute.

Social security financing statutes determine the general conditions of their financial equilibrium and, taking into account anticipated revenue, set expenditure objectives subject to the conditions and with the reservations provided for by an organic statute.

Programming statutes [lois des programmation] determine the objectives of the action of the State.

The multiannual directions for public finances are defined by programming statutes. They are in line with the objective of a balance of accounts of the public administration. The provisions of the present Article may be specified and completed by an organic statute.

Article 34-1. The chambers may pass resolutions under the conditions set by an organic statute [loi organique].
Bills for resolutions of which the Government considers that their adoption or rejection would become a matter of its responsibility or that they contain injunctions against it are inadmissible and may not be included in the agenda.

Article 35. A declaration of war is authorized by Parliament.
The Government informs Parliament of its decision to have the Armed Forces intervene abroad, at the latest three days after the start of the intervention. It specifies the objectives pursued. This information may lead to a debate which is not followed by any vote.
Where the length of the intervention exceeds four months, the Government submits its extension to Parliament for authorization. It may ask the National Assembly to decide in final instance.
If Parliament is not in session after four months have expired, it decides at the opening of the following session.

Article 36. A state of siege is decreed in the Council of Ministers.
Its extension beyond twelve days may only be authorized by Parliament.

Article 37. Matters other than those falling under the scope of statute [loi] are of regulatory nature [réglementaire].
Texts of statutory form enacted with regard to these matters may be modified by decree issued after an opinion by the Council of State [Conseil d'État]. Of these texts, those enacted after the entry into force of the present Constitution may not be modified by decree except if the Constitutional Council [Conseil Constitutionnel] has declared that they are of a regulatory nature pursuant to the foregoing paragraph.

Article 37-1. Statute and regulation may contain, for a limited purpose and time, provisions of an experimental nature.

Article 38. The Government may, in order to implement its programme, request Parliament to authorize, for a limited period of time, the taking of measures by ordinances [ordonnances] which normally fall under the scope of statute.
Ordinances are issued in the Council of Ministers after an opinion by the Council of State. They enter into force upon their publication but become ineffective if the government bill for their ratification is not submitted to Parliament before the date set by the enabling statute. They may only be ratified in an explicit manner.
Upon the expiry of the period of time referred to in the first paragraph of the present Article, ordinances may not be modified except by statute in matters within the scope of statute.

Article 39. The right of initiative for statutes rests both with the Prime Minister and the members of Parliament.

Government bills [projets de loi] are discussed in the Council of Ministers after an opinion by the Council of State and submitted to the bureau of one of the two chambers. Government bills for financial statutes and social security financing statutes are submitted to the National Assembly first. Without prejudice to the first paragraph of Article 44, government bills having as their primary object the organization of the territorial entities are submitted to the Senate first.

The presentation of government bills [projets de loi] submitted to the National Assembly or the Senate meets the conditions set by an organic statute [loi organique].

Government bills may not be included in the agenda if the conference of the presidents of the first chamber seized declares that the rules set by the organic statute have been disregarded. In case of disagreement between the conference of presidents and the Government, the president of the chamber concerned or the Prime Minister may refer the matter to the Constitutional Council which decides within eight days.

Under the conditions stipulated by statute, the president of a chamber may submit to the Council of State [Conseil d'État] a private member's bill submitted by one of the members of that chamber, before its examination in a committee, for its opinion, unless that member objects.

Article 40. Private member's bills [propositions] and amendments formulated by members of Parliament are not admissible if their adoption would have as a consequence either a diminution of public revenue or the creation or aggravation of public expenditure.

Article 41. If it appears, during the legislative process, that a private member's bill or amendment is not a matter of statute or is contrary to a delegation granted by virtue of Article 38, the Government or the president of the chamber seized may oppose it as inadmissible.

In case of disagreement between the Government and the president of the chamber concerned, the Constitutional Council, at the request of either party, rules within a period of eight days.

Article 42. Debate on government bills [projets] and private member's bills [propositions de loi] in the meeting takes place on the basis of the text adopted by the committee seized by application of Article 43 or, by default, the text referred to the chamber.

However, the debate in the meeting on government bills for constitutional amendment statutes [projets de révision constitutionnelle], financial statutes [projets de loi de finances] and social security financing statutes [projets de loi de financement de la sécurité sociale] takes place, in the first reading in front of the first chamber seized, on the basis of the text presented by the Government and, in the other readings, the text transmitted by the other chamber.

The debate in the meeting, in the first reading, of a government bill or a private member's bill may only take place before the first chamber seized after the expiry of a period of six weeks after its submission. It may only take place before the second chamber seized after the expiry of a period of four weeks from the moment of its transmission.

The previous paragraph does not apply if the accelerated procedure has been initiated under the conditions stipulated in Article 45. Nor does it apply to government bills for financial statutes, social security financing statutes and to government bills relating to a state of crisis [états de crise].

Article 43. Government and private member's bills are sent for examination to one of the permanent committees, the number of which is limited to eight in each chamber.

Upon the demand of the Government or the chamber seized, government or private member's bills are sent for examination to a committee set up especially for that purpose.

Article 44. Members of Parliament and the Government have the right of amendment. This right is exercised in the meeting or in a committee under the conditions prescribed in the rules of procedure of the chambers, within the framework determined by an organic statute.

After the opening of the debate, the Government may object to the consideration of any amendment which has not previously been submitted to a committee.

If the Government so demands, the chamber seized decides by a single vote on the whole or part of the debated text, containing only the amendments proposed or accepted by the Government.

Article 45. Every government or private member's bill is considered successively in the two chambers of Parliament with a view to the adoption of an identical text. Without prejudice to the application of Articles 40 and 41, any amendment that has a link, even an indirect one, with the text submitted or transmitted is admissible in the first reading.

Where, as a result of a disagreement between the two chambers, a government or private member's bill could not be adopted after two readings by each chamber or, if the Government has decided to apply the accelerated procedure without the conference of presidents being jointly opposed, after one reading by each of them, the Prime Minister or, for a private member's bill, the presidents of the two chambers acting jointly, have the right to convene a joint committee, composed of an equal number of members of each chamber, charged with the task to propose a text on the provisions still under debate.

The text drafted by the joint committee may be submitted by the Government to the two chambers for adoption. No amendment is admissible except with the consent of the Government.

If the joint committee does not succeed in agreeing on a common text or if this text is not adopted under the conditions provided for by the foregoing paragraph, the Government may, after a new reading by the National Assembly and by the Senate, request the National Assembly to adopt a definitive decision. In that case, the National Assembly may reconsider either the text drafted by the joint committee or the last text adopted by itself, modified, where appropriate, by one or more amendments adopted by the Senate.

Article 46. Statutes which the Constitution defines as organic statutes [lois organiques] are adopted and amended under the following conditions.

The government or private member's bill may not be subjected to deliberation and to a vote of the chambers in the first reading until the expiry of the period fixed in the third paragraph of Article 42. However, if the accelerated procedure has been applied under the conditions stipulated in Article 45, the government or private member's bill may not be subjected to deliberation in the first chamber seized until the expiry of a period of fifteen days after its submission.

The procedure of Article 45 applies. However, failing agreement between the two chambers, the text may be adopted by the National Assembly in final reading only by an absolute majority of its members.

Organic statutes relating to the Senate must be adopted in the same terms by the two chambers.

Organic statutes may not be promulgated until the Constitutional Council has declared their conformity with the Constitution.

Article 47. Parliament adopts government bills for financial statutes under the conditions provided by an organic statute.

If the National Assembly has not reached a decision in the first reading within a period of forty days after the submission of a government bill, the Government seizes the Senate which must reach a decision within a period of fifteen days. Thereafter the procedure of Article 45 is applied.

If Parliament has not reached a decision within a period of seventy days, the provisions of the government bill may be enacted by ordinance.

If a financial statute setting revenues and expenditure for a financial year has not been submitted in time for promulgation before the beginning of that financial year, the Government requests from Parliament, as a matter of urgency, the authorization to collect taxes and make available by decree the funds needed for measures already adopted. The time limits set by the present Article are suspended when Parliament is not in session.

Article 47-1. Parliament adopts government bills for social security financing statutes under the conditions provided by an organic statute. If the National Assembly has not reached a decision in the first reading within a period of twenty days after the submission of a government bill, the Government seizes the Senate which must reach a decision within a period of fifteen days. Thereafter the procedure of Article 45 is applied. If Parliament has not reached a decision within a period of fifty days, the provisions of the government bill may be put into effect by ordinance.

The time limits set by the present Article are suspended when Parliament is not in session and, with respect to each chamber, during the weeks during which it has decided not to meet in conformity with the second paragraph of Article 28.

Article 47-2. The Court of Auditors [Cour des Comptes] assists the Parliament with the control of the action of the Government. It assists the Parliament and the Government with the control of the execution of financial statutes and the implementation of social security financing statutes as well as with the assessment of public policies. With its public reports, it contributes to the informing of the citizens.

The accounts of the public administration are regular and sincere. They provide a picture that faithfully shows the results of their management, their assets and their financial situation.

Article 48. Without prejudice to the application of the last three paragraphs of Article 28, the agenda is fixed by each chamber.

Two weeks of meetings out of four are reserved with priority, in the order that the Government has fixed, for the examination of texts and for debates which it requests to be included in the agenda.

Furthermore, the examination of government bills for financial statutes, social security financing statutes and, subject to the provisions of the following paragraph, texts transmitted by the other chamber at least six weeks earlier, government bills relating to a state of crisis and requests for authorization envisaged by Article 35, is, upon request of the Government, included in the agenda with priority.

One week of meetings out of four is reserved, with priority and in the order fixed by each assembly, for the control of the action of the Government and for the assessment of public policies.

One day of meeting per month is reserved for an agenda determined by each chamber upon the initiative of opposition groups of the chamber concerned, as well as of minority groups.

At least one meeting per week, including during extraordinary sessions provided for in Article 29, is reserved, with priority, for questions of members of Parliament and answers by the Government.

Article 49. The Prime Minister, after deliberation by the Council of Ministers, ties the responsibility of the Government before the National Assembly to the Government's programme or possibly a general policy statement.

The National Assembly invokes the responsibility of the Government by a vote on a motion of censure. Such a motion is only admissible if it is signed by at least one tenth of the members of the National Assembly. The vote may not take place until forty-eight hours have elapsed after the tabling. Solely votes in favour of the motion of censure are counted, which may only be adopted by a majority of the members composing the Assembly. Except in the case stipulated by the paragraph hereunder, a deputy may not be a signatory to more than three motions of censure during one ordinary session and to more than one during one extraordinary session.

The Prime Minister may, after deliberation by the Council of Ministers, make a matter of the responsibility of the Government before the National Assembly the adoption of a government bill for a financial statute or a social security financing statute. In that event, the government bill is considered adopted unless a motion of censure, tabled within the twenty-four hours that follow, is adopted under the conditions provided for by the foregoing paragraph. The Prime Minister may furthermore resort to this procedure for one other government bill or one private member's bill per session.

The Prime Minister has the option to request from the Senate the approval of a general policy statement.

Article 50. When the National Assembly adopts a motion of censure or when it disapproves the programme or a general policy statement of the Government, the Prime Minister must tender the resignation of the Government to the President of the Republic.

Article 50-1. Before one of the chambers the Government may, on its own initiative or at the request of a parliamentary group in the sense of Article 51-1, make a statement on a specified subject that is followed by a debate and that may, if it so decides, be the object of a vote without making it a matter of its responsibility.

Article 51. The closure of an ordinary session or of extraordinary sessions is postponed by operation of law in order to allow, where applicable, the application of Article 49. For that same purpose, supplementary meetings are held by operation of law.

Article 51-1. The rules of procedure of each chamber determine the rights of parliamentary groups constituted within it. It recognizes the rights specific to opposition groups of the chamber concerned as well as to minority groups.

Article 51-2. For the exercise of the controlling and evaluation tasks defined in the first paragraph of Article 24, commissions of inquiry may be created within each chamber in order to gather information under the conditions stipulated by statute.

Statute determines their rules of organization and functioning. The conditions of their establishment are determined by the rules of procedure of each chamber.

Title VI. On international treaties and agreements

Article 52. The President of the Republic negotiates and ratifies treaties [traités].
He is informed of any negotiation for the conclusion of an international agreement [accord international] not subject to ratification.

Article 53. Peace treaties, treaties on trade, treaties or agreements relating to international organization, those which affect the finances of the State, those which modify provisions of statutory nature, those which relate to the status of persons, those which entail the cession, exchange or acquisition of territory, may only be ratified or approved by statute.
They do not take effect until they have been ratified or approved.
No cession, no exchange, no acquisition of territory is valid without the consent of the population concerned.

Article 53-1. The Republic may conclude, with European States bound by commitments identical to its own in matters of asylum and the protection of human rights and fundamental freedoms, agreements determining their respective competences for the consideration of requests for asylum submitted to them.
However, even if, pursuant to these agreements, a request does not fall under its competences, the authorities of the Republic always have the right to grant asylum to any foreigner persecuted for his action in pursuit of freedom or who seeks protection by France for another reason.

Article 53-2. The Republic may recognize the jurisdiction of the International Criminal Court under the conditions provided by the treaty signed on 18 July 1998.

Article 54. If the Constitutional Council, seized by the President of the Republic, by the Prime Minister, by the president of one of the chambers or by sixty deputies or sixty senators, has declared that an international commitment contains a clause contrary to the Constitution, the authorization to ratify or approve the international commitment in question may only be given after amendment of the Constitution.

Article 55. Treaties or agreements duly ratified or approved have, upon their publication, authority superior to that of statutes, subject, with respect to each agreement or treaty, to their application by the other party.

Title VII. The Constitutional Council

Article 56. The Constitutional Council [Conseil Constitutionnel] comprises nine members whose mandate lasts nine years and is not renewable. One third of the Constitutional

Council is renewed every three years. Three of the members are appointed by the President of the Republic, three by the president of the National Assembly, three by the president of the Senate. The procedure stipulated in the last paragraph of Article 13 is applicable to these appointments. The appointments made by the president of each chamber are submitted for an opinion only to the competent permanent committee of the relevant chamber.

In addition to the nine members provided for above, former Presidents of the Republic are by operation of law members of the Constitutional Council for life.

The president is appointed by the President of the Republic. He has the decisive vote in case of a tie.

Article 57. The office of a member of the Constitutional Council is incompatible with that of a minister or a member of Parliament. Other incompatibilities are established by an organic statute.

Article 58. The Constitutional Council ensures the proper conduct of the election of the President of the Republic.

It examines complaints and proclaims the result of the election.

Article 59. The Constitutional Council rules, in case of a challenge, on the proper conduct of the election of deputies and senators.

Article 60. The Constitutional Council ensures the proper conduct of referendums as provided for by Articles 11 and 89 and by Title XV. It proclaims the results thereof.

Article 61. Organic statutes, prior to their promulgation, private member's bills mentioned in Article 11 before they have been submitted to referendum, and the rules of procedure of the parliamentary chambers, before coming into force, must be submitted to the Constitutional Council which rules on their conformity with the Constitution.

For the same purpose, statutes may be referred to the Constitutional Council, before their promulgation, by the President of the Republic, the Prime Minister, the president of the National Assembly, the president of the Senate or sixty deputies or sixty senators.

In the cases provided for by the two foregoing paragraphs, the Constitutional Council must rule within a period of one month. However, at the request of the Government, in cases of urgency, this period is reduced to eight days.

In the same cases, referral to the Constitutional Council suspends the time period for promulgation.

Article 61-1. When, in the course of proceedings before a court, it is submitted that a statutory provision jeopardizes the rights and freedoms which the Constitution guarantees, the Constitutional Council may be seized on that question by reference from the Council of State or the Court of Cassation which decide within a determined period.

An organic statute determines the conditions for the application of the present Article.

Article 62. A provision declared unconstitutional on the basis of Article 61 may neither be promulgated nor implemented.

A provision declared unconstitutional on the basis of Article 61-1 is repealed from the moment of the publication of the decision of the Constitutional Council or a later date established in that decision. The Constitutional Council determines the conditions and limits within which the effects that the provision has created may be called into question. The decisions of the Constitutional Council are not open to any appeal. They are binding on public authority and on all administrative and judicial authorities.

Article 63. An organic statute determines the organization and functioning of the Constitutional Council, the procedure followed before it and, in particular, the time limits for submitting complaints to it.

Title VIII. On the judicial authority

Article 64. The President of the Republic is the guarantor of the independence of the judicial authority.

He is assisted by the High Council of the Judiciary [Conseil Supérieur de la Magistrature].

An organic statute contains the rules governing magistrates.

Judges [magistrats du siège] are irremovable.

Article 65. The High Council of the Judiciary comprises a section competent with regard to judges [magistrats du siège] and one competent with regard to public prosecutors [magistrats du parquet].

The section competent with regard to judges is presided over by the first president of the Court of Cassation [Cour de cassation]. It comprises furthermore five judges and one public prosecutor, one member of the Council of State nominated by the Council of State [Conseil d'État], one advocate [avocat] as well as six distinguished persons who are not members of either Parliament or the judiciary or the administration. The President of the Republic, the president of the National Assembly and the president of the Senate each appoint two distinguished persons. The procedure stipulated in the last paragraph of Article 13 is applicable to the appointment of distinguished persons. The appointments made by the president of each chamber of Parliament are submitted for an opinion only to the competent permanent committee of the relevant chamber.

The section competent with regard to public prosecutors is presided over by the procurator-general at the Court of Cassation. It comprises furthermore five public prosecutors and one judge, as well as the member of the Council of State, the advocate and the six distinguished persons mentioned in the second paragraph.

The section of the High Council of the Judiciary competent with regard to judges submits proposals for the appointments of judges at the Court of Cassation, for those of the first president of a court of appeals [cour d'appel] and for those of the president of a district court [tribunal de grande instance]. The other judges are appointed upon its assent.

The section of the High Council of the Judiciary competent with regard to public prosecutors gives its opinion on appointments that affect public prosecutors.

The section of the High Council of the Judiciary competent with regard to judges rules as a disciplinary council for judges. It then comprises besides the members envisaged in the second paragraph the judge who is a member of the section competent with regard to public prosecutors.

The section of the High Council of the Judiciary competent with regard to public prosecutors gives its opinion on those disciplinary sanctions that affect them. It then comprises besides the members envisaged in the third paragraph, the public prosecutor who is a member of the section competent with regard to judges.

The High Council of the Judiciary meets in plenary composition in order to answer requests for an opinion made by the President of the Republic in application of Article 64. It gives, in the same composition, its opinion on questions regarding the ethics of magistrates as well as on any question regarding the functioning of the justice system on which it is seized by the minister of justice. The plenary composition comprises three of the five judges mentioned in the second paragraph, three of the five public prosecutors mentioned in the third paragraph as well as the member of the Council of State, the advocate and the six distinguished persons mentioned in the second paragraph. It is presided over by the first president of the Court of Cassation who may be substituted by the procurator-general at that Court.

Except in disciplinary matters the minister of justice may participate in the meetings of the sections of the High Council of the Judiciary.

The High Council of the Judiciary may be seized by a person undergoing a trial under the conditions determined by organic statute.

An organic statute determines the conditions for the application of the present Article.

Article 66. No-one may be detained arbitrarily.

The judicial authority, guardian of individual liberty, ensures the observance of this principle under the conditions provided by statute.

Article 66-1. No-one may be sentenced to the death penalty.

Title IX. The High Court

Article 67. The President of the Republic is not liable for any acts committed in this capacity, subject to the provisions of the Articles 53-2 and 68.
He may not, during his mandate and before no French court or administrative authority, be required to testify, nor be the object of a court action, investigatory action, instruction or prosecution. Any period of prescription or foreclosure is suspended.
All actions and proceedings thus barred may be resumed or brought against him upon expiry of a period of one month after the end of his office.

Article 68. The President of the Republic may only be removed from office in case of a breach of his duties manifestly incompatible with the exercise of his mandate. The removal is proclaimed by Parliament sitting as the High Court [Haute Cour].
The proposal to convene the High Court adopted by one of the chambers of Parliament is immediately transmitted to the other, which reaches its decision within fifteen days.
The High Court is chaired by the president of the National Assembly. It rules within a period of one month, by secret ballot, on the removal from office. Its decision is of immediate effect.
The decisions taken in the application of the present Article are taken by two thirds of the members composing the chamber concerned or the High Court. Any delegation of votes is prohibited. Only the votes in favour of the proposal to convene the High Court or of the removal from office are counted.
An organic statute determines the conditions for the application of the present Article.

Title X. On the criminal liability of members of the government

Article 68-1. The members of the government are liable for acts committed in the exercise of their office and qualified as crimes [crime] or misdemeanours [délit] at the time they were committed.
They are tried by the Court of Justice of the Republic [Cour de justice de la République]. The Court of Justice of the Republic is bound by such definition of crimes and misdemeanours as well as by such determination of penalties as follows from statute.

Article 68-2. The Court of Justice of the Republic consists of fifteen judges: twelve parliamentarians elected from among their ranks and in equal number by the National Assembly and by the Senate after each general or partial election of these chambers, and three judges at the Court of Cassation, one of whom presides over the Court of Justice of the Republic.

Any person who claims to be a victim of a crime or misdemeanour committed by a member of the government in the exercise of his office may file a complaint with a petitions committee.

This committee orders either the closure of the procedure or its transmission to the procurator-general at the Court of Cassation for the seizing of the Court of Justice of the Republic.

The procurator-general at the Court of Cassation may also upon his own motion seize the Court of Justice of the Republic upon the assent of the petitions committee.

An organic statute determines the conditions for the application of the present Article.

Article 68-3. The provisions of the present Title are applicable to acts committed before its entry into force.

Title XI. The Economic, Social and Environmental Council

Article 69. The Economic, Social and Environmental Council [Conseil économique, social et environnemental], seized by the Government, gives its opinion on government bills, draft ordinances or draft decrees as well as on private member's bills which are submitted to it.

A member of the Economic, Social and Environmental Council may be appointed by it to present to the parliamentary chambers the opinion of the Council on the government or private member's bills which have been submitted to it.

The Economic, Social and Environmental Council may be seized by way of petition under the conditions determined by organic statute. After examination of the petition, it notifies the Government and Parliament of the follow-up actions that it proposes to take.

Article 70. The Economic, Social and Environmental Council may be consulted by the Government and Parliament on any problem of an economic, social or environmental nature. The Government may equally consult it on government bills for programming statutes defining the multiannual directions for public finances. Any plan or any government bill for a programming statute of an economic, social or environmental nature is submitted to it for its opinion.

Article 71. The composition of the Economic and Social and Environmental Council, the number of whose members may not exceed two hundred and thirty-three, and its rules of procedure are determined by an organic statute.

Title XI bis. The Defender of Rights

Article 71-1. The Defender of Rights guards the respect of rights and liberties by the administrations of the State, the territorial entities, public bodies, as well as by any body charged with a public service task, or with respect to which an organic statute confers competences on him.

He may be seized, under the conditions stipulated by an organic statute, by any person who considers himself harmed by the functioning of a public service or a body envisaged in the first paragraph. He may consider a matter on his own initiative.

An organic statute specifies the competences and the terms of intervention of the Defender of Rights. It determines the conditions under which he may be assisted by a collegiate body in the exercise of some of his competences.

The Defender of Rights is appointed by the President of the Republic for a non-renewable term of six years after application of the procedure stipulated in the last paragraph of Article 13. His functions are incompatible with those of a member of Government and of a member of Parliament. Other incompatibilities are determined by organic statute.

The Defender of Rights gives account of his activity to the President of the Republic and to Parliament.

Title XII. The territorial entities

Article 72. The territorial entities [collectivités territoriales] of the Republic are the municipalities [communes], the departments [départements], the regions [régions], the special-status entities and the overseas entities governed by Article 74. Any other territorial entity is created by statute, where appropriate in place of one or more entities referred to in the present paragraph.

Territorial entities are charged with taking decisions on the entirety of competences that can best be exercised at their level.

Under the conditions provided by statute, the entities administer themselves freely through elected councils and possess regulatory powers [réglementaire] for the exercise of their competences.

Under the conditions provided by organic statute, provided that the essential conditions for the exercise of a public liberty or a constitutionally guaranteed right is not affected, territorial entities or associations thereof may, where such is provided by statute or regulation, as the case may be, derogate on an experimental basis for limited purpose and duration from statutory or regulatory provisions governing the exercise of their competences.

No territorial entity may exercise tutelage over another. However, where the exercise of a competence requires the co-operation of several territorial entities, statute may authorize one of them or one of their associations to organize the modalities of their joint action.

In the territorial entities of the Republic, the representative of the State, representing each of the members of the Government, is responsible for the national interests, administrative supervision and the observance of statutes.

Article 72-1. Statute determines the conditions under which voters in each territorial entity may, by exercising the right of petition, request that a question relevant to its competence be included in the agenda of the deliberative assembly of that entity.

Under the conditions determined by organic statute, government bills for deliberation or acts relevant to the competence of a territorial entity may, on its initiative, by means of referendum, be submitted to the decision of the voters of that entity.

When it is envisaged that a territorial entity be created or provided with a special status or its organization be modified, it may be decided by statute to consult the voters registered in the concerned entities. The modification of the borders of territorial entities may equally give rise to a consultation of the voters under the conditions provided by statute.

Article 72-2. Territorial entities enjoy resources of which they may dispose freely under the conditions determined by statute.

They may receive all or a part of the revenue from taxes of any nature. Statute may authorize them to specify the basis and rate thereof within the limits it determines.

Fiscal revenue and other own resources of the territorial entities represent, for each category of entities, a decisive share of the entirety of their resources. Organic statute determines the conditions under which this rule is given effect.

Any transfer of competences between the State and the territorial entities is accompanied by an allocation of resources equivalent to what had been dedicated to the exercise of those competences. Any creation or extension of competences having as a consequence an increase in expenditures of territorial entities is accompanied by resources determined by statute.

Statute provides for equalization mechanisms designed to promote equality between territorial entities.

Article 72-3. The Republic recognizes, within the French people, the overseas populations in a common ideal of liberty, equality and fraternity.

Guadeloupe, Guiana, Martinique, Réunion, Mayotte, Saint-Barthélemy, Saint-Martin, Saint-Pierre-and-Miquelon, the Islands of Wallis and Futuna and French Polynesia are governed by Article 73 for departments and overseas regions and for territorial entities created by application of the last paragraph of Article 73, and by Article 74 for the other entities.

The status of New Caledonia is governed by Title XIII.

Statute determines the legislative regime and the special organization of the French Southern and Antarctic Territories and of Clipperton.

Article 72-4. No change, regarding the whole or a part of one of the entities mentioned in the second paragraph of Article 72-3, of one towards the other of the regimes provided for by Articles 73 and 74, takes place unless the consent of the voters of the entity or the part of the entity concerned has been obtained beforehand under the conditions provided by the following paragraph. This change of regime is decided on by organic statute.

The President of the Republic, on a proposal of the Government during sessions or on joint proposal of the two chambers, which are published in the Official Journal [Journal officiel], may decide to consult the voters of a territorial entity situated overseas on a question relating to its organization, to its competences or to its legislative regime. Where this consultation concerns a change stipulated in the foregoing paragraph and is organized on proposal of the Government, it makes a statement before each chamber, which is followed by a debate.

Article 73. In the overseas departments and regions, statutes and regulations are applicable by operation of law. They may be the object of adaptations in view of the particular characteristics and constraints of these entities.

These adaptations may be decided by the entities on matters where they exercise their competences and if they were enabled to do so, as the case may be, by statute or by regulation.

By derogation from the first paragraph and in order to take account of their specificities, entities governed by the present Article may be enabled, as the case may be by statute or by regulation, to themselves determine the rules applicable on their territory in a limited number of matters that can fall under the scope of statute or regulation.

These rules may not concern nationality, civil rights, guarantees of civil liberties, the status and capacity of persons, the organization of justice system, criminal law, criminal procedure, foreign policy, defence, public security and order, currency, credit and exchange, as well as electoral law. This enumeration may be specified and completed by organic statute.

The provisions stipulated in the two preceding paragraphs are not applicable to the department and to the region of Réunion.

The enabling provided for in the second and third paragraph is decided, upon request of the entity concerned, subject to the conditions and with the reservations provided by an organic statute. They may not be carried out where the essential conditions for the exercise of a public liberty or a constitutionally guaranteed right is at issue.

The creation by statute of an entity substituting an overseas department and region or the establishment of a single deliberative assembly for those two entities may not take place unless the consent of the voters registered in the territory of these entities has been obtained according to the procedure provided in the second paragraph of Article 72-4.

Article 74. The overseas entities governed by the present Article have a status that takes account of their particular interests within the Republic.

This status is defined by organic statute, adopted after an opinion of the deliberative assembly, which determines:

- the conditions under which statutes and regulations are applicable there;
- the competences of this entity; subject to those already exercised by it, the transfer of competences by the State may not concern the matters enumerated in the fourth paragraph of Article 73, specified and complemented, as the case may be, by organic statute;
- the rules on the organization and functioning of the institutions of the entity and the electoral regime of its deliberative assembly;
- the conditions under which its institutions are consulted on government bills and private member's bills and drafts of ordinances or decrees containing provisions that are specific to the entity as well as to the ratification or approval of international commitments concluded in matters relevant to its competence.

The organic statute may equally determine, for those entities that are provided with autonomy, the conditions under which:
- the Council of State exercises specific judicial review over certain categories of acts of the deliberative assembly effected on the basis of competences that it exercises within the scope of statute;
- the deliberative assembly may amend a statute promulgated after the entry into force of the status of the entity, where the Constitutional Council, seized in particular by the authorities of that entity, has established that the statute has intervened in the scope of competence of that entity;
- measures justified by local needs may be taken by the entity in favour of its population, in matters of access to employment, the right of establishment for the exercise of a professional activity or the protection of land property;
- the entity may participate, under the control of the State, in the exercise of the competences it retains, respecting the guarantees granted to the entire national territory for the exercise of public liberties.

The other modalities of the organization specific to the entities subject to the present Article are determined and amended by statute after consultation of their deliberative assembly.

Article 74-1. In the overseas entities envisaged by Article 74 and in New Caledonia, the Government may, by ordinance, in the matters that remain in the competence of the State, extend, with the necessary adaptations, the provisions of statutory nature in force in Metropolitan France or adapt the provisions of statutory nature in force to the specific organization of the entity concerned, provided that the statute did not explicitly exclude, for the provisions in question, recourse to this procedure.

The ordinances are issued in the Council of Ministers after an opinion of the deliberative assembly concerned and the Council of State. They enter into force upon their publication. They become ineffective in the absence of ratification by Parliament within a period of eighteen months after that publication.

Article 75. The citizens of the Republic who do not have ordinary civil status, only envisaged in Article 34, retain their personal status as long as they have not renounced it.

Article 75-1. Regional languages belong to the heritage of France.

Title XIII. Transitional provisions regarding New Caledonia

Article 76. The population of New Caledonia is called upon to pronounce itself before the 31 December 1998 on the provisions of the agreement signed at Nouméa on 5 May 1998 and published on 27 May 1998 in the Official Journal of the French Republic.
Admitted to participate in the vote are the persons who fulfil the conditions determined in Article 2 of statute no. 88-1028 of 9 November 1988.
The measures necessary for the organization of the vote are taken by decree in consultation with the Council of State [Conseil d'Etat] after having been discussed in the council of ministers.

Article 77. After adoption of the agreement by the vote provided in Article 76, an organic statute, passed after an opinion of the deliberative assembly of New Caledonia, determines, in order to ensure the development of New Caledonia respecting the directions defined by that agreement and in accordance with the terms necessary in order to give it effect:
- the competences of the State that will be transferred definitively to the institutions of New Caledonia, the time scale and the modalities of the transfer, as well as the allocation of the expenditures resulting therefrom;
- the rules of the organization and functioning of the institutions of New Caledonia and in particular the conditions under which certain categories of acts of the deliberative assembly of New Caledonia may be submitted for review to the Constitutional Council [Conseil Constitutionnel] before publication;
- the rules relating to citizenship, to the electoral regime, to employment and to the customary civil status;
- the conditions and time limits within which the population concerned in New Caledonia will be led to pronounce themselves on the attainment of full sovereignty.

The other measures necessary for giving effect of the agreement mentioned in Article 76 are defined by statute.
For the definition of the electoral body called upon to elect the members of the deliberative assemblies of New Caledonia and its provinces, the list to which the agreement mentioned in Article 76 and in Article 188 and 189 of the organic statute no. 99-209 of 19 March 1999 relating to New Caledonia refer is the list drawn up in the course of the vote provided for in Article 76 and including the persons not admitted to participate in it.

Articles 78 to 86. (Repealed)

Title XIV. On the French-speaking World and on Association Agreements

Article 87. The Republic takes part in the development of solidarity and cooperation between the States and peoples which have the French language in common.

Title XV. On the European Union

Article 88-1. The Republic participates in the European Union, constituted by States that have freely chosen to exercise certain of their powers conjointly by virtue of the Treaty on European Union and the Treaty on the Functioning of the European Union as they result from the Treaty signed at Lisbon on 13 December 2007.

Article 88-2. Statute determines the rules regarding the European arrest warrant by application of the acts taken by the institutions of the European Union.

Article 88-3. Subject to reciprocity and in accordance with the terms laid down by the Treaty on European Union signed on 7 February 1992, the right to vote and to stand in municipal elections may be granted only to citizens of the Union residing in France. These citizens may neither exercise the office of mayor or deputy mayor, nor participate in the designation of senatorial electors and in the election of senators. An organic statute adopted in identical terms by both chambers determines the conditions under which the present Article is applied.

Article 88-4. The Government submits to the National Assembly and to the Senate, when they have been transmitted to the Council of the European Union, drafts of or proposals for acts of the European Communities and of the European Union.
In accordance with the terms set by the rules of procedure of each chamber, European resolutions may be adopted, also outside sessions where appropriate, on the drafts and proposals mentioned in the first paragraph, as well as on any document emanating from an institution of the European Union.
Within each parliamentary chamber a committee responsible for European affairs is established.

Article 88-5. Any government bill authorizing the ratification of a Treaty regarding the accession of a State to the European Union and to the European Communities is submitted to referendum by the President of the Republic.

However, by a vote on a motion adopted in identical terms by each assembly by a majority of three fifths, Parliament may authorize the adoption of the government bill in accordance with the procedure stipulated in the third paragraph of Article 89.

[Note: This Article does not apply to accessions made following an intergovernmental conference whose convocation was decided by the European Council before 1 July 2004.]

Article 88-6. The National Assembly or the Senate may adopt a reasoned opinion on the compliance of a draft European legislative act with the principle of subsidiarity. The opinion is addressed by the president of the chamber concerned to the presidents of the European Parliament, of the Council and of the European Commission. The Government is informed of this.
Each chamber may bring an action before the Court of Justice of the European Union against a European legislative act for a violation of the principle of subsidiarity. The action is transmitted to the Court of Justice of the European Union by the Government. To that end, resolutions may be adopted, also outside sessions where appropriate, in accordance with the terms on initiative and debate set by the rules of procedure of each chamber. Upon request of sixty deputies or of sixty senators, the action is brought by operation of law.

Article 88-7. By adoption of a motion passed in identical terms by the National Assembly and the Senate, Parliament may oppose an amendment of the rules for the adoption of acts of the European Union in the cases envisaged, under the simplified treaty revision procedure or judicial cooperation in civil matters, by the Treaty on European Union and the Treaty on the Functioning of the European Union as they result from the Treaty signed at Lisbon on 13 December 2007.

Title XVI. On amendments

Article 89. The right of initiative for a revision of the Constitution lies concurrently with the President of the Republic, upon a proposal by the Prime Minister, and with the members of Parliament.
A government or private member's bill for a revision must be examined under the conditions of the fixed periods determined in the third paragraph of Article 42 and adopted by both chambers in identical terms. The revision is final after having been approved by referendum.
However, a government bill for a revision is not submitted to referendum where the President of the Republic decides to submit it to Parliament convened in Congress [Congrès]; in that case, the government bill for revision is not approved unless it is adopted by

a majority of three fifths of the votes cast. The bureau of the Congress is that of the National Assembly.

No procedure of revision may be initiated or continued where the integrity of the territory is jeopardized.

The republican form of Government may not be the object of a revision.

Title XVII. (Repealed)

5   ELECTORAL CODE [CODE ELECTORAL][4]

Statutory part

Book I. The election of deputies, members of the departmental councils and members of the municipal councils

[*Title I is omitted.*]

Title II. Special provisions regarding the election of deputies

Chapter I. Composition of the National Assembly and the length of the mandate of the deputies

Article LO 119. The number of deputies is five hundred seventy seven.

Article LO 120. The National Assembly is re-elected in full.

Article LO 121. The powers of the National Assembly expire on the third Tuesday of June in the fifth year following its election.

Article LO 122. Save for a case of dissolution, general elections take place within sixty days prior to the expiry of the powers of the National Assembly.

Chapter II. Election procedure

Article L 123. The deputies are elected in single-vote majority voting with two rounds.

Article L 124. The vote takes place in electoral districts.

Article L 125. The electoral districts are determined in conformity with Table 1 annexed to the present Code.
A revision of the borders of the electoral districts takes place, according to demographic developments, after the second general census of the population following the last redistricting.

---

4   As last amended on 15 April 2019. Selected provisions (from the statutory part): Book I: Title II, Chapters I and II, as well as Articles L 162 and L 163 of Chapter V; Book II: Titles I and II, Articles L 283 to L285 of Title III, and Chapter I of Title IV. Translation by Philipp Kiiver & Sascha Hardt.

Article L 126. No-one is elected in the first round of the vote if he has not received:
1. the absolute majority of votes cast;
2. a number of votes equal to one quarter of the number of registered voters.

In the second round, a relative majority suffices.

In case of a tie, the oldest of the candidates is elected.

[Chapters III and IV are omitted.]

Chapter V. Declarations of candidacies

[Articles L 154 to L 161 are omitted.]

Article L 162. The declarations of candidacies for the second round of the vote must be filed before 18.00 hours on the Tuesday that follows the first round.

However if, because of a case of force majeure, the counting of the votes could not be completed in the period prescribed in Article L 175, declarations are accepted until 18.00 hours on Wednesday.

Save for the provisions of Article L 163, no-one may be candidate in the second round if he did not run in the first round and if he did not receive a number of votes at least equal to 12.5 % of the number of registered voters.

In case a single candidate fulfils these conditions, the candidate who has received, after him, the largest number of votes in the first round may proceed to the second.

In case no candidate fulfils these conditions, the two candidates who have received the largest number of votes in the first round may proceed to the second.

A candidate may not present in the second round of the vote any alternate other than the one he designated in his declaration of candidacy for the first round.

The provisions of the second and third paragraph of Article L 157 and those of Article L 159 are applicable to declarations of candidacies for the second round of the vote. In that case, the administrative tribunal decides within a period of twenty-four hours.

Article L 163. Where a candidate dies after the expiry of the period prescribed for filing declarations of candidacies, his alternate becomes candidate and may designate a new alternate.

Where an alternate dies during the same period, the candidate may designate a new alternate.

[The remainder of Book I is omitted.]

Book II. The election of senators of the departments

Title I. Composition of the Senate and the length of the mandate of the senators

Article LO 274. The number of Senators elected within the departments is 326.

Article LO 275. Senators are elected for six years.

Article LO 276. The Senate is re-elected by half. For this purpose, the senators are divided into two classes, 1 and 2, of approximately equal importance, in accordance with Table 5 annexed to the present Code.

Article LO 277. In each class, the mandate of the senators begins at the opening of the ordinary session which follows their election, at which date the mandate of the senators previously in office expires.

Article LO 278. The election of senators takes place within sixty days prior to the date of the beginning of their mandate.

Title II. Composition of the electoral college

Article L 279. The seats of the senators representing the departments are distributed in accordance with Table 6 annexed to the present Code.

Article L 280. The composition of the electoral college charged with electing the senators ensures, in in each department, the representation of the different categories of territorial entities and of the diversity of communities, taking into account the population residing there.
This electoral college is composed of:
1. deputies and senators;
2. members of the regional council [conseillers régionaux] from the departmental section corresponding to the department and the members of the Assembly of Corsica designated under the conditions envisaged by Title III bis of the present Book;

2bis. members of the Assembly of Guyana and the Assembly of Martinique;
3. members of the departmental council [conseillers départementaux];
4. delegates of the municipal councils or the substitutes of these delegates.

Article L 281. The deputies, the members of the regional councils, the members of the Assembly of Corsica, the members of the Assembly of Guyana, the members of the Assebly of Martinique and the members of the departmental councils who have been appointed by the census commissions are registered in the list of senatorial electors and take part in the vote even if their election is contested. In case they are prevented by a major hindrance, they may exercise, upon written request, their right to vote by proxy. The mandatary must be a member of the senatorial electoral college and may not dispose of more than one proxy.

Article L 282. In the case where a member of the departmental council is a deputy, a member of the regional council or a member of the Assembly of Corsica, a replacement is designated for him, upon his proposal, by the president of the departmental council.
In the case where a member of the regional council, a member of the Assembly of Corsica, a member of the Assembly of Guyana or a member of the Assemly of Martinique is a deputy, a replacement is designated for him, upon his proposal, by the president of the regional council, the one of the Assembly of Corsica, the one of the Assembly of Guyana or the one of the Assembly of Martinique.

Title III. Designation of delegates of municipal councils

Article L 283. The decree calling up the senatorial electors determines the day on which the delegates of the municipal councils and their substitutes must be designated. An interval of at least six weeks must separate these elections and the ones of the senators.

Article L 284. In municipalities of less than 9,000 inhabitants, the municipal councils elect from among their members:
- one delegate for municipal councils of nine and eleven members;
- three delegates for municipal councils of fifteen members;
- five delegates for municipal councils of nineteen members;
- seven delegates for municipal councils of twenty-three members;
- fifteen delegates for municipal councils of twenty-seven and twenty-nine members.

In case the municipal council is formed by application of Articles L 2113-6 and L 2113-7 of the General Code of Territorial Entities [code général des collectivités territoriales] regarding mergers of municipalities as worded prior to the enactment of statute no. 2010-1563 on the reform of the territorial entities, the number of delegates is equal to the number to which the former municipalities would have been entitled before the merger.

Article L 285. In municipalities of 9,000 inhabitants and more, all members of the municipal council are delegates ex officio.
Furthermore, in municipalities of more than 30,000 inhabitants, the municipal councils elect additional delegates, namely 1 for every 800 inhabitants in excess of 30,000.

[*The remainder of Title III and Title IIIbis are omitted.*]

Title IV. Election of senators

Chapter I. Election procedure

Article L 294. In departments where two senators or less are elected, the election takes place by majority voting with two rounds.
No-one is elected senator in the first round of the vote if he has not obtained:
1. the absolute majority of votes cast;
2. a number of votes equal to one quarter of registered voters.
    In the second round of the vote, a relative majority suffices. In case of a tie, the oldest of the candidates is elected.

Article L 295. In departments where three senators or more are elected, the election takes place by proportional representation following the rule of largest averages, without spreading votes over multiple lists [panachage] and without preference votes.
On each list, seats are attributed to candidates in the order of nomination.

[*The remainder of the Code is omitted.*]

Germany

6 Basic Law for the Federal Republic of Germany of 23 May 1949[1]

Preamble
Conscious of its responsibility before God and man, inspired by the will to serve world peace as an equal partner in a united Europe, the German people, by virtue of its constituent power, has adopted for itself this Basic Law. Germans in the States of Baden-Württemberg, Bavaria, Berlin, Brandenburg, Bremen, Hamburg, Hesse, Mecklenburg-Western Pomerania, Lower Saxony, North Rhine-Westphalia, Rhineland-Palatinate, Saar, Saxony, Saxony-Anhalt, Schleswig-Holstein and Thuringia have achieved the unity and freedom of Germany in free self-determination. This Basic Law thus applies to the entire German people.

I. The fundamental rights

Article 1. (1) Human dignity is inviolable. To respect and protect it is the duty of all state authority.
(2) The German people therefore acknowledges inviolable and inalienable human rights as the basis of every community of people, of peace and of justice in the world.
(3) The following fundamental rights bind the legislature, the executive and the judiciary as directly applicable law.

Article 2. (1) Everyone has the right to the free development of his personality, as far as he does not infringe on the rights of others and does not violate the constitutional order or the law of morality.
(2) Everyone has the right to life and physical integrity. The freedom of the person is inviolable. These rights may be interfered with only pursuant to a statute.

Article 3. (1) All people are equal before the law.
(2) Men and women have equal rights. The state promotes the actual implementation of equal rights for women and men and takes measures to remove existing disadvantages.

---

1 As last amended by the Act for the Amendment of the Basic Law [Gesetz zur Änderung des Grundgesetzes] of 28 March 2029 (*BGBl.* I p. 404). Translation by Philipp Kiiver, Sascha Hardt, Gereon Rotering &Gisela Kristoferitsch.

(3) No-one may be disadvantaged or preferred because of his sex, his descent, his race, his language, his homeland and origin, his faith, his religious or political views. No-one may be disadvantaged because of his disability.

Article 4. (1) The freedom of faith, of conscience, and the freedom to manifest one's religious and world-view conviction, are inviolable.
(2) The undisturbed exercise of religion is ensured.
(3) No-one may be forced against his conscience into armed military service. Details are regulated by a federal statute.

Article 5. (1) Everyone has the right to freely express and disseminate his opinion in speech, writing and picture and to inform himself without interference from generally accessible sources. The freedom of the press and the freedom of reporting through radio and film are ensured. Censorship does not take place.
(2) These rights find their limits in the regulations of general statutes, in statutory provisions for the protection of the youth and in the right to personal honour.
(3) Art and science, research and teaching are free. The freedom of teaching does not release from the loyalty to the constitution.

Article 6. (1) Marriage and family are placed under the special protection of the state order.
(2) The care and upbringing of children are the natural right of the parents and are an obligation that is primarily theirs. The community of the state watches over their performance.
(3) Children may be separated from the family pursuant to a statute against the will of their custodians only when the custodians fail or when the children are in danger of becoming victims of neglect for other reasons.
(4) Every mother is entitled to the protection and care of the community.
(5) Legislation is to provide children born outside wedlock with conditions for their physical and mental development and their position in society equal to those of children born within wedlock.

Article 7. (1) The entire school system is placed under the supervision of the state.
(2) Custodians have the right to decide over the participation of their child in religion classes.
(3) Religion classes are a regular course at public schools with the exception of non-denominational schools. Without prejudice to the state right of supervision, religious classes are taught in accordance with the principles of the religious communities. No teacher may be obliged against his will to teach religion classes.

(4) The right to establish private schools is ensured. Private schools as a substitute for public schools require the approval of the state and are subject to State legislation. Approval is to be granted when private schools are not inferior to state schools in their teaching aims and facilities as well as the scientific training of their teaching staff, and when a segregation of pupils according to the economic standing of the parents is not promoted. Approval is to be denied when the economic and legal position of the teaching staff is insufficiently secured.

(5) A private primary-cum-secondary school is only to be allowed if the curriculum administration recognizes a special educational interest or, upon custodians' request, if it is to be established as a community school, a denominational school or as a school based on a particular world view and a public primary-cum-secondary school of that kind is lacking in the municipality.

(6) Nursery schools remain abolished.

Article 8. (1) All Germans have the right to assemble peacefully and unarmed without notification or permission.

(2) Regarding gatherings outdoors, this right may be limited by or pursuant to a statute.

Article 9. (1) All Germans have the right to form clubs and societies.

(2) Associations whose purposes or activities run counter to criminal law, or which are aimed against the constitutional order or the idea of understanding between nations, are prohibited.

(3) The right to form associations for the promotion of working and economic conditions is ensured for everyone and for all professions. Agreements that limit or seek to hinder this right are void, measures taken with a view thereto are illegal. Measures in the sense of Articles 12a, 35 (2) and (3), Article 87a (4) and Article 91 may not be directed against industrial dispute action that is taken for the protection and promotion of working and economic conditions by associations in the meaning of the first sentence.

Article 10. (1) The privacy of correspondence as well as the privacy of mail and telecommunications are inviolable.

(2) Limitations may be ordered only pursuant to a statute. If the limitation serves the protection of the liberal-democratic fundamental order or of the integrity or security of the Federation or a State, then statute may provide that it not be notified to those affected and that recourse to the courts be replaced by review by organs and auxiliary organs appointed by the parliament.

Article 11. (1) All Germans enjoy freedom of movement on the entire territory of the Federation.

(2) This right may be limited only by or pursuant to a statute and only for those cases where sufficient means to support life are lacking and where this would result in a special burden on the community or where it is necessary for the aversion of a danger to the integrity or the liberal democratic fundamental order of the Federation or a State, for the countering of an epidemic threat, natural disasters or very serious accidents, for the protection of the youth from neglect or for the prevention of criminal acts.

Article 12. (1) All Germans have the right to freely choose their profession, place of work and of their training. The exercise of a profession may be regulated by or pursuant to a statute.
(2) No-one may be forced to perform a particular work, except within the framework of a regular general public service obligation that is the same for everyone.
(3) Forced labour is permissible only in the context of a court-ordered deprivation of freedom.

Article 12a. (1) Men from the age of eighteen onwards can be obliged to serve in the armed forces, the Federal Border Guard [Bundesgrenzschutz] or in a civil defence organization.
(2) He who refuses armed military service on conscientious grounds may be obliged to serve in an alternative service. The length of the alternative service may not exceed the length of the military service. Details are regulated by a statute which may not compromise the freedom of conscientious decision and which must also provide for an alternative service option which is not connected with the units of the armed forces and the Federal Border Guard.
(3) Persons liable to conscription who have not been drafted in accordance with paragraphs 1 or 2 may in a state of defence, by or pursuant to a statute, be committed to an employment for civilian services for defence purposes including the protection of the civilian population; commitment to public employment is only permissible for the exercise of police tasks or such sovereign tasks of public administration that can be fulfilled only within a public employment. Employments in the meaning of the first sentence may be established with the armed forces, in the context of their supply, as well as in the public administration; commitment to employment in the context of the supply of the civilian population is permissible only to secure its basic needs or to maintain its safety.
(4) If, in a state of defence, the demand for civilian services in the civilian medical and health system as well as in the stationary military hospital system cannot be met on a voluntary basis, women from the age of eighteen until the age of fifty-five may be drafted to such services by or pursuant to a statute. They may in no event be drafted to armed service.
(5) For the time period before the state of defence, obligations under paragraph 3 may only be established within the guidelines of Article 80a (1). For the preparation to services

according to paragraph 3 for which special knowledge or skills are required, by or pursuant to a statute the participation in training courses may be made mandatory. In that respect, the first sentence does not apply.
(6) If, in a state of defence, the demand for workers in the contexts stipulated in paragraph 3, second sentence, cannot be met on a voluntary basis, the freedom of Germans to give up a profession or a place of work may be limited, in order to meet this demand, by or pursuant to a statute. Prior to the beginning of a state of defence, paragraph 5, first sentence, applies mutatis mutandis.

Article 13. (1) The home is inviolable.
(2) Searches may be ordered only by a judge or, in case of an imminent threat, also by other organs provided for by statutes, and may be conducted only in the form stipulated there.
(3) When certain facts support the suspicion that someone has committed a certain very serious crime defined individually by statute, then, for the prosecution of this act, on the basis of a court order, technical means for the acoustic surveillance of homes in which the suspect is presumably staying may be used, if the investigation of the case by other means would be disproportionately burdensome or futile. The measure is to be of a limited duration. The order is to be given by a body staffed with three judges. In case of an imminent threat, it may also be given by a single judge.
(4) To avert acute threats to public safety, especially a threat to the public or to life, technical means for the surveillance of homes may be used only on the basis of a court order. In case of an imminent threat, the measure may also be ordered by another instance stipulated by statute; a court decision must afterwards be obtained without delay.
(5) If technical means are exclusively meant for the protection of persons operating in a home, the measure may be ordered by an instance stipulated by statute. Any other use of the information thus obtained is permissible only for the purpose of criminal prosecution or the aversion of dangers and only if the lawfulness of the measure has been established by a court; in case of an imminent threat, a court decision must afterwards be obtained without delay.
(6) The Federal Government informs the Bundestag annually about the use that has been made of technical means under paragraph 3, under paragraph 4 within the competence of the Federation, and under paragraph 5 in as far as it requires judicial review. A body elected by the Bundestag exercises parliamentary control on the basis of this report. The States ensure an equivalent parliamentary control.
(7) Interferences and limitations may otherwise be effected only for the aversion of a threat to the public or to the life of individual persons, pursuant to a statute also for the prevention of acute threats to public safety and order, especially to address a shortage of housing space, to combat epidemic threats or to protect endangered adolescents.

Article 14. (1) Property and the right of inheritance are ensured. The content and limits thereof are defined by statutes.
(2) Property entails obligations. Its use should also serve the public good.
(3) An expropriation is only permissible for the public good. It may be effected only by or pursuant to a statute which regulates the kind and extent of compensation. The compensation is to be established by justly weighing the interests of the community and of those involved. Recourse to the ordinary courts is open in case of a dispute regarding the amount of the compensation.

Article 15. Land, natural resources and means of production may, for the purpose of socialization, by a statute which regulates the kind and extent of compensation, be transferred into public ownership or into other forms of collective concern. As regards the compensation, Article 14 (3), third and fourth sentence, applies mutatis mutandis.

Article 16. (1) German citizenship may not be withdrawn. A loss of citizenship may occur only pursuant to a statute and, if against the will of the person affected, only when the person affected does not become stateless as a result.
(2) No German may be extradited to a foreign state. By statute a different regime may be established concerning extraditions to a member state of the European Union or an international tribunal, as long as principles of the rule of law are secured.

Article 16a. (1) Those politically persecuted enjoy the right to asylum.
(2) He who arrives from a member state of the European Communities or from another third country where the application of the Convention relating to the status of refugees and the Convention for the protection of human rights and fundamental freedoms is ensured, cannot rely on paragraph 1. The states outside the European Communities to which the conditions of the first sentence apply are designated by a statute which requires the consent of the Bundesrat. In cases stipulated by the first sentence, measures for the termination of a stay may be taken irrespectively of any court actions filed against them.
(3) By a statute which requires the consent of the Bundesrat, states may be designated where, based on the state of the law, the application of the law and the general political circumstances, it appears certain that neither political persecution nor inhuman or degrading punishment or treatment takes place. It is presumed that an alien from such a state is not being persecuted as long as he does not provide facts which support the conclusion that he is being politically persecuted contrary to this presumption.
(4) The execution of measures for the termination of a stay are, in the cases of paragraph 3 and in other cases that are manifestly ill-founded or are presumed manifestly ill-founded, suspended by a court only when serious doubts exist as to the lawfulness of the measure; the scope of review may be limited, and belated submissions be disregarded. Details are to be regulated by statute.

(5) Paragraphs 1 to 4 do not bar any international treaties of member states of the European Communities among themselves and with third countries which, while respecting the obligations under the Convention relating to the status of refugees and the Convention for the protection of human rights and fundamental freedoms, the application of which must be ensured in the contracting states, provide for rules on jurisdiction for the review of applications for asylum, including the mutual recognition of decisions regarding asylum.

Article 17. Everyone has the right, individually or together with others in a group, to address in writing the competent authorities and parliament with petitions or complaints.

Article 17a. (1) Statutes regarding military and alternative service may provide that for members of the armed forces and the alternative service, for the duration of the military or alternative service, the fundamental right to freely express and disseminate one's opinion in speech, writing and picture (Article 5 (1), first sentence, first clause), the fundamental right of freedom of assembly (Article 8) and the right of petition (Article 17) in as far as it grants the right to submit petitions or complaints together with others in a group, be limited.
(2) Statutes which serve the purpose of defence, including the protection of the civilian population, may provide that the fundamental rights of free movement (Article 11) and the inviolability of the home (Article 13) be limited.

Article 18. He who abuses the freedom of expression, in particular the freedom of the press (Article 5 (1)), the freedom of teaching (Article 5 (3)), the freedom of assembly (Article 8), the freedom of association (Article 9), the privacy of the correspondence, the mail and telecommunications (Article 10), property (Article 14) or the right to asylum (Article 16a) in order to fight against the liberal democratic fundamental order, forfeits these fundamental rights. The forfeiture and its scope are established by the Federal Constitutional Court [Bundesverfassungsgericht].

Article 19. (1) In as far as a fundamental right may be limited by or pursuant to a statute in accordance with this Basic Law, such statute must be of a general nature and may not merely apply to an individual case. In addition, the statute must state the fundamental right and the Article concerned.
(2) In no event may a fundamental right be compromised in its essence.
(3) The fundamental rights also cover domestic legal persons, in as far as they are applicable in the light of their nature.
(4) If someone's rights are violated by public authority, he has recourse to the courts. In as far as no other jurisdiction applies, recourse may be had to the ordinary courts. Article 10 (2), second sentence, remains unaffected by this.

II. The Federation and the States

Article 20. (1) The Federal Republic of Germany is a democratic and social federal state.
(2) All state authority derives from the people. It is exercised by the people through elections and votes and through specific organs of the legislature, of executive power and the judiciary.
(3) The legislature is bound by the constitutional order, the executive power and the judiciary by law and justice.
(4) All Germans have the right to resist any person seeking to abolish this order, if no other remedy is available.

Article 20a. The state protects, also under its responsibility for future generations, the natural foundations of life and the animals, within the framework of the constitutional order through legislation and within the guidelines of law and justice through executive power and the judiciary.

Article 21. (1) Political parties contribute to the political will-formation of the people. Their establishment is free. Their internal order must correspond to democratic principles. They must render account about the origin and use of their means as well as about their assets in public.
(2) Political parties which, based on their aims or the conduct of their followers, are committed to jeopardizing or eliminating the liberal democratic fundamental order or to threatening the integrity of the Federal Republic of Germany, are unconstitutional.
(3) Parties which, by reason of their goals or the conduct of their followers, seek to impair or abolish the free democratic basic order or to endanger the existence of the federal Republic of Germany are excluded from state financing. Where this exclusion is established, the tax privilege of these parties and of donations to these parties lapses as well.
(4) The Federal Constitutional Court rules on the question of unconstitutionality pursuant to sub-paragraph (2), as well as on the exclusion from state financing pursuant to sub-paragraph (3).
(5) Details are regulated by federal statutes.

Article 22. (1) The capital of the Federal Republic of Germany is Berlin. The representation of the state as a whole in the capital is a matter for the Federation. Details are regulated by statute.
(2) The federal flag is black-red-gold.

Article 23. (1) With a view to achieving a united Europe, the Federal Republic of Germany participates in the development of the European Union which is committed to democratic, rule-of-law, social, and federal principles and to the principle of subsidiarity, and which guarantees a level of protection of fundamental rights essentially comparable to that afforded by this Basic Law. To this end the Federation may, by a statute with the consent of the Bundesrat, transfer sovereign powers. For the establishment of the European Union, as well as for changes to its treaty foundations and comparable regulations that amend or supplement this Basic Law in its content, or that make such amendments or supplements possible, Article 79 (2) and (3) applies.

(1a) The Bundestag and the Bundesrat have the right to bring an action before the Court of Justice of the European Union if a legislative act of the European Union infringes upon the principle of subsidiarity. The Bundestag is obliged to do so on application by a quarter of its members. A statute which requires the consent of the Bundesrat may, with respect to the exercise of the rights accorded to the Bundestag and the Bundesrat in the treaty framework of the European Union, make deviations from the first sentence of Article 42 (2), first sentence, and Article 52 (3), first sentence.

(2) The Bundestag and, through the Bundesrat, the States, participate in matters concerning the European Union. The Federal Government must inform the Bundestag and the Bundesrat comprehensively and at the earliest possible time.

(3) The Federal Government provides the Bundestag with an opportunity to state its opinion prior to its participation in legislative acts of the European Union. The Federal Government takes into account the statements of opinion of the Bundestag during negotiations. Details are regulated by a statute.

(4) The Bundesrat is to be included in the will-formation of the Federation in as far as it would have had to participate in an equivalent domestic measure or in as far as the States would have been competent domestically.

(5) In as far as, in an area of exclusive competence of the Federation, interests of the States are affected, or in as far as the Federation has otherwise legislative competence, the Federal Government takes into account the statements of opinion of the Bundesrat. If primarily legislative competences of the States, the organization of their authorities or their administrative procedures are affected, the opinion of the Bundesrat must to that extent be given greatest consideration during the will-formation of the Federation; the responsibility of the Federation for the state as a whole must in that context be upheld. In matters that may result in an increase in spending or a decrease in revenue for the Federation, the consent of the Federal Government is required.

(6) If primarily exclusive legislative competences of the States in the areas of schooling, culture or broadcasting are affected, the exercise of the rights that the Federal Republic of Germany has as a member state of the European Union is transferred from the Federation to a representative of the States appointed by the Bundesrat. The exercise of these rights is carried out with the participation of and in coordination with the Federal Government; the responsibility of the Federation for the state as a whole must in that context be upheld.

(7) Details regarding paragraphs 4 to 6 are regulated by a statute that requires the consent of the Bundesrat.

Article 24. (1) The Federation may, by statute, transfer sovereign powers to international organizations.
(1a) In as far as the States are competent for the exercise of state power and the fulfilment of state tasks, they may, with the consent of the Federal Government, transfer sovereign powers to cross-border neighbourhood institutions.
(2) The Federation may, for the preservation of peace, enter into a system of mutual collective security; it will in that context agree to limitations of its sovereign powers which bring about and secure a peaceful and permanent order in Europe and between the nations of the world.
(3) For the settlement of international disputes, the Federation will accede to agreements regarding general, comprehensive and mandatory international arbitration.

Article 25. The general rules of international law are an integral part of federal law. They take precedence over statutes and directly create rights and obligations for the inhabitants of the territory of the Federation.

Article 26. (1) Acts that are capable of and are committed with the intent to disturb the peaceful coexistence of nations, in particular prepare the conduct of a war of aggression, are unconstitutional. They are to be made punishable offences.
(2) Weapons designed for warfare may be produced, transported and brought into circulation only with the consent of the Federal Government. Details are regulated by a federal statute.

Article 27. All German merchant vessels form a uniform merchant fleet.

Article 28. (1) The constitutional order in the States must comply with the principles of a republican, democratic and social state based on the rule of law in the meaning of this Basic Law. In the States, rural counties [Kreise] and municipalities [Gemeinden], the people must have a representative body that is formed in general, direct, free, equal and secret-ballot elections. At elections within rural counties and municipalities, persons with the citizenship of a member state of the European Community, within the guidelines of the law of the European Community, also have the right to vote and may be elected. In municipalities, a municipal assembly may take the place of an elected body.
(2) Municipalities must have the secured right to regulate all affairs of the local community, within the framework of statutes, on their own responsibility. Also associations of municipalities [Gemeindeverbände] have, within the framework of their statutory function, within the guidelines of statutes, the right to self-government. The securing of self-

government also includes the foundations of financial autonomy; part of these foundations is a source of revenue related to economic strength to which municipalities with the right to set tax rates are entitled.

(3) The Federation ensures that the constitutional order of the States complies with fundamental rights and the provisions of paragraphs 1 and 2.

Article 29. (1) The territory of the Federation may be restructured so as to ensure that the States, in the light of their size and capacity, are able to effectively fulfil the tasks vested in them. Account is to be taken of regional attachment, historical and cultural connections, economic opportunity, as well as the requirements of regional planning and zoning.

(2) Measures for the restructuring of the territory of the Federation are effected by a federal statute which requires approval in a referendum [Volksentscheid]. The affected States are to be heard.

(3) The referendum takes place in those States from the territory or from parts of the territory of which a new or a redrawn State is to be formed (affected States). The object of the referendum is the question whether the affected States should continue to exist as before or whether the new or redrawn State should be formed. A referendum in favour of a new or redrawn State is established when majorities vote in favour of the change both within its future territory and within the territories or parts of territories of an affected State whose State affiliation is to be changed. It is not established when a majority within the territory of one of the affected States rejects the change; such rejection is however ineffective if in a part of a territory whose affiliation with the affected State is to be changed, a two-thirds majority votes in favour of the change, except when within the territory of the affected State as a whole a two-thirds majority rejects the change.

(4) If within a contiguous, separated residential and economic area whose parts lie in several States and which has at least one million inhabitants, one-tenth of the population entitled to vote for the Bundestag there demands by popular initiative [Volksbegehren] that for this area a single State affiliation be created, then within two years a federal statute is either to determine whether the State affiliation will be changed in accordance with paragraph 2 or that a consultative referendum [Volksbefragung] will be held in the affected States.

(5) The consultative referendum is aimed at establishing whether a change of State affiliation to be proposed by the statute finds approval. The statute may subject different, yet not more than two proposals to the consultative referendum. If a majority votes in favour of a proposed change of State affiliation, then within two years a federal statute is to determine whether the State affiliation will be changed in accordance with paragraph 2. If a proposal subjected to a consultative referendum receives an approval corresponding with the provisions of paragraph 3, third and fourth sentence, then within two years after the consultative referendum a federal statute regarding the creation of the proposed State is to be adopted, which does no longer require approval by referendum.

(6) A majority in a referendum and in a consultative referendum is the majority of the votes cast, if that includes at least one quarter of the population entitled to vote for the Bundestag. As for the rest, details regarding the referendum, the popular initiative and the consultative referendum are regulated by a federal statute; this statute may also provide that popular initiatives may not be repeated within a time period of five years.

(7) Further changes to the territorial shape of the States may be effected by inter-State agreements [Staatsverträge] between the affected States or by a federal statute with the consent of the Bundesrat, if the territory whose State affiliation is to be changed has no more than 50,000 inhabitants. Details are regulated by a federal statute which requires the consent of the Bundesrat and the approval of the majority of the members of the Bundestag. It must provide for a hearing of the affected municipalities and rural counties.

(8) The States may regulate a restructuring of their territory or parts of their territory, in deviation from the provisions of paragraphs 2 to 7, by inter-State agreement. The affected municipalities and rural counties are to be heard. The inter-State agreement requires approval by referendum in each participating State. If the inter-State agreement concerns parts of the territories of States, the approval may be confined to referendums in these parts of the territories; the fifth sentence, second clause, does not apply. In a referendum the majority of votes cast decides if it includes at least one quarter of the population entitled to vote for the Bundestag; details are regulated by a statute. The inter-State agreement requires the consent of the Bundestag.

Article 30. The exercise of state power and the fulfilment of state tasks is a matter for the States, in as far as this Basic Law does not stipulate or permit otherwise.

Article 31. Federal law prevails over State law.

Article 32. (1) The conduct of relations with foreign states is a matter for the Federation.
(2) Before the conclusion of a treaty which affects the special circumstances of a State, that State is to be heard.
(3) In as far as the States have legislative competence, they may conclude treaties with foreign states with the consent of the Federal Government.

Article 33. (1) Every German has the same citizenship rights and obligations in all States.
(2) Every German has, in view of his aptitude, ability and professional performance, equal access to every public office.
(3) The enjoyment of civil and political rights, the admission to public offices as well as the rights acquired in public service are independent of religious conviction. No-one may be subject to disadvantage due to his adherence or non-adherence to a conviction or world view.

(4) The exercise of sovereign powers as a permanent task is, as a rule, to be transferred to members of the public service who are in a public-law relation of service and loyalty.
(5) The law on the public service is to be regulated and developed further, taking into account the traditional principles of the professional civil service.

Article 34. If someone violates his official duties with respect to a third person in the exercise of a public office entrusted to him, then liability lies in principle with the state or with the entity in the service of which he is. In case of intent or gross negligence, individual liability for indemnity is reserved. For the right to damages and indemnity, recourse to the ordinary courts may not be excluded.

Article 35. (1) All authorities of the Federation and the States provide to each other legal and inter-administrative assistance.
(2) In order to maintain or restore public safety or order, a State may in cases of special significance request forces and facilities of the Federal Border Guard to support its police, if the police could, without such support, not fulfil a task at all or only with great difficulty. For relief in case of a natural disaster or a very serious accident, a State may request police forces of other States, forces and facilities of other administrations as well as the Federal Border Guard and the armed forces.
(3) If the natural disaster or the accident threatens the territory of more than one State, the Federal Government may, in as far as that is necessary for effective relief, give the State governments the order to make police forces available to other States, and use units of the Federal Border Guard and the armed forces to support the police forces. Measures of the Federal Government under the first sentence must at any time be lifted upon request of the Bundesrat, otherwise without delay after the removal of the threat.

Article 36. (1) In the supreme federal authorities, civil servants from all States must be employed in appropriate proportions. Persons employed in the other federal authorities should, as a rule, be drawn from the State in which they serve.
(2) Statutes regarding the military must also take into account the division of the Federation into States and their special regional attachments.

Article 37. (1) If a State does not fulfil its federal duties according to the Basic Law or another federal statute, the Federal Government may, with the consent of the Bundesrat, take the necessary measures to compel that State to fulfil its duties by way of federal enforcement [Bundeszwang].
(2) For the execution of federal enforcement, the Federal Government or its representative has the right to give instructions to all States and their authorities.

III. The Bundestag

Article 38. (1) The members of the German Bundestag are elected in general, direct, free, equal and secret-ballot elections. They are the representatives of the whole people, not bound by orders or instructions, and responsible only to their conscience.
(2) He who has attained the age of eighteen years has the right to vote; he who has reached the age at which majority begins, has the right to be elected.
(3) Details are regulated by a federal statute.

Article 39. (1) The Bundestag is elected, subject to the following provisions, for four years. Its term ends with the convention of a new Bundestag. New elections take place at the earliest forty-six, at the latest forty-eight months after the beginning of a term. In the case of a dissolution of the Bundestag, new elections take place within sixty days.
(2) The Bundestag convenes, at the latest, on the thirtieth day after elections.
(3) The Bundestag determines the end and the beginning of its sessions. The president of the Bundestag may convene it earlier. He is obliged to do so if one-third of the members, the Federal President or the Federal Chancellor so demand.

Article 40. (1) The Bundestag elects its president, his deputy and the secretaries. It adopts its rules of procedure.
(2) The president exercises proprietary and police powers in the Bundestag building. Without his permission, no search or seizure may take place on the premises of the Bundestag.

Article 41. (1) Review of elections is a matter for the Bundestag. It also decides whether a member of the Bundestag has lost his membership.
(2) Complaints against the decision of the Bundestag are admissible before the Federal Constitutional Court.
(3) Details are regulated by a federal statute.

Article 42. (1) The Bundestag deliberates in public. Upon the request of one-tenth of its members or upon request of the Federal Government, the public may be excluded by a two-thirds majority. The decision on the request takes place in a non-public session.
(2) A decision of the Bundestag requires a majority of the votes cast, in as far as this Basic Law does not provide otherwise. For the elections to be carried out by the Bundestag, the rules of procedure may allow for exceptions.
(3) Truthful reports about the public sessions of the Bundestag and its committees do not give rise to any liability.

Article 43. (1) The Bundestag and its committees may demand the presence of any member of the Federal Government.
(2) The members of the Bundesrat and the Federal Government as well as their representatives have access to all sessions of the Bundestag and its committees. They have the right to be heard at all times.

Article 44. (1) The Bundestag has the right and, upon request of one quarter of its members the obligation, to establish an investigative committee [Untersuchungsausschuss] which gathers the necessary evidence in public deliberation. The public may be excluded.
(2) The rules regarding criminal procedure are applicable mutatis mutandis to the gathering of evidence. The privacy of the correspondence, mail and telecommunications remains unaffected.
(3) Courts and administrative authorities are obliged to provide legal and inter-administrative assistance.
(4) The decisions of investigative committees are outside the scope of judicial assessment. In the consideration and qualification of the facts subject to the investigation, the courts are free.

Article 45. The Bundestag establishes a committee for the affairs of the European Union. It may authorize it to exercise the rights of the Bundestag under Article 23 with respect to the Federal Government. It may also authorize it to exercise the rights that have been accorded to the Bundestag in the treaty framework of the European Union.

Article 45a. (1) The Bundestag establishes a committee for foreign affairs and a committee for defence.
(2) The committee for defence also has the rights of an investigative committee. Upon the request of one quarter of its members it has the obligation to make a matter the subject of an investigation.
(3) Article 44 (1) does not apply to the area of defence.

Article 45b. For the protection of fundamental rights and as an auxiliary organ of the Bundestag in the exercise of parliamentary control, a commissioner for the armed forces [Wehrbeauftragter] is appointed. Details are regulated by a federal statute.

Article 45c. (1) The Bundestag establishes a petitions committee which has as its task the consideration of petitions and complaints addressed to the Bundestag under Article 17.
(2) The competences of the committee for the consideration of complaints are regulated by a federal statute.

Article 45d. (1) The Bundestag establishes a body to control the intelligence activities of the Federation.
(2) Details are regulated by a federal statute.

Article 46. (1) A member of the Bundestag may at no time be prosecuted by judicial or disciplinary means or be in any other way held liable outside the Bundestag because of his voting or because of a statement which he made in the Bundestag or in one of its committees. This does not apply to defamatory insults.
(2) A member of the Bundestag may be held liable or arrested because of a punishable act only with the permission of the Bundestag, unless he is arrested as he committed the act or on the following day.
(3) Permission of the Bundestag is furthermore required for any other limitation of the personal freedom of a member of the Bundestag or for the commencement of a procedure against a member of the Bundestag under Article 18.
(4) Any criminal procedure and any procedure under Article 18 against a member of the Bundestag, any detention and any other limitation of his personal freedom must be suspended upon demand of the Bundestag.

Article 47. The members of the Bundestag have the right to refuse to testify regarding persons who have confided information to them in their capacity as members of the Bundestag or to whom they have in that capacity confided information, as well as regarding the information itself. In as far as this right to refuse to testify applies, the seizure of written documents is not permissible.

Article 48. (1) He who runs as a candidate for a seat in the Bundestag has a right to the leave necessary for the preparation of his election.
(2) No-one may be hindered from assuming and exercising the office of a member of the Bundestag. A dismissal or discharge from employment on this ground is not permissible.
(3) The members of the Bundestag have the right to an appropriate allowance that secures their independence. They have the right to the free use of all state-run means of transport. Details are regulated by a federal statute.

Article 49. (Repealed).

IV. The Bundesrat

Article 50. Through the Bundesrat, the States participate in the legislation and administration of the Federation and in matters concerning the European Union.

Article 51. (1) The Bundesrat consists of members of the State governments, which appoint and recall them. They may be represented by other members of their governments.
(2) Each State has at least three votes; States with more than two million inhabitants have four, States with more than six million inhabitants five, States with more than seven million inhabitants six votes.
(3) Each State may send as many members as it has votes. The votes of each State may be cast only as a unit and only by members present or their alternates.

Article 52. (1) The Bundesrat elects its president for one year.
(2) The president convenes the Bundesrat. He must convene it if the representatives of at least two States or the Federal Government so demand.
(3) The Bundesrat takes its decisions with at least a majority of its votes. It adopts its rules of procedure. It deliberates in public. The public may be excluded.
(3a) For matters concerning the European Union, the Bundesrat may establish a European affairs chamber whose decisions are considered decisions of the Bundesrat; the number of votes of the States to be cast as a unit is determined by Article 51 (2).
(4) In the committees of the Bundesrat, other members or representatives of the governments of the States may be members.

Article 53. The members of the Federal Government have the right and, upon demand, the duty to participate in the deliberations of the Bundesrat and its committees. They have the right to be heard at all times. The Bundesrat is to be kept informed by the Federal Government about the conduct of affairs.

IVa. The Joint Committee

Article 53a. (1) Two-thirds of the members of the Joint Committee [Gemeinsamer Ausschuss] comprise members of the Bundestag and one-third members of the Bundesrat. The members of the Bundestag are appointed by the Bundestag according to the relative strength of the political party groups; they may not be members of the Federal Government. Each State is represented by a member of the Bundesrat appointed by it; these members are not bound by any instructions. The establishment of the Joint Committee and its procedures are regulated by rules of procedure which are to be adopted by the Bundestag and which require the consent of the Bundesrat.
(2) The Federal Government must inform the Joint Committee about its planning for the state of defence. The rights of the Bundestag and its committees under Article 43 (1) are not affected.

V. The Federal President

Article 54. (1) The Federal President is elected without debate by the Federal Convention [Bundesversammlung].
Any German may be elected who is entitled to vote for the Bundestag and who has attained the age of forty.
(2) The term of office of the Federal President is five years. A subsequent re-election is permissible only once.
(3) The Federal Convention consists of the members of the Bundestag and an equal number of members who are elected by the parliaments of the States on the basis of proportional representation.
(4) The Federal Convention convenes, at the latest, thirty days before the expiry of the term of office of the Federal President, and in case of an early termination thirty days after that moment at the latest. It is convened by the president of the Bundestag.
(5) After the expiry of a term, the period under paragraph 4, first sentence, begins with the first convention of the Bundestag.
(6) He who has received the votes of a majority of the members of the Federal Convention is elected. If after two ballots such majority is not obtained by any candidate, then he who receives the most votes in a further ballot is elected.
(7) Details are regulated by a federal statute.

Article 55. (1) The Federal President may not be a member of the Federal Government or of a legislative body of the Federation or of a State.
(2) The Federal President may not exercise any other remunerated office, he may pursue no trade or profession and may not be a member of either the board or the supervisory board of a profit-oriented company.

Article 56. The Federal President, when assuming office, takes the following oath before the assembled members of the Bundestag and the Bundesrat:

> "I swear that I shall dedicate my strength to the well-being of the German people, promote its welfare, protect it from harm, uphold and defend the Basic Law and the legislation of the Federation, fulfil my duties conscientiously, and do justice to all. So help me God."

The oath may also be taken without the religious assertion.

Article 57. The powers of the Federal President, in case he is prevented from exercising his functions or in case of an early termination of his term, are exercised by the president of the Bundesrat.

Article 58. Instructions and orders of the Federal President require for their validity the countersignature by the Federal Chancellor or the competent federal minister. This does not apply to the appointment and dismissal of the Federal Chancellor, the dissolution of the Bundestag under Article 63 and the request under Article 69 (3).

Article 59. (1) The Federal President represents the Federation under international law. He concludes, in the name of the Federation, treaties with foreign states. He accredits and receives envoys.
(2) Treaties which regulate the political relations of the Federation, or which refer to objects of federal legislation, require the consent or participation of the organs competent for such federal legislation in the form of a federal statute. For administrative agreements, the regulations regarding the federal administration apply mutatis mutandis.

Article 59a. (Repealed).

Article 60. (1) The Federal President appoints and dismisses federal judges, federal civil servants, officers and non-commissioned officers, as far as statutory regulations do not provide otherwise.
(2) He exercises, in individual cases, the right of pardon for the Federation.
(3) He may transfer these competences to other authorities.
(4) Paragraphs 2 to 4 of Article 46 apply to the Federal President mutatis mutandis.

Article 61. (1) The Bundestag or the Bundesrat may impeach the Federal President for an intentional violation of the Basic Law or another federal statute before the Federal Constitutional Court. The motion to impeach must be tabled by at least a quarter of the members of the Bundestag or a quarter of the votes of the Bundesrat. The decision to impeach requires a majority of two-thirds of the members of the Bundestag or two-thirds of the votes of the Bundesrat. The prosecution is conducted by a representative of the impeaching organ.
(2) If the Federal Constitutional Court establishes that the Federal President is guilty of having committed an intentional violation of the Basic Law or another federal statute, it may declare that he is removed from office. By interim order after impeachment it may rule that he is prevented from exercising his functions.

VI. The Federal Government

Article 62. The Federal Government consists of the Federal Chancellor [Bundeskanzler] and the federal ministers.

Article 63. (1) The Federal Chancellor is elected, on the proposal of the Federal President, by the Bundestag without debate.
(2) He who receives the votes of a majority of the members of the Bundestag is elected. The person elected is to be appointed by the Federal President.
(3) If the nominee is not elected, the Bundestag may within fourteen days after the ballot, by the votes of more than half of its members, elect a Federal Chancellor.
(4) If no election is successful within this period, a new ballot takes place without delay, in which he who receives the most votes is elected. If the person elected receives the votes of a majority of the members of the Bundestag, the Federal President must appoint him within seven days after the election. If the person elected does not receive such a majority, then within seven days the Federal President must either appoint him or dissolve the Bundestag.

Article 64. (1) The federal ministers are appointed and dismissed by the Federal President on the proposal of the Federal Chancellor.
(2) The Federal Chancellor and the federal ministers, when assuming office, take the oath as stipulated in Article 56 before the Bundestag.

Article 65. The Federal Chancellor determines the guidelines of policy and bears responsibility for that. Within these guidelines, each federal minister directs his portfolio autonomously and on his own responsibility. The Federal Government rules in case of disagreements between federal ministers. The Federal Chancellor directs its affairs according to rules of procedure as adopted by the Federal Government and approved by the Federal President.

Article 65a. (1) The federal minister of defence has the command over the armed forces.
(2) (Repealed).

Article 66. The Federal Chancellor and the federal ministers may not exercise any other remunerated office, they may pursue no trade or profession and may not be a member of either the board or, without consent of the Bundestag, the supervisory board of a profit-oriented company.

Article 67. (1) The Bundestag may express its lack of confidence in the Federal Chancellor only by electing a successor by the vote of a majority of its members and by requesting the Federal President to dismiss the Federal Chancellor. The Federal President must comply with the request and appoint the person elected.
(2) Forty-eight hours must pass between the motion and the election.

Article 68. (1) If a motion of the Federal Chancellor for a vote of confidence is not supported by the majority of the members of the Bundestag, the Federal President may, on the proposal of the Federal Chancellor, dissolve the Bundestag within twenty-one days. The right of dissolution lapses as soon as the Bundestag elects another Federal Chancellor by the vote of a majority of its members.
(2) Forty-eight hours must pass between the motion and the vote.

Article 69. (1) The Federal Chancellor appoints a federal minister as his deputy.
(2) The office of the Federal Chancellor ends in any event with the convention of a new Bundestag, the office of a federal minister ends also with any other termination of the office of the Federal Chancellor.
(3) On the request of the Federal President, the Federal Chancellor is obliged, and on the request of the Federal Chancellor or the Federal President a federal minister is obliged to continue the affairs until the appointment of a successor.

VII. The legislation of the Federation

Article 70. (1) The States have the right to legislate in as far as this Basic Law does not confer legislative power on the Federation.
(2) The delimitation of competences between the Federation and the States is guided by the provisions of this Basic Law regarding exclusive and concurrent legislation.

Article 71. In the area of exclusive legislative power of the Federation, the States have power to legislate only when and in as far as they are expressly authorized to do so by a federal statute.

Article 72. (1) In the area of concurrent legislative power, the States have power to legislate so long as and to the extent that the Federation has not exercised its legislative power through a statute.
(2) The Federation has legislative power in the areas of Article 74 (1) no. 4, 7, 11, 13, 15, 19a, 20, 22, 25 and 26 when and to the extent that the bringing about of equivalent living standards throughout the territory of the Federation or the upholding of legal or economic unity in the interest of the state as a whole require a federal statutory regulation.
(3) If the Federation has made use of its legislative competence, the States may by statute adopt regulations that deviate therefrom regarding:
1. hunting (except the law on hunting permits);
2. nature conservation and landscape management (except the general principles of nature conservation, the law on the protection of species or maritime nature conservation);
3. the distribution of land;

4. regional planning;
5. water resources (except regulations on substances and facilities);
6. admissions to higher education and higher education diplomas.

   Federal statutes in these areas enter into force at the earliest six months after their publication, in as far as nothing is provided otherwise with the consent of the Bundesrat. In the areas of the first sentence, in the relation between federal law and State law the later statute prevails.

(4) A federal statute may determine that a federal statutory regulation a need for which in the sense of paragraph 2 no longer exists, may be replaced by State law.

Article 73. (1) The Federation has exclusive legislative power regarding:
1. foreign relations as well as defence including the protection of the civilian population;
2. citizenship in the Federation;
3. free movement, the passport regime, population registers and identity documents, immigration, emigration and extradition;
4. currency, the money and coinage regime, measures and weights as well as the determination of the time;
5. the unity of the customs and trade area, trade and navigation agreements, the free movement of goods and the movement of goods and capital with foreign states including customs and border protection;

   5a. the protection of German cultural assets from transfers abroad;
6. air traffic;

   6a. rail traffic which falls entirely or predominantly under the ownership of the Federation (the railways of the Federation), the construction, maintenance and operation of tracks of the railways of the Federation as well as the levying of charges for the use of these tracks;
7. post and telecommunications;
8. legal relations of persons in the service of the Federation and of directly federal entities of public law;
9. intellectual property, copyright and publishing law;

   9a. the protection from the dangers of international terrorism by the Federal Criminal Investigations Police Office [Bundeskriminalpolizeiamt] in cases where a danger transcending State borders is at hand, where the jurisdiction of a State police authority is not apparent or where a supreme State authority requests a takeover of jurisdiction;
10. the cooperation between the Federation and the States
    a. regarding criminal police investigation,
    b. for the protection of the liberal democratic fundamental order, the integrity and security of the Federation or a State (domestic intelligence [Verfassungsschutz]) and

c. for the protection against attempts within the territory of the Federation which jeopardize, through the use of force or preparatory acts with such aim, the external interests of the Federal Republic of Germany,
as well as the establishment of a Federal Criminal Investigations Police Office and the international fight against crime;
11. statistics for federal purposes;
12. the law on weapons and explosives;
13. care for those disabled in war and surviving dependants of war dead, and support for former prisoners of war;
14. the production and use of nuclear energy for peaceful purposes, the establishment and operation of facilities serving these purposes, the protection against dangers arising from the release of nuclear energy or from ionizing radiation, and the disposal of radioactive material.
(2) Statutes under paragraph 1 no. 9a require the consent of the Bundesrat.

Article 74. (1) Concurrent legislative power extends to the following areas:
1. private law, criminal law, the court system, judicial procedure (except the law on the execution of detentions pending criminal investigation), the advocacy, the notary and legal advice system;
2. the civil status registry;
3. the law on associations;
4. the law on the sojourn and establishment of aliens;
5. (repealed);
6. the affairs of refugees and expellees;
7. public welfare (except the law on homes);
8. (repealed);
9. war damages and reparations;
10. war graves and the graves of other victims of war and victims of tyranny;
11. commercial law (mining, industry, energy, crafts, trade, commerce, banking and stock exchange, private insurance) except the law on the closing times for shops, on bars and restaurants, on gambling halls, on acting performance by persons, fairs, exhibitions and markets;
12. labour law including the organization of enterprises, work safety and job agency services, as well as social security including unemployment insurance;
13. the regulation of education allowances and the promotion of scientific research;
14. the law on expropriation in as far as it is relevant in the areas of Articles 73 and 74;
15. the transfer of land, natural resources and means of production into public ownership or other forms of collective concern;
16. the prevention of abuses of economically powerful positions;

17. the promotion of agricultural and forestry production (except the law on rearrangements of terrain), the securing of food supply, the import and export of agricultural and forestry products, high-seas and coastal fisheries and coastal protection;
18. the transfer of urban real estate, land law (except the law on contributions for land development) and the law on housing allowances, the law on old debt relief, the law on homebuilding premiums, the law on homebuilding for miners and miner settlement law;
19. measures against human and animal diseases that are dangerous to the public or communicable, the admission to medical and other healing professions and the healing services, as well as the law on the pharmacy system, medicines, medical products, cures, narcotics and poisons;

19a. the securing of the economic viability of hospitals and the regulation of hospital charges;

20. the law on food including the animals used for the production thereof, the law on recreational consumables, on commodities for use and on feed, as well as the safety in the trade in agricultural and forestry seeds and seedlings, the protection of plants against diseases and pests as well as animal protection;
21. high-seas and coastal shipping as well as naval signalling, inland navigation, meteorological services, shipping routes and inland waterways serving general traffic;
22. road traffic, motor transport, the construction and maintenance of country roads for long-distance traffic, as well as the levying and distribution of fees or charges for the use of public roads by vehicle;
23. railways, which are not railways of the Federation, with the exception of mountain railways;
24. waste management, air pollution control and noise abatement (except protection from behaviour-related noise);
25. state liability;
26. the medically assisted creation of human life, the analysis and artificial modification of genetic information as well as regulations concerning transplantation of organs, tissues and cells;
27. the rights and obligations deriving from the status of civil servants of States, municipalities and other public-law entities as well as judges in the States except careers, salary and support;
28. hunting;
29. nature conservation and landscape management;
30. the distribution of land;
31. regional planning;
32. water resources;
33. admissions to higher education and higher education diplomas.

(2) Statutes under paragraph 1 no. 25 and 27 require the consent of the Bundesrat.

Articles 74a and 75. (Repealed).

Article 76. (1) Bills are introduced in the Bundestag by the Federal Government, from the floor of the Bundestag, or by the Bundesrat.
(2) Bills of the Federal Government must first be transmitted to the Bundesrat. The Bundesrat is entitled to give a reaction to such bills within six weeks. If it demands for important reasons, especially with regard to the size of a bill, an extension of the period, then the period is nine weeks. The Federal Government may transmit a bill, which it has by way of exception, when transmitting it to the Bundesrat, qualified as particularly urgent, to the Bundestag after three weeks or, if the Bundesrat has made a demand pursuant to the third sentence, after six weeks, even when it has not yet received the reaction of the Bundesrat; it must in that case transmit the reaction of the Bundesrat to the Bundestag without delay. In the case of bills for an amendment of this Basic Law and for the transfer of sovereign powers pursuant to Article 23 or Article 24, the period for a reaction is nine weeks; the fourth sentence does not apply.
(3) Bills of the Bundesrat must be transmitted to the Bundestag by the Federal Government within six weeks. The Federal Government, when transmitting them, is to give a statement of its opinion. If it demands for important reasons, especially with regard to the size of a bill, an extension of the period, the period is nine weeks. If the Bundesrat has by way of exception qualified a bill as particularly urgent, the period is three weeks or, if the Federal Government has made a demand pursuant to the third sentence, six weeks. In the case of bills for an amendment of this Basic Law and for the transfer of sovereign powers pursuant to Article 23 or Article 24, the period is nine weeks; the fourth sentence does not apply. The Bundestag must deliberate and decide on the bills within a reasonable time.

Article 77. (1) Federal statutes are adopted by the Bundestag. They must, after their adoption, be transmitted to the Bundesrat by the president of the Bundestag without delay.
(2) The Bundesrat may, within three weeks after receiving an adopted bill, demand that a committee for the joint consideration of bills, composed of members of the Bundestag and of the Bundesrat, be convened. The composition and procedure of this committee is regulated by rules of procedure which are adopted by the Bundestag and which require the consent of the Bundesrat. The members of the Bundesrat sent to this committee are not bound by instructions. If a statute requires the consent of the Bundesrat, then also the Bundestag and the Federal Government may demand a convention. If the committee proposes an amendment to the adopted bill, the Bundestag must decide again.
(2a) In as far as a statute requires the consent of the Bundesrat, the Bundesrat, if a demand under paragraph 2, first sentence, is not made or the conciliation procedure is concluded without any proposals for an amendment to the adopted bill, must decide on its consent within a reasonable time.

(3) In as far as a statute does not require the consent of the Bundesrat, the Bundesrat, once the procedure under paragraph 2 is completed, may within two weeks object to a statute adopted by the Bundestag. The period for objection starts, in the case under paragraph 2, last sentence, with the receipt of the new decision adopted by the Bundestag, and in all other cases with the receipt of the statement of the chairman of the committee stipulated under paragraph 2 that the procedure before the committee has been concluded.

(4) If the objection is adopted by the majority of the votes of the Bundesrat, it may be rejected by a decision of the majority of the members of the Bundestag. If the Bundesrat has adopted the objection by a majority of at least two-thirds of its votes, then its rejection by the Bundestag requires a two-thirds majority, including at least a majority of the members of the Bundestag.

Article 78. A statute adopted by the Bundestag is successfully completed if the Bundesrat consents to it or does not make a demand pursuant to Article 77 (2) or does not enter an objection within the period stipulated in Article 77 (3) or withdraws such objection, or if the objection is overridden by the Bundestag.

Article 79. (1) The Basic Law may be amended only by a statute which expressly amends or supplements its text. In the case of international treaties which have as their object a peace settlement, the preparation of a peace settlement or the phasing out of an occupation regime, or which are intended to serve the defence of the Federal Republic, a clarification that the provisions of the Basic Law do not preclude the conclusion and entry into force of such treaties requires only a supplement to the text of the Basic Law which is confined to such clarification.

(2) Any such statute requires the approval by two-thirds of the members of the Bundestag and two-thirds of the votes of the Bundesrat.

(3) Any amendment to this Basic Law affecting the division of the Federation into States, the participation of the States in principle in the legislative process, or the principles laid down in Articles 1 and 20, is inadmissible.

Article 80. (1) By statute, the Federal Government, a federal minister or the State governments may be authorized to adopt ordinances [Rechtsverordnungen]. In that case, the content, purpose and scope of the given authorization must be determined in the statute. The legal basis must be stated in the ordinance. If by statute it is provided that an authorization may be delegated further, then such authorization of a delegation requires an ordinance.

(2) The consent of the Bundesrat is required, save for federal statutory regulations providing otherwise, for ordinances of the Federal Government or a federal minister regarding the principles and charges for the use of the facilities of the post and telecommunica-

tions system, regarding the principles of the levying of charges for the use of the facilities of the railways of the Federation, regarding the construction and operation of railways, as well as ordinances based on federal statutes which require the consent of the Bundesrat or which are executed by the States on behalf of the Federation or as their own affairs.

(3) The Bundesrat may transmit to the Federal Government proposals for the adoption of ordinances which require its consent.

(4) In as far as State governments are authorized to adopt ordinances by federal statute or pursuant to federal statutes, the States are also competent to regulate by statute.

Article 80a. (1) If this Basic Law or a federal statute regarding defence including the protection of the civilian population provides that regulations may be applied only within the guidelines of this Article, then such application except in a state of defence is only permissible when the Bundestag has declared the beginning of a state of tension [Spannungsfall] or when it has approved such application explicitly. The declaration of a state of tension and the special approval in the cases of Article 12a (5), first sentence, and (6), second sentence, require a majority of two-thirds of votes cast.

(2) Measures pursuant to regulations under paragraph 1 must be lifted when the Bundestag so demands.

(3) By deviation from paragraph 1, the application of such regulations is permissible also on the basis and within the guidelines of a decision that is taken by an international body in the framework of an alliance treaty with the consent of the Federal Government. Measures under this paragraph must be lifted when the Bundestag by the majority of its members so demands.

Article 81. (1) If in the case of Article 68 the Bundestag is not dissolved, the Federal President may, upon request of the Federal Government with the consent of the Bundesrat, declare a legislative emergency [Gesetzgebungsnotstand] for a bill if the Bundestag rejects it although the Federal Government has qualified it as urgent. The same applies when a bill has been rejected although the Federal Chancellor had linked it to a motion under Article 68.

(2) If the Bundestag rejects the bill after the declaration of a legislative emergency again or if it adopts it in a version qualified as unacceptable by the Federal Government, then the statute is deemed adopted if the Bundesrat consents to it. The same applies when the bill has not been adopted by the Bundestag within four weeks after the new introduction.

(3) During the term of office of a Federal Chancellor, also any other bill rejected by the Bundestag may be adopted within a period of six months following the first declaration of a legislative emergency under paragraphs 1 and 2. After the period has lapsed, during the term of office of that same Federal Chancellor another declaration of a legislative emergency is not permissible.

(4) The Basic Law may be neither amended nor wholly or partly suspended or rendered inapplicable by a statute that has been adopted under paragraph 2.

Article 82. (1) Statutes completed in accordance with the provisions of this Basic Law are, after counter-signature, certified by the Federal President and published in the Federal Law Gazette [Bundesgesetzblatt]. Ordinances are certified by the organ which adopts them and are, save for other statutory regulations, published in the Federal Law Gazette.
(2) All statutes and all ordinances are to determine the day of entry into force. If such a provision is lacking, they enter into force on the fourteenth day after the end of the day when the Federal Law Gazette has been published.

VIII. The execution of federal statutes and the federal administration

Article 83. The States execute federal statutes as their own affairs in as far as this Basic Law does not otherwise provide or permit.

Article 84. (1) Where the States execute federal statutes as their own affairs, they regulate the establishment of authorities and the administrative procedure. Where federal statutes provide otherwise, the States may make adopt regulations in deviation therefrom. Where a State has adopted a deviating regulation pursuant to the second sentence, subsequent federal regulations regarding the establishment of authorities and the administrative procedure relating to this enter into force in that State at the earliest six months after their publication, in as far as nothing is provided otherwise with the consent of the Bundesrat. Article 72 (3) third sentence applies mutatis mutandis. In exceptional cases the Federation may, because of a special need for uniform federal regulation, regulate the administrative procedure without a possibility of deviation for the States. Such statutes require the consent of the Bundesrat. A federal statute may not delegate tasks to municipalities and associations of municipalities.
(2) The Federal Government may, with the consent of the Bundesrat, issue general administrative regulations.
(3) The Federal Government exercises supervision to ensure that the States execute federal statutes in accordance with applicable law. The Federal Government may, for this purpose, send agents to the highest State authorities, with their consent or, if such consent is refused, with the consent of the Bundesrat, also to subordinate authorities.
(4) Should shortcomings which the Federal Government has established in the execution of federal statutes in the States not be corrected, the Bundesrat decides, at the request of the Federal Government or the State concerned, whether the State has violated the law. The decision of the Bundesrat may be challenged before the Federal Constitutional Court.
(5) The Federal Government may, by federal statute which requires the consent of the Bundesrat, be granted authorization, for the execution of federal statutes, to issue indivi-

dual instructions in particular cases. They are, unless the Federal Government considers the matter urgent, to be addressed to the highest States authorities.

Article 85. (1) Where the States execute federal statutes on behalf of the Federation, the establishment of the authorities remains the concern of the States, unless federal statutes with the consent of the Bundesrat provide otherwise. A federal statute may not delegate tasks to municipalities and associations of municipalities.
(2) The Federal Government may, with the consent of the Bundesrat, issue general administrative regulations. It may regulate the uniform training of civil servants and employees. The heads of intermediate authorities are to be appointed with its approval.
(3) The State authorities are subordinate to the instructions of the competent highest federal authorities. The instructions are, unless the Federal Government considers the matter urgent, to be addressed to the highest State authorities. Execution of the instructions is to be ensured by the highest State authorities.
(4) Federal supervision extends to the lawfulness and expediency of execution. The Federal Government may, for this purpose, require reporting and submission of files and send agents to all authorities.

Article 86. Where the Federation executes statutes by direct federal administration or by directly federal entities or institutions of public law, the Federal Government issues, to the extent that a statute does not provide details, the general administrative regulations. It regulates, unless statute provides otherwise, the establishment of the authorities.

Article 87. (1) The Foreign Service [Auswärtiger Dienst], the Federal Revenue Administration [Bundesfinanzverwaltung] and, pursuant to Article 89, the administration of the federal waterways and navigation are managed by direct federal administration with a dedicated administrative substructure. By federal statute federal border guard authorities [Bundesgrenzschutzbehörden], and central offices for police information and communications, for the criminal police and for the collection of documents for the purposes of domestic intelligence [Verfassungsschutz] and of protection against endeavours on federal territory which, through the use of force or preparatory acts thereto endanger the foreign interests of the Federal Republic of Germany, may be established.
(2) Social insurance institutions whose competence extends beyond the territory of one State are managed as directly federal entities of public law. Social insurance institutions whose competence extends beyond the territory of one State but not more than three States are managed in deviation from the first sentence as directly State entities of public law if the supervising State is determined by the States involved.
(3) In addition, for matters on which the Federation is competent to legislate, independent higher federal authorities as well as new directly federal entities and institutions of public law may be established by federal statute. Where new tasks arise for the Federation

in matters on which it has the power to legislate, then in cases of urgent need federal authorities at the intermediate and lower levels may be established with the consent of the Bundesrat and of the majority of the members of the Bundestag.

Article 87a. (1) The Federation establishes armed forces for the purpose of defence. Their numerical strength and the general outline of their organization must follow from the budget.
(2) Except for defence, the armed forces may only be deployed to the extent explicitly permitted by this Basic Law.
(3) The armed forces have, in a state of defence and in a state of tension [Spannungsfall], the competence to protect civilian objects and to perform tasks of traffic control to the extent that this is required for the accomplishment of their defence mission. Furthermore, during a state of defence or a state of tension the armed forces may also be assigned to protect civilian objects so as to support police measures; in such case the armed forces cooperate with the competent authorities.
(4) In order to avert an imminent danger to the existence or liberal democratic fundamental order of the Federation or of a State, the Federal Government may, if the conditions of Article 91 (2) are fulfilled and the police forces as well as the Federal Border Guard [Bundesgrenzschutz] are not sufficient, deploy the armed forces to support the police and the Federal Border Guard in protecting civilian objects and in fighting organized and militarily armed insurgents. The deployment of the armed forces is to be discontinued if the Bundestag or the Bundesrat so demands.

Article 87b. (1) The Federal Armed Forces Administration [Bundeswehrverwaltung] is managed by direct federal administration with a dedicated administrative substructure. It performs tasks of personnel management and tasks to cover the immediate material requirements of the armed forces. Tasks related to the maintenance of injured persons or construction work may only be delegated to the Federal Armed Forces Administration by federal statute which requires the consent of the Bundesrat. The consent of the Bundesrat is furthermore required for statutes to the extent that they authorize the Federal Armed Forces Administration to interfere with the rights of third parties; this does not apply to statutes in the area of personnel management.
(2) In addition, federal statutes concerning defence, including recruitment for military service and the protection of the civilian population may, with the consent of the Bundesrat, provide that they be executed, wholly or in part, by direct federal administration with a dedicated administrative substructure or by the States on behalf of the Federation. Where such statutes are executed by the States on behalf of the Federation, they may, with the consent of the Bundesrat, provide that the powers appertaining to the Federation and the competent supreme federal authorities pursuant to Article 85 are delegated wholly or in part to higher federal authorities; in such case it may be provided that these authorities

do not require the consent of the Bundesrat in issuing general administrative regulations pursuant to Article 85 (2) first sentence.

Article 87c. Statutes that are enacted pursuant to Article 73 (1) no. 14, may, with the consent of the Bundesrat, provide that they be executed by the States on behalf of the Federation.

Article 87d. (1) The air traffic administration is managed by federal administration. Tasks related to air traffic control may also be executed by foreign air traffic organizations that are authorized pursuant to European Community law. Details are regulated by a federal statute.
(2) A federal statute requiring the consent of the Bundesrat may delegate tasks relating to air traffic administration to the States as commissioned administration [Auftragsverwaltung].

Article 87e. (1) The railway transport administration for railways of the Federation is managed by direct federal administration. By federal statute tasks relating to the railway transport administration may be delegated to the States as their own affairs.
(2) The Federation discharges tasks relating to the railway transport administration extending beyond the area of the railways of the Federation that are delegated to it by federal statute.
(3) Railways of the Federation are managed as commercial enterprises established under private law. These are owned by the Federation, to the extent that the activities of the commercial enterprise comprise the construction, maintenance and the operation of railroads. The transfer of federal shares in these commercial enterprises under to the second sentence is effected pursuant to a statute; the majority of the shares remains with the Federation. Details are regulated by a federal statute.
(4) The Federation ensures that account be taken of the benefit of the general public, especially the transportation needs, in developing and maintaining the federal railroad network of the railways of the Federation as well as in their transportation services on that railroad network, to the extent that they do not concern local passenger rail services. Details are regulated by a federal statute.
(5) Statutes enacted pursuant to paragraphs 1 to 4 require the consent of the Bundesrat. The consent of the Bundesrat is furthermore required for statutes which regulate the dissolution, merger and splitting-up of railway enterprises of the Federation, the transfer of railway tracks of the railways of the Federation to third parties as well as the abandonment of railroad tracks of railways of the Federation or which affect local passenger rail services.

Article 87f. (1) Within the guidelines of a federal statute requiring the consent of the Bundesrat, the Federation ensures area-wide adequate and sufficient services in the area of post and telecommunications.
(2) Services within the meaning of paragraph 1 are provided as private commercial activities by the enterprises that emerged from the special asset German Federal Post Office [Deutsche Bundespost] and by other private providers. Sovereign tasks in the area of post and telecommunications are performed by direct federal administration.
(3) Without prejudice to paragraph 2 second sentence, the Federation, in the form of a directly federal institution of public law, performs particular tasks with respect to the enterprises that emerged from the special asset German Federal Post Office within the guidelines of a federal statute.

Article 88. The Federation establishes a currency bank and bank of issue as the Federal Bank [Bundesbank]. Its tasks and powers may, within the framework of the European Union, be transferred to the European Central Bank, which is independent and committed to the primary goal of securing price stability.

Article 89. (1) The Federation is the owner of the former Reich waterways.
(2) The Federation manages the federal waterways through its own authorities. It performs the state tasks of inland navigation extending beyond the area of a single State and the tasks of maritime navigation which are assigned to it by statute. It may assign the management of federal waterways, to the extent that they lie within the territory of one State, upon request to that State as commissioned administration. If a waterway touches the territory of several States, the Federation may commission the State which is designated by the States concerned.
(3) In the administration, development and new construction of waterways, the requirements of land and water management are to be observed in agreement with the States.

Article 90. (1) The Federation remains the owner of the federal motorways [Bundesautobahnen] and other federal roads of long-distance traffic. This ownership is inalienable.
(2) The management of the federal motorways is conducted in federal administration. For the discharge of its tasks, the Federation may make use of a corporation under private law. This corporation is held in inalienable ownership of the Federation. A direct or indirect participation of third parties in this corporation and its subsidiaries is precluded. A participation of private parties in the context of public-private partnerships is precluded with regard to road networks encompassing the entire federal motorway network or the entire network of other federal long-distance roads within a State, or substantial parts thereof. Details are laid down in a federal statute.

(3) The States or the self-regulatory bodies [Selbstverwaltungskörperschaften] competent pursuant to State law manage the remaining federal roads of long-distance traffic on behalf of the Federation.
(4) Upon request of a State, the Federation may take the remaining federal roads of long-distance traffic, as far as they are located on the territory of that State, into federal administration.

Article 91. (1) In order to avert an imminent danger to the existence or the liberal democratic fundamental order of the Federation or of a State, a State may request the services of the police forces of other States as well as forces and institutions of other administrations and of the Federal Border Guard [Bundesgrenzschutz].
(2) If the State where such danger is imminent is not itself prepared or able to combat the danger, the Federal Government may place the police in that State and police forces of other States under its own authority and deploy units of the Federal Border Guard. The order is to be lifted after the removal of the danger and, otherwise, at any time upon the demand of the Bundesrat. Where the danger extends to the territory of more than one State, the Federal Government may, to the extent that this is necessary for the effective combating, issue instructions to the State governments; the first and second sentence remain unaffected.

VIIIa. Joint tasks

Article 91a. (1) The Federation participates in the fulfilment of the tasks of the States in the following areas, if these tasks are important for the whole and the participation of the Federation is necessary for the improvement of living standards (joint tasks):
1. improvement of regional economic structure,
2. improvement of agricultural structure and coastal protection.
(2) By federal statute with the consent of the Bundesrat, joint tasks as well as the details of coordination are determined.
(3) The Federation bears in the cases of paragraph 1 no. 1 half of the costs in each State. In the cases of paragraph 1 no. 2, the Federation bears at least half; the contribution must be fixed uniformly for all States. Details are regulated by statute. The making available of funds remains a matter for the adoption of the budgets of the Federation and the States.

Article 91b. (1) The Federation and the States may, on the basis of agreements in cases of importance that transcends regions, cooperate in the promotion of science, research, and teaching. Agreements which relating predominantly to universities [Hochschulen], require the approval of all states. The latter does not apply to agreements relating to research buildings, including large equipment.

(2) The Federation and the States may cooperate on the basis of agreements for the assessment of the effectiveness of the educational system in international comparison and on reports and recommendations in that matter.
(3) The allocation of the financial burden is regulated in the agreement.

Article 91c. (1) The Federation and the States may cooperate in the planning, establishment and operation of the information systems needed for the fulfilment of their tasks.
(2) The Federation and the States may on the basis of agreements establish the standards and security requirements necessary for the communication between their information systems. Agreements concerning the principles of the cooperation pursuant to the first sentence may provide for individual tasks, circumscribed with regard to their content and extent, that details enter into force for the Federation and the States with the consent of a qualified majority to be determined by the agreement. They require the consent of the Bundestag and the parliaments of the participating States; the right to terminate these agreements may not be excluded. The agreements also regulate the bearing of burdens.
(3) The States may furthermore agree on the joint operation of information systems and the establishment of dedicated institutions.
(4) The Federation establishes a connecting network in order to connect the information systems of the Federation and of the States. The details regarding the establishment and the operation of the connecting network are regulated by federal statute which requires the consent of the Bundesrat.
(5) Comprehensive access by information technology to the administrative services of the Federation and the States is regulated by federal statute with the consent of the Bundesrat.

Article 91d. The Federation and the States may, in order to determine and promote the performance of their administrations, conduct comparative studies and publish the results.

Article 91e. (1) In the execution of federal statutes in the area of basic social security for jobseekers, the Federation and the States or the municipalities and associations of municipalities competent under State law cooperate, as a rule, in joint institutions.
(2) The Federation may allow that a limited number of municipalities and associations of municipalities, on their request and with the consent of the supreme State authority, excercises the tasks under paragraph 1 alone. The necessary expenditure including administrative costs are borne by the Federation, to the extent that in an execution of statutes pursuant to paragraph 1 the tasks are to be exercised by the Federation.
(3) Details are regulated by a federal statute which requires the consent of the Bundesrat.

IX. The judiciary

Article 92. Judicial power is vested in the judges; it is exercised by the Federal Constitutional Court, by the federal courts provided for in this Basic Law, and by the courts of the States.

Article 93. (1) The Federal Constitutional Court [Bundesverfassungsgericht] rules:
1. on the interpretation of this Basic Law in the event of disputes concerning the extent of the rights and duties of a supreme federal body or of other parties vested with rights of their own by this Basic Law or by the rules of procedure of a supreme federal body;
2. in the event of disagreements or doubts regarding the formal or substantive compatibility of federal law or State law with this Basic Law, or the compatibility of State law with other federal law, on application of the Federal Government, a State government or one-quarter of the members of the Bundestag;

    2a. in the event of disagreements whether a statute complies with the conditions under Article 72 (2) on application of the Bundesrat, a State government or the parliament of a State;
3. in the event of disagreements regarding the rights and duties of the Federation and the States, especially as regards the execution of federal law by the States and the performance of federal supervision;
4. in other public-law disputes between the Federation and the States, between different States, or within one State, in as far as another recourse is not available;

    4a. on constitutional complaints, which may be filed by any person with the allegation that one of his fundamental rights or one of his rights contained in Article 20 (4), 33, 38, 101, 103 and 104 has been violated by public authority;

    4b. on constitutional complaints of municipalities or associations of municipalities based on a violation of the right to self-government pursuant to Article 28 by a statute, or by State legislation yet only in as far as no complaint may be filed with the State constitutional court;

    4c. on objections of associations to their non-recognition as a party for elections of the Bundestag;
5. in the other cases provided by this Basic Law.

(2) The Federal Constitutional Court furthermore rules on the application of the Bundesrat, a State government or the parliament of a State whether in the case of Article 72 (4) the need for a federal statutory regulation under Article 72 (2) no longer exists or whether in the cases of Article 125a (2), first sentence, federal law could no longer be adopted. The finding that the need has ceased to exist or that federal law could no longer be adopted replaces a federal statute under Article 72 (4) or Article 125a (2), second sentence. An application under the first sentence is admissible only when a bill under Article 72 (4) or Article 125a (2), second sentence, has been rejected in the Bundestag or

is not deliberated and decided upon within one year or when such bill has been rejected in the Bundesrat.
(3) The Federal Constitutional Court furthermore becomes active in the other cases assigned by federal statute.

Article 94. (1) The Federal Constitutional Court is composed of federal judges and other members. Half of the members of the Federal Constitutional Court are elected by the Bundestag and half by the Bundesrat. They may not be members of the Bundestag, the Bundesrat, the Federal Government or equivalent bodies of a State.
(2) A federal statute regulates its organization and its procedures and determines in which cases its decisions have statutory force. It may make the prior exhaustion of judicial remedies a precondition for constitutional complaints and stipulate a special admissibility procedure.

Article 95. (1) For the areas of general, administrative, tax, labour and social-security jurisdiction, the Federation establishes as supreme courts the Federal Supreme Court [Bundesgerichtshof], the Federal Administrative Court, the Federal Tax Court, the Federal Labour Court and the Federal Social-Security Court.
(2) The appointment of judges at these courts is decided by the federal minister competent for the respective subject-matter together with a judicial nomination committee [Richterwahlausschuss] which is composed of the ministers from the States competent for the respective subject-matter and an equal number of members who are elected by the Bundestag.
(3) For the upholding of the unity of jurisprudence, a Joint Chamber of the courts stipulated in paragraph 1 must be established. Details are regulated by a federal statute.

Article 96. (1) The Federation may establish a federal court for intellectual property law.
(2) The Federation may establish courts of military criminal justice for the armed forces as federal courts. They may exercise criminal law jurisdiction only in a state of defence as well as over members of the armed forces who are deployed abroad or are serving on board of warships. Details are regulated by a federal statute. These courts fall within the competence of the Federal minister of justice. Their salaried judges must possess the qualifications to be a judge.
(3) The supreme court for the courts stipulated in paragraphs 1 and 2 is the Federal Supreme Court.
(4) The Federation may, for persons in a public-law service relation to it, establish federal courts to decide in disciplinary and complaint procedures.
(5) For criminal procedures in the following areas, a federal statute with the consent of the Bundesrat may provide that State courts are to exercise the jurisdiction of the Federation:

1. genocide;
2. crimes against humanity under international criminal law;
3. war crimes;
4. other acts that are capable of and are committed with the intent to disturb the peaceful coexistence of nations (Article 26 (1));
5. protection of the state.

Article 97. (1) Judges are independent and are subject only to the law.
(2) Judges who are salaried and appointed permanently may be dismissed or suspended in their function permanently or temporarily or be transferred to another post or made to retire before the expiry of their term against their will only by virtue of a judicial decision and only for reasons and in the form provided by statutes. Legislation may determine age limits upon the reaching of which judges appointed for life retire. In the context of changes to the organization of courts or their districts, judges may be transferred to another court or removed from office, yet only while preserving their full salary.

Article 98. (1) The legal position of federal judges is to be regulated by a special federal statute.
(2) If a federal judge violates, in the exercise of his office or outside, the principles of the Basic Law or the constitutional order of a State, then the Federal Constitutional Court may order by a two-thirds majority upon request of the Bundestag that the judge be transferred to a different post or be made to retire. In case of an intentional violation, dismissal may be ordered.
(3) The legal position of judges in the States is to be regulated by special State statutes, in as far as Article 74 (1) no. 27 does not provide otherwise.
(4) The States may provide that the State minister of justice decides together with a judicial nomination committee over the appointment of judges in the States.
(5) The States may, as regards State judges, provide for a regulation corresponding to paragraph 2. State constitutional law in force remains unaffected. The Federal Constitutional Court may decide over the prosecution of a judge.

Article 99. By State statute, the Federal Constitutional Court may be assigned the jurisdiction to decide in constitutional disputes within one State, and the supreme courts stipulated in Article 95 (1) may be assigned last-instance jurisdiction to decide in cases where the application of State law is of the issue.

Article 100. (1) If a court concludes that a statute on the validity of which its decision depends is unconstitutional, then the proceedings are to be stayed, and, where a violation of the constitution of a State is of the issue, a decision is to be obtained from the State court which is competent for constitutional disputes, or, when a violation of this Basic

Law is of the issue, a decision from the Federal Constitutional Court is to be obtained. The same applies where a violation of this Basic Law by State law or an incompatibility between State statute and a federal statute is of the issue.

(2) If in a judicial dispute it is doubtful whether a rule of international law is part of federal law and whether it directly creates rights and obligations for individuals (Article 25), then the court must obtain a decision from the Federal Constitutional Court.

(3) If the constitutional court of a State wishes to deviate from a decision of the Federal Constitutional Court or the constitutional court of another State in the interpretation of the Basic Law, then the constitutional court must obtain a decision from the Federal Constitutional Court.

Article 101. (1) Extraordinary tribunals are inadmissible. No-one may be deprived of his right to a lawful judge.
(2) Courts for special subject-areas may be established only by statute.

Article 102. The death penalty is abolished.

Article 103. (1) Before a court, everyone has the right to a hearing in accordance with the law.
(2) An act may be punished only when the liability to punishment was determined by statute before the act was committed.
(3) No-one may be punished several times on the basis of general criminal statutes for the same act.

Article 104. (1) The freedom of a person may be limited only pursuant to a formal statute and only in accordance with the form prescribed therein. Detained persons may not be abused either psychologically or physically.
(2) The permissibility and continuation of a deprivation of freedom is decided only by a judge. In all cases of a deprivation of freedom that are not based on a court order, a judicial decision must be obtained without delay. The police may, based on their own powers, detain no-one any longer than until the end of the day following the arrest. Details must be regulated statutorily.
(3) Everyone provisionally detained based on the suspicion of a criminal act must, at the latest on the day following the arrest, be brought before a judge who must inform him of the reasons for the arrest, question him, and give him an opportunity to object. The judge must, without delay, either issue a written arrest warrant stating the reasons, or order a release.
(4) A relative [Angehöriger] of the detainee or a person of his trust must be notified without delay of any judicial decision regarding the order or continuation of a deprivation of freedom.

X. The finances system

Article 104a. (1) The Federation and the States bear the costs resulting from the exercise of their tasks separately to the extent that this Basic Law does not provide otherwise.
(2) Where the States act on behalf of the Federation, the Federation bears the costs resulting therefrom.
(3) Federal statutes that confer pecuniary benefits and are executed by the States may provide that the pecuniary benefits are borne wholly or in part by the Federation. Where the statute provides that the Federation bears half of the costs or more, it is executed on behalf of the Federation.
(4) Federal statutes that establish obligations for the States to provide pecuniary benefits, benefits in kind with pecuniary value, or comparable services with respect to third parties and that are executed by the States as their own affairs or pursuant to paragraph 3, second sentence, on behalf of the Federation, require the consent of the Bundesrat, if the costs resulting therefrom are to be borne by the States.
(5) The Federation and the States bear the administrative costs arising for their administrative authorities and are liable to each other for ensuring a proper administration. Details are regulated by a federal statute which requires the consent of the Bundesrat.
(6) The Federation and the States bear the burdens of a violation of supranational or international-law obligations of Germany according to the domestic distribution of responsibilities and tasks. In cases of financial corrections of the European Union affecting several States, the Federation and the States bear these burdens at a ratio of 15 to 85. In such case the collectivity of the States bears 35 percent of the total burdens in mutual solidarity pursuant to a general key; 50 percent are borne by the States that caused the burdens, proportionate to the amount of the funds received. Details are regulated by a federal statute which requires the consent of the Bundesrat.

Article 104b. (1) The Federation may, to the extent that this Basic Law confers legislative competences upon it, grant financial aids to the States for particularly significant investments of the States and municipalities (associations of municipalities) that are required to
1. avert a disturbance of the macro-economic equilibrium or to
2. equalize diverging economic strengths in the federal territory or to
3. stimulate economic growth.
    In deviation from the first sentence, the Federation may, in cases of natural disasters or exceptional emergencies that are beyond the state's control and substantially compromise the state financial situation, grant financial aids even without legislative competences.
(2) Details, particularly the kinds of investments to be supported, are regulated by federal statute which requires the consent of the Bundesrat, or pursuant to the Federal Budget Act [Bundeshaushaltsgesetz] by administrative agreement. The federal statute or the ad-

ministrative agreement may contain provisions on the configuration of the respective State programmes for the use of the financial aid. The determination of criteria for the configuration of the State programmes takes place in agreement with the States concerned. In order to guarantee the expedient use of funds, the federal government may demand the submission of reports and documents and conduct investigations in all authorities. The federal funds are granted in addition to the States' own resources. They are to be granted for a limited time period and to be reviewed at regular intervals with respect to their use. The financial aids are to be administered with annual sums decreasing over time.

(3) The Bundestag, the Federal Government and the Bundesrat are, upon request, to be informed about the execution of the measures and the improvements achieved.

Article 104c. The Federation may grant the States financial aid for investments of national importance, as well as for special temporary expenditures immediately linked with the latter, made by the States and municipalities (municipal associations) for the purpose of enhancing the capacity of the municipal educational infrastructure. Articles 104b (2) clauses 1 to 3, 5, 6, and sub-paragraph (3) apply mutatis mutandis. To guarantee the expedient use of funds, the Federal Government may demand reports and, with regard to specific causes [anlassbezogen], the submission of documents.

Article 104d. The Federation may grant the States financial aid for investments of national importance made by the States and municipalities (municipal associations) in the area of social housing. Article 104b (2) clause 1 to 5, as well as sub-paragraph (2) apply mutatis mutandis.

Article 105. (1) The Federation has exclusive legislative power regarding customs duties and fiscal monopolies.
(2) The Federation has concurrent legislative power regarding other taxes where it is entitled, wholly or in part, to the revenue generated by these taxes, or where the conditions of Article 72 (2) are met.
(2a) The States have competence to legislate regarding local consumption and expenditure taxes for as long as and to the extent that they are not equivalent to taxes regulated by federal statute. They have competence to determine the tax rate of the real estate acquisition tax.
(3) Federal statutes regarding taxes whose revenue flows wholly or in part to the States or the municipalities (associations of municipalities) require the consent of the Bundesrat.

Article 106. (1) The Federation is entitled to the yield of fiscal monopolies and to the revenue from the following taxes:
1. customs duties;

2. consumption taxes, to the extent that they are not due to the States pursuant to paragraph 2 or jointly to the Federation and the States pursuant to paragraph 3 or to the municipalities pursuant to paragraph 6;
3. the road freight transportation tax, the motor vehicle tax and other traffic taxes related to motorized transportation;
4. capital transactions taxes, the insurance tax and the exchange tax;
5. one-time levies on property and compensation levies raised for the implementation of the equalization of burdens;
6. the supplementary levy on the income tax and corporation tax;
7. levies within the framework of the European Communities.

(2) The States are entitled to the revenue from the following taxes:
1. the property tax;
2. the inheritance tax;
3. the traffic taxes to the extent that they are not due to the Federation pursuant to paragraph 1 or jointly to the Federation and the States pursuant to paragraph 3;
4. the beer tax;
5. the levies of casinos.

(3) The revenue from the income tax, the corporation tax and the turnover tax is due to the Federation and the States jointly (joint taxes) to the extent that pursuant to paragraph 5 the revenue from the income tax and pursuant to paragraph 5a the revenue from the turnover tax is not allocated with the municipalities. The revenue from the income tax and the corporation tax is shared equally between the Federation and the States. The respective shares of the Federation and the States in the revenue from the turnover tax are determined by a federal statute that requires the consent of the Bundesrat. This determination is to be based on the following principles:

1. Within the framework of current revenues, the Federation and the States have an equal claim to recover their necessary expenditures. The extent of these expenditures is to be determined with regard to multi-annual financial planning.
2. The coverage requirements of the Federation and the States are to be coordinated in such way that a fair balance is achieved, an excessive burden on the taxpayers is avoided, and uniformity of living standards throughout the federal territory is maintained.

    In addition, in the determination of the respective shares of the Federation and the States in the revenue from the turnover tax, losses in tax revenue incurred by the States from 1 January 1996 because of the consideration of children in income tax law are also to be taken into account. Details are regulated by the federal statute enacted pursuant to the third sentence.

(4) The respective shares of the Federation and the States in the turnover tax is to be determined anew when the ratio between revenue and expenditure of the Federation and the States develops in a substantially different manner; losses of revenue that are addi-

tionally taken into account under paragraph 3, fifth sentence, in determining the respective shares in the turnover tax remain disregarded in that context. Where additional tasks are assigned to or revenue is withdrawn from the States by federal statute, then the additional burden may be compensated by federal grants pursuant to a federal statute which requires the consent of the Bundesrat, if it is limited to a short time period. In the statute, the principles for calculating these grants and for their distribution among the States are to be established.

(5) The municipalities receive a share in the revenue of the income tax that is to be passed on by the States to their municipalities on the basis of the income tax payments of their inhabitants. Details are regulated by a federal statute which requires the consent of the Bundesrat. It may provide that municipalities may establish rate factors [Hebesatz] for the municipalities' share.

(5a) The municipalities receive a share in the revenue of the turnover tax from 1 January 1998. It is passed on by the States on the basis of a geographical and economic key. Details are regulated by a federal statute requiring the consent of the Bundesrat.

(6) The revenue from the real property tax and the trade tax is due to the municipalities; revenue from local consumption and expenditure taxes is due to the municipalities or, in accordance with State legislation, to the associations of municipalities. Municipalities are to be granted the right to establish rate factors for the real property tax and the trade tax within the framework of the statutes. Where there are no municipalities in a State, revenue from the real property tax and the trade tax as well as revenue from local consumption and expenditure taxes is due to the State. The Federation and the States may, by virtue of an apportionment, share in the revenue from the trade tax. Details regarding the apportionment are regulated by a federal statute which requires the consent of the Bundesrat. In accordance with State legislation, the real property tax and the trade tax as well as the municipalities' share of the revenue from the income tax and turnover tax may be taken as a calculation basis for determining apportionments.

(7) From the State' share of the total revenue from joint taxes, a percentage to be determined by State legislation flows to the municipalities and associations of municipalities collectively. For the rest, State legislation determines whether and to what extent revenues from State taxes are due to municipalities (associations of municipalities).

(8) Where the Federation arranges for special facilities in individual States or municipalities (associations of municipalities) which directly result in an increase of expenditure or a loss of revenue (special burdens) for these States or municipalities (associations of municipalities), the Federation grants the necessary compensation where and to the extent that States or municipalities (associations of municipalities) cannot reasonably be expected to bear the special burdens. Compensations from third parties and financial benefits arising for the States or municipalities (associations of municipalities) from the facilities are to be taken into account in granting the compensation.

(9) Revenues and expenditures of municipalities (associations of municipalities) are considered to be States revenues and expenditures for the purposes of this Article.

Article 106a. The States are entitled, from 1 January 1996, to a sum from the tax revenue of the Federation for local public transport. Details are regulated by a federal statute which requires the consent of the Bundesrat. The sum pursuant to the first sentence is not taken into account in the assessment of financial strength pursuant to Article 107 (2).

Article 106b. The States are entitled from 1 July 2009 to a sum from the tax revenue of the Federation in consequence of the transfer of the motor vehicle tax to the Federation. Details are regulated by a federal statute which requires the consent of the Bundesrat.

Article 107. (1) The revenue from State taxes and the States' share of revenue from the income tax and the corporation tax belongs to the individual States to the extent that the taxes are collected by tax authorities within their territories (local revenue). A federal statute which requires the consent of the Bundesrat is to make more detailed provisions for the corporation tax and the wage tax regarding the delimitation as well as the manner and scope of the disaggregation of the local revenue. The statute may also make provision for the delimitation and disaggregation of local revenue from other taxes.
Subject to provisions pursuant to sub-paragraph (2), the individual States are entitled to the States' share of revenue from the turnover tax in accordance with their population numbers.
(2) It is to be ensured by federal statute requiring the consent of the Bundesrat that the diverging financial powers of the States are appropriately aligned; in this, the financial power and financial requirements of municipalities (associations of municipalities) are to be taken into account. For this purpose, deductions [Abschläge] from and supplements [Zuschläge] to the respective financial power in the distribution of the States' shares in the revenue of the turnover tax are to be regulated in the statute. The conditions for the granting of supplements and the making of deductions as well as the standards for the amounts of these supplements and deductions are to be laid down in the statute. For the purpose of evaluating financial power, mining royalties [bergrechtliche Förderabgabe] may only partially be taken into account. The statute may also stipulate that the Federation provides grants from its own funds to financially weak States in order to complement the coverage of their general financial requirements (supplementary grants). Independently of the standards pursuant to clauses 1 to 3, grants may also be accorded to financially weak [leistungsschwach] States whose municipalities (associations of municipalities) have a particularly low fiscal capacity [Steuerkraft] (municipal fiscal capacity grants), as well as to financially weak states whose share in subsidy funds pursuant to Article 91b lies below their population share.

Article 108. (1) Customs duties, fiscal monopolies, consumption taxes regulated by federal legislation including the import turnover tax, as well as the motor vehicle tax and other traffic taxes related to motorized transportation from 1 July 2009 onwards and charges within the framework of the European Communities are administered by federal tax authorities. The organization of these authorities is regulated by a federal statute. Where intermediate authorities are established, their heads are appointed in consultation with the State governments.

(2) The remaining taxes are administered by State tax authorities. The organization of these authorities and the uniform training of their civil servants may be regulated by a federal statute which requires the consent of the Bundesrat. Where intermediate authorities are established, their heads are appointed in agreement with the Federal Government.

(3) Where State tax authorities administer taxes that flow, wholly or in part, to the Federation, they act on behalf of the Federation. Article 85 (3) and (4) applies with the proviso that the Federal Government is substituted by the Minister of Finance.

(4) A federal statute which requires the consent of the Bundesrat may provide for a collaboration in the administration of taxes between federal and State tax authorities as well as in the case of taxes under Paragraph 1 for administration by State tax authorities or in the case of other taxes for their administration by federal tax authorities if and to the extent that the execution of tax laws will thereby be substantially facilitated or improved. For the taxes flowing exclusively to the municipalities (associations of municipalities), the administration that State tax authorities are entitled to may be delegated by the States to the municipalities (associations of municipalities) wholly or in part. The federal statute pursuant to clause 1 may stipulate, with regard to a cooperation between the Federation and the States, that, with the consent of a majority defined in the statute, rules for the execution of tax statutes become mandatory for all States.

(4a) A federal statute requiring the consent of the Bundesrat may, with the consent of the States concerned, provide for a cooperation of State financial authorities and a cross-State conferral of competences to the State financial authorities of one or several States in the administration of taxes falling under sub-paragraph (2), if and as far as the execution of the tax statutes is thereby substantially improved or simplified. The bearing of the costs may be regulated by federal statute.

(5) The procedures to be applied by federal tax authorities are regulated by a federal statute. The procedures to be applied by State tax authorities, or, as provided by the second sentence of paragraph 4, by municipalities (associations of municipalities) may be regulated by a federal statute which requires the consent of the Bundesrat.

(6) Financial jurisdiction is uniformly regulated by a federal statute.

(7) The Federal Government may issue general administrative rules, which require the consent of the Bundesrat to the extent that the administration is incumbent upon State tax authorities or municipalities (associations of municipalities).

Article 109. (1) The Federation and the States are autonomous and independent from one another in their budget management.
(2) The Federation and the States jointly fulfil the responsibilities of the Federal Republic of Germany arising from legal acts of the European Community on the basis of Article 104 of the Treaty establishing the European Community for compliance with budgetary discipline and, within this framework, take due account of the requirements of the macro-economic equilibrium.
(3) The budgets of the Federation and the States are in principle to be balanced without revenue from credits. The Federation and the States may provide regulations regarding the consideration that is symmetrical for the upturn and downturn of the effects of an economic development that is deviating from the normal situation as well as an exception for natural disasters or exceptional emergencies that are beyond the state's control and that substantially compromise the state financial situation. For the exception, a corresponding redemption regulation is to be provided. Further details for the budget of the Federation are regulated by Article 115 with the proviso that the first sentence is complied with if the revenue from credits does not exceed 0.35 percent in proportion to the nominal gross domestic product. Details for the budgets of the States are regulated by them within the framework of their constitutional competences with the proviso that the first sentence is only complied with if no revenue from credits is admitted.
(4) By federal statute which requires the consent of the Bundesrat, common principles applying to the budgetary law, to budget management in line with cyclical economic requirements and to multi-annual financial planning may be established for the Federation and the States.
(5) Sanctions imposed by the European Community in relation to the provisions of Article 104 of the Treaty establishing the European Community for compliance with budgetary discipline are borne by the Federation and the States in a ratio of 65 to 35. The collectivity of the States bears 35 percent of the burdens allocated with the States in mutual solidarity and in proportion to their population; 65 percent of the burdens allocated with to the States is borne by the States in accordance with their share of causation. Details are regulated by a federal statute which requires the consent of the Bundesrat.

Article 109a. (1) In order to avoid budgetary emergencies, a federal statute, which requires the consent of the Bundesrat, regulates
1. the continuous supervision of the budget management of the Federation and the States by a common panel (stability council [Stabilitätsrat]),
2. the requirements and the procedures for determining an imminent budgetary emergency,
3. the principles for establishing and executing restructuring programmes to avoid budgetary emergencies.

The decisions of the stability council and the underlying documentation of the deliberations are to be published.

(2) As of the year 2020, the stability council is charged with monitoring compliance with the provisions of Article 109 (3) by the Federation and the States. The monitoring is guided by the provisions and processes resulting from legal acts on the basis of the Treaty on the Functioning of the European Union for compliance with budgetary discipline.

(3) The decisions of the stability council and the underlying documents must be published.

Article 110. (1) All revenues and expenditures of the Federation are to be included in the budget; for federal enterprises and special assets only allocations or withdrawals need to be included. The budget is to be balanced for revenues and expenditures.

(2) The budget is established for one or more fiscal years divided by years, in a budget statute before the beginning of the first fiscal year. Parts of the budget may apply to different periods of time, divided by fiscal years.

(3) Bills pursuant to the first sentence of paragraph 2 as well as bills to amend the budget statute and the budget are to be submitted to the Bundesrat simultaneously with their transmission to the Bundestag; the Bundesrat is entitled to give a reaction on the bills within six weeks or, in the case of amendment bills, within three weeks.

(4) The budget statute may only contain provisions relating to revenues and expenditures of the Federation and to the period for which the budget statute is enacted. The budget statute may prescribe that its provisions expire only upon publication of the next budget statute or, in the event of an authorization pursuant to Article 115, at a later date.

Article 111. (1) If, by the end of a fiscal year, the budget for the following year has not been established by a statute, the Federal Government is authorized, until its entry into force, to make all expenditures that are necessary
a. to maintain statutory institutions and to carry out statutory measures,
b. to fulfil the legal obligations of the Federation,
c. to continue constructions, acquisitions and other services, or to continue to grant benefits for these purposes, to the extent that amounts have already been approved in the budget of a previous year.

(2) To the extent that revenues not based upon specific statutes from taxes, charges or other sources or the operational capital reserves do not cover the expenditures referred to in paragraph 1, the Federal Government may mobilize the funds necessary for sustaining operational management up to a maximum of one quarter of the total amount of the previous budget by way of a credit.

Article 112. Expenditures in excess of or outside the budgetary planning require the consent of the Minister of Finance. It may only be granted in the case of an unforeseen and irrefutable necessity. Details may be regulated by a federal statute.

Article 113. (1) Statutes which increase the expenditures of the budget proposed by the Federal Government or which comprise or will bring about in the future new expenditures require the consent of the Federal Government. The same applies to statutes that comprise or will bring about in the future decreases in revenue. The Federal Government may demand that the Bundestag suspend its decision-making on these statutes. In such case the Federal Government is to transmit a statement to the Bundestag within six weeks.
(2) The Federal Government may, within four weeks after the Bundestag has adopted this statute, demand that it make a decision again.
(3) Where the statute has become effective pursuant to Article 78, the Federal Government may withhold its consent only within six weeks and only after having initiated the procedure provided for in the third and fourth sentence of paragraph 1 or in paragraph 2. Upon the expiry of that period, consent is deemed to have been given.

Article 114. (1) The Minister of Finance is to render annually to the Bundestag and to the Bundesrat an account of all revenues and expenditures as well as of assets and debts during the following fiscal year, for the relief of the Federal Government.
(2) The Federal Court of Audit [Bundesrechnungshof], whose members enjoy judicial independence, audits the account as well as the economic efficiency and regularity of the federal budget and operational management. For the purposes of the audit pursuant to clause 1, the Federal Court of Audit may also survey entities outside the federal administration; this also applies in cases in which the Federation accords earmarked funds to the States for the performance of State tasks. It is to report annually directly to the Bundestag and to the Bundesrat in addition to the Federal Government. In all other respects, the competences of the Federal Court of Audit are regulated by federal statute.

Article 115. (1) The raising of credit and the assumption of co-signing of obligations, of guarantees or of other commitments which may lead to expenditures in future fiscal years require authorization to a quantified or quantifiable amount by a federal statute.
(2) Revenues and expenditures are in principle to be balanced without revenues from credits. This principle is complied with if the revenues from credits do not exceed 0.35 percent in proportion to the nominal gross domestic product. In addition, for an economic development that is deviating from the normal situation, the effects on the budget are to be considered symmetrically for the upturn and the downturn. Deviations in the effective raising of credit from the credit maximum permissible pursuant to the first through third sentences are registered on a control account; burdens that exceed the

threshold of 1.5 percent in proportion to the nominal gross domestic product are to be reduced in line with the economic development. Details, especially the correction of revenues and expenditures for financial transactions and the procedure for calculating the maximum limit of the annual net borrowing taking into account the economic developments on the basis of a procedure for economic development correction as well as the control and the offsetting of deviations in the effective raising of credit from the maximum limit, are regulated by a federal statute. In the case of natural disasters or exceptional emergencies that are beyond the state's control and that substantially compromise the state financial situation, these maximum credit limits may be exceeded on the basis of a decision of the majority of the members of the Bundestag. The decision is to be connected with a redemption plan. The redemption of the credits raised pursuant to the sixth sentence is to take place within an adequate timeframe.

Xa. State of defence

Article 115a. (1) The finding that the territory of the Federation is being attacked by force of arms or that there is an imminent threat of such an attack (state of defence) is pronounced by the Bundestag with the consent of the Bundesrat. The finding is pronounced on request of the Federal Government and requires a majority of two-thirds of votes cast, including at least the majority of the members of the Bundestag.
(2) If the situation imperatively requires immediate action and insurmountable impediments prevent the timely convention of the Bundestag or if it does not have capacity to take decisions, then the Joint Committee pronounces the finding with a majority of two-thirds of votes cast, including a majority if its members.
(3) The finding is published by the Federal President in accordance with Article 82 in the Federal Law Gazette. If this cannot be done in time, the publication takes place in another manner; it must later be effected in the Federal Law Gazette as soon as the circumstances permit.
(4) If the territory of the Federation is being attacked by force of arms and the competent federal organs are incapable of immediately pronouncing a finding under paragraph 1, first sentence, such finding is deemed pronounced and published as from the time when the attack started. The Federal President specifies that time as soon as the circumstances permit.
(5) If the finding of a state of defence has been published and the territory of the Federation is being attacked by force of arms, the Federal President may, with the consent of the Bundestag, make declarations under international law regarding the existence of a state of defence. Under the conditions of paragraph 2, the position of the Bundestag is assumed by the Joint Committee.

Article 115b. With the publication of the state of defence, the command over the armed forces passes to the Federal Chancellor.

Article 115c. (1) The Federation has the right of concurrent legislation for the state of defence also in the matters that fall within the legislative power of the States. These statutes require the consent of the Bundesrat.
(2) To the extent that the circumstances during the state of defence so require, for the state of defence a statute may
1. in case of expropriations in deviation from Article 14 (3) second sentence, regulate the compensation provisionally,
2. regarding deprivations of freedom, provide for a time limit deviating from Article 104 (2) third sentence and (3) first sentence, at most however one of four days, for the case that a judge could not act within the time limit applied in normal times.

(3) To the extent that it is necessary for the aversion of a present or immediately threatening attack, for the state of defence by federal statute with the consent of the Bundesrat the administration and the finances system of the Federation and the States may be regulated in deviation from the sections VIII, VIIIa and X, in which case the viability of the States, municipalities and associations of municipalities, especially in a financial perspective, is to be respected.
(4) Federal statutes in the sense of Paragraph 1 and 2 no. 1 may for the purpose of the preparation of their execution already be applied before the beginning of the state of defence.

Article 115d. (1) Regarding legislation of the Federation in a state of defence, the provisions of Paragraphs 2 and 3 apply in deviation from Article 76 (2), Article 77 (1) second sentence and (2) to (4), Article 78 and Article 82 (1).
(2) Bills of the Federal Government which it has qualified as urgent are to be transmitted to the Bundesrat at the same time as their submission to the Bundestag. The Bundestag and the Bundesrat immediately deliberate on these bills jointly. In as far as the consent of the Bundesrat is required for a statute, the majority of its votes are required for the adoption of the statute. Details are regulated by rules of procedure which are adopted by the Bundestag and which require the consent of the Bundesrat.
(3) For the publication of statutes, Article 115a (3) second sentence applies mutatis mutandis.

Article 115e. (1) If the Joint Committee declares in a state of defence with a majority of two thirds of the votes cast, at least with the majority of its members, that an insurmountable impediment prevent the timely convention of the Bundestag or that it does not have capacity to take decisions, the Joint Committee has the position of Bundestag and Bundesrat and exercises their rights unitarily.

(2) By statute of the Joint Committee the Basic Law may neither be amended nor wholly or partly suspended or rendered inapplicable. The Joint Committee is not entitled to adopt statutes under Article 23 (1) second sentence, Article 24 (1) or Article 29.

Article 115f. (1) The Federal Government may, in a state of defence, in as far as the circumstances so require,
1. use the Federal Border Guard throughout the entire territory of the Federation;
2. give orders, besides to the federal administration, also to the State governments and, if it considers it to be urgent, to the State authorities and transfer this power to members of the State governments to be determined by it.

(2) The Bundestag, the Bundesrat and the Joint Committee are to be informed of the measures taken under Paragraph 1 immediately.

Article 115g. The constitutional position and the fulfilment of the constitutional tasks of the Federal Constitutional Court and its judges may not be jeopardized. The statute regarding the Federal Constitutional Court may be amended by a statute of the Joint Committee only to the extent that this is also in the opinion of the Federal Constitutional Court required in order to maintain the capacity of the Court to function. Until the adoption of such a statute the Federal Constitutional Court may take the measures necessary for maintaining the capacity of the Court to function. The Federal Constitutional Court takes decisions under the second and third sentence by majority of the judges present.

Article 115h. (1) Electoral terms of the Bundestag or the parliaments of the States expiring during a state of defence end six months after the termination of the state of defence. The term of the Federal President expiring during a state of defence as well as the exercise of his powers in case of early termination of his term by the president of the Bundesrat end nine months after the termination of the state of defence. The term of a member of the Federal Constitutional Court expiring during a state of defence ends six months after the termination of the state of defence.

(2) Where a new election of a Federal Chancellor by the Joint Committee becomes necessary, it elects a new Federal Chancellor by a majority of its members; the Federal President submits a proposal to the Joint Committee. The Joint Committee may express its lack of confidence in the Federal Chancellor only by electing a successor by the vote of two-thirds of its members.

(3) For the duration of the state of defence, a dissolution of the Bundestag is excluded.

Article 115i. (1) If the competent federal organs are incapable of taking the measures necessary for the aversion of the danger and the situation imperatively requires an immediate autonomous action in certain parts of the territory of the Federation, the State governments or authorities or representatives appointed by them are authorized to take measures in the sense of Article 115f (1) in matters within their competence.

(2) Measures under Paragraph 1 may at any time be repealed by the Federal Government, in relation to State authorities and subordinated federal authorities also by the prime ministers of the States.

Article 115k. (1) For the duration of their applicability, statutes under Articles 115c, 115e and 115g and ordinances that are adopted pursuant such statutes render conflicting law inapplicable. This does not apply to earlier law that has been adopted pursuant to Articles 115c, 115e and 115g.

(2) Statutes that the Joint Committee has adopted and ordinances that were adopted pursuant to such statutes expire at the latest six months after the termination of the state of defence.

(3) Statutes that contain rules deviating from Articles 91a, 91b, 104a, 106 and 107 apply at the latest until the end of the second fiscal year following the termination of the state of defence. They may, after the termination of the state of defence, be amended by federal statute with the consent of the Bundesrat, in order to lead over to the regime under sections VIIIa and X.

Article 115l. (1) The Bundestag may at any time with the consent of the Bundesrat repeal statutes of the Joint Committee. The Bundesrat may demand that the Bundestag decide on this matter. Other measures taken for the aversion of the danger by the Joint Committee or the Federal Government are to be lifted when the Bundestag and the Bundesrat so decide.

(2) The Bundestag may at any time with the consent of the Bundesrat, by a decision which is to be published by the Federal President, declare the state of defence terminated. The Bundesrat may demand that the Bundestag decide on this matter. The state of defence is to be declared terminated immediately when the conditions for its declaration are no longer present.

(3) The conclusion of peace is decided by federal statute.

XI. Transitional and final provisions

Article 116. (1) German within the meaning of this Basic Law is, subject to other statutory provisions, he who has the German citizenship or who, as a refugee or expellee of German ethnicity or as his spouse or descendant found admittance to the territory of the German Reich as it existed on 31 December 1937.

(2) Former German citizens, who, between 30 January 1933 and 8 May 1945, had their citizenship revoked for political, racial or religious reasons, and their descendants, are, on

application, to be re-naturalised. They are considered as not denaturalized if they, after 8 May 1945, took up residence in Germany and have not expressed a contrary intention.

Article 117. (1) Law contrary to Article 3 (2) remains in force until its adaptation to that provision of the Basic Law, but not for longer than until 31 March 1953.
(2) Statutes which limit the right to freedom of movement due to the current shortage of living space remain in force until their repeal by federal statute.

Article 118. The reorganization in the territories comprising the States of Baden, Württemberg-Baden and Württemberg-Hohenzollern may be effected, in derogation from the provisions of Article 29, by agreement between the States concerned. If no agreement is reached, the reorganization will be regulated by federal statute which must provide for a consultative referendum.

Article 118a. The reorganization in the territory comprising the States of Berlin and Brandenburg may be effected, in derogation from the provisions of Article 29, by agreement, with the participation of their eligible voters, between the States concerned..

Article 119. In matters relating to refugees and expellees, in particular as regards their distribution among the States, the federal government, until the adoption of a settlement by federal statute, may, with the consent of the Bundesrat, issue ordinances having the force of statute. For special cases, the federal government may be authorized to issue individual instructions. These instructions are, unless in case of an imminent danger, to be addressed to the highest States authorities.

Article 120. (1) The Federation bears the expenses for occupation costs and other internal and external burdens resulting from the war, in accordance with the more detailed federal statutes. To the extent that these burdens resulting from the war have been regulated by federal statutes by 1 October 1969, the Federation and the States bear such expenses in the proportion established by such federal statutes. To the extent that expenditures for burdens resulting from the war which neither have been nor are regulated by federal statutes have been assumed by 1 October 1965 by the States, municipalities (associations of municipalities) or other agencies performing functions of the States or municipalities, the Federation is not obliged to assume expenditures of this nature even after that date. The Federation bears the supplementary contributions towards the expenses of social security, including unemployment insurance and unemployment assistance. The distribution of burdens resulting from the war between the Federation and the States regulated by this paragraph does not affect the statutory regulation of compensation claims for effects of the war.
(2) Revenues pass to the Federation at the same time as it takes over the expenditures.

Article 120a. (1) The statutes concerning the implementation of the equalization of burdens may, with the consent of the Bundesrat, stipulate that in the field of equalization payments they will be executed partly by the Federation and partly by the States on behalf of the Federation and that the powers appertaining to the federal government and the competent highest federal authorities pursuant to Article 85 are delegated to the Federal Equalization of Burdens Office [Bundesausgleichsamt]. The Federal Equalization of Burdens Office does not require the consent of the Bundesrat in the exercise of these competences; its instructions are, except in cases of urgency, to be directed to the highest States authorities (State equalization of burdens offices).
(2) Article 87 (3), second sentence, remains unaffected.

Article 121. A majority of the members of the Bundestag and the Federal Convention within the meaning of this Basic Law is the majority of their statutory number.

Article 122. (1) From the convention of the Bundestag onwards, statutes are exclusively enacted by the legislative bodies recognized by this Basic Law.
(2) Legislative bodies and entities participating in the legislative process in an advisory capacity whose competence expires pursuant to paragraph 1 are dissolved from that moment.

Article 123. (1) Law predating the convention of the Bundestag remains in force to the extent that it does not conflict with the Basic Law.
(2) Treaties concluded by the German Reich, which pursuant to this Basic Law concern matters falling within the competence of State legislation, if under general principles of law they are and continue to be valid, remain in force, subject to all rights and objections of the parties, until new treaties are concluded by the authorities competent pursuant to this Basic Law or until their termination is otherwise effected by virtue of provisions contained in them.

Article 124. Law concerning matters falling within the exclusive legislative competence of the Federation becomes federal law within its scope of application.

Article 125. Law concerning matters falling within concurrent legislative powers of the Federation becomes federal law within its scope of application,
1. insofar as it applies uniformly within one or more occupation zones,
2. insofar as it is law by which after 8 May 1945 former Reich law has been amended.

Article 125a. (1) Law which has been enacted as federal law, but due to the amendment of Article 74 (1), the insertion of Article 84 (1) seventh sentence, Article 85 (1) second sentence or Article 105 (2a) second sentence or due to the repeal of Articles 74a, 75 or 98

(3) second sentence could no longer be enacted as federal law remains in force as federal law. It may be replaced by State law.

(2) Law which has been enacted pursuant to Article 72 (2) in the version applicable until 15 November 1994, but which due to the amendment of Article 72 (2) could no longer be enacted as federal law, remains in force as federal law. By federal statute it may be stipulated that it may be replaced by State law.

(3) Law which has been enacted as State law but due to the amendment of Article 73 could no longer be enacted as State law remains in force as State law. It may be replaced by federal law.

Article 125b. (1) Law which has been enacted pursuant to Article 75 in the version applicable until 1 September 2006 and which also after this date could be enacted as federal law, remains in force. Competences and obligations of the States to legislate remain in place in that respect. With respect to the areas mentioned in Article 72 (3) first sentence, the States may adopt regulations in deviation from this law; in the areas of Article 72 (3) first sentence, nos. 2, 5 and 6 however only when and to the extent that the Federation has exercised its legislative powers after 1 September 2006, in the cases of numbers 2 and 5 from 1 January 2010 at the latest, in the case of number 6 from 1 August 2008 at the latest.

(2) The States may adopt regulations in deviation from federal legal provisions that have been enacted pursuant to Article 84 (1) in the version applicable until 1 September 2006, they may adopt regulations in deviation from regulations regarding administrative procedure until 31 December 2008 however only if after 1 September 2006 regulations regarding administrative procedure have been amended in the relevant federal statute.

Article 125c. (1) Law which has been enacted pursuant to Article 91a (2) in conjunction with paragraph 1 no. 1 in the version applicable until 1 September 2006 remains in force until 31 December 2006.

(2) The legal provisions in the areas of municipal traffic financing and promotion of social housing created pursuant to Article 104a (4) in the version applicable until 1 September 2006 remain in force until 31 December 2006. The legal provisions created in the area of municipal traffic financing for the special programmes pursuant to § 6 (1) Municipal Traffic Financing Act [Gemeindeverkehrsfinanzierungsgesetz], as well as those created with the Act on Federal Financial Aid Pursuant to Article 104a of the Basic Law to the States of Bremen, Hamburg, Mecklenburg-Western Pommerania, Lower Saxony, as well as Schleswig-Holstein for Sea Ports [Gesetz über Finanzhilfen des Bundes nach Artikel 104a Absatz 4 des Grundgesetzes an die Länder … für Seehäfen] of 20 December 2001 pursuant to Article 104a (4) in the version in force until 1 September 2006 remain valid until repealed. An amendment of the Municipal Traffic Financing Act is permissible. The remaining legal provisions created pursuant to Article 104a (4) in the version in

force until 1 September 2006 remain in force until 31 December 2019, as far as no earlier time is or has been set for their expiry.
(3) Article 104b (2) clause 5 is only to be applied to provisions that enter into force after 31 December 2019.

Article 126. Disagreements about the continuance of law as federal law are resolved by the Federal Constitutional Court.

Article 127. The federal government may, with the consent of the governments of the States concerned, within one year after the promulgation of this Basic Law, enact law of the Bizone administration [Vereinigtes Wirtschaftsgebiet], to the extent that it remains in force as federal law under Article 124 or 125, in the States of Baden, Greater Berlin, Rhineland-Palatinate and Württemberg-Hohenzollern..

Article 128. To the extent that law remaining in force provides for powers to issue instructions within the meaning of Article 84 (5), they remain in force until statutory regulation provides otherwise.

Article 129. (1) To the extent that legal provisions that remain in force as federal law contain an authorization to enact ordinances or general administrative regulations or to issue administrative acts, it passes to the authorities henceforth competent in the subject matter. In cases of doubt, the federal government decides in agreement with the Bundesrat; the decision is to be published.
(2) To the extent that legal provisions that remain in force as State law contain such an authorization, it is exercised by the authorities competent under State law.
(3) To the extent that legal provisions within the meaning of paragraphs 1 and 2 authorize their amendment or supplementation or the enactment of legal provisions in the place of statutes, such authorization is expired.
(4) The provisions of paragraphs 1 and 2 apply mutatis mutandis where legal provisions refer to provisions no longer in force or to institutions no longer existent.

Article 130. (1) Administrative bodies and other institutions serving the public administration or the administration of justice that are not based on State law or agreements between States as well as the administration of the South West German Railways and the administrative board for postal and telecommunications services for the French occupation zone are subordinate to the federal government. The latter regulates with the consent of the Bundesrat their transfer, dissolution or liquidation.
(2) The supreme disciplinary superior of the members of these administrations and institutions is the competent federal minister.

(3) Institutions and entities under public law not directly subordinate to a State and not based on agreements between the States are under the supervision of the competent supreme federal authority.

Article 131. The legal relationships of persons including refugees and expellees who on 8 May 1945 were employed in the public service, who have left it for reasons related to other than to civil servant or labour agreement law and who have not yet been employed or not in a position corresponding to their former one, are to be regulated by federal statute. The same applies mutatis mutandis to persons including refugees and expellees who on 8 May 1945 were entitled to support and who for reasons related to other than to civil servant or labour agreement law no longer receive support or equivalent support. Until the entry into force of the federal statute, no legal entitlements may be claimed save for other regulations under State law.

Article 132. (1) Civil servants and judges who, on the moment of the entry into force of this Basic Law, are appointed for life, may within six months after the first convention of the Bundestag be retired, suspended or transferred to an office with a lower salary if they lack the personal or professional aptitude required for their office. This provision applies mutatis mutandis to employees with a non-terminable employment. In the case of employees whose employment can be terminated, periods of notice exceeding those set by labour agreement may be terminated within the same time period.
(2) This provision does not apply to members of the public service who are not affected by the provisions regarding the "Liberation from National Socialism and Militarism" or who are recognized victims of National Socialism, unless an important personal ground obtains.
(3) Those affected may have recourse to the courts pursuant to Article 19 (4).
(4) Details are regulated by an ordinance of the federal government which requires the consent of the Bundesrat.

Article 133. The Federation succeeds to the rights and obligations of the Bizone administration [Vereinigtes Wirtschaftsgebiet].

Article 134. (1) The assets of the Reich in principle become federal assets.
(2) To the extent that they were, pursuant to their originally intended use, to be used principally for administrative tasks which pursuant to this Basic Law are not administrative tasks of the Federation, they are to be transferred free of charge to the authorities now competent and, to the extent that they, pursuant to their current and not merely temporary use, serve for administrative tasks that pursuant to this Basic Law are now to be performed by the States, they are to be transferred to the States. The Federation may also transfer other assets to the States.

(3) Assets that were placed at the disposal of the Reich free of charge by States and municipalities (associations of municipalities) become assets of the States and municipalities (associations of municipalities) again, to the extent that the Federation does not require them for its own administrative tasks.
(4) Details are regulated by a federal statute which requires the consent of the Bundesrat.

Article 135. (1) If after 8 May 1945 and before the entry into force of this Basic Law the affiliation of a territory to a State has changed, then the State to which the territory now belongs is entitled to the assets of the State to which it previously belonged that are located in that territory.
(2) The assets of no longer existing States and other entities and institutions under public law, to the extent that, pursuant to their originally intended use, they were to be used principally for administrative tasks or, pursuant to their current and not merely temporary use, serve principally administrative tasks, pass to the State or entity or institution under public law that now performs these tasks.
(3) Land property of no longer existing States including appurtenances pass to the State within which it is located to the extent that it is not already included among the assets within the meaning of paragraph 1.
(4) To the extent that an overriding interest of the Federation or the particular interest of a territory so requires, arrangements deviating from the provisions of paragraphs 1 to 3 of this Article may be adopted by federal statute.
(5) In all other respects, the succession and disposition of assets, to the extent that it has not been resolved by 1 January 1952 by agreement between the States or entities or institutions under public law concerned, is regulated by a federal statute which requires the consent of the Bundesrat.
(6) Holdings of the former State of Prussia in private-law enterprises pass to the Federation. Details are regulated by a federal statute which may also deviate from this provision.
(7) To the extent that assets which would fall to a State or entity or institution under public law pursuant to paragraphs 1 to 3 had been used by the beneficiary by a State statute, pursuant to a State statute or in any other manner at the entry into force of this Basic Law, the transfer of assets is considered to have taken place before the use.

Article 135a. (1) By federal legislation reserved pursuant to Article 134 (4) and Article 135 (5) it may be provided that the following do not have to be fulfilled or do not have to be fulfilled in full:
1. liabilities of the Reich as well as liabilities of the former State of Prussia and other no longer existing entities and institutions under public law,
2. liabilities of the Federation or other entities or institutions under public law which are related to the passing of assets pursuant to Article 89, 90, 134 and 135 and liabilities of

these legal bodies that are based on measures taken by the legal bodies designated under subparagraph 1,
3. liabilities of the States and municipalities (associations of municipalities) which have arisen from measures which these legal bodies have taken before 1 August 1945 in order to implement orders of the occupying powers or to remedy a state of emergency resulting from the war within the framework of the administrative tasks incumbent upon or delegated by the Reich.

(2) Paragraph 1 applies mutatis mutandis to liabilities of the German Democratic Republic or its legal bodies as well as to liabilities of the Federation or other entities or institutions under public law which are related to the passing of assets of the German Democratic Republic to the Federation, States and municipalities, and to liabilities arising from measures of the German Democratic Republic or its legal bodies.

Article 136. (1) The Bundesrat convenes for the first time on the day of the first convention of the Bundestag.
(2) Until the election of the first Federal President, his competences are exercised by the president of the Bundesrat. He does not have the right to dissolve the Bundestag.

Article 137. (1) The right of civil servants, employees in the public service, professional soldiers, temporary volunteer soldiers and judges to run in elections in the Federation, in the States and the municipalities may be restricted by statute.
(2) The electoral law to be adopted by the Parliamentary Council [Parlamentarischer Rat] applies to the election of the first Bundestag, the first Federal Convention and the first Federal President of the Federal Republic.
(3) The competence of the Federal Constitutional Court pursuant to Article 42 (2) is, until its establishment, exercised by the German High Court for the Bizone [Deutsches Obergericht für das Vereinigte Wirtschaftsgebiet] which decides in accordance with its own rules of procedure.

Article 138. Changes to the constitutions of the profession of notary public as it now exists in the States of Baden, Bavaria, Württemberg-Baden and Württemberg-Hohenzollern require the consent of the governments of these States.

Article 139. The legal provisions enacted for the "Liberation of the German People from National Socialism and Militarism" [Befreiung des deutschen Volkes vom Nationalsozialismus und Militarismus] are not affected by the provisions of this Basic Law.

Article 140. The provisions of Articles 136, 137, 138, 139 and 141 of the German Constitution of 11 August 1919 are part of this Basic Law.

Article 141. Article 7 (3) first sentence does not apply in any State where State law providing otherwise was in force on 1 January 1949.

Article 142. Notwithstanding the provision of Article 31, provisions of State constitutions remain in force to the extent that they guarantee fundamental rights in conformity with Articles 1 to 18 of this Basic Law.

Article 142a. (Repealed).

Article 143. (1) Law in the territory specified in Article 3 of the Unification Treaty [Einigungsvertrag] may deviate from the provisions of this Basic Law at the latest until 31 December 1992, to the extent and so long as, due to the differing circumstances, a complete adaptation to the order of the Basic Law cannot be achieved yet. Deviations may not violate Article 19 (2) and must be compatible with the principles stipulated in Article 79 (3).
(2) Deviations from Titles II, VIII, VIIIa, IX, X and XI are permissible at the latest until 31 December 1995.
(3) Notwithstanding paragraphs 1 and 2, Article 41 of the Unification Treaty and provisions for its implementation remain in force to the extent that they provide that interference with property in the territory specified in Article 3 of that Treaty cannot be reversed.

Article 143a. (1) The Federation has exclusive legislative competence in all matters arising from the transformation of the federal railways administered by the Federation into commercial enterprises. Article 87e (5) applies mutatis mutandis. Civil servants of the federal railways may be assigned by statute, without prejudice to their legal status or the responsibility of the employer, to provide services for railways of the Federation organized under private law.
(2) The Federation executes statutes enacted pursuant to paragraph 1.
(3) The performance of the tasks relating to local public railway transport of the former federal railways is the responsibility of the Federation until 31 December 1995. The same applies to the corresponding tasks of the Rail Transport Administration [Eisenbahnverkehrsverwaltung]. Details are regulated by a federal statute that requires the consent of the Bundesrat.

Article 143b. (1) The special assets of the German Federal Post Office [Deutsche Bundespost] is transformed into private-law enterprises pursuant to a federal statute. The Federation has exclusive legislative competence in all matters arising herefrom.
(2) The exclusive rights of the Federation existing before the transformation may be conferred by a federal statute for a transitional period on the enterprises that succeed

the postal service of the German Federal Post Office [Deutsche Bundespost Postdienst] and the telecommunications service of the German Federal Post Office [Deutsche Bundespost Telekom]. The majority interest in the enterprise that succeeds the postal service of the German Federal Post Office may be surrendered by the Federation at the earliest five years after the entry into force of the statute. To do so requires a federal statute with the consent of the Bundesrat.

(3) The federal civil servants employed by the German Federal Post Office are employed by the private enterprises without prejudice to their legal status and the responsibility of their employer. The enterprises exercise employer's authority. Details are regulated by a federal statute.

Article 143c. (1) The States are entitled from 1 January 2007 until 31 December 2019 to receive amounts out of the federal budget annually for the discontinuation of the Federation's share in financing due to the abolition of the joint tasks of upgrading and constructing universities including university hospitals and educational guidance and due to the abolition of financial aid for the improvement of the traffic situation of the municipalities and for social housing subsidies. Until 31 December 2013, these amounts are calculated on the basis of the average financing shares of the Federation in the 2000 to 2008 frame of reference.

(2) The amounts are, until 31 December 2013, distributed among the States as follows:
1. as annual fixed amounts whose height is calculated on the basis of the average share of each State over the time period of 2000 to 2003;
2. for a specific purpose of the responsibilities under the previous mixed financing.

(3) The Federation and the States review until the end of 2013 to what extent the financing means the States have been assigned under paragraph 1 are still suitable and necessary for the performance of the States' tasks. From 1 January 2014 onwards, the purpose-bound appropriation designated in paragraph 2 (2) of the financing means assigned pursuant to paragraph 1 will lapse; the investment-related appropriation of the median volume remains valid. The agreements from the Second Solidarity Agreement [Solidarpakt II] remain unaffected.

(4) Details are regulated by a federal statute that requires the consent of the Bundesrat.

Article 143d. (1) Articles 109 and 115 in the version applicable until 31 July 2009 are to be applied for the last time to the 2010 fiscal year. Articles 109 and 115 in the version applicable as from 1 August 2009 are to be applied for the first time to the 2011 fiscal year; credit authorizations existing on 31 December 2010 for special assets [Sondervermögen] already established remain unaffected. The States may, in the period from 1 January 2011 to 31 December 2019, deviate from the target of Article 109 (3) in accordance with the applicable provisions of State law. The States' budgets are to be shaped in such way that in the 2020 fiscal year the target under Article 109 (3) fifth sentence is met. The

Federation may, in the time period from 1 January 2011 to 31 December 2015 deviate from the target of Article 115 (2) second sentence. The reduction of the existing deficit shall begin in the 2011 fiscal year. The annual budgets are to be shaped in such way that in the 2016 fiscal year the target under Article 115 (2) second sentence is met; details are regulated by a federal statute.

(2) As an aid for compliance with the target under Article 109 (3) from 1 January 2020 onwards, the States of Berlin, Bremen, Saarland, Saxony-Anhalt and Schleswig-Holstein may be granted a total of 800 million euros in consolidation aids per year out of the federal budget for the time period of 2011 to 2019. Thereof, 300 million euros are allotted to Bremen, 260 million euros to Saarland, and 80 million euros each to Berlin, Saxony-Anhalt and Schleswig-Holstein. The aids are provided on the basis of an administrative agreement pursuant to a federal statute with the consent of the Bundesrat. The granting of aids presupposes a complete clearing of the financing deficits by the end of 2020. Details, in particular the annual stages of reduction of the financing deficit, the supervision of the reduction of the financing deficits by the Stability Council [Stabilitätsrat] as well as consequences in case of non-compliance with the stages of reduction are regulated by a federal statute with the consent of the Bundesrat and an administrative agreement. A simultaneous granting of consolidation aids and stabilization aids due to an extreme budgetary emergency is excluded.

(3) The financing burden resulting from the granting of consolidation aids is distributed in equal parts between the Federation and the States, in the case of the latter from their share of the turnover tax. Details are regulated by a federal statute with the consent of the Bundesrat.

(4) To facilitate the autonomous compliance with the provisions of Article 109 (3) in the future, the States of Bremen and Saarland may, as of 1 January 2020, be granted restructuring aid [Sanierungshilfen] of an annual total of 800 million Euros from the budget of the Federation. The States take measures for the reduction of their excessive debt, as well as for the enhancement of their economic and financial power. Details are laid down in a federal statute that requires the consent of the Bundesrat. The simultaneous granting of this restructuring aid and restructuring aid on the basis of an extreme budgetary emergency is precluded.

Article 143e. (1) By way of derogation from Article 90 (2), the federal motorways [Bundesautobahnen] will be held in delegated administration [Auftragsverwaltung] by the States or the self-regulatory bodies competent under State law until 31 December 2020 at the latest. The Federation regulates the transition from delegated to federal administration pursuant to Article 90 (2) and (4) by means of federal statute with the consent of the Bundesrat.

(2) Upon the request by a State, to be submitted before 31 December 2018, the Federation shall, by way of derogation from Article 90 (4), take the remaining federal roads of

long-distance traffic, as far as they are located on the territory of that State, into federal administration with effect as of 1 January 2021.

(3) A federal statute with the consent of the Bundesrat may provide that a State, upon request, takes charge of planning permit and planning approval procedures [Planfeststellung und Plangenehmigung] for the construction and for the alteration of federal motorways and other federal roads of long-distance traffic, which the Federation has taken into federal administration pursuant to Article 90 (4) or Article 143e (2), on behalf of the Federation, and under which conditions a re-transfer of these tasks can take place.

Article 143f. Article 143d, the Act on the Financial Equalisation between the Federation and the States [Gesetz über den Finanzausgleich zwischen Bund und Ländern], as well as other statutes adopted on the basis of Article 107 (2) in its version applicable as of 1 January 2020 shall expire, if after 31 December 2030 the Federal Government, the Bundestag, or at least three States jointly have demanded negotiations regarding a rearrangement of the federal financial relations [bundesstaatliche Finanzbeziehungen] and, upon the lapse of five years after notification of the demand for negotiations of the Federal Government, the Bundestag, or the States to the Federal President, no statutory rearrangement of the federal financial relations has entered into force. The day of expiry is to be announced in the federal gazette.

Article 143g. For the regulation of the distribution of tax revenue [Steuerertragsverteilung], the financial equalisation scheme between the Länder [Länderfinanzausgleich], and the federal supplementary grants [Bundesergänzungszuweisungen] until 31 December 2019, Article 107 continues to apply in its version applicable until the entry into force of the Act for the Amendment of the Basic Law of 13 July 2017.

Article 144. (1) This Basic Law requires ratification by the representative assemblies in two thirds of the States in which it is to apply initially.

(2) To the extent that the application of this Basic Law is subject to restrictions in one of the States listed in Article 23 or in a part of these States, that State or that part of the State has the right to send representatives to the Bundestag pursuant to Article 38 and to the Bundesrat pursuant to Article 50.

Article 145. (1) The Parliamentary Council [Parlamentarischer Rat], with the participation of the representatives of Greater Berlin, declares the adoption of this Basic Law in public session, promulgates and publishes it.

(2) This Basic Law enters into force at the end of the day on which it is published.

(3) It is to be published in the Federal Law Gazette [Bundesgesetzblatt].

Article 146. This Basic Law, which since the completion of the unity and freedom of Germany applies to the entire German people, shall cease to apply on the day on which a constitution enters into force which has been freely adopted by the German people.

7   FEDERAL ELECTIONS ACT [BUNDESWAHLGESETZ][2]

I. Electoral system

§ 1. (1) The German Bundestag is composed, subject to the deviations resulting from this Act, of 598 members. They are elected in general, direct, free, equal and secret-ballot elections by the Germans entitled to vote, according to the principle of proportional representation combined with person-based voting.
(2) 299 of the members of the Bundestag are elected upon electoral district candidacies within electoral districts and the other members upon State candidacies (State lists).

§ 2. (1) The electoral territory is the territory of the Federal Republic of Germany.
(2) The division of the electoral territory into electoral districts is based on the Annex to this Act.
(3) Each electoral district is, for the purposes of polling, divided into polling districts.

§ 3. (1) During the division of electoral districts, the following principles must be observed:
1. The State borders must be respected.
2. The number of electoral districts in the individual States must correspond as far as possible to their share of the population. It is established with the same calculation method which is applied to the distribution of seats to the State lists in accordance with § 6 (2), second to seventh sentence.
3. The population size of an electoral district should not deviate from the average population size of electoral districts by more than 15 per cent, above or below; if the deviation is more than 25 per cent, a re-delimitation of the district must take place.
4. An electoral district is to form a contiguous area.
5. The borders of municipalities, rural counties and autonomous cities are to be respected if possible.
During the calculation of population numbers, aliens (§ 2 (1) Sojourn Act [Aufenthaltsgesetz]) are not taken into account.
(2) The Federal President appoints a permanent electoral district commission. It consists of the president of the Federal Statistics Office [Statistisches Bundesamt], one judge at the Federal Administrative Court [Bundesverwaltungsgericht] and five other members.
(3) The electoral district commission has the task to report on changes of population numbers in the electoral territory and to submit whether and which changes in the division of electoral districts it considers necessary in view thereof. It may submit in its report

---

2   As last amended by federal statute of 10 July 2018 (*BGBl.* I p. 1116). Selected provisions: Chapter I (§§ 1-7); §12. Translation by Sascha Hardt.

proposals for changes also for other reasons. Regarding its proposals for changes in the division of electoral districts it must respect the principles stipulated in paragraph 1; if following the calculation under paragraph 1 no. 2, several possible affiliations with electoral districts may result, it draws up proposals on that matter.

(4) The report of the electoral district commission must be submitted to the Federal Ministry of Internal Affairs within fifteen months following the beginning of the term of the German Bundestag. The Federal Ministry of Internal Affairs transmits it without delay to the German Bundestag and publishes a reference to the publication as a Bundestag printed paper [Bundestagsdrucksache] in the Federal Gazette [Bundesanzeiger]. Upon request of the Federal Ministry of Internal Affairs, the electoral district committee must submit a supplementary report; for this case, the second sentence applies mutatis mutandis.

(5) If State borders are being redrawn in accordance with statutory provisions regarding the procedure on further changes to the territorial shape of the States under Article 29 (7) of the Basic Law, then the borders of the affected electoral districts also change accordingly. If in the receiving State two or more electoral districts are affected or if an exclave of a State is created, then the electoral district affiliation of the new part of the State is determined by the electoral district affiliation of the municipality, municipal district or autonomous area to which it has been attached. Changes to State borders which are carried out after the end of the thirty-second month following the beginning of the term have an effect on the division of electoral districts only in the following term.

§ 4. Each voter has two votes, a first vote for the election of a member of the Bundestag from the electoral district, and a second vote for the election of a State list.

§ 5. In each electoral district, one member of the Bundestag is elected. The candidate who receives the most votes is elected. In case of a tie, a lot to be drawn by the district returning officer [Kreiswahlleiter] decides.

§ 6. (1) For the distribution of seats to be filled from State lists, the second votes cast for each State list are added. The second votes of those voters who have cast their first votes for a candidate who was successful in his electoral district and who has been put forward in accordance with § 20 (3) or by a political party which is not eligible for the allocation of seats pursuant to paragraph 3 or for which no State list was admitted in the respective State are not taken into account. The number of successful electoral district candidates stipulated in the second sentence is subtracted from the total number of members of the Bundestag (§1 (1)).

(2) In a first distribution, the total number of seats (§1 (1)) is initially allocated, pursuant to the calculation method described in the second to seventh sentence, to the States according to their share of the population (§3 (1)) and in each State the number of seats

remaining there pursuant to paragraph 1, third sentence, is subsequently allocated to the State lists on the basis of the second votes to be taken into account. Each State list receives as many seats as result from the division of the sum of the second votes it received by an allocation divisor. Decimals under 0.5 are rounded down to the whole number below, those over 0.5 are rounded up to the whole number above. Decimals which are equal to 0.5 are rounded off either upwards or downwards so as to maintain the total number of seats to be distributed; if this results in several possible allocations of seats, the lot, to be drawn by the federal returning officer [Bundeswahlleiter], decides. The allocation divisor must be determined in such a way that, in total, as many seats are allocated to State lists as there are seats available. For that purpose, first the total number of second votes of all State lists to be taken into account is divided by the total number of seats remaining pursuant to paragraph 1, third sentence. If, after this, more seats are allocated to the State lists than there are seats available, then the distribution divisor must be raised so that the number of available seats is obtained in the calculation; if too few seats are allocated to the State lists, the distribution divisor is to be lowered accordingly.

(3) In the allocation of the seats to the State lists, only parties which have received at least five per cent of the valid second votes cast in the electoral territory or which have won a seat in at least three electoral districts are taken into account. The first sentence does not apply to lists submitted by parties of national minorities.

(4) From the number of seats thus determined for each State list the number of seats won by the party in the electoral districts of the state (§5) is subtracted. Seats won in the electoral districts remain in the hands of a party, even if their number exceeds that determined pursuant to paragraph 2 and 3.

(5) The number of seats remaining pursuant to paragraph 1, third sentence, is raised until every party receives at least as many seats in the second distribution pursuant to paragraph 6, first sentence, as have been allocated to it in the first distribution pursuant to paragraph 2 and 3 in addition to the seats won in electoral districts which cannot be subtracted, pursuant to paragraph 4, first sentence, from the number of seats determined for the State list. The total number of seats (§1 (1)) increases by the difference.

(6) The seats to be allocated pursuant to paragraph 5, first sentence, are in any event distributed nationwide, according to the number of second votes to be taken into account, among the parties to be taken into account pursuant to paragraph 3, using the calculation method described in paragraph 2, second to seventh sentence. Within the parties, the seats are distributed, according to the number of second votes to be taken into account, to the State lists, using the calculation method described in paragraph 2, second to seventh sentence; each State list is allocated at least the number of seats won by the party in the electoral districts of the State. From the number of seats determined for each State list the number of seats won by the party in the electoral districts of the State (§5) is subtracted. The remaining seats are filled from the State list in the order specified therein. Candidates who have been elected in an electoral district are not considered on

the state list. If a State list is allocated more seats than candidates are nominated, these seats remain vacant.

(7) If, in the distribution pursuant to paragraph 2 to 6, a party which has received more than half of the second votes cast for all parties to be taken into account does not receive more than half of the seats, it is allocated additional seats until it holds one seat more than half of the seats. Within the party, the seats are distributed pursuant to paragraph 6, second to sixth sentence. In such a case, the total number of seats (§1 (1)) determined pursuant to paragraph 5 increases by the difference.

§ 7. (Repealed).

[Chapter II is omitted.]

Chapter III. Franchise and right to stand as a candidate

§ 12, (1) The right to vote is enjoyed by all Germans within the meaning of Article 116 (1) of the Basic Law who
1. have completed the eighteenth year of age,
2. have been domiciled for at least three months or otherwise habitually reside within the Federal Republic of Germany,
3. have not been excluded from the right to vote pursuant to § 13.

(2) The right to vote is further enjoyed, in case of fulfilment of the remaining requirements, by those Germans within the meaning of Article 116 (1) of the Basic Law who, on election day, reside outside of the Federal Republic of Germany, as far as they
1. have, after completion of their fourteenth year of age, been uninterruptedly domiciled for at least three month or otherwise habitually resided in the Federal Republic of Germany, where this sojourn has taken place less than twenty-five years ago, or
2. have personally and immediately acquired familiarity with the political circumstances in the Federal Republic of Germany for other reasons and are affected by them.
    A former domicile or former residence within the territory referred to in Article 3 of the Unification Treaty [Einigungsvertrag] is also deemed to be a domicile or habitual residence within the meaning of clause 1. In the case of the return to the Federal Republic of Germany of a person enjoying the right to vote pursuant to clause 1, the three-month period of sub-paragraph (1) no. 2 does not apply.

(3) A domicile within the meaning of the law is any enclosed space used for habitation and sleeping. However, caravans [Wohnwagen] and houseboats [Wohnschiffe] are only to be deemed domiciles, if they are not or only occasionally moved.

(4) As far as they are not and have not been domiciled in the Federal Republic of Germany, the following are deemed domiciles within the meaning of sub-paragraph (1) no. 2 or (2) no. 1:

1. for seafarers [Seeleute] and members of their household, the ship inhabited by them, as far as the latter is entitled to fly the federal flag pursuant to the Act on the Law of the Flag [Flaggenrechtsgesetz] in its respective current version,
2. for inland sailors [Binnenschiffer] and members of their household, the ship inhabited by them, as far as the latter is registered in a ship register in the Federal Republic of Germany,
3. for persons deprived of their liberty by judicial order and for other institutionalised persons [Untergebrachte], the correctional facility or corresponding institution.

(5) In calculating the three-month period pursuant to sub-paragraph (1) no. 2 and (2) no. 1, the day on which the domicile was taken or the residence was begun is to be taken into account.

[The remainder of the Act is omitted.]

The Netherlands

8   Charter for the Kingdom of the Netherlands [Statuut voor het Koninkrijk der Nederlanden] of 28 October 1954[1]

Preamble

The Netherlands, Aruba, Curacao and Saint Martin,
noting that the Netherlands, Suriname and the Netherlands Antilles in 1954 have declared by free will to accept a new legal order in the Kingdom of the Netherlands, in which they conduct their own interests autonomously and pursue their common interests on a basis of equality and accord each other assistance, and have resolved in mutual consultation to adopt the Charter for the Kingdom;
noting that the connection with Surinam under the Charter has come to an end as per 25 November 1975 by virtue of an amendment of the Charter by Kingdom Statute of 22 November 1975, Stb. 617, PbNA 233;
noting that Aruba has declared by free will to accept this legal order as a country as per 1 January 1986 for a period of ten years and as per 1 January 1996 for an indefinite period;
considering that Curacao and Saint Martin have both declared by free will to accept this legal order as countries; have resolved in mutual consultation to adopt the Charter for the Kingdom as follows.

§ 1. General provisions

Article 1. The Kingdom comprises the countries of the Netherlands, Aruba, Curacao and Saint Martin.

Article 1a. The crown of the Kingdom is held by inheritance by Her Majesty Queen Juliana, Princess of Orange-Nassau, and, by succession, by her lawful successors.

Article 2. (1) The King heads the government of the Kingdom and of each of the countries. He is inviolable, the ministers are responsible.
(2) The King is represented in Aruba, Curacao and Saint Martin by the Governor [Gouverneur]. The competences, duties and responsibility of the Governor as representative of the government of the Kingdom are regulated by Kingdom Statute [rijkswet] or, where applicable, by Kingdom Ordinance [algemene maatregel van rijksbestuur].

---

1   As last amended by Kingdom Statute [Rijkswet] of 1 November 2017 (*Stb.* 426). Translation by Philipp Kiiver & Sascha Hardt.

(3) Kingdom Statute regulates that which relates to the appointment and the dismissal of the Governor. The appointment and the dismissal are effected by the King as head of the Kingdom.

Article 3. (1) Notwithstanding what is provided elsewhere in the Charter, matters for the Kingdom are:
a. the maintenance of the independence and the defence of the Kingdom;
b. foreign relations;
c. Dutch citizenship;
d. the regulation of chivalric orders as well as the flag and the coat of arms of the Kingdom;
e. the regulation of the nationality of vessels and the laying down of conditions regarding the safety and navigation of seagoing vessels which fly the flag of the Kingdom, except sailing vessels;
f. oversight over the general rules regarding the admission and expulsion of Dutch citizens;
g. the laying down of general conditions for the admission and expulsion of aliens;
h. extradition.
(2) Other matters may in mutual consultation be declared to be matters for the Kingdom. In that context, Article 55 applies mutatis mutandis.

Article 4. (1) Royal authority is exercised in matters for the Kingdom by the King as head of the Kingdom.
(2) Legislative authority is exercised in matters for the Kingdom by the legislator of the Kingdom. In cases of bills for Kingdom Statutes, consideration takes place with due regard to Articles 15 to 21.

Article 5. (1) The monarchy and the succession to the throne, the organs of the Kingdom referred to in the Charter, the exercise of royal and legislative authority in matters for the Kingdom are regulated, in as far as that is not provided for by the Charter, by the Constitution [Grondwet] for the Kingdom.
(2) The Constitution respects the provisions of the Charter.
(3) To a proposal for an amendment of the Constitution containing provisions regarding matters for the Kingdom, as well as to bills stating that there is reason to consider such a proposal, Articles 15 to 20 apply.

§ 2. The conduct of matters for the Kingdom

Article 6. (1) The matters for the Kingdom are conducted in cooperation between the Netherlands, Aruba, Curacao and Saint Martin in accordance with the following provisions.
(2) During the conduct of these matters, organs of the countries are involved where possible.

Article 7. The council of ministers of the Kingdom is composed of the ministers appointed by the King and the Minister Plenipotentiary [Gevolmachtigde Minister] appointed by the government of Aruba, Curacao and Saint Martin, respectively.

Article 8. (1) The Ministers Plenipotentiary act on behalf of the governments of their country, which appoint and dismiss them. They must be Dutch citizens.
(2) The government of the country involved determines who replaces the Minister Plenipotentiary in case of his being hindered or absent. That which is provided in this Charter regarding the Minister Plenipotentiary applies mutatis mutandis with respect to his substitute.

Article 9. (1) The Minister Plenipotentiary, before assuming his office, takes an oath or makes a promise of allegiance to the King and the Charter before the Governor. The formula for the oath or promise is established by Kingdom Ordinance.
(2) When in the Netherlands, the Minister Plenipotentiary takes the oath or makes the promise before the King.

Article 10. (1) The Minister Plenipotentiary participates in the deliberations in the meetings of the council of ministers and of the permanent bodies and special commissions of the council regarding matters for the Kingdom which affect the country in question.
(2) The governments of Aruba, Curacao and Saint Martin each have the right – if a certain subject-matter calls for such action – to also let a minister with an advisory vote participate next to the Minister Plenipotentiary in the deliberations stipulated in the preceding paragraph.

Article 11. (1) Proposals for an amendment of the Constitution containing provisions regarding matters for the Kingdom affect Aruba, Curacao and Saint Martin.
(2) As regards defence, it is assumed that the defence of the territory of Aruba, Curacao or Saint Martin, as well as agreements or understandings regarding an area that belongs to their sphere of interests, affect Aruba, Curacao and Saint Martin, respectively.
(3) As regards foreign affairs, it is assumed that foreign affairs where the interests of Aruba, Curacao or Saint Martin are involved, or where the conduct thereof can have

serious consequences for these interests, affect Aruba, Curacao and Saint Martin, respectively.

(4) The determination of the contribution to the costs referred to in Article 35 affects Aruba, Curacao and Saint Martin, respectively.

(5) Proposals for naturalization are only considered to affect Aruba, Curacao and Saint Martin if persons are concerned who reside in the country in question.

(6) The governments of Aruba, Curacao and Saint Martin may state which matters for the Kingdom other than those stipulated in the first to fourth paragraph affect their country.

Article 12. (1) If the Minister Plenipotentiary of Aruba, Curacao or Saint Martin, indicating his reasons based on which he expects serious detriment to his country, has declared that his country should not be bound by a proposed instrument containing generally binding regulations, such instrument may not be adopted in a way that it applies in the country in question, unless this would be incompatible with the ties of the country within the Kingdom.

(2) If the Minister Plenipotentiary of Aruba, Curacao or Saint Martin has serious objections to the initial opinion of the council of ministers regarding the requirement of binding nature as stipulated in the first paragraph, or regarding any other matter in the consideration of which he has participated, then upon his request deliberations are continued, if necessary with due regard to a time limit to be determined by the council of ministers.

(3) The deliberations referred to above are conducted between the prime-minister, two ministers, the Minister Plenipotentiary and a minister or special plenipotentiary to be nominated by the government involved.

(4) If several Ministers Plenipotentiary wish to participate in continued deliberations, then these deliberations are conducted between these Ministers Plenipotentiary, an equal number of ministers and the prime-minister. The second paragraph of Article 10 applies mutatis mutandis.

(5) The council of ministers decides in accordance with the result of the continued deliberations. If the opportunity for continued deliberations has not been seized within the specified time limit, then the council of ministers takes its decision.

Article 12a. By Kingdom Statute provisions are adopted for the treatment of such disputes as stipulated by Kingdom Statute between the Kingdom and the countries.

Article 13. (1) There is a Council of State of the Kingdom [Raad van State van het Koninkrijk].

(2) If the government of Aruba, Curacao or Saint Martin makes known such wish, the King appoints a member to the Council of State for Aruba, Curacao and Saint Martin,

respectively, whose appointment is effected in agreement with the government of the country involved. His dismissal is effected after consultation with that government.

(3) The members of the Council of State for Aruba, Curacao and Saint Martin participate in the activities of the Council of State in case the Council or a division of the Council is heard regarding bills for Kingdom Statutes and Kingdom Ordinances which shall apply in Aruba, Curacao and Saint Martin, respectively, or regarding other matters which, in accordance with Article 11, affect Aruba, Curacao and Saint Martin, respectively.

(4) By Kingdom Ordinance, regulations may be adopted with respect to the mentioned members of the Council of State that deviate from the provisions of the Council of State Act [Wet op de Raad van State].

Article 14. (1) Regulations regarding matters for the Kingdom – in as far as the relevant matter is not regulated in the Constitution and save for international regulations and that which is provided in the third paragraph – are established by Kingdom Statute [rijkswet] or, in cases where that is applicable, by Kingdom Ordinance [algemene maatregel van rijksbestuur]. The Kingdom Statute or the Kingdom Ordinance may charge other organs with, or leave to other organs, the establishment of more detailed regulations. The charging of or leaving to the countries is effected with respect to the legislator or the government of the countries.

(2) If the regulation is not reserved for Kingdom Statute, it may be effected by Kingdom Ordinance.

(3) Regulations regarding matters for the Kingdom which do not apply in Aruba, Curacao or Saint Martin are established by statute [wet] or ordinance [algemene maatregel van bestuur].

(4) The naturalization of persons resident in Aruba, Curacao or Saint Martin is effected by or pursuant to Kingdom Statute.

Article 15. (1) The King transmits a bill for a Kingdom Statute, simultaneously with its introduction in the States-General, to the representative bodies of Aruba, Curacao and Saint Martin.

(2) In case of a proposal for a bill for a Kingdom Statute emanating from the States-General, the transmission of the bill by the Second Chamber [Tweede Kamer] is effected immediately after it has been introduced in the Chamber.

(3) The Minister Plenipotentiary of Aruba, Curacao or Saint Martin has the right to propose to the Second Chamber to make a proposal for a bill for a Kingdom Statute.

Article 16. The representative body of the country where the regulation shall apply has the right to scrutinize it before the public consideration of the bill in the Second Chamber and, if necessary within a time period determined for that purpose, to issue a written report on it.

Article 17. (1) The Minister Plenipotentiary of the country where the regulation shall apply is offered the opportunity to attend the oral consideration of the bill for a Kingdom Statute in the Chambers of the States-General and to provide such information to the Chambers as he considers appropriate.

(2) The representative body of the country where the regulation shall apply may decide, for the consideration of a specific matter in the States-General, to delegate one or more special delegates who also have the right to attend the oral consideration and to provide information in that context.

(3) The Ministers Plenipotentiary and the special delegates are not liable to judicial prosecution for that which they have said in the meeting of the Chambers of the States-General or which they have submitted to them in writing.

(4) The Ministers Plenipotentiary and the special delegates have the right, during the consideration in the Second Chamber, to propose amendments to the bill.

Article 18. (1) The Minister Plenipotentiary of the country where the regulation shall apply is given the opportunity, before the final vote on a bill for a Kingdom Statute in the Chambers of the States-General, to give a statement regarding that bill. If the Minister Plenipotentiary declares his opposition to the bill, he may also request the Chamber to postpone the vote until the following meeting. If the Second Chamber, after the Minister Plenipotentiary has declared his opposition to the bill, adopts it with a majority smaller than three-fifths of the number of votes cast, the consideration is suspended and further deliberations regarding the bill take place in the council of ministers.

(2) If special delegates are attending the meeting of the Chambers, the right stipulated in the first paragraph also applies to the delegate nominated by the representative body for that purpose.

Article 19. Articles 17 and 18 apply mutatis mutandis to the consideration in the joint session of the States-General.

Article 20. By Kingdom Statute, further regulations may be established regarding that which is provided in Articles 15 to 19.

Article 21. If, after concluded deliberations with the Ministers Plenipotentiary of Aruba, Curacao and Saint Martin, in case of war or in other special cases where action must be taken swiftly, it is impossible in the opinion of the King to wait for the result of the scrutiny stipulated in Article 16, the provision of that Article may be deviated from.

Article 22. (1) The government of the Kingdom ensures the publication of Kingdom Statutes and Kingdom Ordinances. It is effected where the regulation shall apply in the official journal. The governments of the countries provide the necessary assistance in that context.

(2) They enter into force on the moment to be stipulated by or pursuant to these regulations.

(3) The enactment formula of Kingdom Statutes and of Kingdom Ordinances states that the provisions of the Charter for the Kingdom have been respected.

Article 23. (1) The jurisdiction of the Supreme Court of the Netherlands [Hoge Raad der Nederlanden] as regards disputes in Aruba, Curacao and Saint Martin, as well as on Bonaire, Saint Eustatius and Saba, is regulated by Kingdom Statute.

(2) If the government of Aruba, Curacao or Saint Martin so requests, by that Kingdom Statute the possibility is opened for a member, an extraordinary member or an advisory member to be added to the Court.

Article 24. (1) Agreements with foreign states and with international organizations which affect Aruba, Curacao or Saint Martin are submitted, simultaneously with the submission to the States-General, to the representative body of Aruba, Curacao and Saint Martin, respectively.

(2) In case the agreement is submitted to the States-General for tacit approval, the Minister Plenipotentiary may, within the period set for the Chambers of the States-General for that purpose, express the wish that the agreement be submitted to explicit approval by the States-General.

(3) The preceding paragraphs apply mutatis mutandis with respect to the termination of international agreements, the first paragraph applies with the provision that the intention of termination is notified to the representative body of Aruba, Curacao and Saint Martin, respectively.

Article 25. (1) The King does not commit Aruba, Curacao or Saint Martin to international economic and financial agreements if the government of the country, indicating the reasons based on which it expects serious detriment from the commitment to the country, has declared that the country should not be committed.

(2) The King does not terminate international economic and financial agreements as regards Aruba, Curacao or Saint Martin if the government of the country, indicating the reasons based on which it expects serious detriment from the termination to the country, has declared that for the country a termination should not take place. Termination may nevertheless be effected if it is incompatible with the provisions of the agreement that the country be excluded from the termination.

Article 26. If the government of Aruba, Curacao or Saint Martin expresses the wish that an international economic or financial agreement should be concluded which is to apply exclusively to the country involved, the government of the Kingdom shall cooperate with a view to such an agreement unless this would be incompatible with the ties of the country within the Kingdom.

Article 27. (1) Aruba, Curacao and Saint Martin are involved as early as possible in the preparation of agreements with foreign states which affect them in accordance with Article 11. They are also involved in the execution of agreements which affect them thus and which are binding upon them.
(2) The Netherlands, Aruba, Curacao and Saint Martin adopt a mutual provision on the cooperation between the countries regarding the adoption of regulations or other measures which are necessary for the execution of agreements with foreign states.
(3) If the interests of the Kingdom are affected by the continued absence of regulations or other measures which are necessary for the execution of an agreement with foreign states in one of the countries, whereas the agreement can be approved for that country only when the regulations or other measures are ready, a Kingdom Ordinance, or if necessary a Kingdom Statute may provide in which manner that agreement shall be executed.
(4) If the regulations or other measures for the execution of the agreement in question are adopted by the country, the Kingdom Ordinance or the Kingdom Statute will be repealed.

Article 28. On the basis of international agreements concluded by the Kingdom, Aruba, Curacao and Saint Martin may, if such wish exists, join international organizations as members.

Article 29. (1) The acquisition or guarantee of a credit outside the Kingdom in the name of or at the expense of one of the countries takes place in agreement with the government of the Kingdom.
(2) The council of ministers agrees with the acquisition or guarantee of such credit unless this would be contrary to the interests of the Kingdom.

Article 30. (1) Aruba, Curacao and Saint Martin provide the armed forces that are present in their territory with help and assistance which they require in the fulfillment of their task.
(2) By country statute, rules are established to ensure that the armed forces of the Kingdom in Aruba, Curacao and Saint Martin can fulfill their task.

Article 31. (1) Persons who are resident in Aruba, Curacao and Saint Martin may be obliged to serve in the armed forces or in civilian service only by country statute.
(2) It is reserved to the Regulation of State [Staatsregeling] to determine that servicemen serving in the armed forces may be deployed abroad without their consent only pursuant to country statute.

Article 32. In the armed forces for the defence of Aruba, Curacao and Saint Martin as far as possible persons shall be included who are resident in these countries.

Article 33. (1) For the purposes of defence, the confiscation of property and use of goods, the limitation of property and usage rights, the requisition of services and quartering is effected only under observance of general rules to be laid down by Kingdom Statute which also contain provisions regarding compensation.
(2) In that Kingdom Statute, further regulation is assigned where possible to country institutions.

Article 34. (1) The King may, for the maintenance of external or internal security, in case of war or threat of war or where a threat to or disruption of internal order and peace can lead to a substantial infringement on the interests of the Kingdom, declare each part of the territory in state of war or in state of siege.
(2) By or pursuant to Kingdom Statute the manner is determined in which such declaration is effected and the consequences are regulated.
(3) In this regulation is may be provided that and in which manner competences of bodies of civilian authority regarding public order and policing pass wholly or partly to other bodies of civilian authority or to military authority and that the civilian authorities in that latter case are subordinate to military authorities. Regarding the passing of competences, consultation with the government of the affected country takes place where possible. In that regulation it may be deviated from provisions regarding the freedom of the press, the right of association and assembly as well as the inviolability of the home and the respect for correspondence.
(4) For the territory declared in state of siege, in case of war in a manner determined by Kingdom Statute, military penal law and military penal jurisdiction may be wholly or partly declared applicable to everyone.

Article 35. (1) Aruba, Curacao and Saint Martin share, in accordance with their economic strength, the costs connected to the maintenance of the independence and defence of the Kingdom as well as the costs connected to the maintenance of other affairs of the Kingdom to the extent that this benefits Aruba, Curacao and Saint Martin respectively.
(2) The share for Aruba, Curacao and Saint Martin, respectively, stipulated in the first paragraph, is determined by the council of ministers for one fiscal year or for several consecutive fiscal years. Article 12 applies mutatis mutandis, with the exception that decisions are taken by unanimity.
(3) Where the determination stipulated in the second paragraph does not take place in time, pending that, for the duration of at most one fiscal year, the share determined in accordance with that paragraph for the previous fiscal year applies.

(4) The preceding paragraphs do not apply to measures for which special arrangements have been established.

§ 3. Mutual assistance, consultation and cooperation

Article 36. The Netherlands, Aruba, Curacao and Saint Martin provide to each other aid and assistance.

Article 36a. (Repealed).

Article 37. (1) The Netherlands, Aruba, Curacao and Saint Martin shall conduct as much consultation as possible regarding all matters where the interests of two or more of the countries are affected. For that purpose, special representatives may be appointed and common institutions may be established.
(2) As matters in the meaning of this Article are considered, among other things:
a. the promotion of cultural and social ties between the countries;
b. the promotion of effective economic, financial and monetary relations between the countries;
c. questions regarding the coinage and monetary system, banking and foreign-currency policy;
d. the promotion of economic resilience through mutual aid and assistance by the countries;
e. the exercise of professions and businesses by Dutch citizens in the countries;
f. matters regarding aviation, including the policy on unregulated air transportation;
g. matters regarding shipping;
h. cooperation in the field of telegraphy, telephony and radio communications.

Article 38. (1) The Netherlands, Aruba, Curacao and Saint Martin may establish regulations between each other.
(2) In mutual consultation it may be provided that such regulations and the change thereof are established by Kingdom Statute or Kingdom Ordinance.
(3) Regarding matters of private law and criminal law of an inter-regional or international nature, regulations may be established by Kingdom Statute if agreement over such regulations exists between the governments of the countries involved.
(4) The matter of the relocation of the seat of legal persons is regulated by Kingdom Statute. On this regulation, agreement between the governments of the countries is required.

Article 38a. The countries may, through mutual regulations, adopt provisions for the treatment of disputes between them. The second paragraph of Article 38 applies.

Article 39. (1) Private and commercial law, civil procedure, criminal law, criminal procedure, copyright law, industrial property, the office of the notary, as well as provisions regarding measures and weights are regulated as far as possible in an equivalent manner in the Netherlands, Aruba, Curacao and Saint Martin.
(2) A proposal for a far-reaching change in the existing legislation on this matter is not introduced in the representative body – or taken into consideration by the representative body – before the governments in the other countries have been given the opportunity to express their views in that matter.

Article 40. Judgments given by the judge in the Netherlands, Aruba, Curacao or Saint Martin, and orders issued by him, as well as engrossments of authentic acts issued there, may be executed in the entire Kingdom with due regard to the legal provisions of the country where the execution takes place.

§ 4. The constitutional system of the countries

Article 41. (1) The Netherlands, Aruba, Curacao and Saint Martin conduct their own affairs autonomously.
(2) The matters for the Kingdom are among the subjects of concern for the countries.

Article 42. (1) In the Kingdom, the constitutional system of the Netherlands is regulated in the Constitution [Grondwet], the one of Aruba, Curacao and Saint Martin in the Regulation of State [Staatsregeling] of Aruba, of Curacao and of Saint Martin.
(2) The Regulations of State of Aruba, of Curacao and of Saint Martin are established by country statute [landsverordening]. Each proposal for an amendment of the Regulation of State indicates clearly the proposed amendment. The representative body may not adopt the bill for such a country statute unless by two-thirds of votes cast.

Article 43. (1) Each of the countries ensures the realization of the fundamental human rights and freedoms, legal certainty and proper administration.
(2) The guarantee of these rights, freedoms, legal certainty and proper administration is a matter for the Kingdom.

Article 44. (1) A country statute for an amendment of the Regulation of State regarding:
a. the Articles relating to the fundamental human rights and freedoms;
b. the provisions relating to the competences of the Governor;
c. the Articles relating to the competences of the representative bodies of the countries;
d. the Articles relating to the judiciary,
is transmitted to the government of the Kingdom. It does not enter into force until after the government of the Kingdom has expressed its consent herein.

(2) A bill for a country statute regarding the preceding provisions is not presented to the representative body, nor taken into consideration by that body by way of a private member's initiative, until the opinion of the government of the Kingdom is obtained.

Article 45. Amendments to the Constitution [Grondwet] regarding:
a. the Articles relating to the fundamental human rights and freedoms;
b. the provisions relating to the competences of the government;
c. the Articles relating to the competences of the representative body;
d. the Articles relating to the judiciary,
   are – notwithstanding the provisions of Article 5 – considered to affect Aruba, Curacao and Saint Martin in the meaning of Article 10.

Article 46. (1) The representative bodies are elected by the residents of the country involved who are Dutch citizens, who have reached an age to be determined by the countries, which may not be higher than 25 years. Each voter only casts one vote. The elections are free and secret. If a necessity thereto appears, the countries may establish restrictions. Every Dutch citizen may run in elections, with the provision that the countries may establish a requirement of residence and an age limit.
(2) The countries may confer the right to elect representative bodies to Dutch citizens who are not residents of the country involved, as well as the right to elect representative bodies and the right to run in elections to residents of the country involved who are not Dutch citizens, in any case provided that in that context at least the requirements for residents who are also Dutch citizens are observed.

Article 47. (1) The ministers and the members of the representative body in the countries, before assuming their office, take an oath or make a promise of allegiance to the King and the Charter.
(2) The ministers and the members of the representative body in Aruba, Curacao and Saint Martin take the oath or make the promise before the representative of the King.

Article 48. The countries respect the provisions of the Charter in their legislation and administration.

Article 49. By Kingdom Statute, regulations may be established regarding the binding effect of legislative measures which are incompatible with the Charter, an international regulation, a Kingdom Statute or a Kingdom Ordinance.

Article 50. (1) Legislative and administrative measures in Aruba, Curacao and Saint Martin which are incompatible with the Charter, an international regulation, a Kingdom Statute or a Kingdom Ordinance, or with interests the promotion or safeguarding of

which is a matter for the Kingdom, may be suspended or annulled by the King as the head of the Kingdom by way of reasoned decree. The proposal for an annulment is issued by the council of ministers.
(2) For the Netherlands, this matter is regulated, where necessary, in the Constitution.

Article 51. (1) If an organ in Aruba, Curacao or Saint Martin does not, or does insufficiently perform what it must perform pursuant to the Charter, an international regulation, a Kingdom Statute or a Kingdom Ordinance, then a Kingdom Ordinance, while stating the legal grounds and reasons on which it is based, may determine in which manner this shall be performed.
(2) For the Netherlands, this matter is regulated, where necessary, in the Constitution.

Article 52. Country statute may confer competences with respect to country affairs, with the approval of the King, to the King as head of the Kingdom and to the Governor as an organ of the Kingdom.

Article 53. If Aruba, Curacao or Saint Martin express such wish, the independent supervision of the spending of funds in accordance with the budget of Aruba, Curacao and Saint Martin, respectively, is exercised by the General Chamber of Audit [Algemene Rekenkamer]. In that case, regulations are established after consultation with the Chamber of Audit by Kingdom Statute regarding the cooperation between the Chamber of Audit and the country involved. Thereafter, the government of the country may, upon a proposal from the representative body, appoint someone who is given the opportunity to participate in the deliberations on all matters of the country involved.

§ 5. Transitional and final provisions

Article 54. (Repealed)

Article 55. (1) Amendments to this Charter are effected by Kingdom Statute.
(2) A proposal for an amendment adopted by the States-General is not approved by the King until it has been accepted by Aruba, Curacao and Saint Martin. Such acceptance is effected by country statute. Such country statute is not adopted until it has been approved by the Parliaments [Staten] in two readings. If the bill is adopted in the first reading by two-thirds of the votes cast, the adoption is effective immediately. The second reading takes place within one month after the bill has been adopted in first reading.
(3) If and in as far as a proposal for an amendment of the Charter deviates from the Constitution [Grondwet], the proposal is considered in such manner as the Constitution prescribes for proposals for an amendment of the Constitution, with the exception that

both Chambers may adopt the proposed amendment in second reading by an absolute majority of votes cast.

Article 56. Authorities, binding statutes, decrees and decisions existing on the moment of the entry into force of the Charter remain in place until they are replaced by others under observance of this Charter. To the extent that the Charter itself regulates any matter differently, the regulation by the Charter applies.

Article 57. Statutes and ordinances which applied in the Netherlands Antilles have the status of Kingdom Statute or Kingdom Ordinance, respectively, with the exception that, to the extent that they may pursuant to the Charter be amended by country statute, they have the status of country statute.

Article 57a. Existing Kingdom Statutes, statutes, country statutes, Kingdom Ordinances, ordinances and other regulations which are incompatible with an amendment of the Charter remain in force until a provision for this is adopted in accordance with the Charter.

Article 58. (1) Aruba may declare by country statute that it wishes to terminate the legal order laid down by the Charter regarding Aruba.
(2) The proposal for such country statute is accompanied, when tabled, by an outline of a future constitution including at least provisions regarding fundamental rights, government, representative body, legislation and administration, judiciary and amendment of the constitution.
(3) Parliament may only adopt the proposal by a majority of two thirds of the votes of the sitting members.

Article 59. (1) Within six months after the Parliament of Aruba has adopted the proposal stipulated in Article 58 a referendum regulated by country statute is held whereby those entitled to vote may voice their opinion on the adopted proposal.
(2) The adopted proposal is adopted as country statute only if in the referendum a majority of those entitled to vote has voted in favour of the proposal.

Article 60. (1) After the adoption of the country statute in accordance with Articles 58 and 59 and the approval of the future constitution by the Parliament of Aruba by a majority of two thirds of the votes of the sitting members, by royal decree the moment of the termination of the legal order laid down by the Charter regarding Aruba is established in accordance with the wishes of the government of Aruba.

(2) That moment lies at the latest one month after the date of the adoption of the constitution. That adoption takes place at the latest one year after the date of the referendum stipulated in Article 59.

[Articles 60a to 60c are omitted.]

Article 61. The Charter enters into force on the moment of its ceremonial declaration, after it has been affirmed by the King.
Before the affirmation takes place, the Charter requires, for the Netherlands, approval in a manner provided by the Constitution; for Suriname and the Netherlands Antilles by a decision of the representative body.
This decision is taken by two thirds of votes cast. If such majority is not obtained, the Parliament is dissolved and it is decided by the new Parliament by an absolute majority of votes cast.

Article 62. (Repealed)

9   CONSTITUTION FOR THE KINGDOM OF THE NETHERLANDS [GRONDWET VOOR HET KONINKRIJK DER NEDERLANDEN] OF 24 AUGUST 1815[2]

Chapter 1. Fundamental rights

Article 1. All persons in the Netherlands are treated equally in equal circumstances. Discrimination on the grounds of religion, belief, political opinion, race, sex or any other ground is not permissible.

Article 2. (1) Statute regulates who is a Dutch citizen.
(2) Statute regulates the admission and expulsion of aliens.
(3) Extradition may only be effected pursuant to a treaty. Further regulations regarding extradition are provided by statute.
(4) Everyone has the right to leave the country, save for cases provided by statute.

Article 3. All Dutch citizens are eligible for appointment in the public service on an equal footing.

Article 4. Every Dutch citizen has the equal right to elect the members of general representative bodies as well as to be elected member of these bodies, save for limitations and exceptions provided by statute.

Article 5. Everyone has the right to submit petitions in writing to the competent authorities.

Article 6. (1) Everyone has the right to freely express his religion or belief, individually or in community with others, save for everybody's responsibility according to law.
(2) Statute may, regarding the exercise of this right outside of buildings and closed locations, provide for regulations for the protection of health, in the interest of traffic and for the combat against and prevention of disorder.

Article 7. (1) No-one requires prior permission in order to publish thoughts or feelings via the press, save for everybody's responsibility according to law.
(2) Statute provides for regulations regarding radio and television. There is no supervision in advance of the content of a radio or television broadcast.
(3) For the publication of thoughts or feelings via means other than the ones stipulated in the preceding paragraphs, no-one requires prior permission regarding the content thereof, save for everybody's responsibility according to law. Statute may regulate the render-

---

2   As last amended by statute of 16 January 2019 (*Stb.* 33). Translation by Philipp Kiiver & Sascha Hardt.

ing of displays accessible to persons younger than sixteen years of age for the protection of good morals.
(4) The preceding paragraphs do not apply to commercial advertisement.

Article 8. The right of association is recognized. By statute this right may be limited in the interest of the public order.

Article 9. (1) The right of assembly and demonstration is recognized, save for everybody's responsibility according to law.
(2) Statute may provide for regulations for the protection of health, in the interest of traffic and for the combat against and prevention of disorder.

Article 10. (1) Everyone has, save for limitations to be provided by or pursuant to statute, the right to respect for his private life.
(2) Statute provides for regulations for the protection of private life in the context of the recording and transmission of personal data.
(3) Statute provides for regulations regarding the entitlements of persons to insight into the data recorded on them and into the use made thereof, as well as to a correction of such data.

Article 11. Everyone has, save for limitations to be provided by or pursuant to statute, the right to inviolability of his body.

Article 12. (1) The entry into a home without consent of the occupant is permissible only in cases provided by or pursuant to statute, by those who are designated to that end by or pursuant to statute.
(2) An entry in accordance with the preceding paragraph requires prior identification and notification of the purpose of the entry, save for exceptions provided by statute.
(3) A written report on the entry is delivered to the occupant as soon as possible. If the entry has been effected in the interest of national security or of criminal prosecution, the delivery of the report may be postponed in accordance with regulations to be provided by statute. In cases to be provided by statute, the delivery may be omitted if the interest of national security is permanently incompatible with such delivery.

Article 13. (1) The privacy of the correspondence is inviolable except, in cases provided by statute, by order of a judge.
(2) The privacy of telephone and telegraph communications is inviolable except, in cases provided by statute, by or with the authorization of those designated to that end by statute.

Article 14. (1) Expropriation may be effected only in the general interest and for a previously guaranteed compensation, all of which in accordance with regulations to be provided by or pursuant to statute.
(2) Compensation need not be guaranteed beforehand if in a case of emergency immediate expropriation is called for.
(3) In cases provided by or pursuant to statute there is a right to compensation or partial compensation if, in the general interest, by competent authorities property is being destroyed or made unusable or the exercise of ownership rights is being limited.

Article 15. (1) Save for cases provided by or pursuant to statute, no-one may be deprived of his freedom.
(2) He who is deprived of his freedom on a basis other than upon court order may request his release to a judge. In that case he is heard by the judge within a period to be provided by statute. The judge orders immediate release if he considers the deprivation of freedom unlawful.
(3) The trial of him who is deprived of his freedom with a view thereto, takes place within reasonable time.
(4) He who is lawfully deprived of his freedom may be limited in the exercise of his fundamental rights in as far as such exercise is not compatible with the deprivation of freedom.

Article 16. No act is punishable except by virtue of a prior statutory criminal provision.

Article 17. No-one may against his will be barred from access to the judge that statute accords him.

Article 18. (1) Everyone may be aided in court and in administrative appeal.
(2) Statute provides for regulations regarding the provision of legal aid to persons of limited means.

Article 19. (1) The promotion of sufficient employment is a subject of concern for the state authority.
(2) Statute provides for regulations regarding the legal position of those who are engaged in an employment and regarding their protection therein, as well as regarding co-determination.
(3) The right of every Dutch citizen to a free choice of his occupation is recognized, save for limitations provided by or pursuant to statute.

Article 20. (1) The securing of means of subsistence of the population and the promotion of welfare is a subject of concern for the state authority.

(2) Statute provides for regulations regarding entitlements to social security.
(3) Dutch citizens in this country who cannot provide for their own subsistence have a right to state assistance to be regulated by statute.

Article 21. Concern of the state authority is directed at the habitability of the land and the protection and improvement of the environment.

Article 22. (1) State authority takes measures to promote public health.
(2) The promotion of sufficient living space is a subject of concern for the state authority.
(3) It creates conditions for social and cultural development and for leisure activity.

Article 23. (1) Education is a subject of permanent concern for the government.
(2) Teaching is free, save for state supervision and, as regards forms of education designated by statute, the monitoring of the competence and morality of those who teach, all of which is to be regulated by statute.
(3) Public education is regulated by statute with due respect to the religion or belief of everyone.
(4) In each of the public entities referred to in article 132a, sufficient public primary education is offered by the state in a sufficient number of public schools. In accordance with regulations to be provided by statute, deviations from this provision may be permitted as long as an opportunity to receive such education is provided, whether or not in a public school.
(5) The requirements of the appropriateness to be applied to education to be financed wholly or partly from the public purse are regulated by statute with due respect for, as far as special education [bijzonder onderwijs] is concerned, the freedom of underlying direction.
(6) These requirements are regulated for primary education in such manner that the appropriateness of special education financed wholly from the public purse and of public education is equally ensured. In the context of such regulation, in particular the freedom of special education regarding the choice of means of teaching and employment of teachers is respected.
(7) Special primary education which complies with the conditions to be provided by statute is financed from the public purse under the same criteria as public education. Statute provides the conditions under which contributions from the public purse are granted to special secondary and higher secondary education.
(8) The government reports annually to the States-General on the state of the education system.

Chapter 2. Government

§1. The King

Article 24. The crown is vested by hereditary succession in the lawful successors of King William I, Prince of Orange-Nassau.

Article 25. The crown passes, in the case of the death of the King, by virtue of hereditary succession to his lawful descendants, in which case the oldest child takes precedence, with further passage of the crown taking place according to the same rule. When there are no descendants of his own, the crown passes in an equal manner to the lawful descendants first of his parent, then of his grandparent, in the line of hereditary succession as long as they are blood relatives not more than thrice removed from the deceased King.

Article 26. The child which a woman carries at the moment of the death of the King is deemed already born for the purposes of hereditary succession. If it is stillborn, it is deemed never to have existed.

Article 27. Abdication leads to hereditary succession in accordance with the rules provided in the preceding Articles. Children born after the abdication, and their descendants, are excluded from hereditary succession.

Article 28. (1) The King who enters into a marriage without approval granted by statute thereby abdicates.
(2) If someone who can inherit the crown from the King enters into such marriage, then he is, together with the children born within that marriage, and their descendants, excluded from hereditary succession.
(3) The States-General deliberate and decide on a bill to grant approval in joint session.

Article 29. (1) If exceptional circumstances so require, one or more persons may be excluded from hereditary succession by statute.
(2) The bill for that purpose is submitted by or on behalf of the King. The States-General deliberate and decide on the matter in joint session. They may adopt the bill only with at least two-thirds of the number of votes cast.

Article 30. (1) If there is a prospect that there shall be no successor, he may be appointed by statute. The bill for that purpose is submitted by or on behalf of the King. After the submission of the bill, the Chambers are dissolved. The new Chambers deliberate and decide on the matter in joint session. They may adopt the bill only with at least two-thirds of the number of votes cast.

(2) If at the death of the King or at abdication there is no successor, the Chambers are dissolved. The new Chambers convene within four months after the death or abdication in joint session in order to decide on the appointment of a King. They may appoint a successor only with at least two-thirds of the number of votes cast.

Article 31. (1) An appointed King may be succeeded by hereditary succession only by his lawful descendants.
(2) The provisions regarding hereditary succession and the first paragraph of this Article apply mutatis mutandis to an appointed successor as long as he is not yet King.

Article 32. After the King has assumed the exercise of royal authority, he is as soon as possible sworn in and inaugurated in the capital city of Amsterdam in a public joint session of the States-General. He swears or promises allegiance to the Constitution and loyal exercise of his office. Statute provides further regulations.

Article 33. The King exercises royal authority only after he has attained the age of eighteen years.

Article 34. Statute regulates parental authority and guardianship over the King who is a minor and the supervision thereof. The States-General deliberate and decide on the matter in joint session.

Article 35. (1) If the council of ministers concludes that the King is incapable of exercising royal authority, it reports this, submitting the advice of the Council of State requested on the matter, to the States-General, which convene on the matter in a joint session.
(2) If the States-General share this conclusion, they declare that the King is incapable of exercising royal authority. Such declaration is published by order of the chairman of the session and enters into force immediately.
(3) As soon as the King is capable again of exercising royal authority, this is declared by statute. The States-General deliberate and decide on the matter in joint session. Immediately after the publication of this statute, the King resumes the exercise of royal authority.
(4) Statute regulates, where necessary, the supervision over the person of the King if he is declared incapable of exercising royal authority. The States-General deliberate and decide on the matter in joint session.

Article 36. The King may temporarily suspend the exercise of royal authority and resume such exercise by virtue of a statute, the bill for which is submitted by or on behalf of himself. The States-General deliberate and decide on the matter in joint session.

Article 37. (1) Royal authority is exercised by a regent:
a. as long as the King has not attained the age of eighteen years;
b. if a child not yet born can be called to take over the crown;
c. if the King has been declared incapable of exercising royal authority;
d. if the King has temporarily suspended the exercise of royal authority;
e. as long as after the death of the King or his abdication there is no successor.
(2) The regent is appointed by statute. The States-General deliberate and decide on the matter in joint session.
(3) In the cases stipulated in the first paragraph under c. and d., the descendant of the King who is his presumed successor is regent by operation of law, if he has attained the age of eighteen years.
(4) The regent swears or promises allegiance to the Constitution and loyal exercise of his office in a joint session of the States-General. Statute provides further regulations regarding regency and may provide for succession and replacement therein. The States-General deliberate and decide on the matter in joint session.
(5) Articles 35 and 36 apply to the regent mutatis mutandis.

Article 38. As long as the exercise of royal authority is not secured, it is exercised by the Council of State [Raad van State].

Article 39. Statute regulates who is a member of the royal house.

Article 40. (1) The King annually receives allowances charged to the Kingdom in accordance with rules to be provided by statute. That statute determines which other members of the royal house receive allowances charged to the Kingdom and regulates these allowances.
(2) The allowances charged to the Kingdom received by them, as well as assets which serve the exercise of their function, are exempt from personal taxation. Furthermore, what the King or his presumed successor receives from a member of the royal house by virtue of inheritance or gift, is exempt from inheritance, transfer and gift taxation. Further exemption from taxation may be granted by statute.
(3) The Chambers of the States-General may adopt bills for statutes stipulated in the preceding paragraphs only with at least two-thirds of the number of votes cast.

Article 41. The King organizes, with due respect for the public interest, his household.

§ 2. King and ministers

Article 42. (1) The government comprises the King and the ministers.
(2) The King is inviolable; the ministers are responsible.

Article 43. The Prime-Minister [minister-president] and the other ministers are appointed and dismissed by royal decree.

Article 44. (1) Ministries are established by royal decree. They are placed under the direction of a minister.
(2) Furthermore, ministers may be appointed who are not charged with directing a ministry.

Article 45. (1) The ministers together form the council of ministers [ministerraad].
(2) The Prime-Minister is chairman of the council of ministers.
(3) The council of ministers deliberates and decides on general government policy and promotes the unity of that policy.

Article 46. (1) Secretaries of state may be appointed by royal decree.
(2) A secretary of state [staatssecretaris] assumes, in the cases where the minister finds it necessary and with due regard to his instructions, his position as minister. The secretary of state is in that context responsible, notwithstanding the responsibility of the minister.

Article 47. All statutes and royal decrees are signed by the King and by one or more ministers or secretaries of state.

Article 48. The royal decree whereby a Prime-Minister is appointed, is signed also by him. The royal decrees whereby the other ministers and the secretaries of state are appointed or dismissed are signed also by the Prime-Minister.

Article 49. In a manner provided by statute, the ministers and secretaries of state, when assuming office, take an oath or make a declaration and promise before the King of their integrity, and swear or promise allegiance to the Constitution and loyal exercise of their office.

Chapter 3. States-General

§1. Organization and composition

Article 50. The States-General [Staten-Generaal] represent the entire Dutch people.

Article 51. (1) The States-General consist of the Second Chamber [Tweede Kamer] and the First Chamber [Eerste Kamer].

(2) The Second Chamber consists of one hundred and fifty members.
(3) The First Chamber consists of seventy-five members.
(4) In a joint session, the two Chambers are considered as one.

Article 52. (1) The term of session of both Chambers is four years.
(2) If for the provincial assemblies [provinciale staten] a term other than four years is established by statute, the term of session of the First Chamber is changed accordingly.

Article 53. (1) The members of both Chambers are elected on the basis of proportional representation within the limits to be provided by statute.
(2) Elections take place by secret ballot.

Article 54. (1) The members of the Second Chamber are elected directly by Dutch citizens who have attained the age of eighteen years, save for exceptions to be provided by statute with regard to Dutch citizens who are not residents.
(2) He who has been convicted to a prison sentence of at least one year for a criminal act so designated by statute in a final court judgment and who has at the same time been disqualified from the right to vote is excluded from the vote.

Article 55. The members of the First Chamber are elected by the members of the provincial assemblies [provinciale staten] and the members of an electoral college as referred to in article 132a (3). The elections take place, save for the event of a dissolution of the Chamber, within three months following the elections of the members of the provincial assemblies.

Article 56. In order to be able to become a member of the States-General, it is required that one be a Dutch citizen, have attained the age of eighteen years, and not be disqualified from the right to vote.

Article 57. (1) No-one may be a member of both Chambers.
(2) A member of the Second Chamber may not at the same time be a minister, secretary of state, member of the Council of State, member of the General Chamber of Audit, National Ombudsman or substitute ombudsman, or a member of or procurator-general or advocate-general at the Supreme Court.
(3) Nevertheless, a minister or secretary of state, who has tendered his resignation, may combine this office with a membership of the States-General, until a decision has been taken regarding that resignation.
(4) Statute may provide with regard to other public offices that they may not be exercised at the same time as the membership of the States-General or of one of the Chambers.

Article 57a. Statute regulates the temporary replacement of a member of the States-General because of pregnancy and delivery as well as because of illness.

Article 58. Each Chamber examines the letters patent of its newly appointed members and decides, with due regard to the regulations to be provided by statute, on disputes that arise with respect to the letters patent or the election itself.

Article 59. Everything else regarding the right to vote and the elections is regulated by statute.

Article 60. In a manner provided by statute, the members of the Chambers, when assuming their office, take an oath or make a declaration and promise in the assembly of their integrity, and swear or promise allegiance to the Constitution and loyal exercise of their office.

Article 61. (1) Each of the Chambers appoints a president from among the members.
(2) Each of the Chambers appoints a secretary. He and the other administrative staff of the Chambers may not at the same time be members of the States-General.

Article 62. The president of the First Chamber has the chairmanship over the joint session.

Article 63. Financial consideration for members and former members of the States-General and their surviving dependants are regulated by statute. The Chambers may adopt a bill on this matter only with at least two-thirds of the number of votes cast.

Article 64. (1) Each of the Chambers may be dissolved by royal decree.
(2) Each decree on such dissolution also contains an order for new elections to the dissolved Chamber and for the convention of the newly elected Chamber within three months.
(3) The dissolution takes effect on the day when the newly elected Chamber convenes.
(4) Statute determines the duration of the term of session of a Second Chamber operating after dissolution; the period may not be longer than five years. The term of session of a First Chamber operating after dissolution ends on the moment when the term of the dissolved Chamber would have ended.

§ 2. Procedures

Article 65. Annually, on the third Tuesday of September or at an earlier moment to be determined by statute, an explanation is given by or on behalf of the King in a joint session of the States-General regarding the policies to be pursued by the government.

Article 66. (1) The meetings of the States-General are public.
(2) The doors are closed when a tenth part of the number of members present so demand or when the president deems it necessary.
(3) The Chamber or the Chambers in joint session, respectively, then decide whether they should deliberate and decide with closed doors.

Article 67. (1) The Chambers may, each separately and in joint session, deliberate and decide only if more than half of the number of members in office is present at the meeting.
(2) Decisions are taken by a majority of votes.
(3) The members vote without any instructions.
(4) Matters are voted on orally and by individual calls when one member so demands.

Article 68. The ministers and the secretaries of state provide the Chambers, separately and in joint session, orally or in writing the information demanded by one or more members, where such provision is not in conflict with the interest of the state.

Article 69. (1) The ministers and the secretaries of state have access to the meetings and may participate in deliberations.
(2) They may be invited by the Chambers, separately and in joint session, to be present at the meeting.
(3) They may be assisted at the meeting by persons designated by them for that purpose.

Article 70. Both Chambers, both separately and in joint session, have the right of inquiry (enquête) to be regulated by statute.

Article 71. The members of the States-General, the ministers, the secretaries of state and other persons who participate in deliberations may not be prosecuted or held liable for what they have said in the meetings of the States-General or in committees thereof, or for what they have submitted to them in writing.

Article 72. The Chambers, both separately and in joint session, adopt rules of procedure.

Chapter 4. Council of State, General Chamber of Audit, National Ombudsman and permanent advisory bodies

Article 73. (1) The Council of State [Raad van State] or a division of the Council is heard on bills and drafts for ordinances [algemene maatregelen van bestuur] as well as proposals for the ratification of treaties by the States-General. In cases to be provided by statute, such hearing may be omitted.
(2) The Council or a division of the Council is charged with the investigation in administrative disputes that are decided by royal decree, and proposes a decision.
(3) Statute may charge the Council or a division of the Council with deciding in administrative disputes.

Article 74. (1) The King is the president of the Council of State. The presumed successor of the King is a member of the Council by operation of law after having attained the age of eighteen years. By or pursuant to statute, other members of the royal house may be granted membership of the Council.
(2) The members of the Council are appointed for life by royal decree.
(3) They are dismissed upon their own request and because they have attained an age to be provided by statute.
(4) In cases provided by statute they may be suspended or dismissed by the Council.
(5) Statute regulates the further details of their legal position.

Article 75. (1) Statute regulates the organization, composition and competence of the Council of State.
(2) By statute, also other tasks may be assigned to the Council or a division of the Council.

Article 76. The General Chamber of Audit [Algemene Rekenkamer] is charged with investigating the revenue and expenditure of the Kingdom.

Article 77. (1) The members of the General Chamber of Audit are appointed by royal decree for life from a proposal of three persons drawn up by the Second Chamber of the States-General.
(2) They are dismissed upon their own request and because they have attained an age to be provided by statute.
(3) In cases provided by statute they may be suspended or dismissed by the Supreme Court [Hoge Raad].
(4) Statute regulates the further details of their legal position.

Article 78. (1) Statute regulates the organization, composition and competence of the General Chamber of Audit.
(2) By statute, also other tasks may be assigned to the General Chamber of Audit.

Article 78a. (1) The National Ombudsman, upon request or on his own motion, conducts investigations into the conduct of administrative authorities of the Kingdom and of other administrative authorities designated by or pursuant to statute.
(2) The National Ombudsman and a substitute ombudsman are appointed for a term to be provided by statute by the Second Chamber of the States-General. They are dismissed upon their own request and because they have attained an age to be provided by statute. In cases provided by statute they may be suspended or dismissed by the Second Chamber of the States-General. Statute regulates the further details of their legal position.
(3) Statutes regulates the competence and procedures of the National Ombudsman.
(4) By or pursuant to statute, also other tasks may be assigned to the National Ombudsman.

Article 79. (1) Permanent advisory bodies in matters of legislation and administration of the Kingdom are established by or pursuant to statute.
(2) Statute regulates the organization, composition and competence of such bodies.
(3) By or pursuant to statute, also tasks other than advisory ones may be assigned to such bodies.

Article 80. (1) The opinions of the bodies stipulated in this chapter are published in accordance with procedures to be provided by statute.
(2) Opinions given on the matter of bills which are introduced by or on behalf of the King are, save for exceptions to be provided by statute, transmitted to the States-General.

Chapter 5. Legislation and administration

§ 1. Statutes and other regulations

Article 81. Statutes [wetten] are adopted jointly by the government and the States-General.

Article 82. (1) Bills may be introduced by or on behalf of the King and by the Second Chamber of the States-General.
(2) Bills for which deliberation in the States-General in joint session is prescribed may be introduced by or on behalf of the King and, as far as the relevant Articles of Chapter 2 allow, by the joint session.

(3) Bills to be introduced by the Second Chamber or the joint session, respectively, are tabled by one or more of the members.

Article 83. Bills introduced by or on behalf of the King are transmitted to the Second Chamber or, if deliberation in the States-General in joint session is prescribed, to that assembly.

Article 84. (1) As long as a bill introduced by or on behalf of the King has not yet been adopted by the Second Chamber or the joint session, respectively, it may be amended by it, on the proposal of one or more members, and by the government.
(2) As long as the Second Chamber or the joint session, respectively, has not yet adopted a bill to be introduced by itself, it may be amended by it on the proposal of one or more members and by the member or members who have tabled the bill.

Article 85. As soon as the Second Chamber has adopted a bill or has decided to introduce a bill, it transmits it to the First Chamber, which considers it as transmitted to it by the Second Chamber. The Second Chamber may instruct one or more of its members to defend a bill introduced by it in the First Chamber.

Article 86. (1) As long as a bill has not yet been adopted by the States-General, it may be withdrawn by or on behalf of the initiator.
(2) As long as the Second Chamber or the joint session, respectively, has not yet adopted a bill to be introduced by it, it may be withdrawn by the member or members who have tabled it.

Article 87. (1) A bill becomes a statute as soon as it has been adopted by the States-General and confirmed by the King.
(2) The King and the States-General inform each other of their decision regarding any bill.

Article 88. Statute regulates the publication and entry into force of statutes. They do not enter into force before they have been published.

Article 89. (1) Ordinances [algemene maatregelen van bestuur] are adopted by royal decree.
(2) Regulations to be enforced by sanctions are provided there only pursuant to statute. Statute regulates the sanctions to be imposed.
(3) Statute regulates the publication and entry into force of ordinances. They do not enter into force before they have been published.

(4) The second and third paragraph apply mutatis mutandis to other generally binding regulations adopted by the Kingdom.

§ 2. Further provisions

Article 90. The government promotes the development of the international legal order.

Article 91. (1) The Kingdom is not bound by treaties and they are not terminated without prior approval of the States-General. Statute provides the cases where no such approval is required.
(2) Statute provides the manner in which approval is given and may provide for tacit approval.
(3) If a treaty contains provisions which deviate from the Constitution or necessitate such deviation, the Chambers may give approval only with at least two-thirds of the number of votes cast.

Article 92. Subject, where necessary, to the provisions of Article 91 (3), legislative, executive and judicial powers may be conferred upon international organizations by or pursuant to a treaty.

Article 93. Provisions of treaties and of decisions of international organizations, which by virtue of their content can be binding upon everyone, become binding after they have been published.

Article 94. Statutory regulations in force within the Kingdom are not applicable if such application is incompatible with provisions of treaties and decisions of international organizations that are binding on everyone.

Article 95. Statute provides regulations regarding the publication of treaties and decisions of international organizations.

Article 96. (1) The Kingdom is not declared to be in a state of war unless after prior consent of the States-General.
(2) Such consent is not required when consultation with the States-General has proven to be impossible as a result of a state of war existing in fact.
(3) The States-General deliberate and decide on the matter in a joint session.
(4) The provisions of the first and the third paragraph apply mutatis mutandis to a declaration that a war has ended.

Article 97. (1) For the purposes of defence and for the protection of the interests of the Kingdom, as well as for the upholding and promotion of the international legal order, there are armed forces.
(2) The government has the supreme command over the armed forces.

Article 98. (1) The armed forces consist of volunteers and may also comprise conscripts.
(2) Statute regulates compulsory military service and the power to defer drafting into actual service.

Article 99. Statute regulates exemption from military service because of serious conscientious objections.

Article 99a. In accordance with regulations to be provided by statute, obligations may be imposed for the purposes of civil defence.

Article 100. (1) The government provides the States-General with information in advance regarding the deployment or the making available of the armed forces for the upholding and promotion of the international legal order. That includes information in advance regarding the deployment or the making available of the armed forces for humanitarian assistance in case of an armed conflict.
(2) The first paragraph does not apply if pressing reasons prevent the provision of information in advance. In that case, information is provided as soon as possible.

Articles 101 and 102. (Repealed).

Article 103. (1) Statute regulates in which cases, for the maintenance of external and internal security, a state of emergency to be designated as such by statute may be declared by royal decree; statute regulates the consequences.
(2) In that context, deviations are permissible from the constitutional provisions regarding the competences of the governments of the provinces, municipalities, public entities as referred to in article 132a and water boards, from the fundamental rights regulated in Article 6, in as far as the exercise of the right stipulated in that Article outside buildings and closed locations is concerned, 7, 8, 9, 12 (2) and (3) and 13, as well as from Article 113 (1) and (3).
(3) Immediately after the declaration of a state of emergency and then, as long as it has not been lifted by royal decree, each time they consider it necessary, the States-General decide on the continuation thereof; they deliberate and decide on the matter in joint session.

Article 104. Taxes of the Kingdom are raised by virtue of a statute. Other charges of the Kingdom are regulated by statute.

Article 105. (1) The budget of the revenue and expenditure of the Kingdom is established by statute.
(2) Annually, bills for general budget statutes are introduced by or on behalf of the King on the moment provided in Article 65.
(3) Account for the revenue and expenditure of the Kingdom is given to the States-General in accordance with the provisions of statute. The accounts approved by the General Chamber of Audit are submitted to the States-General.
(4) Statute provides regulations regarding the administration of the finances of the Kingdom.

Article 106. Statute regulates the monetary system.

Article 107. (1) Statute regulates private law, criminal law and civil and criminal procedure in general codes, save for the power to regulate certain subject-matters in separate statutes.
(2) Statute provides general rules of administrative law.

Article 108. (Repealed).

Article 109. Statute regulates the legal position of civil servants. It also provides regulations regarding their protection at work and regarding co-determination.

Article 110. The state respects openness in the exercise of its tasks in accordance with regulations to be provided by statute.

Article 111. Chivalric orders are established by statute.

Chapter 6. Judiciary

Article 112. (1) The judiciary is charged with adjudicating in disputes over rights and claims of private law.
(2) Statute may assign the adjudication in disputes which did not arise from private law relations either to the judiciary or to courts which do not form part of the judiciary. Statute regulates the procedures and the consequences of decisions.

Article 113. (1) The judiciary is furthermore charged with adjudicating on criminal acts.
(2) Disciplinary jurisdiction established by the state is regulated by statute.
(3) A sentence of deprivation of freedom may be imposed only by the judiciary.
(4) For adjudication outside the Netherlands and for military criminal law, statute may provide deviating regulations.

Article 114. The death penalty may not be imposed.

Article 115. With regard to disputes stipulated in Article 112 (2), administrative appeal may be allowed.

Article 116. (1) Statute designates the courts that form part of the judiciary.
(2) Statute regulates the organization, composition and competence of the judiciary.
(3) Statute may provide that persons not belonging to the judiciary participate in the jurisprudence thereof.
(4) Statute regulates the supervision by members of the judiciary charged with jurisprudence to be exercised over the exercise of the office of such members and of persons stipulated in the preceding paragraph.

Article 117. (1) The members of the judiciary charged with jurisprudence and the procurator-general at the Supreme Court are appointed by royal decree for life.
(2) They are dismissed upon their own request and because they have attained an age to be provided by statute.
(3) In cases provided by statute they may be suspended or dismissed by a court forming part of the judiciary designated by statute.
(4) Statute regulates the further details of their legal position.

Article 118. (1) The members of the Supreme Court [Hoge Raad] of the Netherlands are appointed from a proposal of three persons drawn up by the Second Chamber of the States-General.
(2) The Supreme Court is charged, in the cases and within the boundaries provided by statute, with cassation of judicial decisions because of a violation of the law.
(3) By statute, also other tasks may be assigned to the Supreme Court.

Article 119. The members of the States-General, the ministers and the secretaries of state are prosecuted for crimes committed in office, also after their leaving office, before the Supreme Court. The order to prosecute is given by royal decree or by a decision of the Second Chamber.

Article 120. The judge does not enter into a review of the constitutionality of statutes and treaties.

Article 121. Save for cases provided by statute, trials are conducted in public and judgments contain the reasons on which they are based. The judgment is handed down in public.

Article 122. (1) Pardon is granted by royal decree after the advice of a court designated by statute and with due regard to regulations to be provided by or pursuant to statute.
(2) Amnesty is granted by or pursuant to statute.

Chapter 7. Provinces, municipalities, Caribbean public entities, water boards, and other public entities

Article 123. (1) By statute, provinces [provincies] and municipalities [gemeenten] may be dissolved and new ones may be established.
(2) Statute regulates the change of provincial and municipal borders.

Article 124. (1) For provinces and municipalities, the power of regulation and administration regarding their local affairs [huishouding] is left to their governments.
(2) Regulation and administration may be demanded of the governments of provinces and municipalities by or pursuant to statute.

Article 125. (1) The head of the province and the municipality is the provincial assembly [provinciale staten] and the municipal council [gemeenteraad], respectively. Their meetings are public, save for exceptions to be regulated by statute.
(2) The government [bestuur] of the province also includes the provincial executive [gedeputeerde staten] and the King's Commissioner, the government of the municipality also includes the board of burgomaster and aldermen and the burgomaster.

Article 126. Statute may provide that the King's Commissioner is charged with the execution of an official instruction given by the government.

Article 127. The provincial assembly and the municipal council adopt, save for exceptions provided by statute or by them pursuant to statute, the provincial and the municipal ordinances [verordeningen], respectively.

Article 128. Save for the cases stipulated in Article 123, the conferral of powers within the meaning of Article

124 (1) to organs other than the ones stipulated in Article 125 may be effected only by the provincial assembly and the municipal council, respectively.

Article 129. (1) The members of the provincial assembly and of the municipal council are elected directly by Dutch citizens who are at the same time residents of the province or municipality, respectively, who fulfil the conditions that apply to elections of the Second Chamber of the States-General. For membership the same conditions apply.
(2) The members are elected on the basis of proportional representation within the limits to be provided by statute.
(3) Articles 53 (2) and 59 apply. Article 57a applies mutatis mutandis.
(4) The term of session of the provincial assembly and the municipal council is four years, save for exceptions to be provided by statute.
(5) Statute provides which offices may not be exercised simultaneously with membership. Statute may provide that disqualifications derive from family relation or marriage and that the commission of acts designated by statute may lead to a loss of membership.
(6) Members vote without instructions.

Article 130. Statute may confer the right to elect the members of the municipal council and the right to be a member of the municipal council to residents who are not Dutch citizens, as long as they at least fulfil the conditions that apply to residents who are also Dutch citizens.

Article 131. The King's Commissioner and the burgomaster are appointed, suspended, and dismissed in a manner provided for by statute. Pursuant to statute, more detailed rules can be imposed regarding the procedures to be followed therein.

Article 132. (1) Statute regulates the organization of provinces and municipalities as well as the composition and competence of their governments.
(2) Statute regulates supervision of these governments.
(3) Decisions of these governments may be subjected to supervision in advance only in cases to be provided by or pursuant to statute.
(4) Annulment of decisions of these governments may only be effected by royal decree because of a violation of the law or the general interest.
(5) Statute regulates provisions in case of a non-performance with regard to regulation and administration demanded by virtue of Article 124 (2). By statute, provisions in deviation from Articles 125 and 127 may be effected in case the government of a province or a municipality grossly neglects its tasks.
(6) Statute provides which taxes may be raised by the governments of provinces and municipalities and regulates their financial relation with the Kingdom.

Article 132a. (1) By law, other territorial public entities than provinces and municipalities may be created and dissolved in the Caribbean part of the Netherlands.
(2) Articles 124, 125, and 127 to 132 apply mutatis mutandis to these public entities.
(3) In these public entities, elections are held for an electoral college for the First Chamber. Article 129 applies mutatis mutandis.
(4) For these public entities, rules can be imposed and other specific measures can be taken with a view to special circumstances by which these public entities differ significantly from the European part of the Netherlands.

Article 133. (1) The dissolution and establishment of water boards [waterschappen], the regulation of their tasks and organization, as well as the composition of their governing bodies is effected, in accordance with regulations to be provided by statute, by provincial ordinance, in as far as nothing is provided otherwise by or pursuant to statute.
(2) Statute regulates the regulatory and other competences of the governing bodies of water boards, as well as the public character of their meetings.
(3) Statute regulates the provincial and further supervision of these governing bodies. Annulment of decisions of these governing bodies may be effected only because of a violation of the law or the general interest.

Article 134. (1) By or pursuant to statute, public entities for professions and enterprises and other public entities may be established and dissolved.
(2) Statute regulates the tasks and the organization of these public entities, the composition and competence of their governing bodies, as well as the public character of their meetings. By or pursuant to statute, regulatory competence may be conferred upon their governing bodies.
(3) Statute regulates the supervision of these governing bodies. Annulment of decisions of these governing bodies may be effected only because of a violation of the law or the general interest.

Article 135. Statute provides regulations for provisions in cases where two or more public entities are involved. In that context, the establishment of a new public entity may be provided for, in which case Article 134 (2) and (3) applies.

Article 136. Disputes between public entities are resolved by royal decree, unless they fall under the jurisdiction of the judiciary or such resolution is assigned by statute to others.

Chapter 8. Revision of the Constitution

Article 137. (1) A statute declares that an amendment of the Constitution as it proposes shall be considered.

(2) The Second Chamber may, whether or not upon such proposal introduced by or on behalf of the King, split a bill for such a statute.
(3) After the publication of the statute stipulated in the first paragraph, the Second Chamber is dissolved.
(4) After the new Second Chamber has convened, both Chambers consider in second reading the proposal for an amendment stipulated in the first paragraph. They may adopt it only with at least two-thirds of the number of votes cast.
(5) The Second Chamber may, whether or not upon such proposal introduced by or on behalf of the King, split a proposal for an amendment with at least two-thirds of the number of votes cast.

Article 138. (1) Before the proposals for an amendment of the Constitution adopted in second reading are confirmed by the King, by statute:
a. the adopted proposals and the provisions of the Constitution left unchanged may be adjusted to one another as far as necessary;
b. the division and position of chapters, sections and Articles as well as the titles may be modified.
(2) The Chambers may adopt a bill containing provisions stipulated in the first paragraph, sub a., only with at least two-thirds of the number of votes cast.

Article 139. The amendments of the Constitution, adopted by the States-General and confirmed by the King, enter into force immediately after they have been published.

Article 140. Existing statutes and other regulations and decisions which are incompatible with an amendment of the Constitution remain in force until a provision on that matter is effected in accordance with the Constitution.

Article 141. The text of the revised Constitution is published by royal decree, in which context chapters, sections and Articles may be renumbered and references be changed accordingly.

Article 142. The Constitution may by statute be brought into line with the Charter for the Kingdom of the Netherlands [Statuut voor het Koninkrijk der Nederlanden]. Articles 139, 140 and 141 apply mutatis mutandis.

[*The supplementary provisions are omitted.*]

10   Elections Act [Kieswet][3]

[Part I is omitted.]

Part II. The elections of the members of the Second Chamber of the States-General, of provincial assemblies and of the municipal councils

[Chapters B to O are omitted.]

Chapter P. The establishment of the election results by the central polling office

§ 1. General provision

Article P 1. Immediately after the records of all main polling offices have been received, the central polling office starts carrying out the activities for the establishment and publication of the results of the elections. If elections of the municipal council or the provincial assembly of a province which forms a single polling district is concerned, the central elections office starts these activities immediately after the activities stipulated in Articles O 1 and O 2 have been concluded.

§ 2. The distribution of seats

[Articles P2 to P4 are omitted.]

Article P 5.
(1) The central polling office divides the sum of the number of votes of all lists by the number of seats to be distributed.
(2) The quotient thus obtained is called electoral divisor.

Article P 6. A list is assigned a seat so many times as the electoral divisor is accommodated in the number of votes of that list.

Article P 7. (1) The remaining seats, which are called rest seats, are, if the number of seats to be distributed is nineteen or more, consecutively assigned to those lists which after assignment of a seat have the largest average number of votes per assigned seat. If averages are equal, the lot decides where necessary.

---

[3] As last amended by statute of 17 May 2017 (*Stb.* 284). Selected provisions: Articles P1, P5 to P7, P9, P10, P15, P19, P19a, U1, U2 (1), U3, U7 to U10 and U15. Translation by Philipp Kiiver & Sascha Hardt.

(2) If the election of the members of the Second Chamber is concerned, lists the number of votes of which is lower than the electoral divisor are not entitled to such assignment.

[Article P 8 is omitted.]

Article P 9. If a list which has received an absolute majority of votes cast is assigned a number of seats that is smaller than the absolute majority of seats to be distributed, that list is assigned one additional seat and, at the same time, one seat is forfeited that had been assigned to the list which had received a seat for the smallest average or the smallest remainder. If two or more lists had received a seat for the same smallest average or the smallest remainder, the lot decides.

Article P 10. If in the application of the preceding provisions a list would have to be assigned more seats than there are candidates, the remaining seat or seats pass by continued application of these provisions to one or more of the other lists on which candidates appear to whom no seat has been assigned.

[Articles P 11 to P 14 are omitted.]

§ 3. The assignment of the seats to the candidates

Article P 15. (1) In the order of the number of votes cast for them, those candidates are elected who, on the common lists on which they appear, have received a number of votes that is larger than 25% of the electoral divisor, as far as that group of lists or that list no being part of a group of lists has been allocated sufficient seats. If numbers are equal, the lot decides where necessary.
(2) If the number of seats to be distributed in the elections is lower than nineteen, then, in the application of the first paragraph, not 25% of the electoral divisor but half of the electoral divisor shall be applied.

[Articles P 16 to P 18 are omitted.]

Article P 19. (1) The central polling office ranks, with respect to each list, the candidates appearing thereon in such manner that the candidates to whom a seat is assigned by application of Article P 15 come on top, in the order in which the seats have been assigned.
(2) Subsequently, in the order of the numbers of votes cast for them, candidates appearing on the list are ranked who have, on the common lists on which they appear, received a number of votes that is larger than 25% of the electoral divisor or larger than half of the

electoral divisor, respectively, but who have not been declared elected by application of Article P 15 (1) or (2), respectively. If numbers are equal, the order of the list decides.
(3) Finally, in the order of the list, the other candidates appearing on the list are ranked.
(4) Article P 18 remains inapplicable in the ranking.
(5) Save for elections of the members of municipal councils with nine or eleven members, the ranking shall be omitted as far as lists or numbers of identical lists are concerned on which no candidates have been declared elected and which do not form part of a combination of lists or group of lists to which one or more seats have been assigned.

Article P 19a. If a candidate is deceased, he is left out of consideration in the application of this section.

[*The remainder of Chapter P is omitted.*]

Part III. The election of the members of the First Chamber of the States-General

[*Chapters Q to T are omitted.*]

Chapter U. The establishment of the election results by the central polling office

§ 1. General provisions

Article U 1. Immediately after the records have been received, the central polling office starts carrying out the activities for the establishment and publication of the results of the elections.

Article U 2. (1) Each vote counts, depending on the province where it has been cast, as a number of votes that is equal to the number that is obtained by dividing the population number of the province by one hundred times the number of members of which the provincial assembly is composed. The quotient is thereafter rounded towards a full number upwards if a fraction is greater than 1/2 and downwards if a fraction is less than 1/2. This number is called the vote value.

[*The remainder of Article U2 is omitted.*]

§ 2. The distribution of seats

Article U 3. With respect to each province, the central polling office multiplies the numbers of votes cast for each candidate and the numbers of votes of the lists by the vote value that applies to that province. For the establishment of the result of the election, the products thus obtained count as the number of votes cast for each candidate or the number of votes of the lists, respectively.

[*Articles U 4 to U 6 are omitted.*]

Article U 7. (1) The central polling office divides the sum of the number of votes of all lists by the number of seats to be distributed.
(2) The quotient thus obtained is called electoral divisor.

Article U 8. A list is assigned a seat so many times as the electoral divisor is accommodated in the number of votes of that list.

Article U 9. The remaining seats, which are called rest seats, are consecutively assigned to those lists which after assignment of a seat have the largest average number of votes per assigned seat. If averages are equal, the lot decides where necessary.

Article U 10. If in the application of the preceding provisions a list would have to be assigned more seats than there are candidates, the remaining seat or seats pass by continued application of these provisions to one or more of the other lists on which candidates appear to whom no seat has been assigned.

[*Articles U 11 to U 14 are omitted.*]

§ 3. The assignment of the seats to the candidates

Article U 15. (1) Those candidates from the list are elected who are designated as such by application, mutatis mutandis, of Articles P 15 to P 18 and P 19a, on the understanding that, by way of derogation from
Article P 15 (1) first sentence, those candidates are elected who have received a number of votes larger than the electoral divisor.
(2) The ranking of candidates is carried out in accordance with the provisions of Article P 19 (1), (3), and (4), on the understanding that no ranking takes place where lists are concerned from which no candidates have been declared elected and which are not part of a group of lists to which one or more seats have been allocated.

[*The remainder of the Act is omitted.*]

United Kingdom

11 Bill of Rights 1689[1]

Whereas the Lords Spirituall and Temporall and Comons assembled at Westminster lawfully fully and freely representing all the Estates of the People of this Realme did upon the thirteenth day of February in the yeare of our Lord one thousand six hundred eighty eight present unto their Majesties then called and known by the Names and Stile of William and Mary Prince and Princesse of Orange being present in their proper Persons a certaine Declaration in Writing made by the said Lords and Comons in the Words following viz

Whereas the late King James the Second by the Assistance of diverse evill Councellors Judges and Ministers imployed by him did endeavour to subvert and extirpate the Protestant Religion and the Lawes and Liberties of this Kingdome.

By Assumeing and Exerciseing a Power of Dispensing with and Suspending of Lawes and the Execution of Lawes without Consent of Parlyament.

By Committing and Prosecuting diverse Worthy Prelates for humbly Petitioning to be excused from Concurring to the said Assumed Power.

By issueing and causeing to be executed a Commission under the Great Seale for Erecting a Court called The Court of Commissioners for Ecclesiasticall Causes.

By Levying Money for and to the Use of the Crowne by pretence of Prerogative for other time and in other manner then the same was granted by Parlyament.

By raising and keeping a Standing Army within this Kingdome in time of Peace without Consent of Parlyament and Quartering Soldiers contrary to Law.

By causing severall good Subjects being Protestants to be disarmed at the same time when Papists were both Armed and Imployed contrary to Law.

By Violating the Freedome of Election of Members to serve in Parlyament.

By Prosecutions in the Court of Kings Bench for Matters and Causes cognizable onely in Parlyament and by diverse other Arbitrary and Illegall Courses.

And whereas of late yeares Partiall Corrupt and Unqualifyed Persons have beene returned and served on Juryes in Tryalls and particularly diverse Jurors in Tryalls for High Treason which were not Freeholders,

And excessive Baile hath beene required of Persons committed in Criminall Cases to elude the Benefitt of the Lawes made for the Liberty of the Subjects.

---

1 An Act declareing the Rights and Liberties of the Subject and Setleing the Succession of the Crowne [As amended]. Selected provisions: first part.

And excessive Fines have beene imposed.

And illegall and cruell Punishments inflicted.

And severall Grants and Promises made of Fines and Forfeitures before any Conviction or Judgement against the Persons upon whome the same were to be levyed. All which are utterly directly contrary to the knowne Lawes and Statutes and Freedome of this Realme.

And whereas the said late King James the Second haveing Abdicated the Government and the Throne being thereby Vacant His Hignesse the Prince of Orange (whome it hath pleased Almighty God to make the glorious Instrument of Delivering this Kingdome from Popery and Arbitrary Power) did (by the Advice of the Lords Spirituall and Temporall and diverse principall Persons of the Commons) cause Letters to be written to the Lords Spirituall and Temporall being Protestants and other Letters to the severall Countyes Cityes Universities Burroughs and Cinque Ports for the Choosing of such Persons to represent them as were of right to be sent to Parlyament to meete and sitt at Westminster upon the two and twentyeth day of January in this Yeare one thousand six hundred eighty and eight in order to such an Establishment as that their Religion Lawes and Liberties might not againe be in danger of being Subverted, Upon which Letters Elections haveing beene accordingly made.

And thereupon the said Lords Spirituall and Temporall and Commons pursuant to their respective Letters and Elections being now assembled in a full and free Representative of this Nation taking into their most serious Consideration the best meanes for attaining the Ends aforesaid Doe in the first place (as their Auncestors in like Case have usually done) for the Vindicating and Asserting their auntient Rights and Liberties, Declare

That the pretended Power of Suspending of Laws or the Execution of Laws by Regall Authority without Consent of Parlyament is illegall.

That the pretended Power of Dispensing with Laws or the Execution of Laws by Regall Authoritie as it hath beene assumed and exercised of late is illegall.

That the Commission for erecting the late Court of Commissioners for Ecclesiasticall Causes and all other Commissions and Courts of like nature are Illegall and Pernicious.

That levying Money for or to the Use of the Crowne by pretence of Prerogative without Grant of Parlyament for longer time or in other manner then the same is or shall be granted is Illegall.

That it is the Right of the Subjects to petition the King and all Commitments and Prosecutions for such Petitioning are Illegall.

That the raising or keeping a standing Army within the Kingdome in time of Peace unlesse it be with Consent of Parlyament is against Law.

That the Subjects which are Protestants may have Arms for their Defence suitable to their Conditions and as allowed by Law.

That Election of Members of Parlyament ought to be free.

That the Freedome of Speech and Debates or Proceedings in Parlyament ought not to be impeached or questioned in any Court or Place out of Parlyament.

That excessive Baile ought not to be required nor excessive Fines imposed nor cruell and unusuall Punishments inflicted.

That Jurors ought to be duely impannelled and returned.

That all Grants and Promises of Fines and Forfeitures of particular persons before Conviction are illegall and void.

And that for Redresse of all Grievances and for the amending strengthening and preserveing of the Lawes Parlyaments ought to be held frequently.

And they doe Claime Demand and Insist upon all and singular the Premises as their undoubted Rights and Liberties and that noe Declarations Judgements Doeings or Proceedings to the Prejudice of the People in any of the said Premisses ought in any wise to be drawne hereafter into Consequence or Example. To which Demand of their Rights they are particularly encouraged by the Declaration of this Highnesse the Prince of Orange as being the onely meanes for obtaining a full Redresse and Remedy therein. Haveing therefore an intire Confidence That his said Highnesse the Prince of Orange will perfect the Deliverance soe farr advanced by him and will still preserve them from the Violation of their Rights which they have here asserted and from all other Attempts upon their Religion Rights and Liberties. The said Lords Spirituall and Temporall and Commons assembled at Westminster doe Resolve That William and Mary Prince and Princesse of Orange be and be declared King and Queene of England France and Ireland and the Dominions thereunto belonging to hold the Crowne and Royall Dignity of the said Kingdomes and Dominions to them the said Prince and Princesse dureing their Lives and the Life of the Survivour of them And that the sole and full Exercise of the Regall Power be onely in and executed by the said Prince of Orange in the Names of the said Prince and Princesse dureing their joynt Lives And after their Deceases the said Crowne and Royall Dignitie of the said Kingdoms and Dominions to be to the Heires of the Body of the said Princesse And for default of such Issue to the Princesse Anne of Denmarke and the Heires of her Body And for default of such Issue to the Heires of the Body of the said Prince of Orange. And the Lords Spirituall and Temporall and Commons doe pray the said Prince and Princesse to accept the same accordingly.

And that the Oathes hereafter mentioned be taken by all Persons of whome the Oathes of Allegiance and Supremacy might be required by Law instead of them And that the said Oathes of Allegiance and Supremacy be abrogated.

I A B doe sincerely promise and sweare That I will be faithfull and beare true Allegiance to their Majestyes King William and Queene Mary Soe helpe me God.

I A B doe sweare That I doe from my Heart Abhorr, Detest and Abjure as Impious and Hereticall this damnable Doctrine and Position That Princes Excommunicated or Deprived by the Pope or any Authority of the See of Rome may be deposed or murdered by their Subjects or any other whatsoever. And I doe declare That noe Forreigne Prince Person Prelate, State or Potentate hath or ought to have any Jurisdiction Power Superiority Preeminence or Authoritie Ecclesiasticall or Spirituall within this Realme Soe helpe me God.

Upon which their said Majestyes did accept the Crowne and Royall Dignitie of the Kingdoms of England France and Ireland and the Dominions thereunto belonging according to the Resolution and Desire of the said Lords and Commons contained in the said Declaration. And thereupon their Majestyes were pleased That the said Lords Spirituall and Temporall and Commons being the two Houses of Parlyament should continue to sitt and with their Majesties Royall Concurrence make effectuall Provision for the Setlement of the Religion Lawes and Liberties of this Kingdome soe that the same for the future might not be in danger againe of being subverted, To which the said Lords Spirituall and Temporall and Commons did agree and proceede to act accordingly.
[*The remainder is omitted.*]

12 Parliaments Act 1911/1949[2]

Whereas it is expedient that provision should be made for regulating the relations between the two Houses of Parliament:
And whereas it is intended to substitute for the House of Lords as it at present exists a Second Chamber constituted on a popular instead of hereditary basis, but such substitution cannot be immediately brought into operation:
And whereas provision will require hereafter to be made by Parliament in a measure effecting such substitution for limiting and defining the powers of the new Second Chamber, but it is expedient to make such provision as in this Act appears for restricting the existing powers of the House of Lords:

Section 1. (1) If a Money Bill, having been passed by the House of Commons, and sent up to the House of Lords at least one month before the end of the session, is not passed by the House of Lords without amendment within one month after it is so sent up to that House, the Bill shall, unless the House of Commons direct to the contrary, be presented to His Majesty and become an Act of Parliament on the Royal Assent being signified, notwithstanding that the House of Lords have not consented to the Bill.
(2) A Money Bill means a Public Bill which in the opinion of the Speaker of the House of Commons contains only provisions dealing with all or any of the following subjects, namely, the imposition, repeal, remission, alteration, or regulation of taxation; the imposition for the payment of debt or other financial purposes of charges on the Consolidated Fund, the National Loans Fund or on money provided by Parliament, or the variation or repeal of any such charges; supply; the appropriation, receipt, custody, issue or audit of accounts of public money; the raising or guarantee of any loan or the repayment thereof; or subordinate matters incidental to those subjects or any of them. In this subsection the expressions "taxation," "public money," and "loan" respectively do not include any taxation, money, or loan raised by local authorities or bodies for local purposes.
(3) There shall be endorsed on every Money Bill when it is sent up to the House of Lords and when it is presented to His Majesty for assent the certificate of the Speaker of the House of Commons signed by him that it is a Money Bill. Before giving his certificate the Speaker shall consult, if practicable, two members to be appointed from the Chairmen's Panel at the beginning of each Session by the Committee of Selection.

Section 2. (1) If any Public Bill (other than a Money Bill or a Bill containing any provision to extend the maximum duration of Parliament beyond five years) is passed by the House of Commons in two successive sessions (whether of the same Parliament or not),

---

2 An Act to make provision with respect to the powers of the House of Lords in relation to those of the House of Commons, and to limit the duration of Parliament [as amended]; An Act to amend the Parliament Act 1911.

and, having been sent up to the House of Lords at least one month before the end of the session, is rejected by the House of Lords in each of those sessions, that Bill shall, on its rejection for the second time by the House of Lords, unless the House of Commons direct to the contrary, be presented to His Majesty and become an Act of Parliament on the Royal Assent being signified thereto, notwithstanding that the House of Lords have not consented to the Bill: Provided that this provision shall not take effect unless one year has elapsed between the date of the second reading in the first of those sessions of the Bill in the House of Commons and the date on which it passes the House of Commons in the second of these sessions.

(2) When a Bill is presented to His Majesty for assent in pursuance of the provisions of this section, there shall be endorsed on the Bill the certificate of the Speaker of the House of Commons signed by him that the provisions of this section have been duly complied with.

(3) A Bill shall be deemed to be rejected by the House of Lords if it is not passed by the House of Lords either without amendment or with such amendments only as may be agreed to by both Houses.

(4) A Bill shall be deemed to be the same Bill as a former Bill sent up to the House of Lords in the preceding session if, when it is sent up to the House of Lords, it is identical with the former Bill or contains only such alterations as are certified by the Speaker of the House of Commons to be necessary owing to the time which has elapsed since the date of the former Bill, or to represent any amendments which have been made by the House of Lords in the former Bill in the preceding session, and any amendments which are certified by the Speaker to have been made by the House of Lords in the second session and agreed to by the House of Commons shall be inserted in the Bill as presented for Royal Assent in pursuance of this section:

Provided that the House of Commons may, if they think fit, on the passage of such a Bill through the House in the second session, suggest any further amendments without inserting the amendments in the Bill, and any such suggested amendments shall be considered by the House of Lords, and, if agreed to by that House, shall be treated as amendments made by the House of Lords and agreed to by the House of Commons; but the exercise of this power by the House of Commons shall not affect the operation of this section in the event of the Bill being rejected by the House of Lords.

Section 3. Any certificate of the Speaker of the House of Commons given under this Act shall be conclusive for all purposes, and shall not be questioned in any court of law.

Section 4. (1) In every Bill presented to His Majesty under the preceding provisions of this Act, the words of enactment shall be as follows, that is to say:

"Be it enacted by the King's most Excellent Majesty, by and with the advice and consent of the Commons in this present Parliament assembled, in accordance with the provisions of the Parliament Acts 1911 and 1949 and by authority of the same, as follows."

(2) Any alteration of a Bill necessary to give effect to this section shall not be deemed to be an amendment of the Bill.

Section 5. In this Act the expression "Public Bill" does not include any Bill for confirming a Provisional Order.

Section 6. Nothing in this Act shall diminish or qualify the existing rights and privileges of the House of Commons.

Section 7. (Repealed by virtue of the Fixed-term Parliaments Act 2011)

Section 8. This Act may be cited as the Parliament Act 1911.

Parliament Act 1949 [An Act to amend the Parliament Act 1911].

Section 1. The Parliament Act, 1911, shall have effect, and shall be deemed to have had effect from the beginning of the session in which the Bill for this Act originated (save as regards that Bill itself), as if –
(a) there had been substituted in subsections (1) and (4) of section two thereof, for the words "in three successive sessions", "for the third time", "in the third of those sessions", "in the third session", and "in the second or third session" respectively, the words "in two successive sessions", "for the second time", "in the second of those sessions", "in the second session", and "in the second session" respectively; and
(b) there had been substituted in subsection (1) of the said section two, for the words "two years have elapsed" the words "one year has elapsed":
Provided that, if a Bill has been rejected for the second time by the House of Lords before the signification of the Royal Assent to the Bill for this Act, whether such rejection was in the same session as that in which the Royal Assent to the Bill for this Act was signified or in an earlier session, the requirement of the said section two that a Bill is to be presented to His Majesty on its rejection for the second time by the House of Lords shall have effect in relation to the Bill rejected as a requirement that it is to be presented to His Majesty as soon as the Royal Assent to the Bill for this Act has been signified, and, notwithstanding that such rejection was in an earlier session, the Royal Assent to the Bill rejected may be signified in the session in which the Royal Assent to the Bill for this Act was signified.

Section 2. (1) This Act may be cited as the Parliament Act 1949.

(2) This Act and the Parliament Act 1911, shall be construed as one and may be cited together as the Parliament Acts 1911 and 1949.

13 Fixed-Term Parliaments Act 2011[3]

Section 1. (1) This section applies for the purposes of the Timetable in rule 1 in Schedule 1 to the Representation of the People Act 1983 and is subject to section 2.
(2) The polling day for the next parliamentary general election after the passing of this Act is to be 7 May 2015.
(3) The polling day for each subsequent parliamentary general election is to be the first Thursday in May in the fifth calendar year following that in which the polling day for the previous parliamentary general election fell.
(4) But, if the polling day for the previous parliamentary general election –
(a) was appointed under section 2(7), and
(a) in the calendar year in which it fell, fell before the first Thursday in May, subsection (3) has effect as if for "fifth" there were substituted "fourth".
(5) The Prime Minister may by order made by statutory instrument provide that the polling day for a parliamentary general election in a specified calendar year is to be later than the day determined under subsection (2) or (3), but not more than two months later.
(6) A statutory instrument containing an order under subsection (5) may not be made unless a draft has been laid before and approved by a resolution of each House of Parliament.
(7) The draft laid before Parliament must be accompanied by a statement setting out the Prime Minister's reasons for proposing the change in the polling day..

Section 2. (1) An early parliamentary general election is to take place if –
(a) the House of Commons passes a motion in the form set out in subsection (2), and
(b) if the motion is passed on a division, the number of members who vote in favour of the motion is a number equal to or greater than two thirds of the number of seats in the House (including vacant seats).
(2) The form of motion for the purposes of subsection (1) (a) is – "That there shall be an early parliamentary general election."
(3) An early parliamentary general election is also to take place if –
(a) the House of Commons passes a motion in the form set out in subsection (4), and
(b) the period of 14 days after the day on which that motion is passed ends without the House passing a motion in the form set out in subsection (5).
(4) The form of motion for the purposes of subsection (3) (a) is – "That this House has no confidence in Her Majesty's Government."
(5) The form of motion for the purposes of subsection (3) (b) is – "That this House has confidence in Her Majesty's Government."

---

[3] An Act to make provision about the dissolution of Parliament and the determination of polling days for parliamentary general elections; and for connected purposes] as last amended by the Recall of MPs Act 2015 (c. 25); Selected provisions: Sections 1 – 3, 6 and 7.

(6) Subsection (7) applies for the purposes of the Timetable in rule 1 in Schedule 1 to the Representation of the People Act 1983.

(7) If a parliamentary general election is to take place as provided for by subsection (1) or (3), the polling day for the election is to be the day appointed by Her Majesty by proclamation on the recommendation of the Prime Minister (and, accordingly, the appointed day replaces the day which would otherwise have been the polling day for the next election determined under section 1).

Section 3. (1) The Parliament then in existence dissolves at the beginning of the 25_{th} working day before the polling day for the next parliamentary general election as determined under section 1 or appointed under section 2, subsection (7).

(2) Parliament cannot otherwise be dissolved.

(3) Once Parliament dissolves, the Lord Chancellor and, in relation to Northern Ireland, the Secretary of State have the authority to have the writs for the election sealed and issued (see rule 3 in Schedule 1 to the Representation of the People Act 1983).

(4) Once Parliament dissolves, Her Majesty may issue the proclamation summoning the new Parliament which may –

(a) appoint the day for the first meeting of the new Parliament;

(b) deal with any other matter which was normally dealt with before the passing of this Act by proclamations summoning new Parliaments (except a matter dealt with by subsection (1) or (3)).

(5) In this section "working day" means any day other than –

(a) a Saturday or Sunday;

(b) a Christmas Eve, Christmas Day or Good Friday;

(c) a day which is a bank holiday under the Banking and Financial Dealings Act 1971 in any part of the United Kingdom;

(d) a day appointed for public thanksgiving or mourning.

(6) But, if –

(a) on a day ("the relevant day") one or more working days are fixed or appointed as bank holidays or days for public thanksgiving or mourning, and

(b) as a result, the day for the dissolution of a Parliament would (apart from this subsection) be brought forward from what it was immediately before the relevant day to a day that is earlier than 30 days after the relevant day, the day or days in question are to continue to be treated as working days (even if the polling day is subsequently changed).

[*Sections 4 is omitted*]

Section 5. (Repealed).

Section 6. (1) This Act does not affect Her Majesty's power to prorogue Parliament.
(2) This Act does not affect the way in which the sealing of a proclamation summoning a new Parliament may be authorised; and the sealing of a proclamation to be issued under section 2 (7) may be authorised in the same way.
(3) The Schedule (which contains consequential amendments etc.) has effect.

Section 7. (1) This Act may be cited as the Fixed-term Parliaments Act 2011.
(2) This Act comes into force on the day it is passed.
(3) An amendment or repeal made by this Act has the same extent as the enactment or relevant part of the enactment to which the amendment or repeal relates.
(4) The Prime Minister must make arrangements –
(a) for a committee to carry out a review of the operation of this Act and, if appropriate in consequence of its findings, to make recommendations for the repeal or amendment of this Act, and
(b) for the publication of the committee's findings and recommendations (if any).
(5) A majority of the members of the committee are to be members of the House of Commons.
(6) Arrangements under subsection (4) (a) are to be made no earlier than 1 June 2020 and no later than 30 November 2020.

14 Human Rights Act 1998[4]

Section 1. (1) In this Act "the Convention rights" means the rights and fundamental freedoms set out in –
(a) Articles 2 to 12 and 14 of the Convention,
(b) Articles 1 to 3 of the First Protocol, and
(c) Article 1 of the Thirteenth Protocol, as read with Articles 16 to 18 of the Convention.
(2) Those Articles are to have effect for the purposes of this Act subject to any designated derogation or reservation (as to which see sections 14 and 15).
(3) The Articles are set out in Schedule 1.
(4) The Secretary of State may by order make such amendments to this Act as he considers appropriate to reflect the effect, in relation to the United Kingdom, of a protocol.
(5) In subsection (4) "protocol" means a protocol to the Convention –
(a) which the United Kingdom has ratified; or
(b) which the United Kingdom has signed with a view to ratification.
(6) No amendment may be made by an order under subsection (4) so as to come into force before the protocol concerned is in force in relation to the United Kingdom.

Section 2. (1) A court or tribunal determining a question which has arisen in connection with a Convention right must take into account any –
(a) judgment, decision, declaration or advisory opinion of the European Court of Human Rights,
(b) opinion of the Commission given in a report adopted under Article 31 of the Convention,
(c) decision of the Commission in connection with Article 26 or 27 (2) of the Convention, or
(d) decision of the Committee of Ministers taken under Article 46 of the Convention,
whenever made or given, so far as, in the opinion of the court or tribunal, it is relevant to the proceedings in which that question has arisen.
(2) Evidence of any judgment, decision, declaration or opinion of which account may have to be taken under this section is to be given in proceedings before any court or tribunal in such manner as may be provided by rules.
(3) In this section "rules" means rules of court or, in the case of proceedings before a tribunal, rules made for the purposes of this section –
(a) by the Lord Chancellor or the Secretary of State, in relation to any proceedings outside Scotland;

---

4 An Act to give further effect to rights and freedoms guaranteed under the European Convention on Human Rights; to make provision with respect to holders of certain judicial offices who become judges of the European Court of Human Rights; and for connected purposes] as last amended by the European Union (Withdrawal) Act 2018 (c. 16). Selected provisions: Sections 1 – 10 and Schedule 2.

(b) by the Secretary of State, in relation to proceedings in Scotland; or
(c) by a Northern Ireland department, in relation to proceedings before a tribunal in Northern Ireland –
   (i) which deals with transferred matters; and
   (ii) for which no rules made under paragraph (a) are in force.

Section 3. (1) So far as it is possible to do so, primary legislation and subordinate legislation must be read and given effect in a way which is compatible with the Convention rights.
(2) This section –
(a) applies to primary legislation and subordinate legislation whenever enacted;
(b) does not affect the validity, continuing operation or enforcement of any incompatible primary legislation; and
(c) does not affect the validity, continuing operation or enforcement of any incompatible subordinate legislation if (disregarding any possibility of revocation) primary legislation prevents removal of the incompatibility.

Section 4. (1) Subsection (2) applies in any proceedings in which a court determines whether a provision of primary legislation is compatible with a Convention right.
(2) If the court is satisfied that the provision is incompatible with a Convention right, it may make a declaration of that incompatibility.
(3) Subsection (4) applies in any proceedings in which a court determines whether a provision of subordinate legislation, made in the exercise of a power conferred by primary legislation, is compatible with a Convention right.
(4) If the court is satisfied –
(a) that the provision is incompatible with a Convention right, and
(b) that (disregarding any possibility of revocation) the primary legislation concerned prevents removal of the incompatibility,
   it may make a declaration of that incompatibility.
(5) In this section "court" means –
(a) the Supreme Court;
(b) the Judicial Committee of the Privy Council;
(c) the Court Martial Appeal Court;
(d) in Scotland, the High Court of Justiciary sitting otherwise than as a trial court or the Court of Session;
(e) in England and Wales or Northern Ireland, the High Court or the Court of Appeal.
(f) the Court of Protection, in any matter being dealt with by the President of the Family Division, the Chancellor of the High Court or a puisne judge on the High Court.

(6) A declaration under this section ("a declaration of incompatibility") –
(a) does not affect the validity, continuing operation or enforcement of the provision in respect of which it is given; and
(b) is not binding on the parties to the proceedings in which it is made.

Section 5. (1) Where a court is considering whether to make a declaration of incompatibility, the Crown is entitled to notice in accordance with rules of court.
(2) In any case to which subsection (1) applies –
(a) a Minister of the Crown (or a person nominated by him),
(b) a member of the Scottish Executive,
(c) a Northern Ireland Minister,
(d) a Northern Ireland department,
is entitled, on giving notice in accordance with rules of court, to be joined as a party to the proceedings.
(3) Notice under subsection (2) may be given at any time during the proceedings.
(4) A person who has been made a party to criminal proceedings (other than in Scotland) as the result of a notice under subsection (2) may, with leave, appeal to the Supreme Court against any declaration of incompatibility made in the proceedings.
(5) In subsection (4) –
"criminal proceedings" includes all proceedings before the Court Martial Appeal Court; and
"leave" means leave granted by the court making the declaration of incompatibility or by the Supreme Court.

Section 6. (1) It is unlawful for a public authority to act in a way which is incompatible with a Convention right.
(2) Subsection (1) does not apply to an act if –
(a) as the result of one or more provisions of primary legislation, the authority could not have acted differently; or
(b) in the case of one or more provisions of, or made under, primary legislation which cannot be read or given effect in a way which is compatible with the Convention rights, the authority was acting so as to give effect to or enforce those provisions.
(3) In this section "public authority" includes –
(a) a court or tribunal, and
(b) any person certain of whose functions are functions of a public nature,
but does not include either House of Parliament or a person exercising functions in connection with proceedings in Parliament.
(4) (Repealed).
(5) In relation to a particular act, a person is not a public authority by virtue only of subsection (3)(b) if the nature of the act is private.

(6) "An act" includes a failure to act but does not include a failure to –
(a) introduce in, or lay before, Parliament a proposal for legislation; or
(b) make any primary legislation or remedial order.

Section 7. (1) A person who claims that a public authority has acted (or proposes to act) in a way which is made unlawful by section 6, subsection (1), may –
(a) bring proceedings against the authority under this Act in the appropriate court or tribunal, or
(b) rely on the Convention right or rights concerned in any legal proceedings,
   but only if he is (or would be) a victim of the unlawful act.
(2) In subsection (1)(a) "appropriate court or tribunal" means such court or tribunal as may be determined in accordance with rules; and proceedings against an authority include a counterclaim or similar proceeding.
(3) If the proceedings are brought on an application for judicial review, the applicant is to be taken to have a sufficient interest in relation to the unlawful act only if he is, or would be, a victim of that act.
(4) If the proceedings are made by way of a petition for judicial review in Scotland, the applicant shall be taken to have title and interest to sue in relation to the unlawful act only if he is, or would be, a victim of that act.
(5) Proceedings under subsection (1)(a) must be brought before the end of –
(a) the period of one year beginning with the date on which the act complained of took place; or
(b) such longer period as the court or tribunal considers equitable having regard to all the circumstances,
   but that is subject to any rule imposing a stricter time limit in relation to the procedure in question.
(6) In subsection (1)(b) "legal proceedings" includes –
(a) proceedings brought by or at the instigation of a public authority; and
(b) an appeal against the decision of a court or tribunal.
(7) For the purposes of this section, a person is a victim of an unlawful act only if he would be a victim for the purposes of Article 34 of the Convention if proceedings were brought in the European Court of Human Rights in respect of that act.
(8) Nothing in this Act creates a criminal offence.
(9) In this section "rules" means –
(a) in relation to proceedings before a court or tribunal outside Scotland, rules made by the Lord Chancellor or the Secretary of State for the purposes of this section or rules of court,
(b) in relation to proceedings before a court or tribunal in Scotland, rules made by the Secretary of State for those purposes,
(c) in relation to proceedings before a tribunal in Northern Ireland –

(i) which deals with transferred matters; and

(ii)

for which no rules made under paragraph (a) are in force,

rules made by a Northern Ireland department for those purposes,

and includes provision made by order under section 1 of the Courts and Legal Services Act 1990.

(10) In making rules, regard must be had to section 9.

(11) The Minister who has power to make rules in relation to a particular tribunal may, to the extent he considers it necessary to ensure that the tribunal can provide an appropriate remedy in relation to an act (or proposed act) of a public authority which is (or would be) unlawful as a result of section 6 (1), by order add to –

(a) the relief or remedies which the tribunal may grant; or

(b) the grounds on which it may grant any of them.

(12) An order made under subsection (11) may contain such incidental, supplemental, consequential or transitional provision as the Minister making it considers appropriate.

(13) "The Minister" includes the Northern Ireland department concerned.

Section 8. (1) In relation to any act (or proposed act) of a public authority which the court finds is (or would be) unlawful, it may grant such relief or remedy, or make such order, within its powers as it considers just and appropriate.

(2) But damages may be awarded only by a court which has power to award damages, or to order the payment of compensation, in civil proceedings.

(3) No award of damages is to be made unless, taking account of all the circumstances of the case, including –

(a) any other relief or remedy granted, or order made, in relation to the act in question (by that or any other court), and

(b) the consequences of any decision (of that or any other court) in respect of that act, the court is satisfied that the award is necessary to afford just satisfaction to the person in whose favour it is made.

(4) In determining –

(a) whether to award damages, or

(b) the amount of an award,

the court must take into account the principles applied by the European Court of Human Rights in relation to the award of compensation under Article 41 of the Convention.

(5) A public authority against which damages are awarded is to be treated –

(a) in Scotland, for the purposes of section 3 of the Law Reform (Miscellaneous Provisions) (Scotland) Act 1940 as if the award were made in an action of damages in which the authority has been found liable in respect of loss or damage to the person to whom the award is made;

(b) for the purposes of the Civil Liability (Contribution) Act 1978 as liable in respect of damage suffered by the person to whom the award is made.

(6) In this section –

"court" includes a tribunal;

"damages" means damages for an unlawful act of a public authority; and

"unlawful" means unlawful under section 6 (1).

Section 9. (1) Proceedings under section 7(1)(a) in respect of a judicial act may be brought only –

(a) by exercising a right of appeal;

(b) on an application (in Scotland a petition) for judicial review; or

(c) in such other forum as may be prescribed by rules.

(2) That does not affect any rule of law which prevents a court from being the subject of judicial review.

(3) In proceedings under this Act in respect of a judicial act done in good faith, damages may not be awarded otherwise than to compensate a person to the extent required by Article 5(5) of the Convention.

(4) An award of damages permitted by subsection (3) is to be made against the Crown; but no award may be made unless the appropriate person, if not a party to the proceedings, is joined.

(5) In this section –

"appropriate person" means the Minister responsible for the court concerned, or a person or government department nominated by him;

"court" includes a tribunal;

"judge" includes a member of a tribunal, a justice of the peace (or, in Northern Ireland, a lay magistrate) and a clerk or other officer entitled to exercise the jurisdiction of a court;

"judicial act" means a judicial act of a court and includes an act done on the instructions, or on behalf, of a judge; and

"rules" has the same meaning as in section 7 (9).

Section 10. (1) This section applies if –

(a) a provision of legislation has been declared under section 4 to be incompatible with a Convention right and, if an appeal lies –

  (i) all persons who may appeal have stated in writing that they do not intend to do so;

  (ii) the time for bringing an appeal has expired and no appeal has been brought within that time; or

  (iii) an appeal brought within that time has been determined or abandoned; or

(b) it appears to a Minister of the Crown or Her Majesty in Council that, having regard to a finding of the European Court of Human Rights made after the coming into force of this section in proceedings against the United Kingdom, a provision of legislation is incompatible with an obligation of the United Kingdom arising from the Convention.

(2) If a Minister of the Crown considers that there are compelling reasons for proceeding under this section, he may by order make such amendments to the legislation as he considers necessary to remove the incompatibility.

(3) If, in the case of subordinate legislation, a Minister of the Crown considers –

(a) that it is necessary to amend the primary legislation under which the subordinate legislation in question was made, in order to enable the incompatibility to be removed, and

(b) that there are compelling reasons for proceeding under this section,

he may by order make such amendments to the primary legislation as he considers necessary.

(4) This section also applies where the provision in question is in subordinate legislation and has been quashed, or declared invalid, by reason of incompatibility with a Convention right and the Minister proposes to proceed under paragraph 2(b) of Schedule 2.

(5) If the legislation is an Order in Council, the power conferred by subsection (2) or (3) is exercisable by Her Majesty in Council.

(6) In this section "legislation" does not include a Measure of the Church Assembly or of the General Synod of the Church of England.

(7) Schedule 2 makes further provision about remedial orders.

[*The remainder of the Act proper and Schedule 1 are omitted.*]

Schedule 2 (Remedial Orders)

Paragraph 1. (1) A remedial order may –

(a) contain such incidental, supplemental, consequential or transitional provision as the person making it considers appropriate;

(b) be made so as to have effect from a date earlier than that on which it is made;

(c) make provision for the delegation of specific functions;

(d) make different provision for different cases.

(2) The power conferred by sub-paragraph (1) (a) includes –

(a) power to amend primary legislation (including primary legislation other than that which contains the incompatible provision); and

(b) power to amend or revoke subordinate legislation (including subordinate legislation other than that which contains the incompatible provision).

(3) A remedial order may be made so as to have the same extent as the legislation which it affects.

(4) No person is to be guilty of an offence solely as a result of the retrospective effect of a remedial order.

Paragraph 2. No remedial order may be made unless –
(a) a draft of the order has been approved by a resolution of each House of Parliament made after the end of the period of 60 days beginning with the day on which the draft was laid; or
(b) it is declared in the order that it appears to the person making it that, because of the urgency of the matter, it is necessary to make the order without a draft being so approved.

Paragraph 3. (1) No draft may be laid under paragraph 2(a) unless –
(a) the person proposing to make the order has laid before Parliament a document which contains a draft of the proposed order and the required information; and
(b) the period of 60 days, beginning with the day on which the document required by this sub-paragraph was laid, has ended.
(2) If representations have been made during that period, the draft laid under paragraph 2(a) must be accompanied by a statement containing –
(a) a summary of the representations; and
(b) if, as a result of the representations, the proposed order has been changed, details of the changes.

Paragraph 4. (1) If a remedial order ("the original order") is made without being approved in draft, the person making it must lay it before Parliament, accompanied by the required information, after it is made.
(2) If representations have been made during the period of 60 days beginning with the day on which the original order was made, the person making it must (after the end of that period) lay before Parliament a statement containing –
(a) a summary of the representations; and
(b) if, as a result of the representations, he considers it appropriate to make changes to the original order, details of the changes.
(3) If sub-paragraph (2) (b) applies, the person making the statement must –
(a) make a further remedial order replacing the original order; and
(b) lay the replacement order before Parliament.
(4) If, at the end of the period of 120 days beginning with the day on which the original order was made, a resolution has not been passed by each House approving the original or replacement order, the order ceases to have effect (but without that affecting anything previously done under either order or the power to make a fresh remedial order).

Paragraph 5. In this Schedule –
"representations" means representations about a remedial order (or proposed remedial order) made to the person making (or proposing to make) it and includes any relevant Parliamentary report or resolution; and

"required information" means –
(a) an explanation of the incompatibility which the order (or proposed order) seeks to remove, including particulars of the relevant declaration, finding or order; and
(b) a statement of the reasons for proceeding under section 10 and for making an order in those terms.

Paragraph 6. In calculating any period for the purposes of this Schedule, no account is to be taken of any time during which –
(a) Parliament is dissolved or prorogued; or
(b) both Houses are adjourned for more than four days.

Paragraph 7. (1) This paragraph applies in relation to –
(a) any remedial order made, and any draft of such an order proposed to be made, –
  (i) by the Scottish Ministers; or
  (ii) within devolved competence (within the meaning of the Scotland Act 1998) by Her Majesty in Council; and
(b) any document or statement to be laid in connection with such an order (or proposed order).
(2) This Schedule has effect in relation to any such order (or proposed order), document or statement subject to the following modifications.
(3) Any reference to Parliament, each House of Parliament or both Houses of Parliament shall be construed as a reference to the Scottish Parliament.
(4) Paragraph 6 does not apply and instead, in calculating any period for the purposes of this Schedule, no account is to be taken of any time during which the Scottish Parliament is dissolved or is in recess for more than four days.

[*The remaining Schedules are omitted.*]

15   CONSTITUTIONAL REFORM ACT 2005[5]

Part 1: The Rule of Law

Section 1. This Act does not adversely affect—
(a) the existing principle of the rule of law, or
(b) the Lord Chancellor's existing constitutional role in relation to that principle.

[*Part 2 is omitted.*]

Part 3: The Supreme Court

Section 23. (1) There is to be a Supreme Court of the United Kingdom.
(2) The Court consists of the persons appointed as its judges by Her Majesty by letters patent, but no appointment may cause the full-time equivalent number of judges of the Court at any time to be more than 12.
(3) Her Majesty may from time to time by Order in Council amend subsection (2) so as to increase or further increase the maximum full-time equivalent number of judges of the Court.
(4) No recommendation may be made to Her Majesty in Council to make an Order under subsection (3) unless a draft of the Order has been laid before and approved by resolution of each House of Parliament.
(5) Her Majesty may by letters patent appoint one of the judges to be President and one to be Deputy President of the Court.
(6) The judges other than the President and Deputy President are to be styled "Justices of the Supreme Court".
(7) The Court is to be taken to be duly constituted despite any vacancy in the office of President or Deputy President.
(8) For the purposes of this section, the full-time equivalent number of judges of the Court is to be calculated by taking the number of full-time judges and adding, for each judge who is not a full-time judge, such fraction as is reasonable.

Section 24. On the commencement of section 23—
(a) the persons who immediately before that commencement are Lords of Appeal in Ordinary become judges of the Supreme Court.
(b) the person who immediately before that commencement is the senior Lord of Appeal in Ordinary becomes the President of the Court, and

---

5   As last amended in its relevant parts by the Courts Reform (Scotland) Act 2014 (asp 18). Selected provisions: Part 1; Part 3, Sections 23-33, 35, 41, and 42.

(c) the person who immediately before that commencement is the second senior Lord of Appeal in Ordinary becomes the Deputy President of the Court.

Section 25. (1) A person is not qualified to be appointed a judge of the Supreme Court unless he has (at any time)—
(a) held high judicial office for a period of at least 2 years,
(b) satisfied the judicial-appointment eligibility condition on a 15-year basis, or
(c) been a qualifying practitioner for a period of at least 15 years.
(2) A person is a qualifying practitioner for the purposes of this section at any time when—
(a) (repealed),
(b) he is an advocate in Scotland or a solicitor entitled to appear in the Court of Session and the High Court of Justiciary, or
(c) he is a member of the Bar of Northern Ireland or a solicitor of the Court of Judicature of Northern Ireland.

Section 26. (1) This section applies to a recommendation for an appointment to one of the following offices—
(a) judge of the Supreme Court;
(b) President of the Court;
(c) Deputy President of the Court.
(2) A recommendation may be made only by the Prime Minister.
(3) The Prime Minister—
(a) must recommend any person who is selected as a result of the convening of a selection commission under this section;
(b) may not recommend any other person.
(4) Where a person who is not a judge of the Court is recommended for appointment as President or Deputy President, the recommendation must also recommend the person for appointment as a judge.
(5) If there is a vacancy in the office of President of the Court or in the office of Deputy President of the Court, or it appears to him that there will soon be such a vacancy, the Lord Chancellor must convene a selection commission for the selection of a person to be recommended.
(5A) If—
(a) the full-time equivalent number of judges of the Court is less than the maximum specified in section 23(2), or it appears to the Lord Chancellor that the full-time equivalent number of judges of the Court will soon be less than that maximum, and
(b) the Lord Chancellor, or the senior judge of the Court, after consulting the other considers it desirable that a recommendation be made for an appointment to the office of judge of the Court,

the Lord Chancellor must convene a selection commission for the selection of a person to be recommended.

(5B) In subsection (5A)(b) "the senior judge of the Court" means—

(a) the President of the Court, or

(b) if there is no President, the Deputy President, or

(c) if there is no President and no Deputy President, the senior ordinary judge.

(6) Schedule 8 is about selection commissions.

(7) Subsections (5) and (5A) are subject to Schedule 8 (cases where duty to convene a selection commission are suspended).

(7A) For the purposes of this section and Schedule 8, a person is selected as a result of the convening of a selection commission if the person's selection is the final outcome of—

(a) the selection process mentioned in section 27(1) being applied by the commission, and

(b) any process provided for by regulations under section 27A being applied in the particular case.

(8) Section 27 applies where a selection commission is convened under this section.

Section 27. (1) The commission must—

(a) determine the selection process to be applied by it,

(b) apply the selection process, and

(c) make a selection accordingly.

(1A) The commission must have an odd number of members not less than five.

(1B) The members of the commission must include—

(a) at least one who is non-legally-qualified,

(b) at least one judge of the Court,

(c) at least one member of the Judicial Appointments Commission,

(d) at least one member of the Judicial Appointments Board for Scotland, and

(e) at least one member of the Northern Ireland Judicial Appointments Commission, and more than one of the requirements may be met by the same person's membership of the commission.

(1C) If the commission is convened for the selection of a person to be recommended for appointment as President of the Court—

(a) its members may not include the President of the Court, and

(b) it is to be chaired by one of its non-legally-qualified members.

(1D) If the commission is convened for the selection of a person to be recommended for appointment as Deputy President of the Court, its members may not include the Deputy President of the Court.

(2) (Repealed.)

(3) (Repealed.)

(4) Subsections (5) to (10) apply to any selection under this section or regulations under section 27A.

(5) Selection must be on merit.

(5A) Where two persons are of equal merit—

(a) section 159 of the Equality Act 2010 (positive action: recruitment etc) does not apply in relation to choosing between them, but

(b) Part 5 of that Act (public appointments etc) does not prevent the commission from preferring one of them over the other for the purpose of increasing diversity within the group of persons who are the judges of the Court.

(6) A person may be selected only if he meets the requirements of section 25.

(7) A person may not be selected if he is a member of the commission.

(8) In making selections for the appointment of judges of the Court the commission must ensure that between them the judges will have knowledge of, and experience of practice in, the law of each part of the United Kingdom.

(9) The commission must have regard to any guidance given by the Lord Chancellor as to matters to be taken into account (subject to any other provision of this Act) in making a selection.

(10) Any selection must be of one person only.

(11) For the purposes of this section a person is non-legally-qualified if the person—

(a) does not hold, and has never held, any of the offices listed in Schedule 1 to the House of Commons Disqualification Act 1975 (judicial offices disqualifying for membership of the House of Commons), and

(b) is not practising or employed as a lawyer, and never has practised or been employed as a lawyer.

Section 27A. (1) The Lord Chancellor must by regulations made with the agreement of the senior judge of the Supreme Court—

(a) make further provision about membership of selection commissions convened under section 26,

(b) make further provision about the process that is to be applied in any case where a selection commission is required to be convened under section 26, and

(c) secure that, in every such case, there will come a point in the process when a selection has to be accepted, either unconditionally or subject only to matters such as the selected person's willingness and availability, by or on behalf of the Lord Chancellor.

(2) The regulations may in particular—

(a) provide for process additional to the selection process applied by a selection commission under section 27(1), including post-acceptance process;

(b) make provision as to things that are, or as to things that are not, to be done by a selection commission—
   (i) as part of the selection process applied by it under section 27(1), or
   (ii) in determining what that process is to be;
(c) provide for the Lord Chancellor to be entitled to require a selection commission to reconsider a selection under section 27(1) or any subsequent selection;
(d) provide for the Lord Chancellor to be entitled to reject a selection under section 27(1) or any subsequent selection;
(e) give other functions to the Lord Chancellor;
(f) provide for particular action to be taken by a selection commission after it has complied with section 27;
(g) provide for the dissolution of a selection commission;
(h) provide for section 16(2)(a) or (b) not to apply in relation to functions of the Lord Chief Justice—
   (i) as a member of a selection commission (including functions of chairing a selection commission), or
   (ii) in relation to the nomination or appointment of members of a selection commission;
(i) provide for a person to cease to be a member of a selection commission where a requirement about the commission's members ceases to be met by the person's membership of the commission;
(j) provide for a person to become a member of a selection commission already convened where another person ceases to be a member of the commission or where a requirement about the commission's members ceases to be met by another person's membership of the commission;
(k) provide for payment to a member of a selection commission of amounts by way of allowances or expenses;
(l) make provision as to what amounts to practice or employment as a lawyer for the purposes of section 27(11)(b).
(3) Before making regulations under this section the Lord Chancellor must consult—
(a) the First Minister in Scotland,
(b) the Northern Ireland Judicial Appointments Commission,
(c) the First Minister for Wales,
(d) the Lord President of the Court of Session,
(e) the Lord Chief Justice of Northern Ireland, and
(f) the Lord Chief Justice of England and Wales.
(4) Regulations under this section—
(a) may make different provision for different purposes;

(b) may make transitory, transitional or saving provision.
(5) In this section "the senior judge", in relation to the Court, has the meaning given by section 26(5B).

Section 27B. (1) Before issuing any selection guidance the Lord Chancellor must—
(a) consult the senior judge of the Supreme Court;
(b) after doing so, lay a draft of the proposed guidance before each House of Parliament.
(2) If the draft is approved by a resolution of each House of Parliament within the 40-day period the Lord Chancellor must issue the guidance in the form of the draft.
(3) In any other case the Lord Chancellor must take no further steps in relation to the proposed guidance.
(4) Subsection (3) does not prevent a new draft of the proposed guidance from being laid before each House of Parliament after consultation with the senior judge of the Court.
(5) Selection guidance comes into force on such date as the Lord Chancellor may appoint by order.
(6) Where selection guidance is in force, the Lord Chancellor may revoke the guidance only by—
(a) new selection guidance issued in accordance with the previous provisions of this section, or
(b) an order made after consulting the senior judge of the Court.
(7) In this section—
"40-day period" in relation to the draft of any proposed selection guidance means—
(a) if the draft is laid before one House on a day later than the day on which it is laid before the other House, the period of 40 days beginning with the later day, and
(b) in any other case, the period of 40 days beginning with the day on which the draft is laid before each House,
no account being taken of any period during which Parliament is dissolved or prorogued or during which both Houses are adjourned for more than 4 days;
"the senior judge", in relation to the Court, has the meaning given by section 26(5B);
"selection guidance" means guidance mentioned in section 27(9).

Section 28. (Repealed.)

Section 29. (Repealed.)

Section 30. (Repealed.)

Section 31. (Repealed.)

Section 32. (1) A person who is appointed as President of the Court must, as soon as may be after accepting office, take the required oaths in the presence of—
(a) the Deputy President, or
(b) if there is no Deputy President, the senior ordinary judge.
(2) A person who is appointed as Deputy President of the Supreme Court must, as soon as may be after accepting office, take the required oaths in the presence of—
(a) the President, or
(b) if there is no President, the senior ordinary judge.
(3) A person who is appointed as a judge of the Supreme Court must, as soon as may be after accepting office, take the required oaths in the presence of—
(a) the President, or
(b) if there is no President, the Deputy President, or
(c) if there is no President and no Deputy President, the senior ordinary judge.
(4) Subsections (1) and (2) apply whether or not the person appointed as President or Deputy President has previously taken the required oaths in accordance with this section after accepting another office.
(5) Subsection (3) does not apply where a person is first appointed as a judge of the Court upon appointment to the office of President or Deputy President.
(6) In this section "required oaths" means—
(a) the oath of allegiance, and
(b) the judicial oath,
   as set out in the Promissory Oaths Act 1868.

Section 33. A judge of the Supreme Court holds that office during good behaviour, but may be removed from it on the address of both Houses of Parliament.

[Section 34 is omitted]

Section 35. (1) A judge of the Supreme Court may at any time resign that office by giving the Lord Chancellor notice in writing to that effect.
(2) The President or Deputy President of the Court may at any time resign that office (whether or not he resigns his office as a judge) by giving the Lord Chancellor notice in writing to that effect.
(3) [omitted]

[Sections 36-39 are omitted.]

Section 40. (1) The Supreme Court is a superior court of record.
(2) An appeal lies to the Court from any order or judgment of the Court of Appeal in England and Wales in civil proceedings.

(3) (Repealed.)

(4) Schedule 9—

(a) transfers other jurisdiction from the House of Lords to the Court.

(b) transfers devolution jurisdiction from the Judicial Committee of the Privy Council to the Court, and

(c) makes other amendments relating to jurisdiction.

(5) The Court has power to determine any question necessary to be determined for the purposes of doing justice in an appeal to it under any enactment.

(6) An appeal under subsection (2) lies only with the permission of the Court of Appeal or the Supreme Court; but this is subject to provision under any other enactment restricting such an appeal.

Section 41. (1) Nothing in this Part is to affect the distinctions between the separate legal systems of the parts of the United Kingdom.

(2) A decision of the Supreme Court on appeal from a court of any part of the United Kingdom, other than a decision on a devolution matter, is to be regarded as the decision of a court of that part of the United Kingdom.

(3) A decision of the Supreme Court on a devolution matter—

(a) is not binding on that Court when making such a decision;

(b) otherwise, is binding in all legal proceedings.

(4) In this section "devolution matter" means—

(a) a question referred to the Supreme Court under section 99 or 112 of the Government of Wales Act 2006, section 33 of the Scotland Act 1998 or section 11 of the Northern Ireland Act 1998;

(b) a devolution issue as defined in Schedule 9 to the Government of Wales Act 2006, Schedule 6 to the Scotland Act 1998 or Schedule 10 to the Northern Ireland Act 1998.

[*The remainder of the act is omitted.*]

16 United Kingdom: Constitutional Reform and Governance Act 2010[6]

[*Part 1 is omitted.*]

Part 2: Ratification of treaties

Section 20. (1) Subject to what follows, a treaty is not to be ratified unless—
(a) a Minister of the Crown has laid before Parliament a copy of the treaty,
(b) the treaty has been published in a way that a Minister of the Crown thinks appropriate, and
(b) period A has expired without either House having resolved, within period A, that the treaty should not be ratified.
(2) Period A is the period of 21 sitting days beginning with the first sitting day after the date on which the requirement in subsection (1) (a) is met.
(3) Subsections (4) to (6) apply if the House of Commons resolved as mentioned in subsection (1) (c) (whether or not the House of Lords also did so).
(4) The treaty may be ratified if—
(a) a Minister of the Crown has laid before Parliament a statement indicating that the Minister is of the opinion that the treaty should nevertheless be ratified and explaining why, and
(b) period B has expired without the House of Commons having resolved, within period B, that the treaty should not be ratified.
(5) Period B is the period of 21 sitting days beginning with the first sitting day after the date on which the requirement in subsection (4) (a) is met.
(6) A statement may be laid under subsection (4) (a) in relation to the treaty on more than one occasion.
(7) Subsection (8) applies if—
(a) the House of Lords resolved as mentioned in subsection (1) (c), but
(b) the House of Commons did not.
(8) The treaty may be ratified if a Minister of the Crown has laid before Parliament a statement indicating that the Minister is of the opinion that the treaty should nevertheless be ratified and explaining why.
(9) "Sitting day" means a day on which both Houses of Parliament sit.

Section 21. (1) A Minister of the Crown may, in relation to a treaty, extend the period mentioned in section 20 (1) (c) by 21 sitting days or less.
(2) The Minister does that by laying before Parliament a statement—
(a) indicating that the period is to be extended, and

---

6   As last amended by the European Union (Withdrawal) Act 2018 (c. 16); Selected provisions: Part 2.

(b) setting out the length of the extension.

(3) The statement must be laid before the period would have expired without the extension.

(4) The Minister must publish the statement in a way the Minister thinks appropriate.

(5) The period may be extended more than once.

Section 22. (1) Section 20 does not apply to a treaty if a Minister of the Crown is of the opinion that, exceptionally, the treaty should be ratified without the requirements of that section having been met.

(2) But a treaty may not be ratified by virtue of subsection (1) after either House has resolved, as mentioned in section 20 (1) (c), that the treaty should not be ratified.

(3) If a Minister determines that a treaty is to be ratified by virtue of subsection (1), the Minister must, either before or as soon as practicable after the treaty is ratified—

(a) lay before Parliament a copy of the treaty,

(b) arrange for the treaty to be published in a way that the Minister thinks appropriate, and

(c) lay before Parliament a statement indicating that the Minister is of the opinion mentioned in subsection (1) and explaining why.

Section 23. (1) (Repealed)

(2) Section 20 does not apply to a treaty in relation to which an Order in Council may be made under one or more of the following—

(a) section 158 of the Inheritance Tax Act 1984 (double taxation conventions);

(b) section 2 of the Taxation (International and Other Provisions) Act 2010 (double taxation arrangements);

(c) section 173 of the Finance Act 2006 (international tax enforcement arrangements).

(2A) Section 20 does not apply to a treaty in relation to which an order may be made under paragraph 66 of Schedule 19 to the Finance Act 2011 (bank levy: arrangements affording double taxation relief).

(2B) Section 20 does not apply to any treaty referred to in section 218(1) of the Finance Act 2012.

(3) Section 20 does not apply to a treaty concluded (under authority given by the government of the United Kingdom) by the government of a British overseas territory, of any of the Channel Islands or of the Isle of Man.

(4) Section 20 does not apply to a treaty a copy of which is presented to Parliament by command of Her Majesty before that section comes into force.

Section 24. In laying a treaty before Parliament under this Part, a Minister shall accompany the treaty with an explanatory memorandum explaining the provisions of the treaty, the reasons for Her Majesty's Government seeking ratification of the treaty, and such other matters as the Minister considers appropriate.

Section 25. (1) In this Part "treaty" means a written agreement—
(a) between States or between States and international organisations, and
(b) binding under international law.
(2) But "treaty" does not include a regulation, rule, measure, decision or similar instrument made under a treaty (other than one that amends or replaces the treaty (in whole or in part)).
(3) In this Part a reference to ratification of a treaty is a reference to an act of a kind specified in subsection (4) which establishes as a matter of international law the United Kingdom's consent to be bound by the treaty.
(4) The acts are—
(a) deposit or delivery of an instrument of ratification, accession, approval or acceptance;
(b) deposit or delivery of a notification of completion of domestic procedures.

[*The remainder of the Act is omitted.*]

17 Scotland Act 1998[7]

Part I. The Scottish Parliament

Section 1. (1) There shall be a Scottish Parliament.

(2) One member of the Parliament shall be returned for each constituency (under the simple majority system) at an election held in the constituency.

(3) Members of the Parliament for each region shall be returned at a general election under the additional member system of proportional representation provided for in this Part and vacancies among such members shall be filled in accordance with this Part.

(4) The validity of any proceedings of the Parliament is not affected by any vacancy in its membership.

(5) Schedule 1 (which makes provision for the constituencies and regions for the purposes of this Act and the number of regional members) shall have effect.

[*Sections 2-27 are omitted.*]

Section 28. (1) Subject to section 29, the Parliament may make laws, to be known as Acts of the Scottish Parliament.

(2) Proposed Acts of the Scottish Parliament shall be known as Bills; and a Bill shall become an Act of the Scottish Parliament when it has been passed by the Parliament and has received Royal Assent.

(3) A Bill receives Royal Assent at the beginning of the day on which Letters Patent under the Scottish Seal signed with Her Majesty's own hand signifying Her Assent are recorded in the Register of the Great Seal.

(4) The date of Royal Assent shall be written on the Act of the Scottish Parliament by the Clerk, and shall form part of the Act.

(5) The validity of an Act of the Scottish Parliament is not affected by any invalidity in the proceedings of the Parliament leading to its enactment.

(6) Every Act of the Scottish Parliament shall be judicially noticed.

(7) This section does not affect the power of the Parliament of the United Kingdom to make laws for Scotland.

(8) But it is recognised that the Parliament of the United Kingdom will not normally legislate with regard to devolved matters without the consent of the Scottish Parliament.

---

7 An Act to provide for the establishment of a Scottish Parliament and Administration and other changes in the government of Scotland; to provide for changes in the constitution and functions of certain public authorities; to provide for the variation of the basic rate of income tax in relation to income of Scottish taxpayers in accordance with a resolution of the Scottish Parliament; to amend the law about parliamentary constituencies in Scotland; and for connected purposes, as last amended by the European Union (Withdrawal) Act 2018 (c. 16). Selected provisions: Sections 1, 28 and 29; Schedule 5, Part I and Part II (Heads A and B).

Section 29. (1) An Act of the Scottish Parliament is not law so far as any provision of the Act is outside the legislative competence of the Parliament.

(2) A provision is outside that competence so far as any of the following paragraphs apply—

(a) it would form part of the law of a country or territory other than Scotland, or confer or remove functions exercisable otherwise than in or as regards Scotland,
(b) it relates to reserved matters,
(c) it is in breach of the restrictions in Schedule 4,
(d) it is incompatible with any of the Convention rights or with EU law,
(e) it would remove the Lord Advocate from his position as head of the systems of criminal prosecution and investigation of deaths in Scotland.

(3) For the purposes of this section, the question whether a provision of an Act of the Scottish Parliament relates to a reserved matter is to be determined, subject to subsection (4), by reference to the purpose of the provision, having regard (among other things) to its effect in all the circumstances.

(4) A provision which—

(a) would otherwise not relate to reserved matters, but
(b) makes modifications of Scots private law, or Scots criminal law, as it applies to reserved matters,

is to be treated as relating to reserved matters unless the purpose of the provision is to make the law in question apply consistently to reserved matters and otherwise.

(5) Subsection (1) is subject to section 30(6).

[*The remainder of the Act is omitted.*]

Schedules
[*Schedules 1-4 are omitted.*]

Schedule 5. Reserved Matters

Part I. General Reservations

The Constitution

Paragraph 1. The following aspects of the constitution are reserved matters, that is—
(a) the Crown, including succession to the Crown and a regency,
(b) the Union of the Kingdoms of Scotland and England,
(c) the Parliament of the United Kingdom,
(d) the continued existence of the High Court of **Justiciary** as a criminal court of first instance and of appeal,

(e) the continued existence of the Court of Session as a civil court of first instance and of appeal.

Paragraph 2. (1) Paragraph 1 does not reserve—
(a) Her Majesty's prerogative and other executive functions,
(b) functions exercisable by any person acting on behalf of the Crown, or
(c) any office in the Scottish Administration.
(2) Sub-paragraph (1) does not affect the reservation by paragraph 1 of honours and dignities or the functions of the Lord Lyon King of Arms so far as relating to the granting of arms; but this sub-paragraph does not apply to the Lord Lyon King of Arms in his judicial capacity.
(3) Sub-paragraph (1) does not affect the reservation by paragraph 1 of the management (in accordance with any enactment regulating the use of land) of the Crown Estate (that is, the property, rights and interests under the management of the Crown Estate Commissioners).
(3A) Sub-paragraph (1) does not affect the reservation by paragraph 1 of the requirements of section 90B(5) to (8).
(4) Sub-paragraph (1) does not affect the reservation by paragraph 1 of the functions of the Security Service, the Secret Intelligence Service and the Government Communications Headquarters.
(5) Sub-paragraph (1) does not affect the reservation by paragraph 1 of the functions exercisable through the Export Credits Guarantee Department.

Paragraph 3. (1) Paragraph 1 does not reserve property belonging to Her Majesty in right of the Crown or belonging to any person acting on behalf of the Crown or held in trust for Her Majesty for the purposes of any person acting on behalf of the Crown.
(2) Paragraph 1 does not reserve the ultimate superiority of the Crown or the superiority of the Prince and Steward of Scotland.
(3) Sub-paragraph (1) does not affect the reservation by paragraph 1 of—
(a) the hereditary revenues of the Crown, other than revenues from **bona vacantia, ultimus haeres** and treasure trove,
(b) the royal arms and standard,
(c) the compulsory acquisition of property held or used by a Minister of the Crown or government department.

Paragraph 4. (1) Paragraph 1 does not reserve property held by Her Majesty in Her private capacity.
(2) Sub-paragraph (1) does not affect the reservation by paragraph 1 of the subject-matter of the Crown Private Estates Acts 1800 to 1873.

United Kingdom

Paragraph 5. Paragraph 1 does not reserve the use of the Scottish Seal.

Political parties

Paragraph 6. The registration and funding of political parties is a reserved matter but this paragraph does not reserve making payments to any political party for the purpose of assisting members of the Parliament who are connected with the party to perform their Parliamentary duties.

Foreign affairs etc.

Paragraph 7. (1) International relations, including relations with territories outside the United Kingdom, the European Union (and their institutions) and other international organisations, regulation of international trade, and international development assistance and co-operation are reserved matters.
(2) Sub-paragraph (1) does not reserve—
(a) observing and implementing international obligations, obligations under the Human Rights Convention and obligations under EU law,
(b) assisting Ministers of the Crown in relation to any matter to which that sub-paragraph applies.

Public service

Paragraph 8. (1) The Civil Service of the State is a reserved matter.
(2) Sub-paragraph (1) does not reserve the subject-matter of—
(a) Part I of the Sheriff Courts and Legal Officers (Scotland) Act 1927 (appointment of sheriff clerks and procurators fiscal etc.),
(b) Part III of the Administration of Justice (Scotland) Act 1933 (officers of the High Court of **Justiciary** and of the Court of Session).

Defence

Paragraph 9. (1) The following are reserved matters—
(a) the defence of the realm,
(b) the naval, military or air forces of the Crown, including reserve forces,
(c) visiting forces,
(d) international headquarters and defence organisations,
(e) trading with the enemy and enemy property.
(2) Sub-paragraph (1) does not reserve—

(a) the exercise of civil defence functions by any person otherwise than as a member of any force or organisation referred to in sub-paragraph (1) (b) to (d) or any other force or organisation reserved by virtue of sub-paragraph (1) (a),

(b) the conferral of enforcement powers in relation to sea fishing.

Treason

Paragraph 10. Treason (including constructive treason), treason felony and misprision of treason are reserved matters.

Part II. Specific reservations

Preliminary

Paragraph 1. The matters to which any of the Sections in this Part apply are reserved matters for the purposes of this Act.

Paragraph 2. A Section applies to any matter described or referred to in it when read with any illustrations, exceptions or interpretation provisions in that Section.

Paragraph 3. Any illustrations, exceptions or interpretation provisions in a Section relate only to that Section (so that an entry under the heading "exceptions" does not affect any other Section).

Reservations

Head A – Financial and Economic Matters

A1. Fiscal, economic and monetary policy
Section A1. Fiscal, economic and monetary policy, including the issue and **circulation** of money, taxes and excise duties, government borrowing and lending, control over United Kingdom public expenditure, the exchange rate and the Bank of England.
Exceptions. Devolved taxes, including their collection and management. Local taxes to fund local authority expenditure (for example, council tax and non-domestic rates).

A2. The currency
Section A2. Coinage, legal tender and bank notes.

A3. Financial services

Section A3. Financial services, including investment business, banking and deposit-taking, collective investment schemes and insurance.

Exception. The subject-matter of section 1 of the Banking and Financial Dealings Act 1971 (bank holidays).

A4. Financial markets

Section A4. Financial markets, including listing and public offers of securities and investments, transfer of securities and insider dealing.

A5. Money laundering

Section A5. The subject-matter of the Money Laundering Regulations 1993, but in relation to any type of business.

Head B – Home Affairs

B1. Misuse of drugs

Section B1. The subject-matter of—
(a) the Misuse of Drugs Act 1971,
(b) sections 12 to 14 of the Criminal Justice (International Co-operation) Act 1990 (substances useful for manufacture of controlled drugs), and
(c) Part V of the Criminal Law (Consolidation) (Scotland) Act 1995 (drug trafficking) and, so far as relating to drug trafficking, the Proceeds of Crime (Scotland) Act 1995.

B2. Data protection

Section B2. The subject-matter of—
(a) the Data Protection Act 1998, and
(b) Council Directive 95/46/EC (protection of individuals with regard to the processing of personal data and on the free movement of such data).
Interpretation. If any provision of the Data Protection Act 1998 is not in force on the principal appointed day, it is to be treated for the purposes of this reservation as if it were.

B3. Elections

Section B3. Elections for membership of the House of Commons, the European Parliament and the Parliament, including the subject-matter of—
(a) the European Parliamentary Elections Act 2002.
(b) the Representation of the People Act 1983 and the Representation of the People Act 1985, and

(b) the Parliamentary Constituencies Act 1986,

so far as those enactments apply, or may be applied, in respect of such membership. Interpretation. Paragraph 5 (1) of Part 3 of this Schedule does not apply to the subject-matter of the European Parliamentary Elections Act 2002; and the reference to the subject-matter of that Act is to be construed as a reference to it as at the date that Act received Royal Assent.

B4. Firearms

Section B4. The subject-matter of the Firearms Acts 1968 to 1997.

Exception. The regulation of air weapons within the meaning given by section 1(3)(b) of the Firearms Act 1968 (which is subject to the following which remain powers of the Secretary of State—

(a) the power to make rules under section 53 of that Act for the purposes of that provision (specially dangerous weapons requiring firearms certificate), and

(b) the power to make an order under section 1(4) of the Firearms (Amendment) Act 1988 (specially dangerous weapons to be prohibited)).

B5. Entertainment

Section B5. The subject-matter of—

(a) the Video Recordings Act 1984, and

(b) sections 1 to 3 and 5 to 16 of the Cinemas Act 1985 (control of exhibitions).

The classification of films for public exhibition by reference to their suitability for viewing by persons generally or above a particular age, with or without any advice as to the desirability of parental guidance.

B6. Immigration and nationality

Section B6. Nationality; immigration, including asylum and the status and capacity of persons in the United Kingdom who are not British citizens; free movement of persons within the European Economic Area; issue of travel documents.

B7. Scientific procedures on live animals

Section B7. The subject-matter of the Animals (Scientific Procedures) Act 1986.

B8. National security, interception of communications, official secrets and terrorism

Section B8. National security.

The interception of communications; but not

(a) the interception of any communication made to or by a person detained at a place of detention, if the communication—

(i) is a written communication and is intercepted there, or

(ii) is intercepted in the course of its transmission by means of a private telecommunication system running there,
(b) the subject matter of Part III of the Police Act 1997 (authorisation to interfere with property etc.) or surveillance not involving interference with property.

The subject-matter of—
(a) the Official Secrets Acts 1911 and 1920, and
(b) the Official Secrets Act 1989, except so far as relating to any information, document or other article protected against disclosure by section 4 (2) (crime) and not by any other provision of sections 1 to 4.

Special powers, and other special provisions, for dealing with terrorism.

Interpretation. "Place of detention" means a prison, young offenders institution, remand centre or legalised police cell (as those expressions are defined for the purposes of the Prisons (Scotland) Act 1989 or a hospital (within the meaning of the given in section 329 (1) of the Mental Health (Care and Treatment) (Scotland) Act 2003; and "person detained", in relation to a hospital, means a person detained there under—
(a) section 24, 25 or 70 of the Mental Health (Scotland) Act 1984;
(b) Part 6 of the Criminal Procedure (Scotland) Act 1995;
(c) the Mental Health (Care and Treatment) (Scotland) Act 2003; or
(d) regulations under—
   (i) subsection (3) of section 116B of the Army Act 1955;
   (ii) subsection (3) of section 116B of the Air Force Act 1955; or
   (iii) section 63B of the Naval Discipline Act 1957.

"Private telecommunication system" has the meaning given in section 261(14) of the Investigatory Powers Act 2016.

B9. Betting, gaming and lotteries
Section B9. Betting, gaming and lotteries.
Exception. In the case of a betting premises licence under the Gambling Act 2005, other than one in respect of a track, the number of gaming machines authorised for which the maximum charge for use is more than £10 (or whether such machines are authorised).

B10. Emergency powers
Section B10. Emergency powers.

B11. Extradition
Section B11. Extradition.

B12. Lieutenancies

Section B12. The subject-matter of the Lieutenancies Act 1997.

Access to information

Public access to information held by public bodies or holders of public offices (including government departments and persons acting on behalf of the Crown).

Exception. Information held by–

(a) the Parliament,
(b) any part of the Scottish Administration,
(c) the Parliamentary corporation,
(d) any Scottish public authority with mixed functions or no reserved functions,
   unless supplied by a Minister of the Crown or government department and held in confidence.

[*The provisions of heads C – L are omitted.*]

[*Schedules 6-9 are omitted.*]

18 Northern Ireland Act 1998[8]

[*Sections 1-3 are omitted.*]

Section 4. (1) In this Act—
"excepted matter" means any matter falling within a description specified in Schedule 2;
"reserved matter" means any matter falling within a description specified in Schedule 3;
"transferred matter" means any matter which is not an excepted or reserved matter.
(2) If at any time after the appointed day it appears to the Secretary of State—
(a) that any reserved matter should become a transferred matter; or
(b) that any transferred matter should become a reserved matter,
he may, subject to subsections (2A) to (3D), lay before Parliament the draft of an Order in Council amending Schedule 3 so that the matter ceases to be or, as the case may be, becomes a reserved matter with effect from such date as may be specified in the Order.
(2A)The Secretary of State shall not lay before Parliament under subsection (2) the draft of an Order amending Schedule 3 so that a policing and justice matter ceases to be a reserved matter unless—
(a) a motion for a resolution praying that the matter should cease to be a reserved matter is tabled by the First Minister and the deputy First Minister acting jointly; and
(b) the resolution is passed by the Assembly with the support of a majority of the members voting on the motion, a majority of the designated Nationalists voting and a majority of the designated Unionists voting.
(3) The Secretary of State shall not lay before Parliament under subsection (2) the draft of any other Order unless the Assembly has passed with cross-community support a resolution praying that the matter concerned should cease to be or, as the case may be, should become a reserved matter.
(3A) The Secretary of State shall not lay before Parliament under subsection (2) the draft of an Order amending paragraph 16 of Schedule 3 (Civil Service Commissioners for Northern Ireland) unless the Secretary of State has, at least three months before laying the draft, laid a report before Parliament.
(3B) The report under subsection (3A) must set out the Secretary of State's view of the effect (if any) that the Order would have on—
(a) the independence of the Civil Service Commissioners for Northern Ireland;
(b) the application of the principle that persons should be selected for appointment to the Northern Ireland Civil Service on merit on the basis of fair and open competition; and

---

[8] An Act to make new provision for the government of Northern Ireland for the purpose of implementing the agreement reached at multi-party talks on Northern Ireland set out in Command Paper 3883, as last amended by the European Union (Withdrawal) Act 2018 (c. 16). Selected provisions: Sections 4-6, 33, 34; Schedules 2 and 3.

(c) the impartiality of the Northern Ireland Civil Service.

(3C) The Secretary of State shall not lay before Parliament under subsection (2) the draft of an Order amending paragraph 42(aa) of Schedule 3 (Northern Ireland Human Rights Commission) unless the Secretary of State has, at least three months before laying the draft, laid a report before Parliament.

(3D) The report under subsection (3C) must set out the Secretary of State's view of the effect (if any) that the Order would have on—

(a) the independence of the Northern Ireland Human Rights Commission;

(b) the application of internationally accepted principles relating to national human rights institutions; and

(c) the relationship between the Northern Ireland Human Rights Commission and the Assembly.

(4) If the draft of an Order laid before Parliament under subsection (2) is approved by resolution of each House of Parliament, the Secretary of State shall submit it to Her Majesty in Council and Her Majesty in Council may make the Order.

(5) In this Act—

"the Assembly" means the New Northern Ireland Assembly, which after the appointed day shall be known as the Northern Ireland Assembly;

"cross-community support", in relation to a vote on any matter, means—

(a) the support of a majority of the members voting, a majority of the designated Nationalists voting and a majority of the designated Unionists voting; or

(b) the support of 60 per cent of the members voting, 40 per cent of the designated Nationalists voting and 40 per cent of the designated Unionists voting;

"designated Nationalist" means a member designated as a Nationalist in accordance with standing orders of the Assembly and "designated Unionist" shall be construed accordingly.

(5A) Standing orders of the Assembly shall provide that a member of the Assembly designated in accordance with the standing orders as a Nationalist, as a Unionist or as Other may change his designation only if—

(a) (being a member of a political party) he becomes a member of a different political party or he ceases to be a member of any political party;

(b) (not being a member of any political party) he becomes a member of a political party.

(6) In this section "policing and justice matter" means a matter falling within a description specified in—

(a) any of paragraphs 9 to 12, 14A to 15A and 17 of Schedule 3; or

(b) any other provision of that Schedule designated for this purpose by an order made by the Secretary of State.

Section 5. (1) Subject to sections 6 to 8, the Assembly may make laws, to be known as Acts.

(2) A Bill shall become an Act when it has been passed by the Assembly and has received Royal Assent.
(3) A Bill receives Royal Assent at the beginning of the day on which Letters Patent under the Great Seal of Northern Ireland signed with Her Majesty's own hand signifying Her Assent are notified to the Presiding Officer.
(4) The date of Royal Assent shall be written on the Act by the Presiding Officer, and shall form part of the Act.
(5) The validity of any proceedings leading to the enactment of an Act of the Assembly shall not be called into question in any legal proceedings.
(6) This section does not affect the power of the Parliament of the United Kingdom to make laws for Northern Ireland, but an Act of the Assembly may modify any provision made by or under an Act of Parliament in so far as it is part of the law of Northern Ireland.

Section 6. (1) A provision of an Act is not law if it is outside the legislative competence of the Assembly.
(2) A provision is outside that competence if any of the following paragraphs apply—
(a) it would form part of the law of a country or territory other than Northern Ireland, or confer or remove functions exercisable otherwise than in or as regards Northern Ireland;
(b) it deals with an excepted matter and is not ancillary to other provisions (whether in the Act or previously enacted) dealing with reserved or transferred matters;
(c) it is incompatible with any of the Convention rights;
(d) it is incompatible with EU law;
(e) it discriminates against any person or class of person on the ground of religious belief or political opinion;
(f) it modifies an enactment in breach of section 7.
(3) For the purposes of this Act, a provision is ancillary to other provisions if it is a provision—
(a) which provides for the enforcement of those other provisions or is otherwise necessary or expedient for making those other provisions effective; or
(b) which is otherwise incidental to, or consequential on, those provisions;
and references in this Act to provisions previously enacted are references to provisions contained in, or in any instrument made under, other Northern Ireland legislation or an Act of Parliament.
(4) Her Majesty may by Order in Council specify functions which are to be treated, for such purposes of this Act as may be specified, as being, or as not being, functions which are exercisable in or as regards Northern Ireland. .

(5) No recommendation shall be made to Her Majesty to make an Order in Council under subsection (4) unless a draft of the Order has been laid before and approved by resolution of each House of Parliament.

Section 6A. (1) An Act of the Assembly cannot modify, or confer power by subordinate legislation to modify, retained EU law so far as the modification is of a description specified in regulations made by a Minister of the Crown.
(2) But subsection (1) does not apply to any modification so far as it would, immediately before exit day, have been within the legislative competence of the Assembly.
(3) A Minister of the Crown must not lay for approval before each House of Parliament a draft of a statutory instrument containing regulations under this section unless—
(a) the Assembly has made a consent decision in relation to the laying of the draft, or
(b) the 40 day period has ended without the Assembly having made such a decision.
(4) For the purposes of subsection (3) a consent decision is—
(a) a decision to agree a motion consenting to the laying of the draft,
(b) a decision not to agree a motion consenting to the laying of the draft, or
(c) a decision to agree a motion refusing to consent to the laying of the draft;
and a consent decision is made when the Assembly first makes a decision falling within any of paragraphs (a) to (c) (whether or not it subsequently makes another such decision).
(5) A Minister of the Crown who is proposing to lay a draft as mentioned in subsection (3) must—
(a) provide a copy of the draft to the relevant Northern Ireland department, and
(b) inform the Presiding Officer that a copy has been so provided.
(6) See also section 96A (duty to make explanatory statement about regulations under this section including a duty to explain any decision to lay a draft without the consent of the Assembly).
(7) No regulations may be made under this section after the end of the period of two years beginning with exit day.
(8) Subsection (7) does not affect the continuation in force of regulations made under this section at or before the end of the period mentioned in that subsection.
(9) Any regulations under this section which are in force at the end of the period of five years beginning with the time at which they came into force are revoked in their application to any Act of the Assembly which receives Royal Assent after the end of that period.
(10) Subsections (3) to (8) do not apply in relation to regulations which only relate to a revocation of a specification.
(11) Regulations under this section may include such supplementary, incidental, consequential, transitional, transitory or saving provision as the Minister of the Crown making them considers appropriate.

(12) In this section—
"the relevant Northern Ireland department" means such Northern Ireland department as the Minister of the Crown concerned considers appropriate;
"the 40 day period" means the period of 40 days beginning with the day on which a copy of the draft instrument is provided to the relevant Northern Ireland department,
and, in calculating that period, no account is to be taken of any time during which the Assembly is dissolved or during which it is in recess for more than four days.

[*Sections 7-32 are omitted.*]

Section 33. (1) The members of the Assembly shall be returned for the parliamentary constituencies in Northern Ireland.
(2) Each constituency shall return five members.
(3) An Order in Council under the Parliamentary Constituencies Act 1986 changing a parliamentary constituency in Northern Ireland shall have effect for the purposes of this Act in relation to—
(a) the first election under section 31 or 32 which takes place after the Order comes into force; and
(b) later elections under that section and by-elections.

Section 34. (1) This section applies to elections of members of the Assembly, including by-elections.
(2) Each vote in the poll at an election shall be a single transferable vote.
(3) A single transferable vote is a vote—
(a) capable of being given so as to indicate the voter's order of preference for the candidates for election as members for the constituency; and
(b) capable of being transferred to the next choice when the vote is not needed to give a prior choice the necessary quota of votes or when a prior choice is eliminated from the list of candidates because of a deficiency in the number of votes given for him.
(4) The Secretary of State may by order make provision about elections or any matter relating to them.
(5) In particular, an order under subsection (4) may make—
(a) provision as to the persons entitled to vote at an election and the registration of such persons;
(b) provision for securing that no person stands as a candidate for more than one constituency at a general election;
(c) provision for determining the date of the poll at a by-election;
(d) provision about deposits.
(6) An order under subsection (4) may apply (with or without modifications) any provision of, or made under, any enactment.

(7) An order under subsection (4) may make different provision for different areas about the conduct of elections, including different provision about the registration of persons entitled to vote at an election.

[*The remainder of the Act is omitted.*]

Schedules

[*Schedule 1 is omitted.*]

Schedule 2: Excepted matters

Paragraph 1. The Crown, including the succession to the Crown and a regency, but not —

(a) functions of the First Minister and deputy First Minister, the Northern Ireland Ministers or the Northern Ireland departments, or functions in relation to Northern Ireland of any Minister of the Crown;
(b) property belonging to Her Majesty in right of the Crown or belonging to a government department or held in trust for Her Majesty for the purposes of a government department (other than property used for the purposes of the armed forces of the Crown or the Ministry of Defence Police);
(c) the foreshore or the sea bed or subsoil or their natural resources so far as vested in Her Majesty in right of the Crown.

Paragraph 2. The Parliament of the United Kingdom; parliamentary elections, including the franchise; disqualifications for membership of that Parliament.

Paragraph 3. International relations, including relations with territories outside the United Kingdom, the European Union (and their institutions) and other international organisations and extradition, and international development assistance and co-operation, but not—
(a) (Repealed)
    (aa) co-operation between the Police Service of Northern Ireland and the Garda Síochána with respect to any of the following matters—
    (i) transfers, secondments, exchanges or training of officers;
    (ii) communications (including liaison and information technology);
    (iii) joint investigations;
    (iv) disaster planning;
(b) the exercise of legislative powers so far as required for giving effect to any agreement or arrangement entered into—

(i) by a Minister or junior Minister participating, by reason of any provision of section 52A or 52B, in a meeting of the North-South Ministerial Council or the British-Irish Council; or
(ii)

by, or in relation to the activities of, any body established for implementing, on the basis mentioned in paragraph 11 of Strand Two of the Belfast Agreement, policies agreed in the North-South Ministerial Council;

(c) observing and implementing international obligations, obligations under the Human Rights Convention and obligations under EU law.

In this paragraph "the Human Rights Convention" means the following as they have effect for the time being in relation to the United Kingdom—

(a) the Convention for the Protection of Human Rights and Fundamental Freedoms, agreed by the Council of Europe at Rome on 4th November 1950; and
(b) any Protocols to that Convention which have been ratified by the United Kingdom.

Paragraph 4. The defence of the realm; trading with the enemy; the armed forces of the Crown but not any matter within paragraph 10 of Schedule 3; war pensions; the Ministry of Defence Police.

Paragraph 5. Control of nuclear, biological and chemical weapons and other weapons of mass destruction.

Paragraph 6. Dignities and titles of honour.

Paragraph 7. Treason but not powers of arrest or criminal procedure.

Paragraph 8. Nationality; immigration, including asylum and the status and capacity of persons in the United Kingdom who are not British citizens; free movement of persons within the European Economic Area; issue of travel documents.

Paragraph 9. The following matters—
(a) taxes or duties under any law applying to the United Kingdom as a whole;
(b) stamp duty levied in Northern Ireland before the appointed day; and
(c) taxes or duties substantially of the same character as those mentioned in sub-paragraph (a) or (b).

Paragraph 9A. Child Trust Funds.

Paragraph 9C. The operation of the Small Charitable Donations Act 2012.

Paragraph 9D. Bonuses under the Savings (Government Contributions) Act 2017.

Paragraph 10. The following matters—
(a) national insurance contributions;
(b) the control and management of the Northern Ireland National Insurance Fund and payments into and out of that Fund;
(c) reductions in and deductions from national insurance contributions;
(d) national insurance rebates;
(e) payments out of public money to money purchase pension schemes;
(f) contributions equivalent premiums;
(g) rights to return to the state pension scheme.
Sub-paragraph (a) includes the determination, payment, collection and return of national insurance contributions and matters incidental to those matters.
Sub-paragraph (b) does not include payments out of the Northern Ireland National Insurance Fund which relate to—
(i) the benefits mentioned in section 143(1) of the Social Security Administration (Northern Ireland) Act 1992, or benefits substantially of the same character as those benefits; or
(ii) administrative expenses incurred in connection with matters not falling within sub-paragraphs (a) to (g).
Sub-paragraphs (b) and (e) do not include payments out of or into the Northern Ireland National Insurance Fund under—
(i) section 172(1)(b), (2)(a) or (7)(c) of the Pension Schemes (Northern Ireland) Act 1993; or
(ii) Article 202, 227, 234 or 252 of the Employment Rights (Northern Ireland) Order 1996.
In this paragraph "contributions equivalent premium" has the meaning given by section 51(2) of the Pension Schemes (Northern Ireland) Act 1993.

Paragraph 10A. Tax credits under Part 1 of the Tax Credits Act 2002.

Paragraph 10B. Health in pregnancy grant, Child benefit and guardian's allowance.

Paragraph 10C. The operation of the Childcare Payments Act 2014.

Paragraph 11. The determination of the remuneration, superannuation and other terms and conditions of service (other than those relating to removal from office) of judges of the Court of Judicature of Northern Ireland, holders of offices listed in column 1 of Schedule 3 to the Judicature (Northern Ireland) Act 1978, county court judges, recorders, resident magistrates, coroners, the Chief and other Social Security Commissioners for

Northern Ireland and the Chief and other Child Support Commissioners for Northern Ireland.

Paragraph 11A. The Supreme Court, but not rights of appeal to the Supreme Court or legal aid for appeals to the Supreme Court.

Paragraph 12. Elections, including the franchise, in respect of the Northern Ireland Assembly, the European Parliament and district councils.
(2) This paragraph does not apply to—
(a) the division of local government districts into areas ("district electoral areas") for the purposes of elections to the councils of those districts,
(b) the determination of the names of district electoral areas, or
(c) the determination of the number of councillors to be elected for a district electoral area or a local government district.

Paragraph 13. The subject-matter of the Political Parties, Elections and Referendums Act 2000 with the exception of Part IX (political donations etc. by companies).
This paragraph does not include the funding of political parties for the purpose of assisting members of the Northern Ireland Assembly connected with such parties to perform their Assembly duties.

Paragraph 14. Coinage, legal tender and bank notes.

Paragraph 15. The National Savings Bank.

Paragraph 16. The subject-matter of the Protection of Trading Interests Act 1980.

Paragraph 17. National security (including the Security Service, the Secret Intelligence Service and the Government Communications Headquarters); special powers and other provisions for dealing with terrorism or subversion; the Technical Advisory Board provided for by section 245 of the Investigatory Powers Act 2016; the subject-matter of—
(a) the Official Secrets Acts 1911 and 1920;
(b) the subject-matter of sections 3 to 10, Schedule 1, Part 2 and Chapter 1 of Part 6 of the Investigatory Powers Act 2016, except so far as relating to the prevention or detection of serious crime (within the meaning of that Act);
(c) the Official Secrets Act 1989, except so far as relating to any information, document or other article protected against disclosure by section 4(2) (crime) and not by any other provision of sections 1 to 4.

Paragraph 18. Nuclear energy and nuclear installations, including nuclear safety, security and safeguards, and liability for nuclear occurrences, but not the subject-matter of—
(a) section 3(5) to (7) of the Environmental Protection Act 1990 (emission limits); or
(b) the Radioactive Substances Act 1993.

Paragraph 19. Regulation of sea fishing outside the Northern Ireland zone (except in relation to Northern Ireland fishing boats).
In this paragraph "Northern Ireland fishing boat" means a fishing vessel which is registered in the register maintained under section 8 of the Merchant Shipping Act 1995 and whose entry in the register specifies a port in Northern Ireland as the port to which the vessel is to be treated as belonging.

Paragraph 20. Regulation of activities in outer space.

Paragraph 20A. Regulation of activities in Antarctica (which for these purposes has the meaning given by section 1 of the Antarctic Act 1994).

Paragraph 21. Any matter with which a provision of the Northern Ireland Constitution Act 1973, other than
section 36(1)(c), solely or mainly deals.

Paragraph 21A. The office and functions of the Advocate General for Northern Ireland.

Paragraph 22. Any matter with which a provision of this Act falling within the following sub-paragraphs solely or mainly deals—
(a) Parts I and II;
(b) Part III except sections 19, 20, 22, 23(2) to (4), 28, 28A, 28B, 28D and 28E;
(c) Part IV except sections 40, 43, 44(8) and 50 and Schedule 5;
(d) in Part V, sections 52A to 52C and 54;
(e) Part VI except sections 57(1) and 67;
(f) in Part VII, sections 69B, 71(1) and (2) and (3) to (5), 74(5) and (6), 76 and 78;
(g) in Part VIII, sections 79 to 83 and Schedule 10.
This paragraph does not apply to—
(i) any matter in respect of which it is stated by this Act that provision may be made by Act of the Assembly;
(ii) any matter to which a description specified in this Schedule or Schedule 3 is stated not to apply; or
(iii) any matter falling within a description specified in Schedule 3.

Schedule 3: Reserved Matters

Paragraph 1. The conferral of functions in relation to Northern Ireland on any Minister of the Crown apart from the Advocate General for Northern Ireland.

Paragraph 2. Property belonging to Her Majesty in right of the Crown or belonging to a department of the Government of the United Kingdom or held in trust for Her Majesty for the purposes of such a department (other than property used for the purposes of the armed forces of the Crown or the Ministry of Defence Police).

Paragraph 3. Navigation, including merchant shipping, but not harbours or inland waters.

Paragraph 4. Civil aviation but not aerodromes.

Paragraph 5. The foreshore and the sea bed and subsoil and their natural resources (except so far as affecting harbours); submarine pipe-lines; submarine cables, including any land line used solely for the purpose of connecting one submarine cable with another.

Paragraph 6. Domicile.

Paragraph 7. The subject-matter of the Postal Services Act 2000.
This paragraph does not include financial assistance for the provision of services (other than postal services and services relating to postal or money orders) to be provided from public post offices.
In this paragraph "postal services" and "public post offices" have the same meanings as in the Postal Services Act 2000.

Paragraph 7A. The alteration of the number of members of the Assembly returned for each constituency.
This paragraph does not include—
(a) the alteration of that number to a number lower than five or higher than six, or
(b) the provision of different numbers for different constituencies.

Paragraph 8. Disqualification for membership of the Assembly; privileges, powers and immunities of the Assembly, its members and committees greater than those conferred by section 50.

Paragraph 9. The following matters—

(a) the subject-matter of Parts 2 and 3 of the Regulation of Investigatory Powers Act 2000, so far as relating to the prevention or detection of crime (within the meaning of that Act) or the prevention of disorder;

(aa) the subject-matter of the following provisions of the Investigatory Powers Act 2016, so far as relating to the prevention or detection of serious crime (within the meaning of that Act)—

(i) sections 3 to 10 and Schedule 1,

(ii) Part 2, and

(iii) Chapter 1 of Part 6;

(ab) the subject-matter of section 11, Parts 3 and 4 and Chapter 2 of Part 6 of the Investigatory Powers Act 2016, so far as relating to the prevention or detection of crime (within the meaning of that Act) or the prevention of disorder;

(ac) the subject-matter of section 12 of, and Schedule 2 to, the Investigatory Powers Act 2016, so far as relating to the prevention or detection of crime (within the meaning of that Act);

(b) in relation to the prevention or detection of crime, the subject-matter of Part 3 of the Police Act 1997;

(c) the operation of—

    (i) sections 21 to 40 of, and Schedules 3 and 4 to, the Justice and Security (Northern Ireland) Act 2007, and

    (ii) section 102 of, and Schedule 12 to, the Terrorism Act 2000;

(d) in relation to terrorism, the exercise of the Royal prerogative of mercy;

(e) the operation of sections 1 to 8 of, and Schedule 1 to, the Justice and Security (Northern Ireland) Act 2007 and the operation of Part 1 of the Criminal Procedure and Investigations Act 1996 where a certificate under section 1 of the 2007 Act has been issued;

(f) in relation to the regulation of drugs or other substances through the criminal law (including offences, exceptions to offences, penalties, powers of arrest and detention, prosecutions and the treatment of offenders) or otherwise in relation to the prevention or detection of crime—

    (i) the subject-matter of the Misuse of Drugs Act 1971;

    (ii) the subject-matter of sections 12 and 13 of the Criminal Justice (International Co-operation) Act 1990;

(g) the National Crime Agency;

(h) in relation to prisons, the accommodation of persons in separated conditions on the grounds of security, safety or good order.

(2) In sub-paragraph (1)(h) "prisons" includes any institution for the detention of persons because of their involvement, or suspected involvement, in crime.

(3) This paragraph does not include any excepted matters or any matter within paragraph 10 of this Schedule.

Paragraph 10. (1) The subject-matter of the Public Processions (Northern Ireland) Act 1998.
(2) In relation to the maintenance of public order, the armed forces of the Crown (including the conferring of powers, authorities, privileges or immunities on members of the armed forces for the purposes of the maintenance of public order).
(3) This paragraph does not include any matter within paragraph 17 of Schedule 2.

Paragraph 11. The operation of the temporary provisions, as defined in section 47 of the Police (Northern Ireland) Act 2000.

Paragraph 11A. (Repealed)

Paragraph 12. (1) Items for the time being specified in Article 45(1) or (2) of the Firearms (Northern Ireland) Order 2004; and the subject-matter of Article 45(10) of that Order.
(2) The security of explosives, including—
(a) the prevention of loss or theft of explosives,
(b) the prevention of the use of explosives for wrongful purposes, and
(c) the detection, identification and traceability of explosives.
This sub-paragraph does not include the security of fireworks, or the licensing of shotfirers, or the subject-matter of section 2 of the Explosives Act (Northern Ireland) 1970.

Paragraph 13. Civil defence.

Paragraph 14. The subject-matter of Part 2 of the Civil Contingencies Act 2004.

Paragraph 14A. (Repealed)

Paragraph 15. (Repealed)

Paragraph 15A. (Repealed)

Paragraph 16. The Civil Service Commissioners for Northern Ireland.

Paragraph 17. (Repealed)

Paragraph 18. The subject-matter of sections 149 to 151 of and Schedules 5 and 5A to the Social Security Administration (Northern Ireland) Act 1992 (Social Security Advisory Committee and Industrial Injuries Advisory Council).

Paragraph 19. The subject-matter of the Vaccine Damage Payment Scheme.

Paragraph 20. Import and export controls and trade with any place outside the United Kingdom but not—
(a) the furtherance of the trade of Northern Ireland or the protection of traders in Northern Ireland against fraud;
(b) services in connection with, or the regulation of, the quality, insurance, transport, marketing or identification of agricultural or food products, including livestock;
(c) the prevention of disease or the control of weeds and pests;
(d) aerodromes and harbours;
(e) any matter within paragraph 4 of Schedule 2.

Paragraph 21. The subject-matter of the National Minimum Wage Act 1998.

Paragraph 22. The subject-matter of the following provisions of the Pension Schemes Act 1993—
(a) section 6 (1), (2) (a) (i), (iii) and (iv) and (b), (3), (4) and (8) (registration of occupational and personal pension schemes);
(b) section 145 (Pensions Ombudsman).

Paragraph 23. The following matters—
(a) financial services, including investment business, banking and deposit-taking, collective investment schemes and insurance;
(b) financial markets, including listing and public offers of securities and investments, transfer of securities and insider dealing.
This paragraph does not include the subject-matter of—
(a) the Industrial and Provident Societies Act Northern Ireland) 1969;
(b) the Credit Unions (Northern Ireland) Order 1985;
(c) the Companies (Northern Ireland) Order 1986;
(d) the Insolvency (Northern Ireland) Order 1989;
(e) the Companies (Northern Ireland) Order 1990;
(f) the Companies (No.2) (Northern Ireland) Order 1990;
(g) the Open-Ended Investment Companies (Investment Companies with Variable Capital) Regulations (Northern Ireland) 1997.

Paragraph 24. The subject-matter of—
(a) the Building Societies Act 1986;
(b) the Friendly Societies Act 1992.

Paragraph 25. The subject-matter of the Money Laundering, Terrorist Financing and Transfer of Funds (Information on the Payer) Regulations 2017, but in relation to any type of business.

Paragraph 25A. (Repealed.)

Paragraph 26. Regulation of anti-competitive practices and agreements; abuse of dominant position; monopolies and mergers.

Paragraph 27. Intellectual property but not the subject-matter of Parts I and II of the Plant Varieties Act 1997 (plant varieties and the Plant Varieties and Seeds Tribunal).

Paragraph 28. Units of measurement and United Kingdom primary standards.

Paragraph 29. Telecommunications; wireless telegraphy; the provision of programme services (within the meaning of the Broadcasting Act 1990); internet services; electronic encryption; the subject matter of Part II of the Wireless Telegraphy Act 1949 (electromagnetic disturbance).

Paragraph 30. The National Lottery (except in so far as any matter within Schedule 2 is concerned).

Paragraph 31. Xenotransplantation.

Paragraph 32. Surrogacy arrangements, within the meaning of the Surrogacy Arrangements Act 1985, including the subject-matter of that Act.

Paragraph 33. The subject-matter of the Human Fertilisation and Embryology Act 1990.

Paragraph 34. Human genetics.

Paragraph 35. Research Councils within the meaning of the Science and Technology Act 1965.

Paragraph 35A. United Kingdom Research and Innovation.

Paragraph 36. Areas in which industry may qualify for assistance under Part III of the Industrial Development Act 1982.

Paragraph 37. Consumer safety in relation to goods.

Paragraph 38. Technical standards and requirements in relation to products in pursuance of an obligation under EU law but not standards and requirements in relation to food, agricultural or horticultural produce, fish or fish products, seeds, animal feeding stuffs, fertilisers or pesticides.

Paragraph 39. The subject-matter of section 3 (5) to (7) of the Environmental Protection Act 1990 (emission limits); the environmental protection technology scheme for research and development in the United Kingdom.

Paragraph 40. The subject-matter of—
(a) the Data Protection Act 1984;
(b) the Data Protection Act 1998; and
(c) Council Directive 95/46/EC (protection of individuals with regard to the processing of personal data and free movement of such data).

Paragraph 41. Oaths and declarations (including all undertakings and affirmations, by whatever name) other than those within section 77 (3).

Paragraph 41A. (1) The division of local government districts into areas ("district electoral areas") for the purposes of elections to the councils of those districts.
(2) The determination of the names of district electoral areas.
(3) The determination of the number of councillors to be elected for a district electoral area or a local government district.

Paragraph 42. Any matter with which a provision of this Act falling within the following sub-paragraphs solely or mainly deals—
(a) in Part III, sections 19, 20, 28, 28A and 28B;
   (aa) in Part VII, sections 68 to 69A, 69C to 70, 71(2A) to (2C) and Schedule 7;
(b) in Part VII, sections 73, 74 (3) and (4), 75 and 77 (1), (2) and (4) to (8) and Schedules 8 and 9;
(c) in Part VIII, sections 90 to 93 and Schedule 11.
This paragraph does not apply to—
(i) any matter in respect of which it is stated by this Act that provision may be made by Act of the Assembly; or
(ii) any matter to which a description specified in this Schedule or Schedule 2 is stated not to apply.

[*The remaining Schedules are omitted.*]

19 GOVERNMENT OF WALES ACT 2006[9]

Part 1: National Assembly for Wales

Section 1. (1) There is to be an Assembly for Wales to be known as the National Assembly for Wales or Cynulliad Cenedlaethol Cymru (referred to in this Act as "the Assembly").
(2) The Assembly is to consist of—
(a) one member for each Assembly constituency (referred to in this Act as "Assembly constituency members"), and
(b) members for each Assembly electoral region (referred to in this Act as "Assembly regional members").
(3) Members of the Assembly (referred to in this Act as "Assembly members") are to be returned in accordance with the provision made by and under this Act for—
(a) the holding of general elections of Assembly members (for the return of the entire Assembly), and
(b) the filling of vacancies in Assembly seats.
(4) The validity of any Assembly proceedings is not affected by any vacancy in its membership.
(5) In this Act "Assembly proceedings" means any proceedings of—
(a) the Assembly,
(b) committees of the Assembly, or
(c) sub-committees of such committees

Section 2. (1) The Assembly constituencies are the constituencies specified in the Parliamentary Constituencies and Assembly Electoral Regions (Wales) Order 2006 (S.I. 2006/1041) as amended by—
(a) the Parliamentary Constituencies and Assembly Electoral
    Regions (Wales) (Amendment) Order 2008 (S.I.2008/1791), and
(b) any Order in Council under the Parliamentary Constituencies Act 1986 giving effect (with or without modifications) to a report falling within section 13(3) or (4) of the Parliamentary Voting System and Constituencies Act 2011.
(2) There are five Assembly electoral regions.
(3) The Assembly electoral regions are as specified in the Parliamentary Constituencies and Assembly Electoral Regions (Wales) Order 2006.
(4) There are four seats for each Assembly electoral region.

---

9 As last amended by the Wales Act 2017 (c. 4). Selected provisions: Part 1, Sections 1,2,6,8 and 9; Part 3, Sections 93 and 94; Part 4, Sections 103,107 and 108; Schedules 7A, Part 1, and 7B, Part 1, Paragraphs 1-5, and Part 2.

[*Sections 3-5 are omitted.*]

Section 6. (1) Each person entitled to vote at a general election in an Assembly constituency has two votes.
(2) One (referred to in this Act as a "constituency vote") is a vote which may be given for a candidate to be the Assembly constituency member for the Assembly constituency.
(3) The other (referred to in this Act as an "electoral region vote") is a vote which may be given for—
(a) a registered political party which has submitted a list of candidates to be Assembly regional members for the Assembly electoral region in which the Assembly constituency is included, or
(b) an individual who is a candidate to be an Assembly regional member for that Assembly electoral region.
(4) The Assembly constituency member for the Assembly constituency is to be returned under the simple majority system.
(5) The Assembly regional members for the Assembly electoral region are to be returned under the additional member system of proportional representation provided for in this Part.
(6) In this Act "registered political party" means a party registered under Part 2 of the Political Parties, Elections and Referendums Act 2000 (c. 41).

[*Section 7 is omitted.*]

Section 8. (1) This section and section 9 are about the return of Assembly regional members for an electoral region at a general election.
(2) The person who is to be returned as the Assembly constituency member for each Assembly constituency in the Assembly electoral region is to be determined before it is determined who are to be returned as the Assembly regional members for the Assembly electoral region.
(3) For each registered political party by which a list of candidates has been submitted for the Assembly electoral region—
(a) there is to be added together the number of electoral region votes given for the party in the Assembly constituencies included in the Assembly electoral region, and
(b) the number arrived at under paragraph (a) is then to be divided by the aggregate of one and the number of candidates of the party returned as Assembly constituency members for any of those Assembly constituencies.
(4) For each individual candidate to be an Assembly regional member for the Assembly electoral region there is to be added together the number of electoral region votes given for the candidate in the Assembly constituencies included in the Assembly electoral region.

(5) The number arrived at—
(a) in the case of a registered political party, under subsection (3) (b), or
(b) in the case of an individual candidate, under subsection (4),
   is referred to in this Act as the electoral region figure for that party or individual candidate.

Section 9. (1) The first seat for the Assembly electoral region is to be allocated to the party or individual candidate with the highest electoral region figure.
(2) The second and subsequent seats for the Assembly electoral region are to be allocated to the party or individual candidate with the highest electoral region figure after any recalculation required by subsection (3) has been carried out.
(3) This subsection requires a recalculation under paragraph (b) of section 8 (3) in relation to a party—
(a) for the first application of subsection (2), if the application of subsection (1) resulted in the allocation of an Assembly seat to the party, or
(b) for any subsequent application of subsection (2), if the previous application of that subsection did so,
   and a recalculation is to be carried out after adding one to the aggregate mentioned in that paragraph.
(4) An individual candidate already returned as an Assembly constituency member or Assembly regional member is to be disregarded.
(5) Seats for the Assembly electoral region which are allocated to a party are to be filled by the persons on the party's list in the order in which they appear on the list. (disregarding anyone already returned as an Assembly constituency member, including anyone whose return is void).
(6) Once a party's list has been exhausted (by the return of persons included on it as Assembly constituency members or by the previous application of subsection (1) or (2)), the party is to be disregarded.
(7) If (on the application of subsection (1) or any application of subsection (2)) the highest electoral region figure is the electoral region figure of two or more parties or individual candidates, the subsection applies to each of them.
(8) However, if subsection (7) would mean that more than the full number of seats for the Assembly electoral region were allocated, subsection (1) or (2) does not apply until—
(a) a recalculation has been carried out under section 8 (3) (b) after adding one to the number of votes given for each party with that electoral region figure, and
(b) one has been added to the number of votes given for each individual candidate with that electoral region figure.
(9) If, after that, the highest electoral region figure is still the electoral region figure of two or more parties or individual candidates, the regional returning officer must decide between them by lots.

Part 3: Assembly Measures

Section 93. (1) The Assembly may make laws, to be known as Measures of the National Assembly for Wales or Mesurau Cynulliad Cenedlaethol Cymru (referred to in this Act as "Assembly Measures").
(2) A proposed Assembly Measure is enacted by being passed by the Assembly and approved by Her Majesty in Council.
(3) The validity of an Assembly Measure is not affected by any invalidity in the Assembly proceedings leading to its enactment.
(4) Every Assembly Measure is to be judicially noticed.
(5) This Part does not affect the power of the Parliament of the United Kingdom to make laws for Wales.

Section 94. (1) Subject to the provisions of this Part, an Assembly Measure may make any provision that could be made by an Act of Parliament.
(2) An Assembly Measure is not law so far as any provision of the Assembly Measure is outside the Assembly's legislative competence.
(3) A provision of an Assembly Measure is within the Assembly's legislative competence only if it falls within subsection (4) or (5).
(4) A provision of an Assembly Measure falls within this subsection if—
(a) it relates to one or more of the matters specified in Part 1 of Schedule 5 and does not fall within any of the exceptions specified in paragraph A1 of Part 2 of that Schedule (whether or not the exception is under a heading corresponding to the field which includes the matter), and
(b) it neither applies otherwise than in relation to Wales nor confers, imposes, modifies or removes (or gives power to confer, impose, modify or remove) functions exercisable otherwise than in relation to Wales.
(5) A provision of an Assembly Measure falls within this subsection if—
(a) it provides for the enforcement of a provision (of that or any other Assembly Measure) which falls within subsection (4) or it is otherwise appropriate for making such a provision effective, or
(b) it is otherwise incidental to, or consequential on, such a provision.
(6) But a provision which falls within subsection (4) or (5) is outside the Assembly's legislative competence if—
(a) it breaches any of the restrictions in paragraphs 1 to 6 of Part 2 of Schedule 5, having regard to any exception in Part 3 of that Schedule from those restrictions,
(b) it extends otherwise than only to England and Wales, or
(c) it is incompatible with the Convention rights or with EU law.
(7) For the purposes of this section the question whether a provision of an Assembly Measure relates to one or more of the matters specified in Part 1 of Schedule 5 (or falls

within any of the exceptions specified in paragraph A1 of Part 2 of that Schedule) is to be determined by reference to the purpose of the provision, having regard (among other things) to its effect in all the circumstances.

[*The remainder of Part 3 is omitted.*]

Part 4: Acts of the Assembly

Section 103. (Repealed.)

[*Sections 104-106 are omitted.*]

Section 107. (1) The Assembly may make laws, to be known as Acts of the National Assembly for Wales or Deddfau Cynulliad Cenedlaethol Cymru (referred to in this Act as "Acts of the Assembly").
(2) Proposed Acts of the Assembly are to be known as Bills; and a Bill becomes an Act of the Assembly when it has been passed by the Assembly and has received Royal Assent.
(3) The validity of an Act of the Assembly is not affected by any invalidity in the Assembly proceedings leading to its enactment.
(4) Every Act of the Assembly is to be judicially noticed.
(5) This Part does not affect the power of the Parliament of the United Kingdom to make laws for Wales.
(6) But it is recognised that the Parliament of the United Kingdom will not normally legislate with regard to devolved matters without the consent of the Assembly.

Section 108. (Repealed.)

Section 108A. (1) An Act of the Assembly is not law so far as any provision of the Act is outside the Assembly's legislative competence.
(2) A provision is outside that competence so far as any of the following paragraphs apply —

(a) it extends otherwise than only to England and Wales;
(b) it applies otherwise than in relation to Wales or confers, imposes, modifies or removes (or gives power to confer, impose, modify or remove) functions exercisable otherwise than in relation to Wales;
(c) it relates to reserved matters (see Schedule 7A);
(d) it breaches any of the restrictions in Part 1 of Schedule 7B, having regard to any exception in Part 2 of that Schedule from those restrictions;
(e) it is incompatible with the Convention rights or with EU law.
(3) But subsection (2)(b) does not apply to a provision that—

(a) is ancillary to a provision of any Act of the Assembly or Assembly Measure or to a devolved provision of an Act of Parliament, and
(a) has no greater effect otherwise than in relation to Wales, or in relation to functions exercisable otherwise than in relation to Wales, than is necessary to give effect to the purpose of that provision.

(4) For this purpose, a provision of an Act of Parliament is ""devolved"" if it would be within the Assembly's legislative competence if it were contained in an Act of the Assembly (ignoring any requirement for consent or consultation imposed under paragraph 8, 10 or 11 of Schedule 7B or otherwise).

(5) In determining what is necessary for the purposes of subsection (3), any power to make laws other than that of the Assembly is disregarded.

(6) The question whether a provision of an Act of the Assembly relates to a reserved matter is determined by reference to the purpose of the provision, having regard (among other things) to its effect in all the circumstances.

(7) For the purposes of this Act a provision is ancillary to another provision if it—
(a) provides for the enforcement of the other provision or is otherwise appropriate for making that provision effective, or
(b) is otherwise incidental to, or consequential on, that provision.

[*The remainder of the Act is omitted.*]

Schedules

[*Schedules 1-6 are omitted.*]

Schedule 7 (Repealed.)

Schedule 7A: Reserved Matters

Part 1: General Reservations

The Constitution

1. The following aspects of the constitution are reserved matters—
(a) the Crown, including succession to the Crown and a regency;
(b) the union of the nations of Wales and England;
(c) the Parliament of the United Kingdom.

2. (1) Paragraph 1 does not reserve—
(a) Her Majesty's executive functions,

(b) functions exercisable by any person acting on behalf of the Crown, or
(c) the use of the Welsh Seal.
(2) Sub-paragraph (1) does not affect the reservation by paragraph 1 of the management (in accordance with any enactment regulating the use of land) of the Crown Estate.
(3) Sub-paragraph (1) does not affect the reservation by paragraph 1 of the functions of the Security Service, the Secret Intelligence Service and the Government Communications Headquarters.
(4) In this paragraph ""executive function"" does not include a function conferred or imposed by or by virtue of any legislation or the prerogative.

3. (1) Paragraph 1 does not reserve property belonging—
(a) to Her Majesty in right of the Crown,
(b) to Her Majesty in right of the Duchy of Lancaster, or
(c) to the Duchy of Cornwall.
(2) Paragraph 1 does not reserve property belonging to any person acting on behalf of the Crown or held in trust for Her Majesty for the purposes of any person acting on behalf of the Crown.
(3) Sub-paragraphs (1) and (2) do not affect the reservation by paragraph 1 of—
(a) the hereditary revenues of the Crown,
(b) the royal arms and standard, or
(c) the compulsory acquisition of property—
    (i) belonging to Her Majesty in right of the Crown;
    (ii) belonging to Her Majesty in right of the Duchy of Lancaster;
    (iii) belonging to the Duchy of Cornwall;
    (iv) held or used by a Minister of the Crown or government department.

4. (1) Paragraph 1 does not reserve property held by Her Majesty in Her private capacity.
(2) Sub-paragraph (1) does not affect the reservation by paragraph 1 of the subject-matter of the Crown Private Estates Acts 1800 to 1873.

Public service

5. The Civil Service of the State is a reserved matter.

Political parties

6. The following are reserved matters—
(a) the registration of political parties;
(b) funding of political parties and of their members and officers;

(c) accounting requirements in relation to political parties;
but this is subject to paragraph 7.

7. Paragraph 6 does not reserve making payments to any political party for the purpose of assisting members of the Assembly who are connected with the party to perform their Assembly duties.

Single legal jurisdiction of England and Wales

8. (1) The following are reserved matters—
(a) courts (including, in particular, their creation and jurisdiction);
(b) judges (including, in particular, their appointment and remuneration);
(c) civil or criminal proceedings (including, in particular, bail, costs, custody pending trial, disclosure, enforcement of orders of courts, evidence, sentencing, limitation of actions, procedure, prosecutors and remedies);
(d) pardons for criminal offences;
(e) private international law;
(f) judicial review of administrative action.
(See also paragraphs 3 and 4 of Schedule 7B (restrictions on modifying private law and criminal law).)
(2) The reference to prosecutors in sub-paragraph (1)(c) does not prevent an Act of the Assembly from making provision about responsibility for the prosecution of devolved offences.
(3) Sub-paragraph (1) does not reserve—
(a) welfare advice to courts in respect of family proceedings in which the welfare of children ordinarily resident in Wales is or may be in question;
(b) representation in respect of such proceedings;
(c) the provision of support (including information and advice), to children ordinarily resident in Wales and their families, in respect of such proceedings;
(d) Welsh family proceedings officers.

Tribunals

9. (1) Tribunals, including—
(a) their membership,
(b) the appointment and remuneration of their members,
(c) their functions and procedure, and

(d) appeals against their decisions,

are a reserved matter.

(2) But this paragraph does not apply to a tribunal (a ""devolved tribunal"") all of whose functions are functions that—

(a) are exercisable only in relation to Wales, and

(b) do not relate to reserved matters.

(3) In the case of a tribunal which has functions that do not relate to reserved matters, sub-paragraph (1) does not reserve any function of deciding an appeal or application which—

(a) relates to a matter that is not a reserved matter, and

(b) is not an appeal against the decision of a tribunal (other than a devolved tribunal),

but it does reserve the tribunal's procedure in relation to that function.

(4) In determining for the purposes of this paragraph whether functions of a tribunal are exercisable only in relation to Wales, no account is taken of any function that—

(a) is exercisable otherwise than in relation to Wales, and

(b) could (apart from paragraph 8 of Schedule 7B) be conferred or imposed by provision falling within the Assembly's legislative competence (by virtue of section 108A(3)).

(5) Where the question whether this paragraph applies to a particular tribunal is relevant to determining whether a provision of an Act of the Assembly is within the Assembly's legislative competence, the time for deciding the question is the time when the Act is passed.

Foreign affairs etc

10. (1) International relations, regulation of international trade, and international development assistance and co-operation are reserved matters.

(2) In sub-paragraph (1) ""international relations"" includes—

(a) relations with territories outside the United Kingdom;

(b) relations with the EU and its institutions;

(c) relations with other international organisations.

(3) But sub-paragraph (1) does not reserve—

(a) observing and implementing international obligations, obligations under the Human Rights Convention and obligations under EU law, or

(b) assisting Ministers of the Crown in relation to any matter to which that sub-paragraph applies.

(4) In this paragraph ""the Human Rights Convention"" means—

(a) the Convention for the Protection of Human Rights and Fundamental Freedoms, agreed by the Council of Europe at Rome on 4th November 1950, and

(b) the Protocols to the Convention,

as they have effect for the time being in relation to the United Kingdom.

Defence

11. The following are reserved matters—
(a) the defence of the realm;
(b) the naval, military or air forces of the Crown, including reserve forces;
(c) visiting forces;
(d) international headquarters and defence organisations;
(e) trading with the enemy and enemy property.

[Parts 2 and 3 are omitted.]

Schedule 7B: General Restrictions

Part 1: General Restrictions

The law on reserved matters

1. (1) A provision of an Act of the Assembly cannot make modifications of, or confer power by subordinate legislation to make modifications of, the law on reserved matters.
(2) ""The law on reserved matters"" means—
(a) any enactment the subject-matter of which is a reserved matter and which is comprised in an Act of Parliament or subordinate legislation under an Act of Parliament, and
(b) any rule of law which is not contained in an enactment and the subject-matter of which is a reserved matter,
and in this sub-paragraph ""Act of Parliament"" does not include this Act.

2. (1) Paragraph 1 does not apply to a modification that—
(a) is ancillary to a provision made (whether by the Act in question or another enactment) which does not relate to reserved matters, and
(b) has no greater effect on reserved matters than is necessary to give effect to the purpose of that provision.
(2) In determining what is necessary for the purposes of this paragraph, any power to make laws other than the power of the Assembly is disregarded.
Private law

3. (1) A provision of an Act of the Assembly cannot make modifications of, or confer power by subordinate legislation to make modifications of, the private law.
(2) ""The private law"" means the law of contract, agency, bailment, tort, unjust enrichment and restitution, property, trusts and succession.

(3) In sub-paragraph (2) the reference to the law of property does not include intellectual property rights relating to plant varieties or seeds but does include the compulsory acquisition of property.
(4) Sub-paragraph (1) does not apply to a modification that has a purpose (other than modification of the private law) which does not relate to a reserved matter.
Criminal law

4. (1) A provision of an Act of the Assembly cannot—
(a) make modifications of, or confer power by subordinate legislation to make modifications of, an offence in a listed category;
(b) create, or confer power by subordinate legislation to create, an offence in a listed category.
(2) The listed categories of offences are—
(a) treason and related offences;
(b) homicide offences (including offences relating to suicide) and other offences against the person (including offences involving violence or threats of violence) that are triable only on indictment;
(c) sexual offences (including offences relating to indecent or pornographic images);
(d) offences of a kind dealt with by the Perjury Act 1911.
(3) A provision of an Act of the Assembly cannot make modifications of, or confer power by subordinate legislation to make modifications of, the law about—
(a) criminal responsibility and capacity,
(b) the meaning of intention, recklessness, dishonesty and other mental elements of offences,
(c) inchoate and secondary criminal liability, or
(d) sentences and other orders and disposals in respect of defendants in criminal proceedings, or otherwise in respect of criminal conduct, and their effect and operation.
(4) For the purposes of this paragraph, a modification of the law relating to defences to an offence is a modification of the offence.
(5) This paragraph does not affect the reservation, by virtue of Schedule 7A, of the creation or modification of offences in relation to reserved matters.
(See also paragraph 8 of that Schedule (single legal jurisdiction of England and Wales).)
Enactments other than this Act

5. (1) A provision of an Act of the Assembly cannot make modifications of, or confer power by subordinate legislation to make modifications of, any of the provisions listed in the table below—

Enactment	Provisions protected from modification
European Communities Act 1972	The whole Act.
Government of Wales Act 1998	Section 144(7).

Human Rights Act 1998	The whole Act.
Civil Contingencies Act 2004	The whole Act.
Energy Act 2008	Section 100 and regulations under that section.
The European Union (Withdrawal) Act 2018	The whole Act.

(2) A provision of an Act of the Assembly cannot, unless it is an oversight provision, make modifications of—
(a) section 146A(1) of the Government of Wales Act 1998, or
(b) sections 2(1) to (3), 3(2) to (4) or 6(2) and (3) of the Public Audit (Wales) Act 2013 (anaw 3),
or confer power by subordinate legislation to do so.

(3) A provision of an Act of the Assembly cannot, unless it is an oversight provision and also a non-governmental committee provision—
(a) make modifications of section 8(1) of the Public Audit (Wales) Act 2013 so far as that section relates to the Auditor General's exercise of functions free from the direction or control of the Assembly or Welsh Government, or
(b) confer power by subordinate legislation to do so.

(4) An ""oversight provision"" is a provision of an Act of the Assembly that—
(a) relates to the oversight or supervision of the Auditor General or of the exercise of the Auditor General's functions, or
(b) is ancillary to a provision falling within paragraph (a).

(5) A ""non-governmental committee provision"" is a provision conferring functions on a committee of the Assembly that—
(a) does not consist of or include members of the Welsh Government, and
(b) is not chaired by an Assembly member who is a member of a political group with an executive role,
or a provision conferring power by subordinate legislation to do so.

(6) A person designated under section 46(5) to exercise the functions of the First Minister is treated as a member of the Welsh Government for the purposes of sub-paragraph (5)(a).

[*Paragraphs 6-12 are omitted.*]

Part 2: General exceptions from Part 1

Restatement

13. (1) Part 1 does not prevent an Act of the Assembly—
(a) restating the law (or restating it with such modifications as are not prevented by that Part), or

(b) repealing or revoking any spent enactment,

or conferring power by subordinate legislation to do so.

(2) For the purposes of paragraph 1, the law on reserved matters includes any restatement in an Act of the Assembly or an Assembly Measure, or subordinate legislation under such an Act or Measure, of the law on reserved matters if the subject-matter of the restatement is a reserved matter.

Subordinate legislation

14. Part 1 does not prevent an Act of the Assembly making modifications of, or conferring power by subordinate legislation to make modifications of, an enactment for or in connection with any of the following purposes—
(a) making different provision about the document by which a power to make, confirm or approve subordinate legislation is to be exercised;
(b) making provision (or no provision) for the procedure, in relation to the Assembly, to which legislation made in the exercise of such a power (or the instrument or other document in which it is contained) is to be subject;
(c) applying any enactment comprised in or made under an Act of the Assembly relating to the documents by which such powers may be exercised.

[*The remaining schedules are omitted.*]

20 European Union (Withdrawal) Act 2018[10]

Repeal of the ECA

1. Repeal of the European Communities Act 1972
The European Communities Act 1972 is repealed on exit day.

Retention of existing EU law

2. Saving for EU-derived domestic legislation
(1) EU-derived domestic legislation, as it has effect in domestic law immediately before exit day, continues to have effect in domestic law on and after exit day.
(2) In this section "EU-derived domestic legislation" means any enactment so far as—
(a) made under section 2(2) of, or paragraph 1A of Schedule 2 to, the European Communities Act 1972,
(b) passed or made, or operating, for a purpose mentioned in section 2(2) (a) or (b) of that Act,
(c) relating to anything—
   (i) which falls within paragraph (a) or (b), or
   (ii) to which section 3(1) or 4(1) applies, or
(d) relating otherwise to the EU or the EEA,
but does not include any enactment contained in the European Communities Act 1972.
(3) This section is subject to section 5 and Schedule 1 (exceptions to savings and incorporation).

3. Incorporation of direct EU legislation
(1) Direct EU legislation, so far as operative immediately before exit day, forms part of domestic law on and after exit day.
(2) In this Act "direct EU legislation" means—
(a) any EU regulation, EU decision or EU tertiary legislation, as it has effect in EU law immediately before exit day and so far as—
   (i) it is not an exempt EU instrument (for which see section 20(1) and Schedule 6),
   (ii) it is not an EU decision addressed only to a member State other than the United Kingdom, and
   (iii) its effect is not reproduced in an enactment to which section 2(1) applies,

---

10 An Act to repeal the European Communities Act 1972 and make other provision in connection with the withdrawal of the United Kingdom from the EU, as last amended by the European Union (Withdrawal) Act 2018 (Exit Day) (Amendment) (No. 2) Regulations 2019. Schedules are omitted.

(b) any Annex to the EEA agreement, as it has effect in EU law immediately before exit day and so far as—
  (i) it refers to, or contains adaptations of, anything falling within paragraph (a), and
  (ii) its effect is not reproduced in an enactment to which section 2(1) applies, or
(c) Protocol 1 to the EEA agreement (which contains horizontal adaptations that apply in relation to EU instruments referred to in the Annexes to that agreement), as it has effect in EU law immediately before exit day.

(3) For the purposes of this Act, any direct EU legislation is operative immediately before exit day if—
(a) in the case of anything which comes into force at a particular time and is stated to apply from a later time, it is in force and applies immediately before exit day,
(b) in the case of a decision which specifies to whom it is addressed, it has been notified to that person before exit day, and
(c) in any other case, it is in force immediately before exit day.

(4) This section—
(a) brings into domestic law any direct EU legislation only in the form of the English language version of that legislation, and
(b) does not apply to any such legislation for which there is no such version,
but paragraph (a) does not affect the use of the other language versions of that legislation for the purposes of interpreting it.

(5) This section is subject to section 5 and Schedule 1 (exceptions to savings and incorporation).

4. Saving for rights etc. under section 2(1) of the ECA

(1) Any rights, powers, liabilities, obligations, restrictions, remedies and procedures which, immediately before exit day—
(a) are recognised and available in domestic law by virtue of section 2(1) of the European Communities Act 1972, and
(b) are enforced, allowed and followed accordingly,
continue on and after exit day to be recognised and available in domestic law (and to be enforced, allowed and followed accordingly).

(2) Subsection (1) does not apply to any rights, powers, liabilities, obligations, restrictions, remedies or procedures so far as they—
(a) form part of domestic law by virtue of section 3, or
(b) arise under an EU directive (including as applied by the EEA agreement) and are not of a kind recognised by the European Court or any court or tribunal in the United Kingdom in a case decided before exit day (whether or not as an essential part of the decision in the case).

(3) This section is subject to section 5 and Schedule 1 (exceptions to savings and incorporation).

5. Exceptions to savings and incorporation

(1) The principle of the supremacy of EU law does not apply to any enactment or rule of law passed or made on or after exit day.

(2) Accordingly, the principle of the supremacy of EU law continues to apply on or after exit day so far as relevant to the interpretation, disapplication or quashing of any enactment or rule of law passed or made before exit day.

(3) Subsection (1) does not prevent the principle of the supremacy of EU law from applying to a modification made on or after exit day of any enactment or rule of law passed or made before exit day if the application of the principle is consistent with the intention of the modification.

(4) The Charter of Fundamental Rights is not part of domestic law on or after exit day.

(5) Subsection (4) does not affect the retention in domestic law on or after exit day in accordance with this Act of any fundamental rights or principles which exist irrespective of the Charter (and references to the Charter in any case law are, so far as necessary for this purpose, to be read as if they were references to any corresponding retained fundamental rights or principles).

(6) Schedule 1 (which makes further provision about exceptions to savings and incorporation) has effect.

6. Interpretation of retained EU law

(1) A court or tribunal—

(a) is not bound by any principles laid down, or any decisions made, on or after exit day by the European Court, and

(b) cannot refer any matter to the European Court on or after exit day.

(2) Subject to this and subsections (3) to (6), a court or tribunal may have regard to anything done on or after exit day by the European Court, another EU entity or the EU so far as it is relevant to any matter before the court or tribunal.

(3) Any question as to the validity, meaning or effect of any retained EU law is to be decided, so far as that law is unmodified on or after exit day and so far as they are relevant to it—

(a) in accordance with any retained case law and any retained general principles of EU law, and

(b) having regard (among other things) to the limits, immediately before exit day, of EU competences.

(4) But—

(a) the Supreme Court is not bound by any retained EU case law,

(b) the High Court of Justiciary is not bound by any retained EU case law when—

   (i) sitting as a court of appeal otherwise than in relation to a compatibility issue (within the meaning given by section 288ZA(2) of the Criminal Procedure (Scotland) Act 1995) or a devolution issue (within the meaning given by paragraph 1 of Schedule 6 to the Scotland Act 1998), or

(ii) sitting on a reference under section 123(1) of the Criminal Procedure (Scotland) Act 1995, and

(c) no court or tribunal is bound by any retained domestic case law that it would not otherwise be bound by.

(5) In deciding whether to depart from any retained EU case law, the Supreme Court or the High Court of Justiciary must apply the same test as it would apply in deciding whether to depart from its own case law.

(6) Subsection (3) does not prevent the validity, meaning or effect of any retained EU law which has been modified on or after exit day from being decided as provided for in that subsection if doing so is consistent with the intention of the modifications.

(7) In this Act—

"retained case law" means—

(a) retained domestic case law, and

(b) retained EU case law;

"retained domestic case law" means any principles laid down by, and any decisions of, a court or tribunal in the United Kingdom, as they have effect immediately before exit day and so far as they—

(a) relate to anything to which section 2, 3 or 4 applies, and

(b) are not excluded by section 5 or Schedule 1,

(as those principles and decisions are modified by or under this Act or by other domestic law from time to time);

"retained EU case law" means any principles laid down by, and any decisions of, the European Court, as they have effect in EU law immediately before exit day and so far as they—

(a) relate to anything to which section 2, 3 or 4 applies, and

(b) are not excluded by section 5 or Schedule 1,

(as those principles and decisions are modified by or under this Act or by other domestic law from time to time);

"retained EU law" means anything which, on or after exit day, continues to be, or forms part of, domestic law by virtue of section 2, 3 or 4 or subsection (3) or (6) above (as that body of law is added to or otherwise modified by or under this Act or by other domestic law from time to time);

"retained general principles of EU law" means the general principles of EU law, as they have effect in EU law immediately before exit day and so far as they—

(a) relate to anything to which section 2, 3 or 4 applies, and

(b) are not excluded by section 5 or Schedule 1,

(as those principles are modified by or under this Act or by other domestic law from time to time).

7. Status of retained EU law

(1) Anything which—

(a) was, immediately before exit day, primary legislation of a particular kind, subordinate legislation of a particular kind or another enactment of a particular kind, and

(b) continues to be domestic law on and after exit day by virtue of section 2,

continues to be domestic law as an enactment of the same kind.

(2) Retained direct principal EU legislation cannot be modified by any primary or subordinate legislation other than—

(a) an Act of Parliament,

(b) any other primary legislation (so far as it has the power to make such a modification), or

(c) any subordinate legislation so far as it is made under a power which permits such a modification by virtue of—

   (i) paragraph 3, 5(3) (a) or (4) (a), 8(3), 10(3) (a) or (4) (a), 11(2) (a) or 12(3) of Schedule 8,

   (ii) any other provision made by or under this Act,

   (iii) any provision made by or under an Act of Parliament passed before, and in the same Session as, this Act, or

   (iv) any provision made on or after the passing of this Act by or under primary legislation.

(3) Retained direct minor EU legislation cannot be modified by any primary or subordinate legislation other than—

(a) an Act of Parliament,

(b) any other primary legislation (so far as it has the power to make such a modification), or

(c) any subordinate legislation so far as it is made under a power which permits such a modification by virtue of—

   (i) paragraph 3, 5(2) or (4) (a), 8(3), 10(2) or (4) (a) or 12(3) of Schedule 8,

   (ii) any other provision made by or under this Act,

   (iii) any provision made by or under an Act of Parliament passed before, and in the same Session as, this Act, or

   (iv) any provision made on or after the passing of this Act by or under primary legislation.

(4) Anything which is retained EU law by virtue of section 4 cannot be modified by any primary or subordinate legislation other than—

(a) an Act of Parliament,

(b) any other primary legislation (so far as it has the power to make such a modification), or

(c) any subordinate legislation so far as it is made under a power which permits such a modification by virtue of—

(i) paragraph 3, 5(3) (b) or (4) (b), 8(3), 10(3) (b) or (4) (b), 11(2) (b) or 12(3) of Schedule 8,

(ii)
any other provision made by or under this Act,

(iii)
any provision made by or under an Act of Parliament passed before, and in the same Session as, this Act, or

(iv)
any provision made on or after the passing of this Act by or under primary legislation.

(5) For other provisions about the status of retained EU law, see—

(a) section 5(1) to (3) (status of retained EU law in relation to other enactments or rules of law),

(b) section 6 (status of retained case law and retained general principles of EU law),

(c) section 15(2) and Part 2 of Schedule 5 (status of retained EU law for the purposes of the rules of evidence),

(d) paragraphs 13 to 16 of Schedule 8 (affirmative and enhanced scrutiny procedure for, and information about, instruments which amend or revoke subordinate legislation under section 2(2) of the European Communities Act 1972 including subordinate legislation implementing EU directives),

(e) paragraphs 19 and 20 of that Schedule (status of certain retained direct EU legislation for the purposes of the Interpretation Act 1978), and

(f) paragraph 30 of that Schedule (status of retained direct EU legislation for the purposes of the Human Rights Act 1998).

(6) In this Act—

"retained direct minor EU legislation" means any retained direct EU legislation which is not retained direct principal EU legislation;

"retained direct principal EU legislation" means—

(a) any EU regulation so far as it—

(i) forms part of domestic law on and after exit day by virtue of section 3, and

(ii) was not EU tertiary legislation immediately before exit day, or

(b) any Annex to the EEA agreement so far as it—

(i) forms part of domestic law on and after exit day by virtue of section 3, and

(ii) refers to, or contains adaptations of, any EU regulation so far as it falls within paragraph (a),

(as modified by or under this Act or by other domestic law from time to time).

Main powers in connection with withdrawal

8. Dealing with deficiencies arising from withdrawal

(1) A Minister of the Crown may by regulations make such provision as the Minister considers appropriate to prevent, remedy or mitigate—

(a) any failure of retained EU law to operate effectively, or

(b) any other deficiency in retained EU law,

arising from the withdrawal of the United Kingdom from the EU.

(2) Deficiencies in retained EU law are where the Minister considers that retained EU law—

(a) contains anything which has no practical application in relation to the United Kingdom or any part of it or is otherwise redundant or substantially redundant,

(b) confers functions on, or in relation to, EU entities which no longer have functions in that respect under EU law in relation to the United Kingdom or any part of it,

(c) makes provision for, or in connection with, reciprocal arrangements between—
   (i) the United Kingdom or any part of it or a public authority in the United Kingdom, and
   (ii) the EU, an EU entity, a member State or a public authority in a member State, which no longer exist or are no longer appropriate,

(d) makes provision for, or in connection with, other arrangements which—
   (i) involve the EU, an EU entity, a member State or a public authority in a member State, or
   (ii) are otherwise dependent upon the United Kingdom's membership of the EU, and which no longer exist or are no longer appropriate,

(e) makes provision for, or in connection with, any reciprocal or other arrangements not falling within paragraph (c) or (d) which no longer exist, or are no longer appropriate, as a result of the United Kingdom ceasing to be a party to any of the EU Treaties,

(f) does not contain any functions or restrictions which—
   (i) were in an EU directive and in force immediately before exit day (including any power to make EU tertiary legislation), and
   (ii) it is appropriate to retain, or

(g) contains EU references which are no longer appropriate.

(3) There is also a deficiency in retained EU law where the Minister considers that there is—

(a) anything in retained EU law which is of a similar kind to any deficiency which falls within subsection (2), or

(b) a deficiency in retained EU law of a kind described, or provided for, in regulations made by a Minister of the Crown.

(4) But retained EU law is not deficient merely because it does not contain any modification of EU law which is adopted or notified, comes into force or only applies on or after exit day.

(5) Regulations under subsection (1) may make any provision that could be made by an Act of Parliament.
(6) Regulations under subsection (1) may (among other things) provide for functions of EU entities or public authorities in member States (including making an instrument of a legislative character or providing funding) to be—
(a) exercisable instead by a public authority (whether or not established for the purpose) in the United Kingdom, or
(b) replaced, abolished or otherwise modified.
(7) But regulations under subsection (1) may not—
(a) impose or increase taxation or fees,
(b) make retrospective provision,
(c) create a relevant criminal offence,
(d) establish a public authority,
(e) be made to implement the withdrawal agreement,
(f) amend, repeal or revoke the Human Rights Act 1998 or any subordinate legislation made under it, or
(g) amend or repeal the Scotland Act 1998, the Government of Wales Act 2006 or the Northern Ireland Act 1998 (unless the regulations are made by virtue of paragraph 21 (b) of Schedule 7 to this Act or are amending or repealing any provision of those Acts which modifies another enactment).
(8) No regulations may be made under this section after the end of the period of two years beginning with exit day.
(9) The reference in subsection (1) to a failure or other deficiency arising from the withdrawal of the United Kingdom from the EU includes a reference to any failure or other deficiency arising from that withdrawal taken together with the operation of any provision, or the interaction between any provisions, made by or under this Act.

9. Implementing the withdrawal agreement

(1) A Minister of the Crown may by regulations make such provision as the Minister considers appropriate for the purposes of implementing the withdrawal agreement if the Minister considers that such provision should be in force on or before exit day, subject to the prior enactment of a statute by Parliament approving the final terms of withdrawal of the United Kingdom from the EU.
(2) Regulations under this section may make any provision that could be made by an Act of Parliament.
(3) But regulations under this section may not—
(a) impose or increase taxation or fees,
(b) make retrospective provision,
(c) create a relevant criminal offence,
(d) establish a public authority, or

(e) amend, repeal or revoke the Human Rights Act 1998 or any subordinate legislation made under it.

(4) No regulations may be made under this section after exit day.

Devolution

10. Continuation of North-South co-operation and the prevention of new border arrangements

(1) In exercising any of the powers under this Act, a Minister of the Crown or devolved authority must—

(a) act in a way that is compatible with the terms of the Northern Ireland Act 1998, and

(b) have due regard to the joint report from the negotiators of the EU and the United Kingdom Government on progress during phase 1 of negotiations under Article 50 of the Treaty on European Union.

(2) Nothing in section 8, 9 or 23(1) or (6) of this Act authorises regulations which—

(a) diminish any form of North-South cooperation provided for by the Belfast Agreement (as defined by section 98 of the Northern Ireland Act 1998), or

(b) create or facilitate border arrangements between Northern Ireland and the Republic of Ireland after exit day which feature physical infrastructure, including border posts, or checks and controls, that did not exist before exit day and are not in accordance with an agreement between the United Kingdom and the EU.

11. Powers involving devolved authorities corresponding to sections 8 and 9

Schedule 2 (which confers powers to make regulations involving devolved authorities which correspond to the powers conferred by sections 8 and 9) has effect.

12. Retaining EU restrictions in devolution legislation etc.

(1) In section 29(2) (d) of the Scotland Act 1998 (no competence for the Scottish Parliament to legislate incompatibly with EU law) for "with EU law" substitute "in breach of the restriction in section 30A(1)".

(2) After section 30 of that Act (legislative competence: supplementary) insert—

"**30A. Legislative competence: restriction relating to retained EU law**

(1) An Act of the Scottish Parliament cannot modify, or confer power by subordinate legislation to modify, retained EU law so far as the modification is of a description specified in regulations made by a Minister of the Crown.

(2) But subsection (1) does not apply to any modification so far as it would, immediately before exit day, have been within the legislative competence of the Parliament.

(3) A Minister of the Crown must not lay for approval before each House of the Parliament of the United Kingdom a draft of a statutory instrument containing regulations under this section unless—
(a) the Scottish Parliament has made a consent decision in relation to the laying of the draft, or
(b) the 40 day period has ended without the Parliament having made such a decision.
(4) For the purposes of subsection (3) a consent decision is—
(a) a decision to agree a motion consenting to the laying of the draft,
(b) a decision not to agree a motion consenting to the laying of the draft, or
(c) a decision to agree a motion refusing to consent to the laying of the draft;
and a consent decision is made when the Parliament first makes a decision falling within any of paragraphs (a) to (c) (whether or not it subsequently makes another such decision).
(5) A Minister of the Crown who is proposing to lay a draft as mentioned in subsection (3) must—
(a) provide a copy of the draft to the Scottish Ministers, and
(b) inform the Presiding Officer that a copy has been so provided.
(6) See also paragraph 6 of Schedule 7 (duty to make explanatory statement about regulations under this section including a duty to explain any decision to lay a draft without the consent of the Parliament).
(7) No regulations may be made under this section after the end of the period of two years beginning with exit day.
(8) Subsection (7) does not affect the continuation in force of regulations made under this section at or before the end of the period mentioned in that subsection.
(9) Any regulations under this section which are in force at the end of the period of five years beginning with the time at which they came into force are revoked in their application to any Act of the Scottish Parliament which receives Royal Assent after the end of that period.
(10) Subsections (3) to (8) do not apply in relation to regulations which only relate to a revocation of a specification.
(11) In this section—
"the 40 day period" means the period of 40 days beginning with the day on which a copy of the draft instrument is provided to the Scottish Ministers,
and, in calculating that period, no account is to be taken of any time during which the Parliament is dissolved or during which it is in recess for more than four days."

(3) In section 108A(2) (e) of the Government of Wales Act 2006 (no competence for the National Assembly for Wales to legislate incompatibly with EU law) for "with EU law" substitute "in breach of the restriction in section 109A(1)".

(4) After section 109 of that Act (legislative competence: supplementary) insert—

"109A. Legislative competence: restriction relating to retained EU law

(1) An Act of the Assembly cannot modify, or confer power by subordinate legislation to modify, retained EU law so far as the modification is of a description specified in regulations made by a Minister of the Crown.

(2) But subsection (1) does not apply to any modification so far as it would, immediately before exit day, have been within the Assembly's legislative competence.

(3) No regulations are to be made under this section unless a draft of the statutory instrument containing them has been laid before, and approved by a resolution of, each House of Parliament.

(4) A Minister of the Crown must not lay a draft as mentioned in subsection (3) unless—

(a) the Assembly has made a consent decision in relation to the laying of the draft, or

(b) the 40 day period has ended without the Assembly having made such a decision.

(5) For the purposes of subsection (4) a consent decision is—

(a) a decision to agree a motion consenting to the laying of the draft,

(b) a decision not to agree a motion consenting to the laying of the draft, or

(c) a decision to agree a motion refusing to consent to the laying of the draft;

and a consent decision is made when the Assembly first makes a decision falling within any of paragraphs (a) to (c) (whether or not it subsequently makes another such decision).

(6) A Minister of the Crown who is proposing to lay a draft as mentioned in subsection (3) must—

(a) provide a copy of the draft to the Welsh Ministers, and

(b) inform the Presiding Officer that a copy has been so provided.

(7) See also section 157ZA (duty to make explanatory statement about regulations under this section including a duty to explain any decision to lay a draft without the consent of the Assembly).

(8) No regulations may be made under this section after the end of the period of two years beginning with exit day.

(9) Subsection (8) does not affect the continuation in force of regulations made under this section at or before the end of the period mentioned in that subsection.

(10) Any regulations under this section which are in force at the end of the period of five years beginning with the time at which they came into force are revoked in their application to any Act of the Assembly which receives Royal Assent after the end of that period.

(11) Subsections (4) to (9) do not apply in relation to regulations which only relate to a revocation of a specification.

(12) In this section—

"the 40 day period" means the period of 40 days beginning with the day on which a copy of the draft instrument is provided to the Welsh Ministers,

and, in calculating that period, no account is to be taken of any time during which the Assembly is dissolved or during which it is in recess for more than four days."

(5) In section 6(2) (d) of the Northern Ireland Act 1998 (no competence for the Northern Ireland Assembly to legislate incompatibly with EU law) for "incompatible with EU law" substitute "in breach of the restriction in section 6A(1)".

(6) After section 6 of that Act (legislative competence) insert—

"**6A. Restriction relating to retained EU law**

(1) An Act of the Assembly cannot modify, or confer power by subordinate legislation to modify, retained EU law so far as the modification is of a description specified in regulations made by a Minister of the Crown.

(2) But subsection (1) does not apply to any modification so far as it would, immediately before exit day, have been within the legislative competence of the Assembly.

(3) A Minister of the Crown must not lay for approval before each House of Parliament a draft of a statutory instrument containing regulations under this section unless—

(a) the Assembly has made a consent decision in relation to the laying of the draft, or

(b) the 40 day period has ended without the Assembly having made such a decision.

(4) For the purposes of subsection (3) a consent decision is—

(a) a decision to agree a motion consenting to the laying of the draft,

(b) a decision not to agree a motion consenting to the laying of the draft, or

(c) a decision to agree a motion refusing to consent to the laying of the draft;

and a consent decision is made when the Assembly first makes a decision falling within any of paragraphs (a) to (c) (whether or not it subsequently makes another such decision).

(5) A Minister of the Crown who is proposing to lay a draft as mentioned in subsection (3) must—

(a) provide a copy of the draft to the relevant Northern Ireland department, and

(b) inform the Presiding Officer that a copy has been so provided.

(6) See also section 96A (duty to make explanatory statement about regulations under this section including a duty to explain any decision to lay a draft without the consent of the Assembly).

(7) No regulations may be made under this section after the end of the period of two years beginning with exit day.

(8) Subsection (7) does not affect the continuation in force of regulations made under this section at or before the end of the period mentioned in that subsection.

(9) Any regulations under this section which are in force at the end of the period of five years beginning with the time at which they came into force are revoked in their application to any Act of the Assembly which receives Royal Assent after the end of that period.

(10) Subsections (3) to (8) do not apply in relation to regulations which only relate to a revocation of a specification.

(11) Regulations under this section may include such supplementary, incidental, consequential, transitional, transitory or saving provision as the Minister of the Crown making them considers appropriate.

(12) In this section—

"the relevant Northern Ireland department" means such Northern Ireland department as the Minister of the Crown concerned considers appropriate;

"the 40 day period" means the period of 40 days beginning with the day on which a copy of the draft instrument is provided to the relevant Northern Ireland department,

and, in calculating that period, no account is to be taken of any time during which the Assembly is dissolved or during which it is in recess for more than four days."

(7) Part 1 of Schedule 3 (which makes corresponding provision in relation to executive competence to that made by subsections (1) to (6) in relation to legislative competence) has effect.

(8) Part 2 of Schedule 3 (which imposes reporting obligations on a Minister of the Crown in recognition of the fact that the powers to make regulations conferred by subsections

(1) to (6) and Part 1 of Schedule 3, and any restrictions arising by virtue of them, are intended to be temporary) has effect.

(9) A Minister of the Crown may by regulations—

(a) repeal any of the following provisions—

    (i) section 30A or 57(4) to (15) of the Scotland Act 1998,

    (ii) section 80(8) to (8L) or 109A of the Government of Wales Act 2006, or

    (iii) section 6A or 24(3) to (15) of the Northern Ireland Act 1998, or

(b) modify any enactment in consequence of any such repeal.

(10) Until all of the provisions mentioned in subsection (9) (a) have been repealed, a Minister of the Crown must, after the end of each review period, consider whether it is appropriate—

(a) to repeal each of those provisions so far as it has not been repealed, or

(b) to revoke any regulations made under any of those provisions so far as they have not been revoked.

(11) In considering whether to exercise the power to make regulations under subsection (9), a Minister of the Crown must have regard (among other things) to—

(a) the fact that the powers to make regulations conferred by the provisions mentioned in subsection (9) (a), and any restrictions arising by virtue of them, are intended to be temporary and, where appropriate, replaced with other arrangements, and

(b) any progress which has been made in implementing those other arrangements.

(12) Part 3 of Schedule 3 (which contains amendments of devolution legislation not dealt with elsewhere) has effect.

(13) In this section—

"arrangement" means any enactment or other arrangement (whether or not legally enforceable);

"review period" means—

(a) the period of three months beginning with the day on which subsection (10) comes into force, and

(b) after that, each successive period of three months.

Parliamentary approval of outcome of EU negotiations

13. Parliamentary approval of the outcome of negotiations with the EU

(1) The withdrawal agreement may be ratified only if—

(a) a Minister of the Crown has laid before each House of Parliament—

    (i) a statement that political agreement has been reached,

    (ii) a copy of the negotiated withdrawal agreement, and

    (iii) a copy of the framework for the future relationship,

(b) the negotiated withdrawal agreement and the framework for the future relationship have been approved by a resolution of the House of Commons on a motion moved by a Minister of the Crown,

(c) a motion for the House of Lords to take note of the negotiated withdrawal agreement and the framework for the future relationship has been tabled in the House of Lords by a Minister of the Crown and—
  (i) the House of Lords has debated the motion, or
  (ii) the House of Lords has not concluded a debate on the motion before the end of the period of five Lords sitting days beginning with the first Lords sitting day after the day on which the House of Commons passes the resolution mentioned in paragraph (b), and

(d) an Act of Parliament has been passed which contains provision for the implementation of the withdrawal agreement.

(2) So far as practicable, a Minister of the Crown must make arrangements for the motion mentioned in subsection (1) (b) to be debated and voted on by the House of Commons before the European Parliament decides whether it consents to the withdrawal agreement being concluded on behalf of the EU in accordance with Article 50(2) of the Treaty on European Union.

(3) Subsection (4) applies if the House of Commons decides not to pass the resolution mentioned in subsection (1) (b).

(4) A Minister of the Crown must, within the period of 21 days beginning with the day on which the House of Commons decides not to pass the resolution, make a statement setting out how Her Majesty's Government proposes to proceed in relation to negotiations for the United Kingdom's withdrawal from the EU under Article 50(2) of the Treaty on European Union.

(5) A statement under subsection (4) must be made in writing and be published in such manner as the Minister making it considers appropriate.

(6) A Minister of the Crown must make arrangements for—

(a) a motion in neutral terms, to the effect that the House of Commons has considered the matter of the statement mentioned in subsection (4), to be moved in that House by a Minister of the Crown within the period of seven Commons sitting days beginning with the day on which the statement is made, and

(b) a motion for the House of Lords to take note of the statement to be moved in that House by a Minister of the Crown within the period of seven Lords sitting days beginning with the day on which the statement is made.

(7) Subsection (8) applies if the Prime Minister makes a statement before the end of 21 January 2019 that no agreement in principle can be reached in negotiations under Article 50(2) of the Treaty on European Union on the substance of—

(a) the arrangements for the United Kingdom's withdrawal from the EU, and

(b) the framework for the future relationship between the EU and the United Kingdom after withdrawal.

(8) A Minister of the Crown must, within the period of 14 days beginning with the day on which the statement mentioned in subsection (7) is made—

(a) make a statement setting out how Her Majesty's Government proposes to proceed, and

(b) make arrangements for—
  (i) a motion in neutral terms, to the effect that the House of Commons has considered the matter of the statement mentioned in paragraph (a), to be moved in that House by a Minister of the Crown within the period of seven Commons sitting days beginning with the day on which the statement mentioned in paragraph (a) is made, and
  (ii) a motion for the House of Lords to take note of the statement mentioned in paragraph (a) to be moved in that House by a Minister of the Crown within the period of seven Lords sitting days beginning with the day on which the statement mentioned in paragraph (a) is made.

(9) A statement under subsection (7) or (8) (a) must be made in writing and be published in such manner as the Minister making it considers appropriate.

(10) Subsection (11) applies if, at the end of 21 January 2019, there is no agreement in principle in negotiations under Article 50(2) of the Treaty on European Union on the substance of—

(a) the arrangements for the United Kingdom's withdrawal from the EU, and

(b) the framework for the future relationship between the EU and the United Kingdom after withdrawal.

(11) A Minister of the Crown must, within the period of five days beginning with the end of 21 January 2019—

(a) make a statement setting out how Her Majesty's Government proposes to proceed, and

(b) make arrangements for—
  (i) a motion in neutral terms, to the effect that the House of Commons has considered the matter of the statement mentioned in paragraph (a), to be moved in that House by a Minister of the Crown within the period of five Commons sitting days beginning with the end of 21 January 2019, and
  (ii) a motion for the House of Lords to take note of the statement mentioned in paragraph (a) to be moved in that House by a Minister of the Crown within the period of five Lords sitting days beginning with the end of 21 January 2019.

(12) A statement under subsection (11) (a) must be made in writing and be published in such manner as the Minister making it considers appropriate

(13) For the purposes of this section—

(a) a statement made under subsection (4), (8) (a) or (11) (a) may be combined with a statement made under another of those provisions,

(b) a motion falling within subsection (6) (a), (8) (b) (i) or (11) (b) (i) may be combined into a single motion with another motion falling within another of those provisions, and

(c) a motion falling within subsection (6) (b), (8) (b) (ii) or (11) (b) (ii) may be combined into a single motion with another motion falling within another of those provisions.

(14) This section does not affect the operation of Part 2 of the Constitutional Reform and Governance Act 2010 (ratification of treaties) in relation to the withdrawal agreement.

(15) In subsection (1) "framework for the future relationship" means the document or documents identified, by the statement that political agreement has been reached, as reflecting the agreement in principle on the substance of the framework for the future relationship between the EU and the United Kingdom after withdrawal.

(16) In this section—

"Commons sitting day" means a day on which the House of Commons is sitting (and a day is only a day on which the House of Commons is sitting if the House begins to sit on that day);

"Lords sitting day" means a day on which the House of Lords is sitting (and a day is only a day on which the House of Lords is sitting if the House begins to sit on that day);

"negotiated withdrawal agreement" means the draft of the withdrawal agreement identified by the statement that political agreement has been reached;

"ratified", in relation to the withdrawal agreement, has the same meaning as it does for the purposes of Part 2 of the Constitutional Reform and Governance Act 2010 in relation to a treaty (see section 25 of that Act);

"statement that political agreement has been reached" means a statement made in writing by a Minister of the Crown which—

(a) states that, in the Minister's opinion, an agreement in principle has been reached in negotiations under Article 50(2) of the Treaty on European Union on the substance of —

   (i) the arrangements for the United Kingdom's withdrawal from the EU, and
   (ii) the framework for the future relationship between the EU and the United Kingdom after withdrawal,

(b) identifies a draft of the withdrawal agreement which, in the Minister's opinion, reflects the agreement in principle so far as relating to the arrangements for withdrawal, and

(c) identifies one or more documents which, in the Minister's opinion, reflect the agreement in principle so far as relating to the framework.

Financial and other matters

14. Financial provision
(1) Schedule 4 (which contains powers in connection with fees and charges) has effect.
(2) A Minister of the Crown, government department or devolved authority may incur expenditure, for the purpose of, or in connection with, preparing for anything about which provision may be made under a power to make subordinate legislation conferred or modified by or under this Act, before any such provision is made.
(3) There is to be paid out of money provided by Parliament—
(a) any expenditure incurred by a Minister of the Crown, government department or other public authority by virtue of this Act, and
(b) any increase attributable to this Act in the sums payable by virtue of any other Act out of money so provided.
(4) Subsection (3) is subject to any other provision made by or under this Act or any other enactment.

15. Publication and rules of evidence
(1) Part 1 of Schedule 5 (which makes provision for the publication by the Queen's Printer of copies of retained direct EU legislation and related information) has effect.
(2) Part 2 of Schedule 5 (which makes provision about rules of evidence) has effect.

16. Maintenance of environmental principles etc.
(1) The Secretary of State must, within the period of six months beginning with the day on which this Act is passed, publish a draft Bill consisting of—
(a) a set of environmental principles,
(b) a duty on the Secretary of State to publish a statement of policy in relation to the application and interpretation of those principles in connection with the making and development of policies by Ministers of the Crown,
(c) a duty which ensures that Ministers of the Crown must have regard, in circumstances provided for by or under the Bill, to the statement mentioned in paragraph (b),
(d) provisions for the establishment of a public authority with functions for taking, in circumstances provided for by or under the Bill, proportionate enforcement action (including legal proceedings if necessary) where the authority considers that a Minister of the Crown is not complying with environmental law (as it is defined in the Bill), and
(e) such other provisions as the Secretary of State considers appropriate.
(2) The set of environmental principles mentioned in subsection (1) (a) must (however worded) consist of—
(a) the precautionary principle so far as relating to the environment,
(b) the principle of preventative action to avert environmental damage,

(c) the principle that environmental damage should as a priority be rectified at source,
(d) the polluter pays principle,
(e) the principle of sustainable development,
(f) the principle that environmental protection requirements must be integrated into the definition and implementation of policies and activities,
(g) public access to environmental information,
(h) public participation in environmental decision-making, and
(i) access to justice in relation to environmental matters.

17. Family unity for those seeking asylum or other protection in Europe
(1) A Minister of the Crown must seek to negotiate, on behalf of the United Kingdom, an agreement with the EU under which, after the United Kingdom's withdrawal from the EU, in accordance with the agreement—
(a) an unaccompanied child who has made an application for international protection to a member State may, if it is in the child's best interests, come to the United Kingdom to join a relative who—
   (i) is a lawful resident of the United Kingdom, or
   (ii) has made a protection claim which has not been decided, and
(b) an unaccompanied child in the United Kingdom, who has made a protection claim, may go to a member State to join a relative there, in equivalent circumstances.
(2) For the purposes of subsection (1) (a) (i) a person is not a lawful resident of the United Kingdom if the person requires leave to enter or remain in the United Kingdom but does not have it.
(3) For the purposes of subsection (1) (a) (ii), a protection claim is decided—
(a) when the Secretary of State notifies the claimant of the Secretary of State's decision on the claim, unless the claimant appeals against the decision, or
(b) if the claimant appeals against the Secretary of State's decision on the claim, when the appeal is disposed of.
(4) In this section—
"application for international protection" has the meaning given by Article 2(h) of Directive 2011/95/EU of the European Parliament and of the Council on standards for the qualification of third-country nationals or stateless persons as beneficiaries of international protection, for a uniform status for refugees or for persons eligible for subsidiary protection, and for the content of the protection granted;
"protection claim" has the same meaning as in Part 5 of the Nationality, Immigration and Asylum Act 2002 (see section 82(2) of that Act);
"relative", in relation to an unaccompanied child, means—
(a) a spouse or civil partner of the child or any person with whom the child has a durable relationship that is similar to marriage or civil partnership, or

(b) a parent, grandparent, uncle, aunt, brother or sister of the child;
"unaccompanied child" means a person under the age of 18 ("the child") who is not in the care of a person who—
(a) is aged 18 or over, and
(b) by law or custom of the country or territory in which the child is present, has responsibility for caring for the child.

18. Customs arrangement as part of the framework for the future relationship

(1) A Minister of the Crown must lay before each House of Parliament a statement in writing outlining the steps taken by Her Majesty's Government, in negotiations under Article 50(2) of the Treaty on European Union, to seek to negotiate an agreement, as part of the framework for the United Kingdom's future relationship with the EU, for the United Kingdom to participate in a customs arrangement with the EU.
(2) The statement under subsection (1) must be laid before both Houses of Parliament before the end of 31 October 2018.

19. Future interaction with the law and agencies of the EU

Nothing in this Act shall prevent the United Kingdom from—
(a) replicating in domestic law any EU law made on or after exit day, or
(b) continuing to participate in, or have a formal relationship with, the agencies of the EU after exit day.

General and final provision

20. Interpretation

(1) In this Act—
"Charter of Fundamental Rights" means the Charter of Fundamental Rights of the European Union of 7 December 2000, as adapted at Strasbourg on 12 December 2007;
"devolved authority" means—
(a) the Scottish Ministers,
(b) the Welsh Ministers, or
(c) a Northern Ireland department;
"domestic law" means—
(a) in section 3, the law of England and Wales, Scotland and Northern Ireland, and
(b) in any other case, the law of England and Wales, Scotland or Northern Ireland;
"the EEA" means the European Economic Area;
"enactment" means an enactment whenever passed or made and includes—
(a) an enactment contained in any Order in Council, order, rules, regulations, scheme, warrant, byelaw or other instrument made under an Act,

(b) an enactment contained in any Order in Council made in exercise of Her Majesty's Prerogative,
(c) an enactment contained in, or in an instrument made under, an Act of the Scottish Parliament,
(d) an enactment contained in, or in an instrument made under, a Measure or Act of the National Assembly for Wales,
(e) an enactment contained in, or in an instrument made under, Northern Ireland legislation,
(f) an enactment contained in any instrument made by a member of the Scottish Government, the Welsh Ministers, the First Minister for Wales, the Counsel General to the Welsh Government, a Northern Ireland Minister, the First Minister in Northern Ireland, the deputy First Minister in Northern Ireland or a Northern Ireland department in exercise of prerogative or other executive functions of Her Majesty which are exercisable by such a person on behalf of Her Majesty,
(g) an enactment contained in, or in an instrument made under, a Measure of the Church Assembly or of the General Synod of the Church of England, and
(h) except in sections 2 and 7 or where there is otherwise a contrary intention, any retained direct EU legislation;

"EU decision" means—
(a) a decision within the meaning of Article 288 of the Treaty on the Functioning of the European Union, or
(b) a decision under former Article 34(2) (c) of the Treaty on European Union;

"EU directive" means a directive within the meaning of Article 288 of the Treaty on the Functioning of the European Union;

"EU entity" means an EU institution or any office, body or agency of the EU;

"EU reference" means—
(a) any reference to the EU, an EU entity or a member State,
(b) any reference to an EU directive or any other EU law, or
(c) any other reference which relates to the EU;

"EU regulation" means a regulation within the meaning of Article 288 of the Treaty on the Functioning of the European Union;

"EU tertiary legislation" means—
(a) any provision made under—
  (i) an EU regulation,
  (ii) a decision within the meaning of Article 288 of the Treaty on the Functioning of the European Union, or
  (iii) an EU directive,
    by virtue of Article 290 or 291(2) of the Treaty on the Functioning of the European Union or former Article 202 of the Treaty establishing the European Community, or

(b) any measure adopted in accordance with former Article 34(2) (c) of the Treaty on European Union to implement decisions under former Article 34(2) (c),

but does not include any such provision or measure which is an EU directive;

"exempt EU instrument" means anything which is an exempt EU instrument by virtue of Schedule 6;

"exit day" means 29 March 2019 at 11.00 p.m. (and see subsections (2) to (5));

"member State" (except in the definitions of "direct EU legislation" and "EU reference") does not include the United Kingdom;

"Minister of the Crown" has the same meaning as in the Ministers of the Crown Act 1975 and also includes the Commissioners for Her Majesty's Revenue and Customs;

"modify" includes amend, repeal or revoke (and related expressions are to be read accordingly);

"Northern Ireland devolved authority" means the First Minister and deputy First Minister in Northern Ireland acting jointly, a Northern Ireland Minister or a Northern Ireland department;

"primary legislation" means—

(a) an Act of Parliament,

(b) an Act of the Scottish Parliament,

(c) a Measure or Act of the National Assembly for Wales, or

(d) Northern Ireland legislation;

"public authority" means a public authority within the meaning of section 6 of the Human Rights Act 1998;

"relevant criminal offence" means an offence for which an individual who has reached the age of 18 (or, in relation to Scotland or Northern Ireland, 21) is capable of being sentenced to imprisonment for a term of more than 2 years (ignoring any enactment prohibiting or restricting the imprisonment of individuals who have no previous convictions);

"retained direct EU legislation" means any direct EU legislation which forms part of domestic law by virtue of section 3 (as modified by or under this Act or by other domestic law from time to time, and including any instruments made under it on or after exit day);

"retrospective provision", in relation to provision made by regulations, means provision taking effect from a date earlier than the date on which the regulations are made;

"subordinate legislation" means—

(a) any Order in Council, order, rules, regulations, scheme, warrant, byelaw or other instrument made under any Act, or

(b) any instrument made under an Act of the Scottish Parliament, Northern Ireland legislation or a Measure or Act of the National Assembly for Wales,

and (except in section 7 or Schedule 2 or where there is a contrary intention) includes any Order in Council, order, rules, regulations, scheme, warrant, byelaw or other instrument made on or after exit day under any retained direct EU legislation;

"tribunal" means any tribunal in which legal proceedings may be brought;
"Wales" and "Welsh zone" have the same meaning as in the Government of Wales Act 2006 (see section 158 of that Act);
"withdrawal agreement" means an agreement (whether or not ratified) between the United Kingdom and the EU under Article 50(2) of the Treaty on European Union which sets out the arrangements for the United Kingdom's withdrawal from the EU.

(2) In this Act references to before, after or on exit day, or to beginning with exit day, are to be read as references to before, after or at 11.00 p.m. on 29 March 2019 or (as the case may be) to beginning with 11.00 p.m. on that day.

(3) Subsection (4) applies if the day or time on or at which the Treaties are to cease to apply to the United Kingdom in accordance with Article 50(3) of the Treaty on European Union is different from that specified in the definition of "exit day" in subsection (1).

(4) A Minister of the Crown may by regulations—

(a) amend the definition of "exit day" in subsection (1) to ensure that the day and time specified in the definition are the day and time that the Treaties are to cease to apply to the United Kingdom, and

(b) amend subsection (2) in consequence of any such amendment.

(5) In subsections (3) and (4) "the Treaties" means the Treaty on European Union and the Treaty on the Functioning of the European Union.

(6) In this Act references to anything which continues to be domestic law by virtue of section 2 include references to anything to which subsection (1) of that section applies which continues to be domestic law on or after exit day (whether or not it would have done so irrespective of that section).

(7) In this Act references to anything which is retained EU law by virtue of section 4 include references to any modifications, made by or under this Act or by other domestic law from time to time, of the rights, powers, liabilities, obligations, restrictions, remedies or procedures concerned.

(8) References in this Act (however expressed) to a public authority in the United Kingdom include references to a public authority in any part of the United Kingdom.

(9) References in this Act to former Article 34(2) (c) of the Treaty on European Union are references to that Article as it had effect at any time before the coming into force of the Treaty of Lisbon.

(10) Any other reference in this Act to—

(a) an Article of the Treaty on European Union or the Treaty on the Functioning of the European Union, or

(b) Article 10 of Title VII of Protocol 36 to those treaties,

includes a reference to that Article as applied by Article 106a of the Euratom Treaty.

[*Section 21 is omitted.*]

22. Regulations

Schedule 7 (which makes provision about the scrutiny by Parliament and the devolved legislatures of regulations under this Act and contains other general provision about such regulations) has effect.

23. Consequential and transitional provision

(1) A Minister of the Crown may by regulations make such provision as the Minister considers appropriate in consequence of this Act.
(2) The power to make regulations under subsection (1) may (among other things) be exercised by modifying any provision made by or under an enactment.
(3) In subsection (2) "enactment" does not include primary legislation passed or made after the end of the Session in which this Act is passed.
(4) No regulations may be made under subsection (1) after the end of the period of 10 years beginning with exit day.
(5) Parts 1 and 2 of Schedule 8 (which contain consequential provision) have effect.
(6) A Minister of the Crown may by regulations make such transitional, transitory or saving provision as the Minister considers appropriate in connection with the coming into force of any provision of this Act (including its operation in connection with exit day).
(7) Parts 3 and 4 of Schedule 8 (which contain transitional, transitory and saving provision) have effect.
(8) The enactments mentioned in Schedule 9 (which contains repeals not made elsewhere in this Act) are repealed to the extent specified.

24. Extent

(1) Subject to subsections (2) and (3), this Act extends to England and Wales, Scotland and Northern Ireland.
(2) Any provision of this Act which amends or repeals an enactment has the same extent as the enactment amended or repealed.
(3) Regulations under section 8(1) or 23 may make provision which extends to Gibraltar —

(a) modifying any enactment which—
  (i) extends to Gibraltar and relates to European Parliamentary elections, or
  (ii) extends to Gibraltar for any purpose which is connected with Gibraltar forming part of an electoral region, under the European Parliamentary Elections Act 2002, for the purposes of such elections, or
(b) which is supplementary, incidental, consequential, transitional, transitory or saving provision in connection with a modification within paragraph (a).

25. Commencement and short title

(1) The following provisions—

(a) sections 8 to 11 (including Schedule 2),

(b) paragraphs 4, 5, 21(2) (b), 48(b), 51(2) (c) and (d) and (4) of Schedule 3 (and section 12(8) and (12) so far as relating to those paragraphs),

(c) sections 13 and 14 (including Schedule 4),

(d) sections 16 to 18,

(e) sections 20 to 22 (including Schedules 6 and 7),

(f) section 23(1) to (4) and (6),

(g) paragraph 41(10), 43 and 44 of Schedule 8 (and section 23(7) so far as relating to those paragraphs),

(h) section 24, and

(i) this section,

come into force on the day on which this Act is passed.

(2) In section 12—

(a) subsection (2) comes into force on the day on which this Act is passed for the purposes of making regulations under section 30A of the Scotland Act 1998,

(b) subsection (4) comes into force on that day for the purposes of making regulations under section 109A of the Government of Wales Act 2006, and

(c) subsection (6) comes into force on that day for the purposes of making regulations under section 6A of the Northern Ireland Act 1998.

(3) In Schedule 3—

(a) paragraph 1(b) comes into force on the day on which this Act is passed for the purposes of making regulations under section 57(4) of the Scotland Act 1998,

(b) paragraph 2 comes into force on that day for the purposes of making regulations under section 80(8) of the Government of Wales Act 2006,

(c) paragraph 3(b) comes into force on that day for the purposes of making regulations under section 24(3) of the Northern Ireland Act 1998,

(d) paragraph 24(2) comes into force on that day for the purposes of making regulations under section 30A of the Scotland Act 1998,

(e) paragraph 24(3) comes into force on that day for the purposes of making regulations under section 57(4) of the Scotland Act 1998,

(f) paragraph 25 comes into force on that day for the purposes of making regulations under section 30A or 57(4) of the Scotland Act 1998,

(g) paragraph 43 comes into force on that day for the purposes of making regulations under section 80(8) or 109A of the Government of Wales Act 2006, and

(h) paragraphs 57 and 58 come into force on that day for the purposes of making regulations under section 6A or 24(3) of the Northern Ireland Act 1998;

and section 12(7) and (12), so far as relating to each of those paragraphs, comes into force on that day for the purposes of making the regulations mentioned above in relation to that paragraph.

(4) The provisions of this Act, so far as they are not brought into force by subsections (1) to (3), come into force on such day as a Minister of the Crown may by regulations appoint; and different days may be appointed for different purposes.

(5) This Act may be cited as the European Union (Withdrawal) Act 2018.

European Union

21 Treaty on European Union[1]

HIS MAJESTY THE KING OF THE BELGIANS, HER MAJESTY THE QUEEN OF DENMARK, THE PRESIDENT OF THE FEDERAL REPUBLIC OF GERMANY, THE PRESIDENT OF IRELAND, THE PRESIDENT OF THE HELLENIC REPUBLIC, HIS MAJESTY THE KING OF SPAIN, THE PRESIDENT OF THE FRENCH REPUBLIC, THE PRESIDENT OF THE ITALIAN REPUBLIC, HIS ROYAL HIGHNESS THE GRAND DUKE OF LUXEMBOURG, HER MAJESTY THE QUEEN OF THE NETHERLANDS, THE PRESIDENT OF THE PORTUGUESE REPUBLIC, HER MAJESTY THE QUEEN OF THE UNITED KINGDOM OF GREAT BRITAIN AND NORTHERN IRELAND[2],

RESOLVED to mark a new stage in the process of European integration undertaken with the establishment of the European Communities,

DRAWING INSPIRATION from the cultural, religious and humanist inheritance of Europe, from which have developed the universal values of the inviolable and inalienable rights of the human person, freedom, democracy, equality and the rule of law,

RECALLING the historic importance of the ending of the division of the European continent and the need to create firm bases for the construction of the future Europe,

CONFIRMING their attachment to the principles of liberty, democracy and respect for human rights and fundamental freedoms and of the rule of law,

CONFIRMING their attachment to fundamental social rights as defined in the European Social Charter signed at Turin on 18 October 1961 and in the 1989 Community Charter of the Fundamental Social Rights of Workers,

DESIRING to deepen the solidarity between their peoples while respecting their history, their culture and their traditions,

DESIRING to enhance further the democratic and efficient functioning of the institutions so as to enable them better to carry out, within a single institutional framework, the tasks entrusted to them,

RESOLVED to achieve the strengthening and the convergence of their economies and to establish an economic and monetary union including, in accordance with the provisions of

---

1 Consolidated version as published in the Official Journal of the European Union on 26 October 2012. Indications and tables of equivalences are omitted.
2 The Republic of Bulgaria, the Czech Republic, the Republic of Estonia, the Republic of Cyprus, The Republic of Latvia, the Republic of Lithuania, the Republic of Hungary, the Republic of Malta, the Republic of Austria, the Republic of Poland, Romania, the Republic of Slovenia, the Slovak Republic, the Republic of Finland and the Kingdom of Sweden have since become members of the European Union.

this Treaty and of the Treaty on the Functioning of the European Union, a single and stable currency,

DETERMINED to promote economic and social progress for their peoples, taking into account the principle of sustainable development and within the context of the accomplishment of the internal market and of reinforced cohesion and environmental protection, and to implement policies ensuring that advances in economic integration are accompanied by parallel progress in other fields,

RESOLVED to establish a citizenship common to nationals of their countries,

RESOLVED to implement a common foreign and security policy including the progressive framing of a common defence policy, which might lead to a common defence in accordance with the provisions of Article 42, thereby reinforcing the European identity and its independence in order to promote peace, security and progress in Europe and in the world,

RESOLVED to facilitate the free movement of persons, while ensuring the safety and security of their peoples, by establishing an area of freedom, security and justice, in accordance with the provisions of this Treaty and of the Treaty on the Functioning of the European Union,

RESOLVED to continue the process of creating an ever closer union among the peoples of Europe, in which decisions are taken as closely as possible to the citizen in accordance with the principle of subsidiarity,

IN VIEW of further steps to be taken in order to advance European integration,

HAVE DECIDED to establish a European Union and to this end have designated as their Plenipotentiaries:

[List of plenipotentiaries not reproduced]

WHO, having exchanged their full powers, found in good and due form, have agreed as follows:

Title I. Common Provisions

Article 1. By this Treaty, the HIGH CONTRACTING PARTIES establish among themselves a EUROPEAN UNION, hereinafter called "the Union", on which the Member States confer competences to attain objectives they have in common.

This Treaty marks a new stage in the process of creating an ever closer union among the peoples of Europe, in which decisions are taken as openly as possible and as closely as possible to the citizen.

The Union shall be founded on the present Treaty and on the Treaty on the Functioning of the European Union (hereinafter referred to as "the Treaties"). Those two Treaties shall have the same legal value. The Union shall replace and succeed the European Community.

Article 2. The Union is founded on the values of respect for human dignity, freedom, democracy, equality, the rule of law and respect for human rights, including the rights of persons belonging to minorities. These values are common to the Member States in a society in which pluralism, non-discrimination, tolerance, justice, solidarity and equality between women and men prevail.

Article 3. (1) The Union's aim is to promote peace, its values and the well-being of its peoples.
(2) The Union shall offer its citizens an area of freedom, security and justice without internal frontiers, in which the free movement of persons is ensured in conjunction with appropriate measures with respect to external border controls, asylum, immigration and the prevention and combating of crime.
(3) The Union shall establish an internal market. It shall work for the sustainable development of Europe based on balanced economic growth and price stability, a highly competitive social market economy, aiming at full employment and social progress, and a high level of protection and improvement of the quality of the environment. It shall promote scientific and technological advance.
It shall combat social exclusion and discrimination, and shall promote social justice and protection, equality between women and men, solidarity between generations and protection of the rights of the child.
It shall promote economic, social and territorial cohesion, and solidarity among Member States.
It shall respect its rich cultural and linguistic diversity, and shall ensure that Europe's cultural heritage is safeguarded and enhanced.
(4) The Union shall establish an economic and monetary union whose currency is the euro.
(5) In its relations with the wider world, the Union shall uphold and promote its values and interests and contribute to the protection of its citizens. It shall contribute to peace, security, the sustainable development of the Earth, solidarity and mutual respect among peoples, free and fair trade, eradication of poverty and the protection of human rights, in particular the rights of the child, as well as to the strict observance and the development of international law, including respect for the principles of the United Nations Charter.
(6) The Union shall pursue its objectives by appropriate means commensurate with the competences which are conferred upon it in the Treaties.

Article 4. (1) In accordance with Article 5, competences not conferred upon the Union in the Treaties remain with the Member States.
(2) The Union shall respect the equality of Member States before the Treaties as well as their national identities, inherent in their fundamental structures, political and constitutional, inclusive of regional and local self-government. It shall respect their essential State

functions, including ensuring the territorial integrity of the State, maintaining law and order and safeguarding national security. In particular, national security remains the sole responsibility of each Member State.

(3) Pursuant to the principle of sincere cooperation, the Union and the Member States shall, in full mutual respect, assist each other in carrying out tasks which flow from the Treaties.

The Member States shall take any appropriate measure, general or particular, to ensure fulfilment of the obligations arising out of the Treaties or resulting from the acts of the institutions of the Union.

The Member States shall facilitate the achievement of the Union's tasks and refrain from any measure which could jeopardise the attainment of the Union's objectives.

Article 5. (1) The limits of Union competences are governed by the principle of conferral. The use of Union competences is governed by the principles of subsidiarity and proportionality.

(2) Under the principle of conferral, the Union shall act only within the limits of the competences conferred upon it by the Member States in the Treaties to attain the objectives set out therein. Competences not conferred upon the Union in the Treaties remain with the Member States.

(3) Under the principle of subsidiarity, in areas which do not fall within its exclusive competence, the Union shall act only if and in so far as the objectives of the proposed action cannot be sufficiently achieved by the Member States, either at central level or at regional and local level, but can rather, by reason of the scale or effects of the proposed action, be better achieved at Union level.

The institutions of the Union shall apply the principle of subsidiarity as laid down in the Protocol on the application of the principles of subsidiarity and proportionality. National Parliaments ensure compliance with the principle of subsidiarity in accordance with the procedure set out in that Protocol.

(4) Under the principle of proportionality, the content and form of Union action shall not exceed what is necessary to achieve the objectives of the Treaties.

The institutions of the Union shall apply the principle of proportionality as laid down in the Protocol on the application of the principles of subsidiarity and proportionality.

Article 6. (1) The Union recognises the rights, freedoms and principles set out in the Charter of Fundamental Rights of the European Union of 7 December 2000, as adapted at Strasbourg, on 12 December 2007, which shall have the same legal value as the Treaties.

The provisions of the Charter shall not extend in any way the competences of the Union as defined in the Treaties.

The rights, freedoms and principles in the Charter shall be interpreted in accordance with the general provisions in Title VII of the Charter governing its interpretation and application and with due regard to the explanations referred to in the Charter, that set out the sources of those provisions.

(2) The Union shall accede to the European Convention for the Protection of Human Rights and Fundamental Freedoms. Such accession shall not affect the Union's competences as defined in the Treaties.

(3) Fundamental rights, as guaranteed by the European Convention for the Protection of Human Rights and Fundamental Freedoms and as they result from the constitutional traditions common to the Member States, shall constitute general principles of the Union's law.

Article 7. (1) On a reasoned proposal by one third of the Member States, by the European Parliament or by the European Commission, the Council, acting by a majority of four fifths of its members after obtaining the consent of the European Parliament, may determine that there is a clear risk of a serious breach by a Member State of the values referred to in Article 2. Before making such a determination, the Council shall hear the Member State in question and may address recommendations to it, acting in accordance with the same procedure.

The Council shall regularly verify that the grounds on which such a determination was made continue to apply.

(2) The European Council, acting by unanimity on a proposal by one third of the Member States or by the Commission and after obtaining the consent of the European Parliament, may determine the existence of a serious and persistent breach by a Member State of the values referred to in Article 2, after inviting the Member State in question to submit its observations.

(3) Where a determination under paragraph 2 has been made, the Council, acting by a qualified majority, may decide to suspend certain of the rights deriving from the application of the Treaties to the Member State in question, including the voting rights of the representative of the government of that Member State in the Council. In doing so, the Council shall take into account the possible consequences of such a suspension on the rights and obligations of natural and legal persons.

The obligations of the Member State in question under the Treaties shall in any case continue to be binding on that State.

(4) The Council, acting by a qualified majority, may decide subsequently to vary or revoke measures taken under paragraph 3 in response to changes in the situation which led to their being imposed.

(5) The voting arrangements applying to the European Parliament, the European Council and the Council for the purposes of this Article are laid down in Article 354 of the Treaty on the Functioning of the European Union.

Article 8. (1) The Union shall develop a special relationship with neighbouring countries, aiming to establish an area of prosperity and good neighbourliness, founded on the values of the Union and characterised by close and peaceful relations based on cooperation.
(2) For the purposes of paragraph 1, the Union may conclude specific agreements with the countries concerned. These agreements may contain reciprocal rights and obligations as well as the possibility of undertaking activities jointly. Their implementation shall be the subject of periodic consultation.

Title II. Provisions on Democratic Principles

Article 9. In all its activities, the Union shall observe the principle of the equality of its citizens, who shall receive equal attention from its institutions, bodies, offices and agencies. Every national of a Member State shall be a citizen of the Union. Citizenship of the Union shall be additional to and not replace national citizenship.

Article 10. (1) The functioning of the Union shall be founded on representative democracy.
(2) Citizens are directly represented at Union level in the European Parliament.
Member States are represented in the European Council by their Heads of State or Government and in the Council by their governments, themselves democratically accountable either to their national Parliaments, or to their citizens.
(3) Every citizen shall have the right to participate in the democratic life of the Union. Decisions shall be taken as openly and as closely as possible to the citizen.
(4) Political parties at European level contribute to forming European political awareness and to expressing the will of citizens of the Union.

Article 11. (1) The institutions shall, by appropriate means, give citizens and representative associations the opportunity to make known and publicly exchange their views in all areas of Union action.
(2) The institutions shall maintain an open, transparent and regular dialogue with representative associations and civil society.
(3) The European Commission shall carry out broad consultations with parties concerned in order to ensure that the Union's actions are coherent and transparent.
(4) Not less than one million citizens who are nationals of a significant number of Member States may take the initiative of inviting the European Commission, within the framework of its powers, to submit any appropriate proposal on matters where citizens consider that a legal act of the Union is required for the purpose of implementing the Treaties.

The procedures and conditions required for such a citizens' initiative shall be determined in accordance with the first paragraph of Article 24 of the Treaty on the Functioning of the European Union.

Article 12. National Parliaments contribute actively to the good functioning of the Union:
(a) through being informed by the institutions of the Union and having draft legislative acts of the Union forwarded to them in accordance with the Protocol on the role of national Parliaments in the European Union;
(b) by seeing to it that the principle of subsidiarity is respected in accordance with the procedures provided for in the Protocol on the application of the principles of subsidiarity and proportionality;
(c) by taking part, within the framework of the area of freedom, security and justice, in the evaluation mechanisms for the implementation of the Union policies in that area, in accordance with Article 70 of the Treaty on the Functioning of the European Union, and through being involved in the political monitoring of Europol and the evaluation of Eurojust's activities in accordance with Articles 88 and 85 of that Treaty;
(d) by taking part in the revision procedures of the Treaties, in accordance with Article 48 of this Treaty;
(e) by being notified of applications for accession to the Union, in accordance with Article 49 of this Treaty;
(f) by taking part in the inter-parliamentary cooperation between national Parliaments and with the European Parliament, in accordance with the Protocol on the role of national Parliaments in the European Union.

Title III. Provisions on the Institutions

Article 13. (1) The Union shall have an institutional framework which shall aim to promote its values, advance its objectives, serve its interests, those of its citizens and those of the Member States, and ensure the consistency, effectiveness and continuity of its policies and actions.
The Union's institutions shall be:
- the European Parliament,
- the European Council,
- the Council,
- the European Commission (hereinafter referred to as "the Commission"),
- the Court of Justice of the European Union,
- the European Central Bank,

– the Court of Auditors.

(2) Each institution shall act within the limits of the powers conferred on it in the Treaties, and in conformity with the procedures, conditions and objectives set out in them. The institutions shall practice mutual sincere cooperation.

(3) The provisions relating to the European Central Bank and the Court of Auditors and detailed provisions on the other institutions are set out in the Treaty on the Functioning of the European Union.

(4) The European Parliament, the Council and the Commission shall be assisted by an Economic and Social Committee and a Committee of the Regions acting in an advisory capacity.

Article 14. (1) The European Parliament shall, jointly with the Council, exercise legislative and budgetary functions. It shall exercise functions of political control and consultation as laid down in the Treaties. It shall elect the President of the Commission.

(2) The European Parliament shall be composed of representatives of the Union's citizens. They shall not exceed seven hundred and fifty in number, plus the President. Representation of citizens shall be degressively proportional, with a minimum threshold of six members per Member State. No Member State shall be allocated more than ninety–six seats.

The European Council shall adopt by unanimity, on the initiative of the European Parliament and with its consent, a decision establishing the composition of the European Parliament, respecting the principles referred to in the first subparagraph.

(3) The members of the European Parliament shall be elected for a term of five years by direct universal suffrage in a free and secret ballot.

(4) The European Parliament shall elect its President and its officers from among its members.

Article 15. (1) The European Council shall provide the Union with the necessary impetus for its development and shall define the general political directions and priorities thereof. It shall not exercise legislative functions.

(2) The European Council shall consist of the Heads of State or Government of the Member States, together with its President and the President of the Commission. The High Representative of the Union for Foreign Affairs and Security Policy shall take part in its work.

(3) The European Council shall meet twice every six months, convened by its President. When the agenda so requires, the members of the European Council may decide each to be assisted by a minister and, in the case of the President of the Commission, by a member of the Commission. When the situation so requires, the President shall convene a special meeting of the European Council.

(4) Except where the Treaties provide otherwise, decisions of the European Council shall be taken by consensus.

(5) The European Council shall elect its President, by a qualified majority, for a term of two and a half years, renewable once. In the event of an impediment or serious misconduct, the European Council can end the President's term of office in accordance with the same procedure.

(6) The President of the European Council:

(a) shall chair it and drive forward its work;

(b) shall ensure the preparation and continuity of the work of the European Council in cooperation with the President of the Commission, and on the basis of the work of the General Affairs Council;

(c) shall endeavour to facilitate cohesion and consensus within the European Council;

(d) shall present a report to the European Parliament after each of the meetings of the European Council.

The President of the European Council shall, at his level and in that capacity, ensure the external representation of the Union on issues concerning its common foreign and security policy, without prejudice to the powers of the High Representative of the Union for Foreign Affairs and Security Policy.

The President of the European Council shall not hold a national office.

Article 16. (1) The Council shall, jointly with the European Parliament, exercise legislative and budgetary functions. It shall carry out policy-making and coordinating functions as laid down in the Treaties.

(2) The Council shall consist of a representative of each Member State at ministerial level, who may commit the government of the Member State in question and cast its vote.

(3) The Council shall act by a qualified majority except where the Treaties provide otherwise.

(4) As from 1 November 2014, a qualified majority shall be defined as at least 55 % of the members of the Council, comprising at least fifteen of them and representing Member States comprising at least 65 % of the population of the Union.

A blocking minority must include at least four Council members, failing which the qualified majority shall be deemed attained.

The other arrangements governing the qualified majority are laid down in Article 238(2) of the Treaty on the Functioning of the European Union.

(5) The transitional provisions relating to the definition of the qualified majority which shall be applicable until 31 October 2014 and those which shall be applicable from 1 November 2014 to 31 March 2017 are laid down in the Protocol on transitional provisions.

(6) The Council shall meet in different configurations, the list of which shall be adopted in accordance with Article 236 of the Treaty on the Functioning of the European Union.

The General Affairs Council shall ensure consistency in the work of the different Council configurations. It shall prepare and ensure the follow-up to meetings of the European Council, in liaison with the President of the European Council and the Commission.

The Foreign Affairs Council shall elaborate the Union's external action on the basis of strategic guidelines laid down by the European Council and ensure that the Union's action is consistent.

(7) A Committee of Permanent Representatives of the Governments of the Member States shall be responsible for preparing the work of the Council.

(8) The Council shall meet in public when it deliberates and votes on a draft legislative act. To this end, each Council meeting shall be divided into two parts, dealing respectively with deliberations on Union legislative acts and non-legislative activities.

(9) The Presidency of Council configurations, other than that of Foreign Affairs, shall be held by Member State representatives in the Council on the basis of equal rotation, in accordance with the conditions established in accordance with Article 236 of the Treaty on the Functioning of the European Union.

Article 17. (1) The Commission shall promote the general interest of the Union and take appropriate initiatives to that end. It shall ensure the application of the Treaties, and of measures adopted by the institutions pursuant to them. It shall oversee the application of Union law under the control of the Court of Justice of the European Union. It shall execute the budget and manage programmes. It shall exercise coordinating, executive and management functions, as laid down in the Treaties. With the exception of the common foreign and security policy, and other cases provided for in the Treaties, it shall ensure the Union's external representation. It shall initiate the Union's annual and multi-annual programming with a view to achieving interinstitutional agreements.

(2) Union legislative acts may only be adopted on the basis of a Commission proposal, except where the Treaties provide otherwise. Other acts shall be adopted on the basis of a Commission proposal where the Treaties so provide.

(3) The Commission's term of office shall be five years.

The members of the Commission shall be chosen on the ground of their general competence and European commitment from persons whose independence is beyond doubt.

In carrying out its responsibilities, the Commission shall be completely independent. Without prejudice to Article 18(2), the members of the Commission shall neither seek nor take instructions from any Government or other institution, body, office or entity. They shall refrain from any action incompatible with their duties or the performance of their tasks.

(4) The Commission appointed between the date of entry into force of the Treaty of Lisbon and 31 October 2014, shall consist of one national of each Member State, including its President and the High Representative of the Union for Foreign Affairs and Security Policy who shall be one of its Vice-Presidents.

(5) As from 1 November 2014, the Commission shall consist of a number of members, including its President and the High Representative of the Union for Foreign Affairs and Security Policy, corresponding to two thirds of the number of Member States, unless the European Council, acting unanimously, decides to alter this number.

The members of the Commission shall be chosen from among the nationals of the Member States on the basis of a system of strictly equal rotation between the Member States, reflecting the demographic and geographical range of all the Member States. This system shall be established unanimously by the European Council in accordance with Article 244 of the Treaty on the Functioning of the European Union.

(6) The President of the Commission shall:

(a) lay down guidelines within which the Commission is to work;

(b) decide on the internal organisation of the Commission, ensuring that it acts consistently, efficiently and as a collegiate body;

(c) appoint Vice-Presidents, other than the High Representative of the Union for Foreign Affairs and Security Policy, from among the members of the Commission.

A member of the Commission shall resign if the President so requests. The High Representative of the Union for Foreign Affairs and Security Policy shall resign, in accordance with the procedure set out in Article 18(1), if the President so requests.

(7) Taking into account the elections to the European Parliament and after having held the appropriate consultations, the European Council, acting by a qualified majority, shall propose to the European Parliament a candidate for President of the Commission. This candidate shall be elected by the European Parliament by a majority of its component members. If he does not obtain the required majority, the European Council, acting by a qualified majority, shall within one month propose a new candidate who shall be elected by the European Parliament following the same procedure.

The Council, by common accord with the President-elect, shall adopt the list of the other persons whom it proposes for appointment as members of the Commission. They shall be selected, on the basis of the suggestions made by Member States, in accordance with the criteria set out in paragraph 3, second subparagraph, and paragraph 5, second subparagraph.

The President, the High Representative of the Union for Foreign Affairs and Security Policy and the other members of the Commission shall be subject as a body to a vote of consent by the European Parliament. On the basis of this consent the Commission shall be appointed by the European Council, acting by a qualified majority.

(8) The Commission, as a body, shall be responsible to the European Parliament. In accordance with Article 234 of the Treaty on the Functioning of the European Union, the European Parliament may vote on a motion of censure of the Commission. If such a motion is carried, the members of the Commission shall resign as a body and the High Representative of the Union for Foreign Affairs and Security Policy shall resign from the duties that he carries out in the Commission.

Article 18. (1) The European Council, acting by a qualified majority, with the agreement of the President of the Commission, shall appoint the High Representative of the Union for Foreign Affairs and Security Policy. The European Council may end his term of office by the same procedure.

(2) The High Representative shall conduct the Union's common foreign and security policy. He shall contribute by his proposals to the development of that policy, which he shall carry out as mandated by the Council. The same shall apply to the common security and defence policy.

(3) The High Representative shall preside over the Foreign Affairs Council.

(4) The High Representative shall be one of the Vice–Presidents of the Commission. He shall ensure the consistency of the Union's external action. He shall be responsible within the Commission for responsibilities incumbent on it in external relations and for coordinating other aspects of the Union's external action. In exercising these responsibilities within the Commission, and only for these responsibilities, the High Representative shall be bound by Commission procedures to the extent that this is consistent with paragraphs 2 and 3.

Article 19. (1) The Court of Justice of the European Union shall include the Court of Justice, the General Court and specialised courts. It shall ensure that in the interpretation and application of the Treaties the law is observed.

Member States shall provide remedies sufficient to ensure effective legal protection in the fields covered by Union law.

(2) The Court of Justice shall consist of one judge from each Member State. It shall be assisted by Advocates–General.

The General Court shall include at least one judge per Member State.

The Judges and the Advocates–General of the Court of Justice and the Judges of the General Court shall be chosen from persons whose independence is beyond doubt and who satisfy the conditions set out in Articles 253 and 254 of the Treaty on the Functioning of the European Union. They shall be appointed by common accord of the governments of the Member States for six years. Retiring Judges and Advocates–General may be reappointed.

(3) The Court of Justice of the European Union shall, in accordance with the Treaties:

(a) rule on actions brought by a Member State, an institution or a natural or legal person;
(b) give preliminary rulings, at the request of courts or tribunals of the Member States, on the interpretation of Union law or the validity of acts adopted by the institutions;
(c) rule in other cases provided for in the Treaties.

Title IV. Provisions on Enhanced Cooperation

Article 20. (1) Member States which wish to establish enhanced cooperation between themselves within the framework of the Union's non-exclusive competences may make use of its institutions and exercise those competences by applying the relevant provisions of the Treaties, subject to the limits and in accordance with the detailed arrangements laid down in this Article and in Articles 326 to 334 of the Treaty on the Functioning of the European Union.

Enhanced cooperation shall aim to further the objectives of the Union, protect its interests and reinforce its integration process. Such cooperation shall be open at any time to all Member States, in accordance with Article 328 of the Treaty on the Functioning of the European Union.

(2) The decision authorising enhanced cooperation shall be adopted by the Council as a last resort, when it has established that the objectives of such cooperation cannot be attained within a reasonable period by the Union as a whole, and provided that at least nine Member States participate in it. The Council shall act in accordance with the procedure laid down in Article 329 of the Treaty on the Functioning of the European Union.

(3) All members of the Council may participate in its deliberations, but only members of the Council representing the Member States participating in enhanced cooperation shall take part in the vote. The voting rules are set out in Article 330 of the Treaty on the Functioning of the European Union.

(4) Acts adopted in the framework of enhanced cooperation shall bind only participating Member States. They shall not be regarded as part of the acquis which has to be accepted by candidate States for accession to the Union.

Title V. General Provisions on the Union's External Action and Specific Provisions on the Common Foreign and Security Policy

Chapter 1. General Provisions on the Union's External Action

Article 21. (1) The Union's action on the international scene shall be guided by the principles which have inspired its own creation, development and enlargement, and which it seeks to advance in the wider world: democracy, the rule of law, the universality and indivisibility of human rights and fundamental freedoms, respect for human dignity, the principles of equality and solidarity, and respect for the principles of the United Nations Charter and international law.

The Union shall seek to develop relations and build partnerships with third countries, and international, regional or global organisations which share the principles referred to in the first subparagraph. It shall promote multilateral solutions to common problems, in particular in the framework of the United Nations.

(2) The Union shall define and pursue common policies and actions, and shall work for a high degree of cooperation in all fields of international relations, in order to:

(a) safeguard its values, fundamental interests, security, independence and integrity;

(b) consolidate and support democracy, the rule of law, human rights and the principles of international law;
(c) preserve peace, prevent conflicts and strengthen international security, in accordance with the purposes and principles of the United Nations Charter, with the principles of the Helsinki Final Act and with the aims of the Charter of Paris, including those relating to external borders;
(d) foster the sustainable economic, social and environmental development of developing countries, with the primary aim of eradicating poverty;
(e) encourage the integration of all countries into the world economy, including through the progressive abolition of restrictions on international trade;
(f) help develop international measures to preserve and improve the quality of the environment and the sustainable management of global natural resources, in order to ensure sustainable development;
(g) assist populations, countries and regions confronting natural or man–made disasters; and
(h) promote an international system based on stronger multilateral cooperation and good global governance.

(3) The Union shall respect the principles and pursue the objectives set out in paragraphs 1 and 2 in the development and implementation of the different areas of the Union's external action covered by this Title and by Part Five of the Treaty on the Functioning of the European Union, and of the external aspects of its other policies.

The Union shall ensure consistency between the different areas of its external action and between these and its other policies. The Council and the Commission, assisted by the High Representative of the Union for Foreign Affairs and Security Policy, shall ensure that consistency and shall cooperate to that effect.

Article 22. (1) On the basis of the principles and objectives set out in Article 21, the European Council shall identify the strategic interests and objectives of the Union.

Decisions of the European Council on the strategic interests and objectives of the Union shall relate to the common foreign and security policy and to other areas of the external action of the Union. Such decisions may concern the relations of the Union with a specific country or region or may be thematic in approach. They shall define their duration, and the means to be made available by the Union and the Member States.

The European Council shall act unanimously on a recommendation from the Council, adopted by the latter under the arrangements laid down for each area. Decisions of the European Council shall be implemented in accordance with the procedures provided for in the Treaties.

(2) The High Representative of the Union for Foreign Affairs and Security Policy, for the area of common foreign and security policy, and the Commission, for other areas of external action, may submit joint proposals to the Council.

Chapter 2. Specific Provisions on the Common Foreign and Security Policy

Section 1. Common Provisions

Article 23. The Union's action on the international scene, pursuant to this Chapter, shall be guided by the principles, shall pursue the objectives of, and be conducted in accordance with, the general provisions laid down in Chapter 1.

Article 24. (1) The Union's competence in matters of common foreign and security policy shall cover all areas of foreign policy and all questions relating to the Union's security, including the progressive framing of a common defence policy that might lead to a common defence.

The common foreign and security policy is subject to specific rules and procedures. It shall be defined and implemented by the European Council and the Council acting unanimously, except where the Treaties provide otherwise. The adoption of legislative acts shall be excluded. The common foreign and security policy shall be put into effect by the High Representative of the Union for Foreign Affairs and Security Policy and by Member States, in accordance with the Treaties. The specific role of the European Parliament and of the Commission in this area is defined by the Treaties. The Court of Justice of the European Union shall not have jurisdiction with respect to these provisions, with the exception of its jurisdiction to monitor compliance with Article 40 of this Treaty and to review the legality of certain decisions as provided for by the second paragraph of Article 275 of the Treaty on the Functioning of the European Union.

(2) Within the framework of the principles and objectives of its external action, the Union shall conduct, define and implement a common foreign and security policy, based on the development of mutual political solidarity among Member States, the identification of questions of general interest and the achievement of an ever-increasing degree of convergence of Member States' actions.

(3) The Member States shall support the Union's external and security policy actively and unreservedly in a spirit of loyalty and mutual solidarity and shall comply with the Union's action in this area.

The Member States shall work together to enhance and develop their mutual political solidarity. They shall refrain from any action which is contrary to the interests of the Union or likely to impair its effectiveness as a cohesive force in international relations. The Council and the High Representative shall ensure compliance with these principles.

Article 25. The Union shall conduct the common foreign and security policy by:
(a) defining the general guidelines;
(b) adopting decisions defining:
    (i) actions to be undertaken by the Union;

(ii) positions to be taken by the Union;
   (iii) arrangements for the implementation of the decisions referred to in points (i) and (ii);
   and by
(c) strengthening systematic cooperation between Member States in the conduct of policy.

Article 26. (1) The European Council shall identify the Union's strategic interests, determine the objectives of and define general guidelines for the common foreign and security policy, including for matters with defence implications. It shall adopt the necessary decisions.

If international developments so require, the President of the European Council shall convene an extraordinary meeting of the European Council in order to define the strategic lines of the Union's policy in the face of such developments.

(2) The Council shall frame the common foreign and security policy and take the decisions necessary for defining and implementing it on the basis of the general guidelines and strategic lines defined by the European Council.

The Council and the High Representative of the Union for Foreign Affairs and Security Policy shall ensure the unity, consistency and effectiveness of action by the Union.

(3) The common foreign and security policy shall be put into effect by the High Representative and by the Member States, using national and Union resources.

Article 27. (1) The High Representative of the Union for Foreign Affairs and Security Policy, who shall chair the Foreign Affairs Council, shall contribute through his proposals to the development of the common foreign and security policy and shall ensure implementation of the decisions adopted by the European Council and the Council.

(2) The High Representative shall represent the Union for matters relating to the common foreign and security policy. He shall conduct political dialogue with third parties on the Union's behalf and shall express the Union's position in international organisations and at international conferences.

(3) In fulfilling his mandate, the High Representative shall be assisted by a European External Action Service. This service shall work in cooperation with the diplomatic services of the Member States and shall comprise officials from relevant departments of the General Secretariat of the Council and of the Commission as well as staff seconded from national diplomatic services of the Member States. The organisation and functioning of the European External Action Service shall be established by a decision of the Council. The Council shall act on a proposal from the High Representative after consulting the European Parliament and after obtaining the consent of the Commission.

Article 28. (1) Where the international situation requires operational action by the Union, the Council shall adopt the necessary decisions. They shall lay down their objectives, scope, the means to be made available to the Union, if necessary their duration, and the conditions for their implementation.

If there is a change in circumstances having a substantial effect on a question subject to such a decision, the Council shall review the principles and objectives of that decision and take the necessary decisions.

(2) Decisions referred to in paragraph 1 shall commit the Member States in the positions they adopt and in the conduct of their activity.

(3) Whenever there is any plan to adopt a national position or take national action pursuant to a decision as referred to in paragraph 1, information shall be provided by the Member State concerned in time to allow, if necessary, for prior consultations within the Council. The obligation to provide prior information shall not apply to measures which are merely a national transposition of Council decisions.

(4) In cases of imperative need arising from changes in the situation and failing a review of the Council decision as referred to in paragraph 1, Member States may take the necessary measures as a matter of urgency having regard to the general objectives of that decision. The Member State concerned shall inform the Council immediately of any such measures.

(5) Should there be any major difficulties in implementing a decision as referred to in this Article, a Member State shall refer them to the Council which shall discuss them and seek appropriate solutions. Such solutions shall not run counter to the objectives of the decision referred to in paragraph 1 or impair its effectiveness.

Article 29. The Council shall adopt decisions which shall define the approach of the Union to a particular matter of a geographical or thematic nature. Member States shall ensure that their national policies conform to the Union positions.

Article 30. (1) Any Member State, the High Representative of the Union for Foreign Affairs and Security Policy, or the High Representative with the Commission's support, may refer any question relating to the common foreign and security policy to the Council and may submit to it, respectively, initiatives or proposals.

(2) In cases requiring a rapid decision, the High Representative, of his own motion, or at the request of a Member State, shall convene an extraordinary Council meeting within 48 hours or, in an emergency, within a shorter period.

Article 31. (1) Decisions under this Chapter shall be taken by the European Council and the Council acting unanimously, except where this Chapter provides otherwise. The adoption of legislative acts shall be excluded.

When abstaining in a vote, any member of the Council may qualify its abstention by making a formal declaration under the present subparagraph. In that case, it shall not be obliged to apply the decision, but shall accept that the decision commits the Union. In a spirit of mutual solidarity, the Member State concerned shall refrain from any action likely to conflict with or impede Union action based on that decision and the other Member States shall respect its position. If the members of the Council qualifying their abstention in this way represent at least one third of the Member States comprising at least one third of the population of the Union, the decision shall not be adopted.

(2) By derogation from the provisions of paragraph 1, the Council shall act by qualified majority:

– when adopting a decision defining a Union action or position on the basis of a decision of the European Council relating to the Union's strategic interests and objectives, as referred to in Article 22(1),
– when adopting a decision defining a Union action or position, on a proposal which the High Representative of the Union for Foreign Affairs and Security Policy has presented following a specific request from the European Council, made on its own initiative or that of the High Representative,
– when adopting any decision implementing a decision defining a Union action or position,
– when appointing a special representative in accordance with Article 33.

If a member of the Council declares that, for vital and stated reasons of national policy, it intends to oppose the adoption of a decision to be taken by qualified majority, a vote shall not be taken. The High Representative will, in close consultation with the Member State involved, search for a solution acceptable to it. If he does not succeed, the Council may, acting by a qualified majority, request that the matter be referred to the European Council for a decision by unanimity.

(3) The European Council may unanimously adopt a decision stipulating that the Council shall act by a qualified majority in cases other than those referred to in paragraph 2.

(4) Paragraphs 2 and 3 shall not apply to decisions having military or defence implications.

(5) For procedural questions, the Council shall act by a majority of its members.

Article 32. Member States shall consult one another within the European Council and the Council on any matter of foreign and security policy of general interest in order to determine a common approach. Before undertaking any action on the international scene or entering into any commitment which could affect the Union's interests, each Member State shall consult the others within the European Council or the Council. Member States shall ensure, through the convergence of their actions, that the Union is able to assert its interests and values on the international scene. Member States shall show mutual solidarity.

When the European Council or the Council has defined a common approach of the Union within the meaning of the first paragraph, the High Representative of the Union for Foreign Affairs and Security Policy and the Ministers for Foreign Affairs of the Member States shall coordinate their activities within the Council.

The diplomatic missions of the Member States and the Union delegations in third countries and at international organisations shall cooperate and shall contribute to formulating and implementing the common approach.

Article 33. The Council may, on a proposal from the High Representative of the Union for Foreign Affairs and Security Policy, appoint a special representative with a mandate in relation to particular policy issues. The special representative shall carry out his mandate under the authority of the High Representative.

Article 34. (1) Member States shall coordinate their action in international organisations and at international conferences. They shall uphold the Union's positions in such forums. The High Representative of the Union for Foreign Affairs and Security Policy shall organise this coordination.

In international organisations and at international conferences where not all the Member States participate, those which do take part shall uphold the Union's positions.

(2) In accordance with Article 24(3), Member States represented in international organisations or international conferences where not all the Member States participate shall keep the other Member States and the High Representative informed of any matter of common interest.

Member States which are also members of the United Nations Security Council will concert and keep the other Member States and the High Representative fully informed. Member States which are members of the Security Council will, in the execution of their functions, defend the positions and the interests of the Union, without prejudice to their responsibilities under the provisions of the United Nations Charter.

When the Union has defined a position on a subject which is on the United Nations Security Council agenda, those Member States which sit on the Security Council shall request that the High Representative be invited to present the Union's position.

Article 35. The diplomatic and consular missions of the Member States and the Union delegations in third countries and international conferences, and their representations to international organisations, shall cooperate in ensuring that decisions defining Union positions and actions adopted pursuant to this Chapter are complied with and implemented.

They shall step up cooperation by exchanging information and carrying out joint assessments.

They shall contribute to the implementation of the right of citizens of the Union to protection in the territory of third countries as referred to in Article 20(2)(c) of the Treaty on the Functioning of the European Union and of the measures adopted pursuant to Article 23 of that Treaty.

Article 36. The High Representative of the Union for Foreign Affairs and Security Policy shall regularly consult the European Parliament on the main aspects and the basic choices of the common foreign and security policy and the common security and defence policy and inform it of how those policies evolve. He shall ensure that the views of the European Parliament are duly taken into consideration. Special representatives may be involved in briefing the European Parliament.

The European Parliament may address questions or make recommendations to the Council or the High Representative. Twice a year it shall hold a debate on progress in implementing the common foreign and security policy, including the common security and defence policy.

Article 37. The Union may conclude agreements with one or more States or international organisations in areas covered by this Chapter.

Article 38. Without prejudice to Article 240 of the Treaty on the Functioning of the European Union, a Political and Security Committee shall monitor the international situation in the areas covered by the common foreign and security policy and contribute to the definition of policies by delivering opinions to the Council at the request of the Council or of the High Representative of the Union for Foreign Affairs and Security Policy or on its own initiative. It shall also monitor the implementation of agreed policies, without prejudice to the powers of the High Representative.

Within the scope of this Chapter, the Political and Security Committee shall exercise, under the responsibility of the Council and of the High Representative, the political control and strategic direction of the crisis management operations referred to in Article 43. The Council may authorise the Committee, for the purpose and for the duration of a crisis management operation, as determined by the Council, to take the relevant decisions concerning the political control and strategic direction of the operation.

Article 39. In accordance with Article 16 of the Treaty on the Functioning of the European Union and by way of derogation from paragraph 2 thereof, the Council shall adopt a decision laying down the rules relating to the protection of individuals with regard to the processing of personal data by the Member States when carrying out activities which fall within the scope of this Chapter, and the rules relating to the free movement of such data. Compliance with these rules shall be subject to the control of independent authorities.

Article 40. The implementation of the common foreign and security policy shall not affect the application of the procedures and the extent of the powers of the institutions laid down by the Treaties for the exercise of the Union competences referred to in Articles 3 to 6 of the Treaty on the Functioning of the European Union.

Similarly, the implementation of the policies listed in those Articles shall not affect the application of the procedures and the extent of the powers of the institutions laid down by the Treaties for the exercise of the Union competences under this Chapter.

Article 41. (1) Administrative expenditure to which the implementation of this Chapter gives rise for the institutions shall be charged to the Union budget.

(2) Operating expenditure to which the implementation of this Chapter gives rise shall also be charged to the Union budget, except for such expenditure arising from operations having military or defence implications and cases where the Council acting unanimously decides otherwise.

In cases where expenditure is not charged to the Union budget, it shall be charged to the Member States in accordance with the gross national product scale, unless the Council acting unanimously decides otherwise. As for expenditure arising from operations having military or defence implications, Member States whose representatives in the Council have made a formal declaration under Article 31(1), second subparagraph, shall not be obliged to contribute to the financing thereof.

(3) The Council shall adopt a decision establishing the specific procedures for guaranteeing rapid access to appropriations in the Union budget for urgent financing of initiatives in the framework of the common foreign and security policy, and in particular for preparatory activities for the tasks referred to in Article 42(1) and Article 43. It shall act after consulting the European Parliament.

Preparatory activities for the tasks referred to in Article 42(1) and Article 43 which are not charged to the Union budget shall be financed by a start–up fund made up of Member States' contributions.

The Council shall adopt by a qualified majority, on a proposal from the High Representative of the Union for Foreign Affairs and Security Policy, decisions establishing:

(a) the procedures for setting up and financing the start–up fund, in particular the amounts allocated to the fund;
(b) the procedures for administering the start–up fund;
(c) the financial control procedures.

When the task planned in accordance with Article 42(1) and Article 43 cannot be charged to the Union budget, the Council shall authorise the High Representative to use the fund. The High Representative shall report to the Council on the implementation of this remit.

Section 2. Provisions on the Common Security and Defence Policy

Article 42. (1) The common security and defence policy shall be an integral part of the common foreign and security policy. It shall provide the Union with an operational capacity drawing on civilian and military assets. The Union may use them on missions outside the Union for peace-keeping, conflict prevention and strengthening international security in accordance with the principles of the United Nations Charter. The performance of these tasks shall be undertaken using capabilities provided by the Member States.

(2) The common security and defence policy shall include the progressive framing of a common Union defence policy. This will lead to a common defence, when the European Council, acting unanimously, so decides. It shall in that case recommend to the Member States the adoption of such a decision in accordance with their respective constitutional requirements.

The policy of the Union in accordance with this Section shall not prejudice the specific character of the security and defence policy of certain Member States and shall respect the obligations of certain Member States, which see their common defence realised in the North Atlantic Treaty Organisation (NATO), under the North Atlantic Treaty and be compatible with the common security and defence policy established within that framework.

(3) Member States shall make civilian and military capabilities available to the Union for the implementation of the common security and defence policy, to contribute to the objectives defined by the Council. Those Member States which together establish multinational forces may also make them available to the common security and defence policy. Member States shall undertake progressively to improve their military capabilities. The Agency in the field of defence capabilities development, research, acquisition and armaments (hereinafter referred to as "the European Defence Agency") shall identify operational requirements, shall promote measures to satisfy those requirements, shall contribute to identifying and, where appropriate, implementing any measure needed to strengthen the industrial and technological base of the defence sector, shall participate in defining a European capabilities and armaments policy, and shall assist the Council in evaluating the improvement of military capabilities.

(4) Decisions relating to the common security and defence policy, including those initiating a mission as referred to in this Article, shall be adopted by the Council acting unanimously on a proposal from the High Representative of the Union for Foreign Affairs and Security Policy or an initiative from a Member State. The High Representative may propose the use of both national resources and Union instruments, together with the Commission where appropriate.

(5) The Council may entrust the execution of a task, within the Union framework, to a group of Member States in order to protect the Union's values and serve its interests. The execution of such a task shall be governed by Article 44.

(6) Those Member States whose military capabilities fulfil higher criteria and which have made more binding commitments to one another in this area with a view to the most demanding missions shall establish permanent structured cooperation within the Union framework. Such cooperation shall be governed by Article 46. It shall not affect the provisions of Article 43.

(7) If a Member State is the victim of armed aggression on its territory, the other Member States shall have towards it an obligation of aid and assistance by all the means in their power, in accordance with Article 51 of the United Nations Charter. This shall not prejudice the specific character of the security and defence policy of certain Member States. Commitments and cooperation in this area shall be consistent with commitments under the North Atlantic Treaty Organisation, which, for those States which are members of it, remains the foundation of their collective defence and the forum for its implementation.

Article 43. (1) The tasks referred to in Article 42(1), in the course of which the Union may use civilian and military means, shall include joint disarmament operations, humanitarian and rescue tasks, military advice and assistance tasks, conflict prevention and peace–keeping tasks, tasks of combat forces in crisis management, including peace–making and post–conflict stabilisation. All these tasks may contribute to the fight against terrorism, including by supporting third countries in combating terrorism in their territories.

(2) The Council shall adopt decisions relating to the tasks referred to in paragraph 1, defining their objectives and scope and the general conditions for their implementation. The High Representative of the Union for Foreign Affairs and Security Policy, acting under the authority of the Council and in close and constant contact with the Political and Security Committee, shall ensure coordination of the civilian and military aspects of such tasks.

Article 44. (1) Within the framework of the decisions adopted in accordance with Article 43, the Council may entrust the implementation of a task to a group of Member States which are willing and have the necessary capability for such a task. Those Member States, in association with the High Representative of the Union for Foreign Affairs and Security Policy, shall agree among themselves on the management of the task.

(2) Member States participating in the task shall keep the Council regularly informed of its progress on their own initiative or at the request of another Member State. Those States shall inform the Council immediately should the completion of the task entail major consequences or require amendment of the objective, scope and conditions deter-

mined for the task in the decisions referred to in paragraph 1. In such cases, the Council shall adopt the necessary decisions.

Article 45. (1) The European Defence Agency referred to in Article 42(3), subject to the authority of the Council, shall have as its task to:
(a) contribute to identifying the Member States' military capability objectives and evaluating observance of the capability commitments given by the Member States;
(b) promote harmonisation of operational needs and adoption of effective, compatible procurement methods;
(c) propose multilateral projects to fulfil the objectives in terms of military capabilities, ensure coordination of the programmes implemented by the Member States and management of specific cooperation programmes;
(d) support defence technology research, and coordinate and plan joint research activities and the study of technical solutions meeting future operational needs;
(e) contribute to identifying and, if necessary, implementing any useful measure for strengthening the industrial and technological base of the defence sector and for improving the effectiveness of military expenditure.
(2) The European Defence Agency shall be open to all Member States wishing to be part of it. The Council, acting by a qualified majority, shall adopt a decision defining the Agency's statute, seat and operational rules. That decision should take account of the level of effective participation in the Agency's activities. Specific groups shall be set up within the Agency bringing together Member States engaged in joint projects. The Agency shall carry out its tasks in liaison with the Commission where necessary.

Article 46. (1) Those Member States which wish to participate in the permanent structured cooperation referred to in Article 42(6), which fulfil the criteria and have made the commitments on military capabilities set out in the Protocol on permanent structured cooperation, shall notify their intention to the Council and to the High Representative of the Union for Foreign Affairs and Security Policy.
(2) Within three months following the notification referred to in paragraph 1 the Council shall adopt a decision establishing permanent structured cooperation and determining the list of participating Member States. The Council shall act by a qualified majority after consulting the High Representative.
(3) Any Member State which, at a later stage, wishes to participate in the permanent structured cooperation shall notify its intention to the Council and to the High Representative.
The Council shall adopt a decision confirming the participation of the Member State concerned which fulfils the criteria and makes the commitments referred to in Articles 1 and 2 of the Protocol on permanent structured cooperation. The Council shall act by a

qualified majority after consulting the High Representative. Only members of the Council representing the participating Member States shall take part in the vote.

A qualified majority shall be defined in accordance with Article 238(3)(a) of the Treaty on the Functioning of the European Union.

(4) If a participating Member State no longer fulfils the criteria or is no longer able to meet the commitments referred to in Articles 1 and 2 of the Protocol on permanent structured cooperation, the Council may adopt a decision suspending the participation of the Member State concerned.

The Council shall act by a qualified majority. Only members of the Council representing the participating Member States, with the exception of the Member State in question, shall take part in the vote.

A qualified majority shall be defined in accordance with Article 238(3)(a) of the Treaty on the Functioning of the European Union.

(5) Any participating Member State which wishes to withdraw from permanent structured cooperation shall notify its intention to the Council, which shall take note that the Member State in question has ceased to participate.

(6) The decisions and recommendations of the Council within the framework of permanent structured cooperation, other than those provided for in paragraphs 2 to 5, shall be adopted by unanimity. For the purposes of this paragraph, unanimity shall be constituted by the votes of the representatives of the participating Member States only.

Title VI. Final Provisions

Article 47. The Union shall have legal personality.

Article 48. (1) The Treaties may be amended in accordance with an ordinary revision procedure. They may also be amended in accordance with simplified revision procedures.
Ordinary revision procedure
(2) The Government of any Member State, the European Parliament or the Commission may submit to the Council proposals for the amendment of the Treaties. These proposals may, inter alia, serve either to increase or to reduce the competences conferred on the Union in the Treaties. These proposals shall be submitted to the European Council by the Council and the national Parliaments shall be notified.

(3) If the European Council, after consulting the European Parliament and the Commission, adopts by a simple majority a decision in favour of examining the proposed amendments, the President of the European Council shall convene a Convention composed of representatives of the national Parliaments, of the Heads of State or Government of the Member States, of the European Parliament and of the Commission. The European Central Bank shall also be consulted in the case of institutional changes in the monetary area. The Convention shall examine the proposals for amendments and shall adopt by con-

sensus a recommendation to a conference of representatives of the governments of the Member States as provided for in paragraph 4.

The European Council may decide by a simple majority, after obtaining the consent of the European Parliament, not to convene a Convention should this not be justified by the extent of the proposed amendments. In the latter case, the European Council shall define the terms of reference for a conference of representatives of the governments of the Member States.

(4) A conference of representatives of the governments of the Member States shall be convened by the President of the Council for the purpose of determining by common accord the amendments to be made to the Treaties.

The amendments shall enter into force after being ratified by all the Member States in accordance with their respective constitutional requirements.

(5) If, two years after the signature of a treaty amending the Treaties, four fifths of the Member States have ratified it and one or more Member States have encountered difficulties in proceeding with ratification, the matter shall be referred to the European Council.

Simplified revision procedures

(6) The Government of any Member State, the European Parliament or the Commission may submit to the European Council proposals for revising all or part of the provisions of Part Three of the Treaty on the Functioning of the European Union relating to the internal policies and action of the Union.

The European Council may adopt a decision amending all or part of the provisions of Part Three of the Treaty on the Functioning of the European Union. The European Council shall act by unanimity after consulting the European Parliament and the Commission, and the European Central Bank in the case of institutional changes in the monetary area. That decision shall not enter into force until it is approved by the Member States in accordance with their respective constitutional requirements.

The decision referred to in the second subparagraph shall not increase the competences conferred on the Union in the Treaties.

(7) Where the Treaty on the Functioning of the European Union or Title V of this Treaty provides for the Council to act by unanimity in a given area or case, the European Council may adopt a decision authorising the Council to act by a qualified majority in that area or in that case. This subparagraph shall not apply to decisions with military implications or those in the area of defence.

Where the Treaty on the Functioning of the European Union provides for legislative acts to be adopted by the Council in accordance with a special legislative procedure, the European Council may adopt a decision allowing for the adoption of such acts in accordance with the ordinary legislative procedure.

Any initiative taken by the European Council on the basis of the first or the second subparagraph shall be notified to the national Parliaments. If a national Parliament makes known its opposition within six months of the date of such notification, the decision referred to in the first or the second subparagraph shall not be adopted. In the absence of opposition, the European Council may adopt the decision.

For the adoption of the decisions referred to in the first and second subparagraphs, the European Council shall act by unanimity after obtaining the consent of the European Parliament, which shall be given by a majority of its component members.

Article 49. Any European State which respects the values referred to in Article 2 and is committed to promoting them may apply to become a member of the Union. The European Parliament and national Parliaments shall be notified of this application. The applicant State shall address its application to the Council, which shall act unanimously after consulting the Commission and after receiving the consent of the European Parliament, which shall act by a majority of its component members. The conditions of eligibility agreed upon by the European Council shall be taken into account.

The conditions of admission and the adjustments to the Treaties on which the Union is founded, which such admission entails, shall be the subject of an agreement between the Member States and the applicant State. This agreement shall be submitted for ratification by all the contracting States in accordance with their respective constitutional requirements.

Article 50. (1) Any Member State may decide to withdraw from the Union in accordance with its own constitutional requirements.

(2) A Member State which decides to withdraw shall notify the European Council of its intention. In the light of the guidelines provided by the European Council, the Union shall negotiate and conclude an agreement with that State, setting out the arrangements for its withdrawal, taking account of the framework for its future relationship with the Union. That agreement shall be negotiated in accordance with Article 218(3) of the Treaty on the Functioning of the European Union. It shall be concluded on behalf of the Union by the Council, acting by a qualified majority, after obtaining the consent of the European Parliament.

(3) The Treaties shall cease to apply to the State in question from the date of entry into force of the withdrawal agreement or, failing that, two years after the notification referred to in paragraph 2, unless the European Council, in agreement with the Member State concerned, unanimously decides to extend this period.

(4) For the purposes of paragraphs 2 and 3, the member of the European Council or of the Council representing the withdrawing Member State shall not participate in the discussions of the European Council or Council or in decisions concerning it.

A qualified majority shall be defined in accordance with Article 238(3)(b) of the Treaty on the Functioning of the European Union.

(5) If a State which has withdrawn from the Union asks to rejoin, its request shall be subject to the procedure referred to in Article 49.

Article 51. The Protocols and Annexes to the Treaties shall form an integral part thereof.

Article 52. (1) The Treaties shall apply to the Kingdom of Belgium, the Republic of Bulgaria, the Czech Republic, the Kingdom of Denmark, the Federal Republic of Germany, the Republic of Estonia, Ireland, the Hellenic Republic, the Kingdom of Spain, the French Republic, the Republic of Croatia, the Italian Republic, the Republic of Cyprus, the Republic of Latvia, the Republic of Lithuania, the Grand Duchy of Luxembourg, the Republic of Hungary, the Republic of Malta, the Kingdom of the Netherlands, the Republic of Austria, the Republic of Poland, the Portuguese Republic, Romania, the Republic of Slovenia, the Slovak Republic, the Republic of Finland, the Kingdom of Sweden and the United Kingdom of Great Britain and Northern Ireland.
(2) The territorial scope of the Treaties is specified in Article 355 of the Treaty on the Functioning of the European Union.

Article 53. This Treaty is concluded for an unlimited period.

Article 54. (1) This Treaty shall be ratified by the High Contracting Parties in accordance with their respective constitutional requirements. The instruments of ratification shall be deposited with the Government of the Italian Republic.
(2) This Treaty shall enter into force on 1 January 1993, provided that all the Instruments of ratification have been deposited, or, failing that, on the first day of the month following the deposit of the Instrument of ratification by the last signatory State to take this step.

Article 55. (1) This Treaty, drawn up in a single original in the Bulgarian, Czech, Danish, Dutch, English, Estonian, Finnish, French, German, Greek, Hungarian, Irish, Italian, Latvian, Lithuanian, Maltese, Polish, Portuguese, Romanian, Slovak, Slovenian, Spanish and Swedish languages, the texts in each of these languages being equally authentic, shall be deposited in the archives of the Government of the Italian Republic, which will transmit a certified copy to each of the governments of the other signatory States.
(2) This Treaty may also be translated into any other languages as determined by Member States among those which, in accordance with their constitutional order, enjoy official status in all or part of their territory. A certified copy of such translations shall be provided by the Member States concerned to be deposited in the archives of the Council.

IN WITNESS WHEREOF the undersigned Plenipotentiaries have signed this Treaty.

EUROPEAN UNION

Done at Maastricht on the seventh day of February in the year one thousand nine hundred and ninety-two.

[*The List of signatories is not reproduced.*]

22   Treaty on the Functioning of the European Union[3]

HIS MAJESTY THE KING OF THE BELGIANS, THE PRESIDENT OF THE FEDERAL REPUBLIC OF GERMANY, THE PRESIDENT OF THE FRENCH REPUBLIC, THE PRESIDENT OF THE ITALIAN REPUBLIC, HER ROYAL HIGHNESS THE GRAND DUCHESS OF LUXEMBOURG, HER MAJESTY THE QUEEN OF THE NETHERLANDS[4],

DETERMINED to lay the foundations of an ever closer union among the peoples of Europe,

RESOLVED to ensure the economic and social progress of their States by common action to eliminate the barriers which divide Europe,

AFFIRMING as the essential objective of their efforts the constant improvements of the living and working conditions of their peoples,

RECOGNISING that the removal of existing obstacles calls for concerted action in order to guarantee steady expansion, balanced trade and fair competition,

ANXIOUS to strengthen the unity of their economies and to ensure their harmonious development by reducing the differences existing between the various regions and the backwardness of the less favoured regions,

DESIRING to contribute, by means of a common commercial policy, to the progressive abolition of restrictions on international trade,

INTENDING to confirm the solidarity which binds Europe and the overseas countries and desiring to ensure the development of their prosperity, in accordance with the principles of the Charter of the United Nations,

RESOLVED by thus pooling their resources to preserve and strengthen peace and liberty, and calling upon the other peoples of Europe who share their ideal to join in their efforts,

DETERMINED to promote the development of the highest possible level of knowledge for their peoples through a wide access to education and through its continuous updating,

and to this end HAVE DESIGNATED as their Plenipotentiaries:

[List of plenipotentiaries not reproduced]

WHO, having exchanged their full powers, found in good and due form, have agreed as follows.

---

3   Consolidated Version as published in the Official Journal of the European Union on 26 October 2012. Selected Parts: Part 1 (Art. 1-7; Part 2 (art. 18-25); Part 5 (art. 205-222); Part 6 (art. 223-334); Part 7 (art. 335-358). Annexes and indications and tables of equivalences are omitted.
4   The Republic of Bulgaria, the Czech Republic, the Kingdom of Denmark, the Republic of Estonia, Ireland, the Hellenic Republic, the Kingdom of Spain, the Republic of Cyprus, the Republic of Latvia, the Republic of Lithuania, the Republic of Hungary, the Republic of Malta, the Republic of Austria, the Republic of Poland, the Portuguese Republic, Romania, the Republic of Slovenia, the Slovak Republic, the Republic of Finland, the Kingdom of Sweden and the United Kingdom of Great Britain and Norther Ireland have since become members of the European Union.

Part One. Principles

Article 1. (1) This Treaty organises the functioning of the Union and determines the areas of, delimitation of, and arrangements for exercising its competences.
(2) This Treaty and the Treaty on European Union constitute the Treaties on which the Union is founded. These two Treaties, which have the same legal value, shall be referred to as "the Treaties".

Title I. Categories and Areas of Union Competence

Article 2. (1) When the Treaties confer on the Union exclusive competence in a specific area, only the Union may legislate and adopt legally binding acts, the Member States being able to do so themselves only if so empowered by the Union or for the implementation of Union acts.
(2) When the Treaties confer on the Union a competence shared with the Member States in a specific area, the Union and the Member States may legislate and adopt legally binding acts in that area. The Member States shall exercise their competence to the extent that the Union has not exercised its competence. The Member States shall again exercise their competence to the extent that the Union has decided to cease exercising its competence.
(3) The Member States shall coordinate their economic and employment policies within arrangements as determined by this Treaty, which the Union shall have competence to provide.
(4) The Union shall have competence, in accordance with the provisions of the Treaty on European Union, to define and implement a common foreign and security policy, including the progressive framing of a common defence policy.
(5) In certain areas and under the conditions laid down in the Treaties, the Union shall have competence to carry out actions to support, coordinate or supplement the actions of the Member States, without thereby superseding their competence in these areas.
Legally binding acts of the Union adopted on the basis of the provisions of the Treaties relating to these areas shall not entail harmonisation of Member States' laws or regulations.
(6) The scope of and arrangements for exercising the Union's competences shall be determined by the provisions of the Treaties relating to each area.

Article 3. (1) The Union shall have exclusive competence in the following areas:
(a) customs union;
(b) the establishing of the competition rules necessary for the functioning of the internal market;
(c) monetary policy for the Member States whose currency is the euro;

(d) the conservation of marine biological resources under the common fisheries policy;
(e) common commercial policy.
(2) The Union shall also have exclusive competence for the conclusion of an international agreement when its conclusion is provided for in a legislative act of the Union or is necessary to enable the Union to exercise its internal competence, or in so far as its conclusion may affect common rules or alter their scope.

Article 4. (1) The Union shall share competence with the Member States where the Treaties confer on it a competence which does not relate to the areas referred to in Articles 3 and 6.
(2) Shared competence between the Union and the Member States applies in the following principal areas:
(a) internal market;
(b) social policy, for the aspects defined in this Treaty;
(c) economic, social and territorial cohesion;
(d) agriculture and fisheries, excluding the conservation of marine biological resources;
(e) environment;
(f) consumer protection;
(g) transport;
(h) trans–European networks;
(i) energy;
(j) area of freedom, security and justice;
(k) common safety concerns in public health matters, for the aspects defined in this Treaty.
(3) In the areas of research, technological development and space, the Union shall have competence to carry out activities, in particular to define and implement programmes; however, the exercise of that competence shall not result in Member States being prevented from exercising theirs.
(4) In the areas of development cooperation and humanitarian aid, the Union shall have competence to carry out activities and conduct a common policy; however, the exercise of that competence shall not result in Member States being prevented from exercising theirs.

Article 5. (1) The Member States shall coordinate their economic policies within the Union. To this end, the Council shall adopt measures, in particular broad guidelines for these policies.
Specific provisions shall apply to those Member States whose currency is the euro.
(2) The Union shall take measures to ensure coordination of the employment policies of the Member States, in particular by defining guidelines for these policies.
(3) The Union may take initiatives to ensure coordination of Member States' social policies.

Article 6. The Union shall have competence to carry out actions to support, coordinate or supplement the actions of the Member States. The areas of such action shall, at European level, be:
(a) protection and improvement of human health;
(b) industry;
(c) culture;
(d) tourism;
(e) education, vocational training, youth and sport;
(f) civil protection;
(g) administrative cooperation.

Title II. Provisions Having General Application

Article 7. The Union shall ensure consistency between its policies and activities, taking all of its objectives into account and in accordance with the principle of conferral of powers.

Article 8. In all its activities, the Union shall aim to eliminate inequalities, and to promote equality, between men and women.

Article 9. In defining and implementing its policies and activities, the Union shall take into account requirements linked to the promotion of a high level of employment, the guarantee of adequate social protection, the fight against social exclusion, and a high level of education, training and protection of human health.

Article 10. In defining and implementing its policies and activities, the Union shall aim to combat discrimination based on sex, racial or ethnic origin, religion or belief, disability, age or sexual orientation.

Article 11. Environmental protection requirements must be integrated into the definition and implementation of the Union's policies and activities, in particular with a view to promoting sustainable development.

Article 12. Consumer protection requirements shall be taken into account in defining and implementing other Union policies and activities.

Article 13. In formulating and implementing the Union's agriculture, fisheries, transport, internal market, research and technological development and space policies, the Union and the Member States shall, since animals are sentient beings, pay full regard to the welfare requirements of animals, while respecting the legislative or administrative provisions and customs of the Member States relating in particular to religious rites, cultural traditions and regional heritage.

Article 14. Without prejudice to Article 4 of the Treaty on European Union or to Articles 93, 106 and 107 of this Treaty, and given the place occupied by services of general economic interest in the shared values of the Union as well as their role in promoting social and territorial cohesion, the Union and the Member States, each within their respective powers and within the scope of application of the Treaties, shall take care that such services operate on the basis of principles and conditions, particularly economic and financial conditions, which enable them to fulfil their missions. The European Parliament and the Council, acting by means of regulations in accordance with the ordinary legislative procedure, shall establish these principles and set these conditions without prejudice to the competence of Member States, in compliance with the Treaties, to provide, to commission and to fund such services.

Article 15. (1) In order to promote good governance and ensure the participation of civil society, the Union's institutions, bodies, offices and agencies shall conduct their work as openly as possible.
(2) The European Parliament shall meet in public, as shall the Council when considering and voting on a draft legislative act.
(3) Any citizen of the Union, and any natural or legal person residing or having its registered office in a Member State, shall have a right of access to documents of the Union's institutions, bodies, offices and agencies, whatever their medium, subject to the principles and the conditions to be defined in accordance with this paragraph.
General principles and limits on grounds of public or private interest governing this right of access to documents shall be determined by the European Parliament and the Council, by means of regulations, acting in accordance with the ordinary legislative procedure.
Each institution, body, office or agency shall ensure that its proceedings are transparent and shall elaborate in its own Rules of Procedure specific provisions regarding access to its documents, in accordance with the regulations referred to in the second subparagraph. The Court of Justice of the European Union, the European Central Bank and the European Investment Bank shall be subject to this paragraph only when exercising their administrative tasks.
The European Parliament and the Council shall ensure publication of the documents relating to the legislative procedures under the terms laid down by the regulations referred to in the second subparagraph.

Article 16. (1) Everyone has the right to the protection of personal data concerning them.
(2) The European Parliament and the Council, acting in accordance with the ordinary legislative procedure, shall lay down the rules relating to the protection of individuals

with regard to the processing of personal data by Union institutions, bodies, offices and agencies, and by the Member States when carrying out activities which fall within the scope of Union law, and the rules relating to the free movement of such data. Compliance with these rules shall be subject to the control of independent authorities.

The rules adopted on the basis of this Article shall be without prejudice to the specific rules laid down in Article 39 of the Treaty on European Union.

Article 17. (1) The Union respects and does not prejudice the status under national law of churches and religious associations or communities in the Member States.
(2) The Union equally respects the status under national law of philosophical and non-confessional organisations.
(3) Recognising their identity and their specific contribution, the Union shall maintain an open, transparent and regular dialogue with these churches and organisations.

Part Two. Non-Discrimination and Citizenship of the Union

Article 18. Within the scope of application of the Treaties, and without prejudice to any special provisions contained therein, any discrimination on grounds of nationality shall be prohibited.
The European Parliament and the Council, acting in accordance with the ordinary legislative procedure, may adopt rules designed to prohibit such discrimination.

Article 19. (1) Without prejudice to the other provisions of the Treaties and within the limits of the powers conferred by them upon the Union, the Council, acting unanimously in accordance with a special legislative procedure and after obtaining the consent of the European Parliament, may take appropriate action to combat discrimination based on sex, racial or ethnic origin, religion or belief, disability, age or sexual orientation.
(2) By way of derogation from paragraph 1, the European Parliament and the Council, acting in accordance with the ordinary legislative procedure, may adopt the basic principles of Union incentive measures, excluding any harmonisation of the laws and regulations of the Member States, to support action taken by the Member States in order to contribute to the achievement of the objectives referred to in paragraph 1.

Article 20. (1) Citizenship of the Union is hereby established. Every person holding the nationality of a Member State shall be a citizen of the Union. Citizenship of the Union shall be additional to and not replace national citizenship.
(2) Citizens of the Union shall enjoy the rights and be subject to the duties provided for in the Treaties. They shall have, inter alia:
(a) the right to move and reside freely within the territory of the Member States;

(b) the right to vote and to stand as candidates in elections to the European Parliament and in municipal elections in their Member State of residence, under the same conditions as nationals of that State;

(c) the right to enjoy, in the territory of a third country in which the Member State of which they are nationals is not represented, the protection of the diplomatic and consular authorities of any Member State on the same conditions as the nationals of that State;

(d) the right to petition the European Parliament, to apply to the European Ombudsman, and to address the institutions and advisory bodies of the Union in any of the Treaty languages and to obtain a reply in the same language.

These rights shall be exercised in accordance with the conditions and limits defined by the Treaties and by the measures adopted thereunder.

Article 21. (1) Every citizen of the Union shall have the right to move and reside freely within the territory of the Member States, subject to the limitations and conditions laid down in the Treaties and by the measures adopted to give them effect.

(2) If action by the Union should prove necessary to attain this objective and the Treaties have not provided the necessary powers, the European Parliament and the Council, acting in accordance with the ordinary legislative procedure, may adopt provisions with a view to facilitating the exercise of the rights referred to in paragraph 1.

(3) For the same purposes as those referred to in paragraph 1 and if the Treaties have not provided the necessary powers, the Council, acting in accordance with a special legislative procedure, may adopt measures concerning social security or social protection. The Council shall act unanimously after consulting the European Parliament.

Article 22. (1) Every citizen of the Union residing in a Member State of which he is not a national shall have the right to vote and to stand as a candidate at municipal elections in the Member State in which he resides, under the same conditions as nationals of that State. This right shall be exercised subject to detailed arrangements adopted by the Council, acting unanimously in accordance with a special legislative procedure and after consulting the European Parliament; these arrangements may provide for derogations where warranted by problems specific to a Member State.

(2) Without prejudice to Article 223(1) and to the provisions adopted for its implementation, every citizen of the Union residing in a Member State of which he is not a national shall have the right to vote and to stand as a candidate in elections to the European Parliament in the Member State in which he resides, under the same conditions as nationals of that State. This right shall be exercised subject to detailed arrangements adopted by the Council, acting unanimously in accordance with a special legislative procedure and after consulting the European Parliament; these arrangements may provide for derogations where warranted by problems specific to a Member State.

Article 23. Every citizen of the Union shall, in the territory of a third country in which the Member State of which he is a national is not represented, be entitled to protection by the diplomatic or consular authorities of any Member State, on the same conditions as the nationals of that State. Member States shall adopt the necessary provisions and start the international negotiations required to secure this protection.

The Council, acting in accordance with a special legislative procedure and after consulting the European Parliament, may adopt directives establishing the coordination and cooperation measures necessary to facilitate such protection.

Article 24. The European Parliament and the Council, acting by means of regulations in accordance with the ordinary legislative procedure, shall adopt the provisions for the procedures and conditions required for a citizens' initiative within the meaning of Article 11 of the Treaty on European Union, including the minimum number of Member States from which such citizens must come.

Every citizen of the Union shall have the right to petition the European Parliament in accordance with Article 227.

Every citizen of the Union may apply to the Ombudsman established in accordance with Article 228.

Every citizen of the Union may write to any of the institutions or bodies referred to in this Article or in Article 13 of the Treaty on European Union in one of the languages mentioned in Article 55(1) of the Treaty on European Union and have an answer in the same language.

Article 25. The Commission shall report to the European Parliament, to the Council and to the Economic and Social Committee every three years on the application of the provisions of this Part. This report shall take account of the development of the Union.

On this basis, and without prejudice to the other provisions of the Treaties, the Council, acting unanimously in accordance with a special legislative procedure and after obtaining the consent of the European Parliament, may adopt provisions to strengthen or to add to the rights listed in Article 20(2). These provisions shall enter into force after their approval by the Member States in accordance with their respective constitutional requirements.

[*Parts 3 and 4 are omitted.*]

Part Five. The Union's External Action

Title I. General Provisions on the Union's External Action

Article 205. The Union's action on the international scene, pursuant to this Part, shall be guided by the principles, pursue the objectives and be conducted in accordance with the general provisions laid down in Chapter 1 of Title V of the Treaty on European Union.

Title II. Common Commercial Policy

Article 206. By establishing a customs union in accordance with Articles 28 to 32, the Union shall contribute, in the common interest, to the harmonious development of world trade, the progressive abolition of restrictions on international trade and on foreign direct investment, and the lowering of customs and other barriers.

Article 207. (1) The common commercial policy shall be based on uniform principles, particularly with regard to changes in tariff rates, the conclusion of tariff and trade agreements relating to trade in goods and services, and the commercial aspects of intellectual property, foreign direct investment, the achievement of uniformity in measures of liberalisation, export policy and measures to protect trade such as those to be taken in the event of dumping or subsidies. The common commercial policy shall be conducted in the context of the principles and objectives of the Union's external action.
(2) The European Parliament and the Council, acting by means of regulations in accordance with the ordinary legislative procedure, shall adopt the measures defining the framework for implementing the common commercial policy.
(3) Where agreements with one or more third countries or international organisations need to be negotiated and concluded, Article 218 shall apply, subject to the special provisions of this Article.
The Commission shall make recommendations to the Council, which shall authorise it to open the necessary negotiations. The Council and the Commission shall be responsible for ensuring that the agreements negotiated are compatible with internal Union policies and rules.
The Commission shall conduct these negotiations in consultation with a special committee appointed by the Council to assist the Commission in this task and within the framework of such directives as the Council may issue to it. The Commission shall report regularly to the special committee and to the European Parliament on the progress of negotiations.
(4) For the negotiation and conclusion of the agreements referred to in paragraph 3, the Council shall act by a qualified majority.
For the negotiation and conclusion of agreements in the fields of trade in services and the commercial aspects of intellectual property, as well as foreign direct investment, the Council shall act unanimously where such agreements include provisions for which unanimity is required for the adoption of internal rules.
The Council shall also act unanimously for the negotiation and conclusion of agreements:

(a) in the field of trade in cultural and audiovisual services, where these agreements risk prejudicing the Union's cultural and linguistic diversity;

(b) in the field of trade in social, education and health services, where these agreements risk seriously disturbing the national organisation of such services and prejudicing the responsibility of Member States to deliver them.

(5) The negotiation and conclusion of international agreements in the field of transport shall be subject to Title VI of Part Three and to Article 218.

(6) The exercise of the competences conferred by this Article in the field of the common commercial policy shall not affect the delimitation of competences between the Union and the Member States, and shall not lead to harmonisation of legislative or regulatory provisions of the Member States in so far as the Treaties exclude such harmonisation.

Title III. Cooperation with Third Countries and Humanitarian Aid

Chapter 1. Development Cooperation

Article 208. (1) Union policy in the field of development cooperation shall be conducted within the framework of the principles and objectives of the Union's external action. The Union's development cooperation policy and that of the Member States complement and reinforce each other.

Union development cooperation policy shall have as its primary objective the reduction and, in the long term, the eradication of poverty. The Union shall take account of the objectives of development cooperation in the policies that it implements which are likely to affect developing countries.

(2) The Union and the Member States shall comply with the commitments and take account of the objectives they have approved in the context of the United Nations and other competent international organisations.

Article 209. (1) The European Parliament and the Council, acting in accordance with the ordinary legislative procedure, shall adopt the measures necessary for the implementation of development cooperation policy, which may relate to multiannual cooperation programmes with developing countries or programmes with a thematic approach.

(2) The Union may conclude with third countries and competent international organisations any agreement helping to achieve the objectives referred to in Article 21 of the Treaty on European Union and in Article 208 of this Treaty.

The first subparagraph shall be without prejudice to Member States' competence to negotiate in international bodies and to conclude agreements.

(3) The European Investment Bank shall contribute, under the terms laid down in its Statute, to the implementation of the measures referred to in paragraph 1.

Article 210. (1) In order to promote the complementarity and efficiency of their action, the Union and the Member States shall coordinate their policies on development cooperation and shall consult each other on their aid programmes, including in international organisations and during international conferences. They may undertake joint action. Member States shall contribute if necessary to the implementation of Union aid programmes.
(2) The Commission may take any useful initiative to promote the coordination referred to in paragraph 1.

Article 211. Within their respective spheres of competence, the Union and the Member States shall cooperate with third countries and with the competent international organisations.

Chapter 2. Economic, Financial and Technical Cooperation with Third Countries

Article 212. (1) Without prejudice to the other provisions of the Treaties, and in particular Articles 208 to 211, the Union shall carry out economic, financial and technical cooperation measures, including assistance, in particular financial assistance, with third countries other than developing countries. Such measures shall be consistent with the development policy of the Union and shall be carried out within the framework of the principles and objectives of its external action. The Union's operations and those of the Member States shall complement and reinforce each other.
(2) The European Parliament and the Council, acting in accordance with the ordinary legislative procedure, shall adopt the measures necessary for the implementation of paragraph 1.
(3) Within their respective spheres of competence, the Union and the Member States shall cooperate with third countries and the competent international organisations. The arrangements for Union cooperation may be the subject of agreements between the Union and the third parties concerned.
The first subparagraph shall be without prejudice to the Member States' competence to negotiate in international bodies and to conclude international agreements.

Article 213. When the situation in a third country requires urgent financial assistance from the Union, the Council shall adopt the necessary decisions on a proposal from the Commission.

Chapter 3. Humanitarian aid

Article 214. (1) The Union's operations in the field of humanitarian aid shall be conducted within the framework of the principles and objectives of the external action of the

Union. Such operations shall be intended to provide ad hoc assistance and relief and protection for people in third countries who are victims of natural or man–made disasters, in order to meet the humanitarian needs resulting from these different situations. The Union's measures and those of the Member States shall complement and reinforce each other.

(2) Humanitarian aid operations shall be conducted in compliance with the principles of international law and with the principles of impartiality, neutrality and non–discrimination.

(3) The European Parliament and the Council, acting in accordance with the ordinary legislative procedure, shall establish the measures defining the framework within which the Union's humanitarian aid operations shall be implemented.

(4) The Union may conclude with third countries and competent international organisations any agreement helping to achieve the objectives referred to in paragraph 1 and in Article 21 of the Treaty on European Union.

The first subparagraph shall be without prejudice to Member States' competence to negotiate in international bodies and to conclude agreements.

(5) In order to establish a framework for joint contributions from young Europeans to the humanitarian aid operations of the Union, a European Voluntary Humanitarian Aid Corps shall be set up. The European Parliament and the Council, acting by means of regulations in accordance with the ordinary legislative procedure, shall determine the rules and procedures for the operation of the Corps.

(6) The Commission may take any useful initiative to promote coordination between actions of the Union and those of the Member States, in order to enhance the efficiency and complementarity of Union and national humanitarian aid measures.

(7) The Union shall ensure that its humanitarian aid operations are coordinated and consistent with those of international organisations and bodies, in particular those forming part of the United Nations system.

Title IV. Restrictive Measures

Article 215. (1) Where a decision, adopted in accordance with Chapter 2 of Title V of the Treaty on European Union, provides for the interruption or reduction, in part or completely, of economic and financial relations with one or more third countries, the Council, acting by a qualified majority on a joint proposal from the High Representative of the Union for Foreign Affairs and Security Policy and the Commission, shall adopt the necessary measures. It shall inform the European Parliament thereof.

(2) Where a decision adopted in accordance with Chapter 2 of Title V of the Treaty on European Union so provides, the Council may adopt restrictive measures under the procedure referred to in paragraph 1 against natural or legal persons and groups or non–State entities.

(3) The acts referred to in this Article shall include necessary provisions on legal safeguards.

Title V. International Agreements

Article 216. (1) The Union may conclude an agreement with one or more third countries or international organisations where the Treaties so provide or where the conclusion of an agreement is necessary in order to achieve, within the framework of the Union's policies, one of the objectives referred to in the Treaties, or is provided for in a legally binding Union act or is likely to affect common rules or alter their scope.
(2) Agreements concluded by the Union are binding upon the institutions of the Union and on its Member States.

Article 217. The Union may conclude with one or more third countries or international organisations agreements establishing an association involving reciprocal rights and obligations, common action and special procedure.

Article 218. (1) Without prejudice to the specific provisions laid down in Article 207, agreements between the Union and third countries or international organisations shall be negotiated and concluded in accordance with the following procedure.
(2) The Council shall authorise the opening of negotiations, adopt negotiating directives, authorise the signing of agreements and conclude them.
(3) The Commission, or the High Representative of the Union for Foreign Affairs and Security Policy where the agreement envisaged relates exclusively or principally to the common foreign and security policy, shall submit recommendations to the Council, which shall adopt a decision authorising the opening of negotiations and, depending on the subject of the agreement envisaged, nominating the Union negotiator or the head of the Union's negotiating team.
(4) The Council may address directives to the negotiator and designate a special committee in consultation with which the negotiations must be conducted.
(5) The Council, on a proposal by the negotiator, shall adopt a decision authorising the signing of the agreement and, if necessary, its provisional application before entry into force.
(6) The Council, on a proposal by the negotiator, shall adopt a decision concluding the agreement.
Except where agreements relate exclusively to the common foreign and security policy, the Council shall adopt the decision concluding the agreement:
(a) after obtaining the consent of the European Parliament in the following cases:
   (i) association agreements;

(ii) agreement on Union accession to the European Convention for the Protection of Human Rights and Fundamental Freedoms;
(iii) agreements establishing a specific institutional framework by organising cooperation procedures;
(iv) agreements with important budgetary implications for the Union;
(v) agreements covering fields to which either the ordinary legislative procedure applies, or the special legislative procedure where consent by the European Parliament is required.

The European Parliament and the Council may, in an urgent situation, agree upon a time–limit for consent.

(b) after consulting the European Parliament in other cases. The European Parliament shall deliver its opinion within a time–limit which the Council may set depending on the urgency of the matter. In the absence of an opinion within that time–limit, the Council may act.

(7) When concluding an agreement, the Council may, by way of derogation from paragraphs 5, 6 and 9, authorise the negotiator to approve on the Union's behalf modifications to the agreement where it provides for them to be adopted by a simplified procedure or by a body set up by the agreement. The Council may attach specific conditions to such authorisation.

(8) The Council shall act by a qualified majority throughout the procedure.

However, it shall act unanimously when the agreement covers a field for which unanimity is required for the adoption of a Union act as well as for association agreements and the agreements referred to in Article 212 with the States which are candidates for accession. The Council shall also act unanimously for the agreement on accession of the Union to the European Convention for the Protection of Human Rights and Fundamental Freedoms; the decision concluding this agreement shall enter into force after it has been approved by the Member States in accordance with their respective constitutional requirements.

(9) The Council, on a proposal from the Commission or the High Representative of the Union for Foreign Affairs and Security Policy, shall adopt a decision suspending application of an agreement and establishing the positions to be adopted on the Union's behalf in a body set up by an agreement, when that body is called upon to adopt acts having legal effects, with the exception of acts supplementing or amending the institutional framework of the agreement.

(10) The European Parliament shall be immediately and fully informed at all stages of the procedure.

(11) A Member State, the European Parliament, the Council or the Commission may obtain the opinion of the Court of Justice as to whether an agreement envisaged is compatible with the Treaties. Where the opinion of the Court is adverse, the agreement envisaged may not enter into force unless it is amended or the Treaties are revised.

Article 219. (1) By way of derogation from Article 218, the Council, either on a recommendation from the European Central Bank or on a recommendation from the Commission and after consulting the European Central Bank, in an endeavour to reach a consensus consistent with the objective of price stability, may conclude formal agreements on an exchange–rate system for the euro in relation to the currencies of third States. The Council shall act unanimously after consulting the European Parliament and in accordance with the procedure provided for in paragraph 3.

The Council may, either on a recommendation from the European Central Bank or on a recommendation from the Commission, and after consulting the European Central Bank, in an endeavour to reach a consensus consistent with the objective of price stability, adopt, adjust or abandon the central rates of the euro within the exchange–rate system. The President of the Council shall inform the European Parliament of the adoption, adjustment or abandonment of the euro central rates.

(2) In the absence of an exchange–rate system in relation to one or more currencies of third States as referred to in paragraph 1, the Council, either on a recommendation from the Commission and after consulting the European Central Bank or on a recommendation from the European Central Bank, may formulate general orientations for exchange–rate policy in relation to these currencies. These general orientations shall be without prejudice to the primary objective of the ESCB to maintain price stability.

(3) By way of derogation from Article 218, where agreements concerning monetary or foreign exchange regime matters need to be negotiated by the Union with one or more third States or international organisations, the Council, on a recommendation from the Commission and after consulting the European Central Bank, shall decide the arrangements for the negotiation and for the conclusion of such agreements. These arrangements shall ensure that the Union expresses a single position. The Commission shall be fully associated with the negotiations.

(4) Without prejudice to Union competence and Union agreements as regards economic and monetary union, Member States may negotiate in international bodies and conclude international agreements.

Title VI. The Union's Relations with International Organisations and Third Countries and Union Delegations

Article 220. (1) The Union shall establish all appropriate forms of cooperation with the organs of the United Nations and its specialised agencies, the Council of Europe, the Organisation for Security and Cooperation in Europe and the Organisation for Economic Cooperation and Development.

The Union shall also maintain such relations as are appropriate with other international organisations.

(2) The High Representative of the Union for Foreign Affairs and Security Policy and the Commission shall implement this Article.

Article 221. (1) Union delegations in third countries and at international organisations shall represent the Union.
(2) Union delegations shall be placed under the authority of the High Representative of the Union for Foreign Affairs and Security Policy. They shall act in close cooperation with Member States' diplomatic and consular missions.

Title VII. Solidarity Clause

Article 222. (1) The Union and its Member States shall act jointly in a spirit of solidarity if a Member State is the object of a terrorist attack or the victim of a natural or man–made disaster. The Union shall mobilise all the instruments at its disposal, including the military resources made available by the Member States, to:
(a)
- prevent the terrorist threat in the territory of the Member States;
- protect democratic institutions and the civilian population from any terrorist attack;
- assist a Member State in its territory, at the request of its political authorities, in the event of a terrorist attack;

(b) assist a Member State in its territory, at the request of its political authorities, in the event of a natural or man–made disaster.
(2) Should a Member State be the object of a terrorist attack or the victim of a natural or man–made disaster, the other Member States shall assist it at the request of its political authorities. To that end, the Member States shall coordinate between themselves in the Council.
(3) The arrangements for the implementation by the Union of the solidarity clause shall be defined by a decision adopted by the Council acting on a joint proposal by the Commission and the High Representative of the Union for Foreign Affairs and Security Policy. The Council shall act in accordance with Article 31(1) of the Treaty on European Union where this decision has defence implications. The European Parliament shall be informed.
For the purposes of this paragraph and without prejudice to Article 240, the Council shall be assisted by the Political and Security Committee with the support of the structures developed in the context of the common security and defence policy and by the Committee referred to in Article 71; the two committees shall, if necessary, submit joint opinions.
(4) The European Council shall regularly assess the threats facing the Union in order to enable the Union and its Member States to take effective action.

Part Six. Institutional and Financial Provisions

Title I. Institutional Provisions

Chapter 1. The Institutions

Section 1. The European Parliament

Article 223. (1) The European Parliament shall draw up a proposal to lay down the provisions necessary for the election of its Members by direct universal suffrage in accordance with a uniform procedure in all Member States or in accordance with principles common to all Member States.
The Council, acting unanimously in accordance with a special legislative procedure and after obtaining the consent of the European Parliament, which shall act by a majority of its component Members, shall lay down the necessary provisions. These provisions shall enter into force following their approval by the Member States in accordance with their respective constitutional requirements.
(2) The European Parliament, acting by means of regulations on its own initiative in accordance with a special legislative procedure after seeking an opinion from the Commission and with the consent of the Council, shall lay down the regulations and general conditions governing the performance of the duties of its Members. All rules or conditions relating to the taxation of Members or former Members shall require unanimity within the Council.

Article 224. The European Parliament and the Council, acting in accordance with the ordinary legislative procedure, by means of regulations, shall lay down the regulations governing political parties at European level referred to in Article 10(4) of the Treaty on European Union and in particular the rules regarding their funding.

Article 225. The European Parliament may, acting by a majority of its component Members, request the Commission to submit any appropriate proposal on matters on which it considers that a Union act is required for the purpose of implementing the Treaties. If the Commission does not submit a proposal, it shall inform the European Parliament of the reasons.

Article 226. In the course of its duties, the European Parliament may, at the request of a quarter of its component Members, set up a temporary Committee of Inquiry to investigate, without prejudice to the powers conferred by the Treaties on other institutions or bodies, alleged contraventions or maladministration in the implementation of Union law, except where the alleged facts are being examined before a court and while the case is still subject to legal proceedings.

The temporary Committee of Inquiry shall cease to exist on the submission of its report. The detailed provisions governing the exercise of the right of inquiry shall be determined by the European Parliament, acting by means of regulations on its own initiative in accordance with a special legislative procedure, after obtaining the consent of the Council and the Commission.

Article 227. Any citizen of the Union, and any natural or legal person residing or having its registered office in a Member State, shall have the right to address, individually or in association with other citizens or persons, a petition to the European Parliament on a matter which comes within the Union's fields of activity and which affects him, her or it directly.

Article 228. (1) A European Ombudsman, elected by the European Parliament, shall be empowered to receive complaints from any citizen of the Union or any natural or legal person residing or having its registered office in a Member State concerning instances of maladministration in the activities of the Union institutions, bodies, offices or agencies, with the exception of the Court of Justice of the European Union acting in its judicial role. He or she shall examine such complaints and report on them.

In accordance with his duties, the Ombudsman shall conduct inquiries for which he finds grounds, either on his own initiative or on the basis of complaints submitted to him direct or through a Member of the European Parliament, except where the alleged facts are or have been the subject of legal proceedings. Where the Ombudsman establishes an instance of maladministration, he shall refer the matter to the institution, body, office or agency concerned, which shall have a period of three months in which to inform him of its views. The Ombudsman shall then forward a report to the European Parliament and the institution, body, office or agency concerned. The person lodging the complaint shall be informed of the outcome of such inquiries.

The Ombudsman shall submit an annual report to the European Parliament on the outcome of his inquiries.

(2) The Ombudsman shall be elected after each election of the European Parliament for the duration of its term of office. The Ombudsman shall be eligible for reappointment.

The Ombudsman may be dismissed by the Court of Justice at the request of the European Parliament if he no longer fulfils the conditions required for the performance of his duties or if he is guilty of serious misconduct.

(3) The Ombudsman shall be completely independent in the performance of his duties. In the performance of those duties he shall neither seek nor take instructions from any Government, institution, body, office or entity. The Ombudsman may not, during his term of office, engage in any other occupation, whether gainful or not.

(4) The European Parliament acting by means of regulations on its own initiative in accordance with a special legislative procedure shall, after seeking an opinion from the Commission and with the consent of the Council, lay down the regulations and general conditions governing the performance of the Ombudsman's duties.

Article 229. The European Parliament shall hold an annual session. It shall meet, without requiring to be convened, on the second Tuesday in March.
The European Parliament may meet in extraordinary part-session at the request of a majority of its component Members or at the request of the Council or of the Commission.

Article 230. The Commission may attend all the meetings and shall, at its request, be heard.
The Commission shall reply orally or in writing to questions put to it by the European Parliament or by its Members.
The European Council and the Council shall be heard by the European Parliament in accordance with the conditions laid down in the Rules of Procedure of the European Council and those of the Council.

Article 231. Save as otherwise provided in the Treaties, the European Parliament shall act by a majority of the votes cast.
The Rules of Procedure shall determine the quorum.

Article 232. The European Parliament shall adopt its Rules of Procedure, acting by a majority of its Members.
The proceedings of the European Parliament shall be published in the manner laid down in the Treaties and in its Rules of Procedure.

Article 233. The European Parliament shall discuss in open session the annual general report submitted to it by the Commission.

Article 234. If a motion of censure on the activities of the Commission is tabled before it, the European Parliament shall not vote thereon until at least three days after the motion has been tabled and only by open vote.
If the motion of censure is carried by a two-thirds majority of the votes cast, representing a majority of the component Members of the European Parliament, the members of the Commission shall resign as a body and the High Representative of the Union for Foreign Affairs and Security Policy shall resign from duties that he or she carries out in the Commission. They shall remain in office and continue to deal with current business until they are replaced in accordance with Article 17 of the Treaty on European Union. In this

case, the term of office of the members of the Commission appointed to replace them shall expire on the date on which the term of office of the members of the Commission obliged to resign as a body would have expired.

Section 2. The European Council

Article 235. (1) Where a vote is taken, any member of the European Council may also act on behalf of not more than one other member.
Article 16(4) of the Treaty on European Union and Article 238(2) of this Treaty shall apply to the European Council when it is acting by a qualified majority. Where the European Council decides by vote, its President and the President of the Commission shall not take part in the vote.
Abstentions by members present in person or represented shall not prevent the adoption by the European Council of acts which require unanimity.
(2) The President of the European Parliament may be invited to be heard by the European Council.
(3) The European Council shall act by a simple majority for procedural questions and for the adoption of its Rules of Procedure.
(4) The European Council shall be assisted by the General Secretariat of the Council.

Article 236. The European Council shall adopt by a qualified majority:
(a) a decision establishing the list of Council configurations, other than those of the General Affairs Council and of the Foreign Affairs Council, in accordance with Article 16(6) of the Treaty on European Union;
(b) a decision on the Presidency of Council configurations, other than that of Foreign Affairs, in accordance with Article 16(9) of the Treaty on European Union.

Section 3. The Council

Article 237. The Council shall meet when convened by its President on his own initiative or at the request of one of its Members or of the Commission.

Article 238. (1) Where it is required to act by a simple majority, the Council shall act by a majority of its component members.
(2) By way of derogation from Article 16(4) of the Treaty on European Union, as from 1 November 2014 and subject to the provisions laid down in the Protocol on transitional provisions, where the Council does not act on a proposal from the Commission or from the High Representative of the Union for Foreign Affairs and Security Policy, the qualified majority shall be defined as at least 72 % of the members of the Council, representing Member States comprising at least 65 % of the population of the Union.

(3) As from 1 November 2014 and subject to the provisions laid down in the Protocol on transitional provisions, in cases where, under the Treaties, not all the members of the Council participate in voting, a qualified majority shall be defined as follows:
(a) A qualified majority shall be defined as at least 55 % of the members of the Council representing the participating Member States, comprising at least 65 % of the population of these States.

A blocking minority must include at least the minimum number of Council members representing more than 35 % of the population of the participating Member States, plus one member, failing which the qualified majority shall be deemed attained;
(b) By way of derogation from point (a), where the Council does not act on a proposal from the Commission or from the High Representative of the Union for Foreign Affairs and Security Policy, the qualified majority shall be defined as at least 72 % of the members of the Council representing the participating Member States, comprising at least 65 % of the population of these States.
(4) Abstentions by Members present in person or represented shall not prevent the adoption by the Council of acts which require unanimity.

Article 239. Where a vote is taken, any Member of the Council may also act on behalf of not more than one other member.

Article 240. (1) A committee consisting of the Permanent Representatives of the Governments of the Member States shall be responsible for preparing the work of the Council and for carrying out the tasks assigned to it by the latter. The Committee may adopt procedural decisions in cases provided for in the Council's Rules of Procedure.
(2) The Council shall be assisted by a General Secretariat, under the responsibility of a Secretary–General appointed by the Council.
The Council shall decide on the organisation of the General Secretariat by a simple majority.
(3) The Council shall act by a simple majority regarding procedural matters and for the adoption of its Rules of Procedure.

Article 241. The Council, acting by a simple majority, may request the Commission to undertake any studies the Council considers desirable for the attainment of the common objectives, and to submit to it any appropriate proposals. If the Commission does not submit a proposal, it shall inform the Council of the reasons.

Article 242. The Council, acting by a simple majority shall, after consulting the Commission, determine the rules governing the committees provided for in the Treaties.

Article 243. The Council shall determine the salaries, allowances and pensions of the President of the European Council, the President of the Commission, the High Representative of the Union for Foreign Affairs and Security Policy, the Members of the Commission, the Presidents, Members and Registrars of the Court of Justice of the European Union, and the Secretary–General of the Council. It shall also determine any payment to be made instead of remuneration.

Section 4. The Commission

Article 244. In accordance with Article 17(5) of the Treaty on European Union, the Members of the Commission shall be chosen on the basis of a system of rotation established unanimously by the European Council and on the basis of the following principles:
(a) Member States shall be treated on a strictly equal footing as regards determination of the sequence of, and the time spent by, their nationals as members of the Commission; consequently, the difference between the total number of terms of office held by nationals of any given pair of Member States may never be more than one;
(b) subject to point (a), each successive Commission shall be so composed as to reflect satisfactorily the demographic and geographical range of all the Member States.

Article 245. The Members of the Commission shall refrain from any action incompatible with their duties. Member States shall respect their independence and shall not seek to influence them in the performance of their tasks.
The Members of the Commission may not, during their term of office, engage in any other occupation, whether gainful or not. When entering upon their duties they shall give a solemn undertaking that, both during and after their term of office, they will respect the obligations arising therefrom and in particular their duty to behave with integrity and discretion as regards the acceptance, after they have ceased to hold office, of certain appointments or benefits. In the event of any breach of these obligations, the Court of Justice may, on application by the Council acting by a simple majority or the Commission, rule that the Member concerned be, according to the circumstances, either compulsorily retired in accordance with Article 247 or deprived of his right to a pension or other benefits in its stead.

Article 246. Apart from normal replacement, or death, the duties of a Member of the Commission shall end when he resigns or is compulsorily retired.
A vacancy caused by resignation, compulsory retirement or death shall be filled for the remainder of the Member's term of office by a new Member of the same nationality appointed by the Council, by common accord with the President of the Commission, after consulting the European Parliament and in accordance with the criteria set out in the second subparagraph of Article 17(3) of the Treaty on European Union.

The Council may, acting unanimously on a proposal from the President of the Commission, decide that such a vacancy need not be filled, in particular when the remainder of the Member's term of office is short.

In the event of resignation, compulsory retirement or death, the President shall be replaced for the remainder of his term of office. The procedure laid down in the first subparagraph of Article 17(7) of the Treaty on European Union shall be applicable for the replacement of the President.

In the event of resignation, compulsory retirement or death, the High Representative of the Union for Foreign Affairs and Security Policy shall be replaced, for the remainder of his or her term of office, in accordance with Article 18(1) of the Treaty on European Union.

In the case of the resignation of all the Members of the Commission, they shall remain in office and continue to deal with current business until they have been replaced, for the remainder of their term of office, in accordance with Article 17 of the Treaty on European Union.

Article 247. If any Member of the Commission no longer fulfils the conditions required for the performance of his duties or if he has been guilty of serious misconduct, the Court of Justice may, on application by the Council acting by a simple majority or the Commission, compulsorily retire him.

Article 248. Without prejudice to Article 18(4) of the Treaty on European Union, the responsibilities incumbent upon the Commission shall be structured and allocated among its members by its President, in accordance with Article 17(6) of that Treaty. The President may reshuffle the allocation of those responsibilities during the Commission's term of office. The Members of the Commission shall carry out the duties devolved upon them by the President under his authority.

Article 249. (1) The Commission shall adopt its Rules of Procedure so as to ensure that both it and its departments operate. It shall ensure that these Rules are published.
(2) The Commission shall publish annually, not later than one month before the opening of the session of the European Parliament, a general report on the activities of the Union.

Article 250. The Commission shall act by a majority of its Members.
Its Rules of Procedure shall determine the quorum.

Section 5. The Court of Justice of the European Union

Article 251. The Court of Justice shall sit in chambers or in a Grand Chamber, in accordance with the rules laid down for that purpose in the Statute of the Court of Justice of the European Union.
When provided for in the Statute, the Court of Justice may also sit as a full Court.

Article 252. The Court of Justice shall be assisted by eight Advocates–General. Should the Court of Justice so request, the Council, acting unanimously, may increase the number of Advocates–General.
It shall be the duty of the Advocate–General, acting with complete impartiality and independence, to make, in open court, reasoned submissions on cases which, in accordance with the Statute of the Court of Justice of the European Union, require his involvement.

Article 253. The Judges and Advocates–General of the Court of Justice shall be chosen from persons whose independence is beyond doubt and who possess the qualifications required for appointment to the highest judicial offices in their respective countries or who are jurisconsults of recognised competence; they shall be appointed by common accord of the governments of the Member States for a term of six years, after consultation of the panel provided for in Article 255.
Every three years there shall be a partial replacement of the Judges and Advocates–General, in accordance with the conditions laid down in the Statute of the Court of Justice of the European Union.
The Judges shall elect the President of the Court of Justice from among their number for a term of three years. He may be re–elected.
Retiring Judges and Advocates–General may be reappointed.
The Court of Justice shall appoint its Registrar and lay down the rules governing his service.
The Court of Justice shall establish its Rules of Procedure. Those Rules shall require the approval of the Council.

Article 254. The number of Judges of the General Court shall be determined by the Statute of the Court of Justice of the European Union. The Statute may provide for the General Court to be assisted by Advocates–General.
The members of the General Court shall be chosen from persons whose independence is beyond doubt and who possess the ability required for appointment to high judicial office. They shall be appointed by common accord of the governments of the Member States for a term of six years, after consultation of the panel provided for in Article 255. The membership shall be partially renewed every three years. Retiring members shall be eligible for reappointment.

The Judges shall elect the President of the General Court from among their number for a term of three years. He may be re-elected.

The General Court shall appoint its Registrar and lay down the rules governing his service.

The General Court shall establish its Rules of Procedure in agreement with the Court of Justice. Those Rules shall require the approval of the Council.

Unless the Statute of the Court of Justice of the European Union provides otherwise, the provisions of the Treaties relating to the Court of Justice shall apply to the General Court.

Article 255. A panel shall be set up in order to give an opinion on candidates' suitability to perform the duties of Judge and Advocate-General of the Court of Justice and the General Court before the governments of the Member States make the appointments referred to in Articles 253 and 254.

The panel shall comprise seven persons chosen from among former members of the Court of Justice and the General Court, members of national supreme courts and lawyers of recognised competence, one of whom shall be proposed by the European Parliament. The Council shall adopt a decision establishing the panel's operating rules and a decision appointing its members. It shall act on the initiative of the President of the Court of Justice.

Article 256. (1) The General Court shall have jurisdiction to hear and determine at first instance actions or proceedings referred to in Articles 263, 265, 268, 270 and 272, with the exception of those assigned to a specialised court set up under Article 257 and those reserved in the Statute for the Court of Justice. The Statute may provide for the General Court to have jurisdiction for other classes of action or proceeding.

Decisions given by the General Court under this paragraph may be subject to a right of appeal to the Court of Justice on points of law only, under the conditions and within the limits laid down by the Statute.

(2) The General Court shall have jurisdiction to hear and determine actions or proceedings brought against decisions of the specialised courts.

Decisions given by the General Court under this paragraph may exceptionally be subject to review by the Court of Justice, under the conditions and within the limits laid down by the Statute, where there is a serious risk of the unity or consistency of Union law being affected.

(3) The General Court shall have jurisdiction to hear and determine questions referred for a preliminary ruling under Article 267, in specific areas laid down by the Statute.

Where the General Court considers that the case requires a decision of principle likely to affect the unity or consistency of Union law, it may refer the case to the Court of Justice for a ruling.

Decisions given by the General Court on questions referred for a preliminary ruling may exceptionally be subject to review by the Court of Justice, under the conditions and within the limits laid down by the Statute, where there is a serious risk of the unity or consistency of Union law being affected.

Article 257. The European Parliament and the Council, acting in accordance with the ordinary legislative procedure, may establish specialised courts attached to the General Court to hear and determine at first instance certain classes of action or proceeding brought in specific areas. The European Parliament and the Council shall act by means of regulations either on a proposal from the Commission after consultation of the Court of Justice or at the request of the Court of Justice after consultation of the Commission. The regulation establishing a specialised court shall lay down the rules on the organisation of the court and the extent of the jurisdiction conferred upon it.
Decisions given by specialised courts may be subject to a right of appeal on points of law only or, when provided for in the regulation establishing the specialised court, a right of appeal also on matters of fact, before the General Court.
The members of the specialised courts shall be chosen from persons whose independence is beyond doubt and who possess the ability required for appointment to judicial office. They shall be appointed by the Council, acting unanimously.
The specialised courts shall establish their Rules of Procedure in agreement with the Court of Justice. Those Rules shall require the approval of the Council.
Unless the regulation establishing the specialised court provides otherwise, the provisions of the Treaties relating to the Court of Justice of the European Union and the provisions of the Statute of the Court of Justice of the European Union shall apply to the specialised courts. Title I of the Statute and Article 64 thereof shall in any case apply to the specialised courts.

Article 258. If the Commission considers that a Member State has failed to fulfil an obligation under the Treaties, it shall deliver a reasoned opinion on the matter after giving the State concerned the opportunity to submit its observations.
If the State concerned does not comply with the opinion within the period laid down by the Commission, the latter may bring the matter before the Court of Justice of the European Union.

Article 259. A Member State which considers that another Member State has failed to fulfil an obligation under the Treaties may bring the matter before the Court of Justice of the European Union.
Before a Member State brings an action against another Member State for an alleged infringement of an obligation under the Treaties, it shall bring the matter before the Commission.

The Commission shall deliver a reasoned opinion after each of the States concerned has been given the opportunity to submit its own case and its observations on the other party's case both orally and in writing.

If the Commission has not delivered an opinion within three months of the date on which the matter was brought before it, the absence of such opinion shall not prevent the matter from being brought before the Court.

Article 260. (1) If the Court of Justice of the European Union finds that a Member State has failed to fulfil an obligation under the Treaties, the State shall be required to take the necessary measures to comply with the judgment of the Court.

(2) If the Commission considers that the Member State concerned has not taken the necessary measures to comply with the judgment of the Court, it may bring the case before the Court after giving that State the opportunity to submit its observations. It shall specify the amount of the lump sum or penalty payment to be paid by the Member State concerned which it considers appropriate in the circumstances.

If the Court finds that the Member State concerned has not complied with its judgment it may impose a lump sum or penalty payment on it.

This procedure shall be without prejudice to Article 259.

(3) When the Commission brings a case before the Court pursuant to Article 258 on the grounds that the Member State concerned has failed to fulfil its obligation to notify measures transposing a directive adopted under a legislative procedure, it may, when it deems appropriate, specify the amount of the lump sum or penalty payment to be paid by the Member State concerned which it considers appropriate in the circumstances.

If the Court finds that there is an infringement it may impose a lump sum or penalty payment on the Member State concerned not exceeding the amount specified by the Commission. The payment obligation shall take effect on the date set by the Court in its judgment.

Article 261. Regulations adopted jointly by the European Parliament and the Council, and by the Council, pursuant to the provisions of the Treaties, may give the Court of Justice of the European Union unlimited jurisdiction with regard to the penalties provided for in such regulations.

Article 262. Without prejudice to the other provisions of the Treaties, the Council, acting unanimously in accordance with a special legislative procedure and after consulting the European Parliament, may adopt provisions to confer jurisdiction, to the extent that it shall determine, on the Court of Justice of the European Union in disputes relating to the application of acts adopted on the basis of the Treaties which create European intellectual property rights. These provisions shall enter into force after their approval by the Member States in accordance with their respective constitutional requirements.

Article 263. The Court of Justice of the European Union shall review the legality of legislative acts, of acts of the Council, of the Commission and of the European Central Bank, other than recommendations and opinions, and of acts of the European Parliament and of the European Council intended to produce legal effects vis-à-vis third parties. It shall also review the legality of acts of bodies, offices or agencies of the Union intended to produce legal effects vis-à-vis third parties.

It shall for this purpose have jurisdiction in actions brought by a Member State, the European Parliament, the Council or the Commission on grounds of lack of competence, infringement of an essential procedural requirement, infringement of the Treaties or of any rule of law relating to their application, or misuse of powers.

The Court shall have jurisdiction under the same conditions in actions brought by the Court of Auditors, by the European Central Bank and by the Committee of the Regions for the purpose of protecting their prerogatives.

Any natural or legal person may, under the conditions laid down in the first and second paragraphs, institute proceedings against an act addressed to that person or which is of direct and individual concern to them, and against a regulatory act which is of direct concern to them and does not entail implementing measures.

Acts setting up bodies, offices and agencies of the Union may lay down specific conditions and arrangements concerning actions brought by natural or legal persons against acts of these bodies, offices or agencies intended to produce legal effects in relation to them.

The proceedings provided for in this Article shall be instituted within two months of the publication of the measure, or of its notification to the plaintiff, or, in the absence thereof, of the day on which it came to the knowledge of the latter, as the case may be.

Article 264. If the action is well founded, the Court of Justice of the European Union shall declare the act concerned to be void.

However, the Court shall, if it considers this necessary, state which of the effects of the act which it has declared void shall be considered as definitive.

Article 265. Should the European Parliament, the European Council, the Council, the Commission or the European Central Bank, in infringement of the Treaties, fail to act, the Member States and the other institutions of the Union may bring an action before the Court of Justice of the European Union to have the infringement established. This Article shall apply, under the same conditions, to bodies, offices and agencies of the Union which fail to act.

The action shall be admissible only if the institution, body, office or agency concerned has first been called upon to act. If, within two months of being so called upon, the institution, body, office or agency concerned has not defined its position, the action may be brought within a further period of two months.

Any natural or legal person may, under the conditions laid down in the preceding paragraphs, complain to the Court that an institution, body, office or agency of the Union has failed to address to that person any act other than a recommendation or an opinion.

Article 266. The institution whose act has been declared void or whose failure to act has been declared contrary to the Treaties shall be required to take the necessary measures to comply with the judgment of the Court of Justice of the European Union.

This obligation shall not affect any obligation which may result from the application of the second paragraph of Article 340.

Article 267. The Court of Justice of the European Union shall have jurisdiction to give preliminary rulings concerning:
(a) the interpretation of the Treaties;
(b) the validity and interpretation of acts of the institutions, bodies, offices or agencies of the Union;

Where such a question is raised before any court or tribunal of a Member State, that court or tribunal may, if it considers that a decision on the question is necessary to enable it to give judgment, request the Court to give a ruling thereon.

Where any such question is raised in a case pending before a court or tribunal of a Member State against whose decisions there is no judicial remedy under national law, that court or tribunal shall bring the matter before the Court.

If such a question is raised in a case pending before a court or tribunal of a Member State with regard to a person in custody, the Court of Justice of the European Union shall act with the minimum of delay.

Article 268. The Court of Justice of the European Union shall have jurisdiction in disputes relating to compensation for damage provided for in the second and third paragraphs of Article 340.

Article 269. The Court of Justice shall have jurisdiction to decide on the legality of an act adopted by the European Council or by the Council pursuant to Article 7 of the Treaty on European Union solely at the request of the Member State concerned by a determination of the European Council or of the Council and in respect solely of the procedural stipulations contained in that Article.

Such a request must be made within one month from the date of such determination. The Court shall rule within one month from the date of the request.

Article 270. The Court of Justice of the European Union shall have jurisdiction in any dispute between the Union and its servants within the limits and under the conditions laid down in the Staff Regulations of Officials and the Conditions of Employment of other servants of the Union.

Article 271. The Court of Justice of the European Union shall, within the limits hereinafter laid down, have jurisdiction in disputes concerning:
(a) the fulfilment by Member States of obligations under the Statute of the European Investment Bank. In this connection, the Board of Directors of the Bank shall enjoy the powers conferred upon the Commission by Article 258;
(b) measures adopted by the Board of Governors of the European Investment Bank. In this connection, any Member State, the Commission or the Board of Directors of the Bank may institute proceedings under the conditions laid down in Article 263;
(c) measures adopted by the Board of Directors of the European Investment Bank. Proceedings against such measures may be instituted only by Member States or by the Commission, under the conditions laid down in Article 263, and solely on the grounds of non–compliance with the procedure provided for in Article 19(2), (5), (6) and (7) of the Statute of the Bank;
(d) the fulfilment by national central banks of obligations under the Treaties and the Statute of the ESCB and of the ECB. In this connection the powers of the Governing Council of the European Central Bank in respect of national central banks shall be the same as those conferred upon the Commission in respect of Member States by Article 258. If the Court finds that a national central bank has failed to fulfil an obligation under the Treaties, that bank shall be required to take the necessary measures to comply with the judgment of the Court.

Article 272. The Court of Justice of the European Union shall have jurisdiction to give judgment pursuant to any arbitration clause contained in a contract concluded by or on behalf of the Union, whether that contract be governed by public or private law.

Article 273. The Court of Justice shall have jurisdiction in any dispute between Member States which relates to the subject matter of the Treaties if the dispute is submitted to it under a special agreement between the parties.

Article 274. Save where jurisdiction is conferred on the Court of Justice of the European Union by the Treaties, disputes to which the Union is a party shall not on that ground be excluded from the jurisdiction of the courts or tribunals of the Member States.

Article 275. The Court of Justice of the European Union shall not have jurisdiction with respect to the provisions relating to the common foreign and security policy nor with respect to acts adopted on the basis of those provisions.

However, the Court shall have jurisdiction to monitor compliance with Article 40 of the Treaty on European Union and to rule on proceedings, brought in accordance with the conditions laid down in the fourth paragraph of Article 263 of this Treaty, reviewing the legality of decisions providing for restrictive measures against natural or legal persons adopted by the Council on the basis of Chapter 2 of Title V of the Treaty on European Union.

Article 276. In exercising its powers regarding the provisions of Chapters 4 and 5 of Title V of Part Three relating to the area of freedom, security and justice, the Court of Justice of the European Union shall have no jurisdiction to review the validity or proportionality of operations carried out by the police or other law-enforcement services of a Member State or the exercise of the responsibilities incumbent upon Member States with regard to the maintenance of law and order and the safeguarding of internal security.

Article 277. Notwithstanding the expiry of the period laid down in Article 263, sixth paragraph, any party may, in proceedings in which an act of general application adopted by an institution, body, office or agency of the Union is at issue, plead the grounds specified in Article 263, second paragraph, in order to invoke before the Court of Justice of the European Union the inapplicability of that act.

Article 278. Actions brought before the Court of Justice of the European Union shall not have suspensory effect. The Court may, however, if it considers that circumstances so require, order that application of the contested act be suspended.

Article 279. The Court of Justice of the European Union may in any cases before it prescribe any necessary interim measures.

Article 280. The judgments of the Court of Justice of the European Union shall be enforceable under the conditions laid down in Article 299.

Article 281. The Statute of the Court of Justice of the European Union shall be laid down in a separate Protocol.
The European Parliament and the Council, acting in accordance with the ordinary legislative procedure, may amend the provisions of the Statute, with the exception of Title I and Article 64. The European Parliament and the Council shall act either at the request of the Court of Justice and after consultation of the Commission, or on a proposal from the Commission and after consultation of the Court of Justice.

Section 6. The European Central Bank

Article 282. (1) The European Central Bank, together with the national central banks, shall constitute the European System of Central Banks (ESCB). The European Central Bank, together with the national central banks of the Member States whose currency is the euro, which constitute the Eurosystem, shall conduct the monetary policy of the Union.
(2) The ESCB shall be governed by the decision-making bodies of the European Central Bank. The primary objective of the ESCB shall be to maintain price stability. Without prejudice to that objective, it shall support the general economic policies in the Union in order to contribute to the achievement of the latter's objectives.
(3) The European Central Bank shall have legal personality. It alone may authorise the issue of the euro. It shall be independent in the exercise of its powers and in the management of its finances. Union institutions, bodies, offices and agencies and the governments of the Member States shall respect that independence.
(4) The European Central Bank shall adopt such measures as are necessary to carry out its tasks in accordance with Articles 127 to 133, with Article 138, and with the conditions laid down in the Statute of the ESCB and of the ECB. In accordance with these same Articles, those Member States whose currency is not the euro, and their central banks, shall retain their powers in monetary matters.
(5) Within the areas falling within its responsibilities, the European Central Bank shall be consulted on all proposed Union acts, and all proposals for regulation at national level, and may give an opinion.

Article 283. (1) The Governing Council of the European Central Bank shall comprise the members of the Executive Board of the European Central Bank and the Governors of the national central banks of the Member States whose currency is the euro.
(2) The Executive Board shall comprise the President, the Vice-President and four other members.
The President, the Vice-President and the other members of the Executive Board shall be appointed by the European Council, acting by a qualified majority, from among persons of recognised standing and professional experience in monetary or banking matters, on a recommendation from the Council, after it has consulted the European Parliament and the Governing Council of the European Central Bank.
Their term of office shall be eight years and shall not be renewable.
Only nationals of Member States may be members of the Executive Board.

Article 284. (1) The President of the Council and a Member of the Commission may participate, without having the right to vote, in meetings of the Governing Council of the European Central Bank.

The President of the Council may submit a motion for deliberation to the Governing Council of the European Central Bank.

(2) The President of the European Central Bank shall be invited to participate in Council meetings when the Council is discussing matters relating to the objectives and tasks of the ESCB.

(3) The European Central Bank shall address an annual report on the activities of the ESCB and on the monetary policy of both the previous and current year to the European Parliament, the Council and the Commission, and also to the European Council. The President of the European Central Bank shall present this report to the Council and to the European Parliament, which may hold a general debate on that basis.

The President of the European Central Bank and the other members of the Executive Board may, at the request of the European Parliament or on their own initiative, be heard by the competent committees of the European Parliament.

Section 7. The Court of Auditors

Article 285. The Court of Auditors shall carry out the Union's audit.
It shall consist of one national of each Member State. Its Members shall be completely independent in the performance of their duties, in the Union's general interest.

Article 286. (1) The Members of the Court of Auditors shall be chosen from among persons who belong or have belonged in their respective States to external audit bodies or who are especially qualified for this office. Their independence must be beyond doubt.

(2) The Members of the Court of Auditors shall be appointed for a term of six years. The Council, after consulting the European Parliament, shall adopt the list of Members drawn up in accordance with the proposals made by each Member State. The term of office of the Members of the Court of Auditors shall be renewable.

They shall elect the President of the Court of Auditors from among their number for a term of three years. The President may be re-elected.

(3) In the performance of these duties, the Members of the Court of Auditors shall neither seek nor take instructions from any government or from any other body. The Members of the Court of Auditors shall refrain from any action incompatible with their duties.

(4) The Members of the Court of Auditors may not, during their term of office, engage in any other occupation, whether gainful or not. When entering upon their duties they shall give a solemn undertaking that, both during and after their term of office, they will respect the obligations arising therefrom and in particular their duty to behave with integrity and discretion as regards the acceptance, after they have ceased to hold office, of certain appointments or benefits.

(5) Apart from normal replacement, or death, the duties of a Member of the Court of Auditors shall end when he resigns, or is compulsorily retired by a ruling of the Court of Justice pursuant to paragraph 6.
The vacancy thus caused shall be filled for the remainder of the Member's term of office. Save in the case of compulsory retirement, Members of the Court of Auditors shall remain in office until they have been replaced.
(6) A Member of the Court of Auditors may be deprived of his office or of his right to a pension or other benefits in its stead only if the Court of Justice, at the request of the Court of Auditors, finds that he no longer fulfils the requisite conditions or meets the obligations arising from his office.
(7) The Council shall determine the conditions of employment of the President and the Members of the Court of Auditors and in particular their salaries, allowances and pensions. It shall also determine any payment to be made instead of remuneration.
(8) The provisions of the Protocol on the privileges and immunities of the European Union applicable to the Judges of the Court of Justice of the European Union shall also apply to the Members of the Court of Auditors.

Article 287. (1) The Court of Auditors shall examine the accounts of all revenue and expenditure of the Union. It shall also examine the accounts of all revenue and expenditure of all bodies, offices or agencies set up by the Union in so far as the relevant constituent instrument does not preclude such examination.
The Court of Auditors shall provide the European Parliament and the Council with a statement of assurance as to the reliability of the accounts and the legality and regularity of the underlying transactions which shall be published in the *Official Journal of the European Union*. This statement may be supplemented by specific assessments for each major area of Union activity.
(2) The Court of Auditors shall examine whether all revenue has been received and all expenditure incurred in a lawful and regular manner and whether the financial management has been sound. In doing so, it shall report in particular on any cases of irregularity.
The audit of revenue shall be carried out on the basis both of the amounts established as due and the amounts actually paid to the Union.
The audit of expenditure shall be carried out on the basis both of commitments undertaken and payments made.
These audits may be carried out before the closure of accounts for the financial year in question.
(3) The audit shall be based on records and, if necessary, performed on the spot in the other institutions of the Union, on the premises of any body, office or agency which manages revenue or expenditure on behalf of the Union and in the Member States, including on the premises of any natural or legal person in receipt of payments from the budget. In the Member States the audit shall be carried out in liaison with national audit

bodies or, if these do not have the necessary powers, with the competent national departments. The Court of Auditors and the national audit bodies of the Member States shall cooperate in a spirit of trust while maintaining their independence. These bodies or departments shall inform the Court of Auditors whether they intend to take part in the audit.

The other institutions of the Union, any bodies, offices or agencies managing revenue or expenditure on behalf of the Union, any natural or legal person in receipt of payments from the budget, and the national audit bodies or, if these do not have the necessary powers, the competent national departments, shall forward to the Court of Auditors, at its request, any document or information necessary to carry out its task.

In respect of the European Investment Bank's activity in managing Union expenditure and revenue, the Court's rights of access to information held by the Bank shall be governed by an agreement between the Court, the Bank and the Commission. In the absence of an agreement, the Court shall nevertheless have access to information necessary for the audit of Union expenditure and revenue managed by the Bank.

(4) The Court of Auditors shall draw up an annual report after the close of each financial year. It shall be forwarded to the other institutions of the Union and shall be published, together with the replies of these institutions to the observations of the Court of Auditors, in the *Official Journal of the European Union*.

The Court of Auditors may also, at any time, submit observations, particularly in the form of special reports, on specific questions and deliver opinions at the request of one of the other institutions of the Union.

It shall adopt its annual reports, special reports or opinions by a majority of its Members. However, it may establish internal chambers in order to adopt certain categories of reports or opinions under the conditions laid down by its Rules of Procedure.

It shall assist the European Parliament and the Council in exercising their powers of control over the implementation of the budget.

The Court of Auditors shall draw up its Rules of Procedure. Those rules shall require the approval of the Council.

Chapter 2. Legal Acts of the Union, Adoption Procedures and other Provisions

Section 1. The Legal Acts of the Union

Article 288. To exercise the Union's competences, the institutions shall adopt regulations, directives, decisions, recommendations and opinions.

A regulation shall have general application. It shall be binding in its entirety and directly applicable in all Member States.

A directive shall be binding, as to the result to be achieved, upon each Member State to which it is addressed, but shall leave to the national authorities the choice of form and methods.

A decision shall be binding in its entirety. A decision which specifies those to whom it is addressed shall be binding only on them.

Recommendations and opinions shall have no binding force.

Article 289. (1) The ordinary legislative procedure shall consist in the joint adoption by the European Parliament and the Council of a regulation, directive or decision on a proposal from the Commission. This procedure is defined in Article 294.

(2) In the specific cases provided for by the Treaties, the adoption of a regulation, directive or decision by the European Parliament with the participation of the Council, or by the latter with the participation of the European Parliament, shall constitute a special legislative procedure.

(3) Legal acts adopted by legislative procedure shall constitute legislative acts.

(4) In the specific cases provided for by the Treaties, legislative acts may be adopted on the initiative of a group of Member States or of the European Parliament, on a recommendation from the European Central Bank or at the request of the Court of Justice or the European Investment Bank.

Article 290. (1) A legislative act may delegate to the Commission the power to adopt non–legislative acts of general application to supplement or amend certain non–essential elements of the legislative act.

The objectives, content, scope and duration of the delegation of power shall be explicitly defined in the legislative acts. The essential elements of an area shall be reserved for the legislative act and accordingly shall not be the subject of a delegation of power.

(2) Legislative acts shall explicitly lay down the conditions to which the delegation is subject; these conditions may be as follows:

(a) the European Parliament or the Council may decide to revoke the delegation;

(b) the delegated act may enter into force only if no objection has been expressed by the European Parliament or the Council within a period set by the legislative act.

For the purposes of (a) and (b), the European Parliament shall act by a majority of its component members, and the Council by a qualified majority.

(3) The adjective "delegated" shall be inserted in the title of delegated acts.

Article 291. (1) Member States shall adopt all measures of national law necessary to implement legally binding Union acts.

(2) Where uniform conditions for implementing legally binding Union acts are needed, those acts shall confer implementing powers on the Commission, or, in duly justified

specific cases and in the cases provided for in Articles 24 and 26 of the Treaty on European Union, on the Council.

(3) For the purposes of paragraph 2, the European Parliament and the Council, acting by means of regulations in accordance with the ordinary legislative procedure, shall lay down in advance the rules and general principles concerning mechanisms for control by Member States of the Commission's exercise of implementing powers.

(4) The word "implementing" shall be inserted in the title of implementing acts.

Article 292. The Council shall adopt recommendations. It shall act on a proposal from the Commission in all cases where the Treaties provide that it shall adopt acts on a proposal from the Commission. It shall act unanimously in those areas in which unanimity is required for the adoption of a Union act. The Commission, and the European Central Bank in the specific cases provided for in the Treaties, shall adopt recommendations.

Section 2. Procedures for the Adoption of Acts and other Provisions

Article 293. (1) Where, pursuant to the Treaties, the Council acts on a proposal from the Commission, it may amend that proposal only by acting unanimously, except in the cases referred to in paragraphs 10 and 13 of Article 294, in Articles 310, 312 and 314 and in the second paragraph of Article 315.

(2) As long as the Council has not acted, the Commission may alter its proposal at any time during the procedures leading to the adoption of a Union act.

Article 294. (1) Where reference is made in the Treaties to the ordinary legislative procedure for the adoption of an act, the following procedure shall apply.

(2) he Commission shall submit a proposal to the European Parliament and the Council.
First reading
(3) The European Parliament shall adopt its position at first reading and communicate it to the Council.

(4) If the Council approves the European Parliament's position, the act concerned shall be adopted in the wording which corresponds to the position of the European Parliament.

(5) If the Council does not approve the European Parliament's position, it shall adopt its position at first reading and communicate it to the European Parliament.

(6) The Council shall inform the European Parliament fully of the reasons which led it to adopt its position at first reading. The Commission shall inform the European Parliament fully of its position.
Second reading
(7) If, within three months of such communication, the European Parliament:

(a) approves the Council's position at first reading or has not taken a decision, the act concerned shall be deemed to have been adopted in the wording which corresponds to the position of the Council;
(b) rejects, by a majority of its component members, the Council's position at first reading, the proposed act shall be deemed not to have been adopted;
(c) proposes, by a majority of its component members, amendments to the Council's position at first reading, the text thus amended shall be forwarded to the Council and to the Commission, which shall deliver an opinion on those amendments.

(8) If, within three months of receiving the European Parliament's amendments, the Council, acting by a qualified majority:

(a) approves all those amendments, the act in question shall be deemed to have been adopted;
(b) does not approve all the amendments, the President of the Council, in agreement with the President of the European Parliament, shall within six weeks convene a meeting of the Conciliation Committee.

(9) The Council shall act unanimously on the amendments on which the Commission has delivered a negative opinion.

Conciliation

(10) The Conciliation Committee, which shall be composed of the members of the Council or their representatives and an equal number of members representing the European Parliament, shall have the task of reaching agreement on a joint text, by a qualified majority of the members of the Council or their representatives and by a majority of the members representing the European Parliament within six weeks of its being convened, on the basis of the positions of the European Parliament and the Council at second reading.

(11) The Commission shall take part in the Conciliation Committee's proceedings and shall take all necessary initiatives with a view to reconciling the positions of the European Parliament and the Council.

(12) If, within six weeks of its being convened, the Conciliation Committee does not approve the joint text, the proposed act shall be deemed not to have been adopted.

Third reading

(13) If, within that period, the Conciliation Committee approves a joint text, the European Parliament, acting by a majority of the votes cast, and the Council, acting by a qualified majority, shall each have a period of six weeks from that approval in which to adopt the act in question in accordance with the joint text. If they fail to do so, the proposed act shall be deemed not to have been adopted.

(14) The periods of three months and six weeks referred to in this Article shall be extended by a maximum of one month and two weeks respectively at the initiative of the European Parliament or the Council.

Special provisions

(15) Where, in the cases provided for in the Treaties, a legislative act is submitted to the ordinary legislative procedure on the initiative of a group of Member States, on a recommendation by the European Central Bank, or at the request of the Court of Justice, paragraph 2, the second sentence of paragraph 6, and paragraph 9 shall not apply.

In such cases, the European Parliament and the Council shall communicate the proposed act to the Commission with their positions at first and second readings. The European Parliament or the Council may request the opinion of the Commission throughout the procedure, which the Commission may also deliver on its own initiative. It may also, if it deems it necessary, take part in the Conciliation Committee in accordance with paragraph 11.

Article 295. The European Parliament, the Council and the Commission shall consult each other and by common agreement make arrangements for their cooperation. To that end, they may, in compliance with the Treaties, conclude interinstitutional agreements which may be of a binding nature.

Article 296. Where the Treaties do not specify the type of act to be adopted, the institutions shall select it on a case–by–case basis, in compliance with the applicable procedures and with the principle of proportionality.

Legal acts shall state the reasons on which they are based and shall refer to any proposals, initiatives, recommendations, requests or opinions required by the Treaties.

When considering draft legislative acts, the European Parliament and the Council shall refrain from adopting acts not provided for by the relevant legislative procedure in the area in question.

Article 297. (1) Legislative acts adopted under the ordinary legislative procedure shall be signed by the President of the European Parliament and by the President of the Council. Legislative acts adopted under a special legislative procedure shall be signed by the President of the institution which adopted them.

Legislative acts shall be published in the *Official Journal of the European Union*. They shall enter into force on the date specified in them or, in the absence thereof, on the twentieth day following that of their publication.

(2) Non–legislative acts adopted in the form of regulations, directives or decisions, when the latter do not specify to whom they are addressed, shall be signed by the President of the institution which adopted them.

Regulations and directives which are addressed to all Member States, as well as decisions which do not specify to whom they are addressed, shall be published in the *Official Journal of the European Union*. They shall enter into force on the date specified in them or, in the absence thereof, on the twentieth day following that of their publication.

Other directives, and decisions which specify to whom they are addressed, shall be notified to those to whom they are addressed and shall take effect upon such notification.

Article 298. (1) In carrying out their missions, the institutions, bodies, offices and agencies of the Union shall have the support of an open, efficient and independent European administration.
(2) In compliance with the Staff Regulations and the Conditions of Employment adopted on the basis of Article 336, the European Parliament and the Council, acting by means of regulations in accordance with the ordinary legislative procedure, shall establish provisions to that end.

Article 299. Acts of the Council, the Commission or the European Central Bank which impose a pecuniary obligation on persons other than States, shall be enforceable.
Enforcement shall be governed by the rules of civil procedure in force in the State in the territory of which it is carried out. The order for its enforcement shall be appended to the decision, without other formality than verification of the authenticity of the decision, by the national authority which the government of each Member State shall designate for this purpose and shall make known to the Commission and to the Court of Justice of the European Union.
When these formalities have been completed on application by the party concerned, the latter may proceed to enforcement in accordance with the national law, by bringing the matter directly before the competent authority.
Enforcement may be suspended only by a decision of the Court. However, the courts of the country concerned shall have jurisdiction over complaints that enforcement is being carried out in an irregular manner.

Chapter 3. The Union's Advisory Bodies

Article 300. (1) The European Parliament, the Council and the Commission shall be assisted by an Economic and Social Committee and a Committee of the Regions, exercising advisory functions.
(2) The Economic and Social Committee shall consist of representatives of organisations of employers, of the employed, and of other parties representative of civil society, notably in socio–economic, civic, professional and cultural areas.
(3) The Committee of the Regions shall consist of representatives of regional and local bodies who either hold a regional or local authority electoral mandate or are politically accountable to an elected assembly.
(4) The members of the Economic and Social Committee and of the Committee of the Regions shall not be bound by any mandatory instructions. They shall be completely independent in the performance of their duties, in the Union's general interest.

(5) The rules referred to in paragraphs 2 and 3 governing the nature of the composition of the Committees shall be reviewed at regular intervals by the Council to take account of economic, social and demographic developments within the Union. The Council, on a proposal from the Commission, shall adopt decisions to that end.

Section 1. The Economic and Social Committee

Article 301. The number of members of the Economic and Social Committee shall not exceed 350.
The Council, acting unanimously on a proposal from the Commission, shall adopt a decision determining the Committee's composition.
The Council shall determine the allowances of members of the Committee.

Article 302. (1) The members of the Committee shall be appointed for five years The Council shall adopt the list of members drawn up in accordance with the proposals made by each Member State. The term of office of the members of the Committee shall be renewable.
(2) The Council shall act after consulting the Commission. It may obtain the opinion of European bodies which are representative of the various economic and social sectors and of civil society to which the Union's activities are of concern.

Article 303. The Committee shall elect its chairman and officers from among its members for a term of two and a half years.
It shall adopt its Rules of Procedure.
The Committee shall be convened by its chairman at the request of the European Parliament, the Council or of the Commission. It may also meet on its own initiative.

Article 304. The Committee shall be consulted by the European Parliament, by the Council or by the Commission where the Treaties so provide. The Committee may be consulted by these institutions in all cases in which they consider it appropriate. It may issue an opinion on its own initiative in cases in which it considers such action appropriate.
The European Parliament, the Council or the Commission shall, if it considers it necessary, set the Committee, for the submission of its opinion, a time limit which may not be less than one month from the date on which the chairman receives notification to this effect. Upon expiry of the time limit, the absence of an opinion shall not prevent further action.
The opinion of the Committee, together with a record of the proceedings, shall be forwarded to the European Parliament, to the Council and to the Commission.

Section 2. The Committee of the Regions

Article 305. The number of members of the Committee of the Regions shall not exceed 350.
The Council, acting unanimously on a proposal from the Commission, shall adopt a decision determining the Committee's composition.
The members of the Committee and an equal number of alternate members shall be appointed for five years. Their term of office shall be renewable. The Council shall adopt the list of members and alternate members drawn up in accordance with the proposals made by each Member State. When the mandate referred to in Article 300(3) on the basis of which they were proposed comes to an end, the term of office of members of the Committee shall terminate automatically and they shall then be replaced for the remainder of the said term of office in accordance with the same procedure. No member of the Committee shall at the same time be a Member of the European Parliament.

Article 306. The Committee of the Regions shall elect its chairman and officers from among its members for a term of two and a half years.
It shall adopt its Rules of Procedure.
The Committee shall be convened by its chairman at the request of the European Parliament, the Council or of the Commission. It may also meet on its own initiative.

Article 307. The Committee of the Regions shall be consulted by the European Parliament, by the Council or by the Commission where the Treaties so provide and in all other cases, in particular those which concern cross–border cooperation, in which one of these institutions considers it appropriate.
The European Parliament, the Council or the Commission shall, if it considers it necessary, set the Committee, for the submission of its opinion, a time limit which may not be less than one month from the date on which the chairman receives notification to this effect. Upon expiry of the time limit, the absence of an opinion shall not prevent further action.
Where the Economic and Social Committee is consulted pursuant to Article 304, the Committee of the Regions shall be informed by the European Parliament, the Council or the Commission of the request for an opinion. Where it considers that specific regional interests are involved, the Committee of the Regions may issue an opinion on the matter. It may issue an opinion on its own initiative in cases in which it considers such action appropriate.
The opinion of the Committee, together with a record of the proceedings, shall be forwarded to the European Parliament, to the Council and to the Commission.

Chapter 4. The European Investment Bank

Article 308. The European Investment Bank shall have legal personality.
The members of the European Investment Bank shall be the Member States.
The Statute of the European Investment Bank is laid down in a Protocol annexed to the Treaties. The Council acting unanimously in accordance with a special legislative procedure, at the request of the European Investment Bank and after consulting the European Parliament and the Commission, or on a proposal from the Commission and after consulting the European Parliament and the European Investment Bank, may amend the Statute of the Bank.

Article 309. The task of the European Investment Bank shall be to contribute, by having recourse to the capital market and utilising its own resources, to the balanced and steady development of the internal market in the interest of the Union. For this purpose the Bank shall, operating on a non–profit–making basis, grant loans and give guarantees which facilitate the financing of the following projects in all sectors of the economy:
(a) projects for developing less–developed regions;
(a) projects for modernising or converting undertakings or for developing fresh activities called for by the establishment or functioning of the internal market, where these projects are of such a size or nature that they cannot be entirely financed by the various means available in the individual Member States;
(c) projects of common interest to several Member States which are of such a size or nature that they cannot be entirely financed by the various means available in the individual Member States.
In carrying out its task, the Bank shall facilitate the financing of investment programmes in conjunction with assistance from the Structural Funds and other Union Financial Instruments.

Title II. Financial Provisions

Article 310. (1) All items of revenue and expenditure of the Union shall be included in estimates to be drawn up for each financial year and shall be shown in the budget.
The Union's annual budget shall be established by the European Parliament and the Council in accordance with Article 314.
The revenue and expenditure shown in the budget shall be in balance.
(2) The expenditure shown in the budget shall be authorised for the annual budgetary period in accordance with the regulation referred to in Article 322.
(3) The implementation of expenditure shown in the budget shall require the prior adoption of a legally binding Union act providing a legal basis for its action and for the im-

plementation of the corresponding expenditure in accordance with the regulation referred to in Article 322, except in cases for which that law provides.

(4) With a view to maintaining budgetary discipline, the Union shall not adopt any act which is likely to have appreciable implications for the budget without providing an assurance that the expenditure arising from such an act is capable of being financed within the limit of the Union's own resources and in compliance with the multiannual financial framework referred to in Article 312.

(5) The budget shall be implemented in accordance with the principle of sound financial management. Member States shall cooperate with the Union to ensure that the appropriations entered in the budget are used in accordance with this principle.

(6) The Union and the Member States, in accordance with Article 325, shall counter fraud and any other illegal activities affecting the financial interests of the Union.

Chapter 1. The Union's Own Resources

Article 311. The Union shall provide itself with the means necessary to attain its objectives and carry through its policies.

Without prejudice to other revenue, the budget shall be financed wholly from own resources.

The Council, acting in accordance with a special legislative procedure, shall unanimously and after consulting the European Parliament adopt a decision laying down the provisions relating to the system of own resources of the Union. In this context it may establish new categories of own resources or abolish an existing category. That decision shall not enter into force until it is approved by the Member States in accordance with their respective constitutional requirements.

The Council, acting by means of regulations in accordance with a special legislative procedure, shall lay down implementing measures for the Union's own resources system in so far as this is provided for in the decision adopted on the basis of the third paragraph. The Council shall act after obtaining the consent of the European Parliament.

Chapter 2. The Multiannual Financial Framework

Article 312. (1) The multiannual financial framework shall ensure that Union expenditure develops in an orderly manner and within the limits of its own resources.
It shall be established for a period of at least five years.
The annual budget of the Union shall comply with the multiannual financial framework.
(2) The Council, acting in accordance with a special legislative procedure, shall adopt a regulation laying down the multiannual financial framework. The Council shall act unanimously after obtaining the consent of the European Parliament, which shall be given by a majority of its component members.

The European Council may, unanimously, adopt a decision authorising the Council to act by a qualified majority when adopting the regulation referred to in the first subparagraph.

(3) The financial framework shall determine the amounts of the annual ceilings on commitment appropriations by category of expenditure and of the annual ceiling on payment appropriations. The categories of expenditure, limited in number, shall correspond to the Union's major sectors of activity.

The financial framework shall lay down any other provisions required for the annual budgetary procedure to run smoothly.

(4) Where no Council regulation determining a new financial framework has been adopted by the end of the previous financial framework, the ceilings and other provisions corresponding to the last year of that framework shall be extended until such time as that act is adopted.

(5) Throughout the procedure leading to the adoption of the financial framework, the European Parliament, the Council and the Commission shall take any measure necessary to facilitate its adoption.

Chapter 3. The Union's Annual Budget

Article 313. The financial year shall run from 1 January to 31 December.

Article 314. The European Parliament and the Council, acting in accordance with a special legislative procedure, shall establish the Union's annual budget in accordance with the following provisions.

(1) With the exception of the European Central Bank, each institution shall, before 1 July, draw up estimates of its expenditure for the following financial year. The Commission shall consolidate these estimates in a draft budget. which may contain different estimates. The draft budget shall contain an estimate of revenue and an estimate of expenditure.

(2) The Commission shall submit a proposal containing the draft budget to the European Parliament and to the Council not later than 1 September of the year preceding that in which the budget is to be implemented.

The Commission may amend the draft budget during the procedure until such time as the Conciliation Committee, referred to in paragraph 5, is convened.

(3) The Council shall adopt its position on the draft budget and forward it to the European Parliament not later than 1 October of the year preceding that in which the budget is to be implemented. The Council shall inform the European Parliament in full of the reasons which led it to adopt its position.

(4) If, within forty–two days of such communication, the European Parliament:

(a) approves the position of the Council, the budget shall be adopted;

(b) has not taken a decision, the budget shall be deemed to have been adopted;

(c) adopts amendments by a majority of its component members, the amended draft shall be forwarded to the Council and to the Commission. The President of the European Parliament, in agreement with the President of the Council, shall immediately convene a meeting of the Conciliation Committee. However, if within ten days of the draft being forwarded the Council informs the European Parliament that it has approved all its amendments, the Conciliation Committee shall not meet.

(5) The Conciliation Committee, which shall be composed of the members of the Council or their representatives and an equal number of members representing the European Parliament, shall have the task of reaching agreement on a joint text, by a qualified majority of the members of the Council or their representatives and by a majority of the representatives of the European Parliament within twenty–one days of its being convened, on the basis of the positions of the European Parliament and the Council.

The Commission shall take part in the Conciliation Committee's proceedings and shall take all the necessary initiatives with a view to reconciling the positions of the European Parliament and the Council.

(6) If, within the twenty–one days referred to in paragraph 5, the Conciliation Committee agrees on a joint text, the European Parliament and the Council shall each have a period of fourteen days from the date of that agreement in which to approve the joint text.

(7) If, within the period of fourteen days referred to in paragraph 6:

(a) the European Parliament and the Council both approve the joint text or fail to take a decision, or if one of these institutions approves the joint text while the other one fails to take a decision, the budget shall be deemed to be definitively adopted in accordance with the joint text; or

(b) the European Parliament, acting by a majority of its component members, and the Council both reject the joint text, or if one of these institutions rejects the joint text while the other one fails to take a decision, a new draft budget shall be submitted by the Commission; or

(c) the European Parliament, acting by a majority of its component members, rejects the joint text while the Council approves it, a new draft budget shall be submitted by the Commission; or

(d) the European Parliament approves the joint text whilst the Council rejects it, the European Parliament may, within fourteen days from the date of the rejection by the Council and acting by a majority of its component members and three–fifths of the votes cast, decide to confirm all or some of the amendments referred to in paragraph 4(c). Where a European Parliament amendment is not confirmed, the position agreed in the Conciliation Committee on the budget heading which is the subject of the amendment shall be retained. The budget shall be deemed to be definitively adopted on this basis.

(8) If, within the twenty–one days referred to in paragraph 5, the Conciliation Committee does not agree on a joint text, a new draft budget shall be submitted by the Commission.

(9) When the procedure provided for in this Article has been completed, the President of the European Parliament shall declare that the budget has been definitively adopted.

(10) Each institution shall exercise the powers conferred upon it under this Article in compliance with the Treaties and the acts adopted thereunder, with particular regard to the Union's own resources and the balance between revenue and expenditure.

Article 315. If, at the beginning of a financial year, the budget has not yet been definitively adopted, a sum equivalent to not more than one twelfth of the budget appropriations for the preceding financial year may be spent each month in respect of any chapter of the budget in accordance with the provisions of the Regulations made pursuant to Article 322; that sum shall not, however, exceed one twelfth of the appropriations provided for in the same chapter of the draft budget.

The Council on a proposal by the Commission, may, provided that the other conditions laid down in the first paragraph are observed, authorise expenditure in excess of one twelfth in accordance with the regulations made pursuant to Article 322. The Council shall forward the decision immediately to the European Parliament.

The decision referred to in the second paragraph shall lay down the necessary measures relating to resources to ensure application of this Article, in accordance with the acts referred to in Article 311.

It shall enter into force thirty days following its adoption if the European Parliament, acting by a majority of its component Members, has not decided to reduce this expenditure within that time–limit.

Article 316. In accordance with conditions to be laid down pursuant to Article 322, any appropriations, other than those relating to staff expenditure, that are unexpended at the end of the financial year may be carried forward to the next financial year only.

Appropriations shall be classified under different chapters grouping items of expenditure according to their nature or purpose and subdivided in accordance with the regulations made pursuant to Article 322.

The expenditure of the European Parliament, the European Council and the Council, the Commission and the Court of Justice of the European Union shall be set out in separate parts of the budget, without prejudice to special arrangements for certain common items of expenditure.

Chapter 4. Implementation of the Budget and Discharge

Article 317. The Commission shall implement the budget in cooperation with the Member States, in accordance with the provisions of the regulations made pursuant to Article 322, on its own responsibility and within the limits of the appropriations, having regard to the principles of sound financial management. Member States shall cooperate with the

Commission to ensure that the appropriations are used in accordance with the principles of sound financial management.

The regulations shall lay down the control and audit obligations of the Member States in the implementation of the budget and the resulting responsibilities. They shall also lay down the responsibilities and detailed rules for each institution concerning its part in effecting its own expenditure.

Within the budget, the Commission may, subject to the limits and conditions laid down in the regulations made pursuant to Article 322, transfer appropriations from one chapter to another or from one subdivision to another.

Article 318. The Commission shall submit annually to the European Parliament and to the Council the accounts of the preceding financial year relating to the implementation of the budget. The Commission shall also forward to them a financial statement of the assets and liabilities of the Union.

The Commission shall also submit to the European Parliament and to the Council an evaluation report on the Union's finances based on the results achieved, in particular in relation to the indications given by the European Parliament and the Council pursuant to Article 319.

Article 319. (1) The European Parliament, acting on a recommendation from the Council, shall give a discharge to the Commission in respect of the implementation of the budget. To this end, the Council and the European Parliament in turn shall examine the accounts, the financial statement and the evaluation report referred to in Article 318, the annual report by the Court of Auditors together with the replies of the institutions under audit to the observations of the Court of Auditors, the statement of assurance referred to in Article 287(1), second subparagraph and any relevant special reports by the Court of Auditors.

(2) Before giving a discharge to the Commission, or for any other purpose in connection with the exercise of its powers over the implementation of the budget, the European Parliament may ask to hear the Commission give evidence with regard to the execution of expenditure or the operation of financial control systems. The Commission shall submit any necessary information to the European Parliament at the latter's request.

(3) The Commission shall take all appropriate steps to act on the observations in the decisions giving discharge and on other observations by the European Parliament relating to the execution of expenditure, as well as on comments accompanying the recommendations on discharge adopted by the Council.

At the request of the European Parliament or the Council, the Commission shall report on the measures taken in the light of these observations and comments and in particular on the instructions given to the departments which are responsible for the implementation of the budget. These reports shall also be forwarded to the Court of Auditors.

Chapter 5. Common provisions

Article 320. The multiannual financial framework and the annual budget shall be drawn up in euro.

Article 321. The Commission may, provided it notifies the competent authorities of the Member States concerned, transfer into the currency of one of the Member States its holdings in the currency of another Member State, to the extent necessary to enable them to be used for purposes which come within the scope of the Treaties. The Commission shall as far as possible avoid making such transfers if it possesses cash or liquid assets in the currencies which it needs.

The Commission shall deal with each Member State through the authority designated by the State concerned. In carrying out financial operations the Commission shall employ the services of the bank of issue of the Member State concerned or of any other financial institution approved by that State.

Article 322. (1) The European Parliament and the Council, acting in accordance with the ordinary legislative procedure, and after consulting the Court of Auditors, shall adopt by means of regulations:
(a) the financial rules which determine in particular the procedure to be adopted for establishing and implementing the budget and for presenting and auditing accounts;
(b) rules providing for checks on the responsibility of financial actors, in particular authorising officers and accounting officers.
(2) The Council, acting on a proposal from the Commission and after consulting the European Parliament and the Court of Auditors, shall determine the methods and procedure whereby the budget revenue provided under the arrangements relating to the Union's own resources shall be made available to the Commission, and determine the measures to be applied, if need be, to meet cash requirements.

Article 323. The European Parliament, the Council and the Commission shall ensure that the financial means are made available to allow the Union to fulfil its legal obligations in respect of third parties.

Article 324. Regular meetings between the Presidents of the European Parliament, the Council and the Commission shall be convened, on the initiative of the Commission, under the budgetary procedures referred to in this Title. The Presidents shall take all the necessary steps to promote consultation and the reconciliation of the positions of the institutions over which they preside in order to facilitate the implementation of this Title.

Chapter 6. Combatting Fraud

Article 325. (1) The Union and the Member States shall counter fraud and any other illegal activities affecting the financial interests of the Union through measures to be taken in accordance with this Article, which shall act as a deterrent and be such as to afford effective protection in the Member States, and in all the Union's institutions, bodies, offices and agencies.
(2) Member States shall take the same measures to counter fraud affecting the financial interests of the Union as they take to counter fraud affecting their own financial interests.
(3) Without prejudice to other provisions of the Treaties, the Member States shall coordinate their action aimed at protecting the financial interests of the Union against fraud. To this end they shall organise, together with the Commission, close and regular cooperation between the competent authorities.
(4) The European Parliament and the Council, acting in accordance with the ordinary legislative procedure, after consulting the Court of Auditors, shall adopt the necessary measures in the fields of the prevention of and fight against fraud affecting the financial interests of the Union with a view to affording effective and equivalent protection in the Member States and in all the Union's institutions, bodies, offices and agencies.
(5) The Commission, in cooperation with Member States, shall each year submit to the European Parliament and to the Council a report on the measures taken for the implementation of this Article.

Title III. Enhanced Cooperation

Article 326. Any enhanced cooperation shall comply with the Treaties and Union law. Such cooperation shall not undermine the internal market or economic, social and territorial cohesion. It shall not constitute a barrier to or discrimination in trade between Member States, nor shall it distort competition between them.

Article 327. Any enhanced cooperation shall respect the competences, rights and obligations of those Member States which do not participate in it. Those Member States shall not impede its implementation by the participating Member States.

Article 328. (1) When enhanced cooperation is being established, it shall be open to all Member States, subject to compliance with any conditions of participation laid down by the authorising decision. It shall also be open to them at any other time, subject to compliance with the acts already adopted within that framework, in addition to those conditions.
The Commission and the Member States participating in enhanced cooperation shall ensure that they promote participation by as many Member States as possible.

(2) The Commission and, where appropriate, the High Representative of the Union for Foreign Affairs and Security Policy shall keep the European Parliament and the Council regularly informed regarding developments in enhanced cooperation.

Article 329. (1) Member States which wish to establish enhanced cooperation between themselves in one of the areas covered by the Treaties, with the exception of fields of exclusive competence and the common foreign and security policy, shall address a request to the Commission, specifying the scope and objectives of the enhanced cooperation proposed. The Commission may submit a proposal to the Council to that effect. In the event of the Commission not submitting a proposal, it shall inform the Member States concerned of the reasons for not doing so.
Authorisation to proceed with the enhanced cooperation referred to in the first subparagraph shall be granted by the Council, on a proposal from the Commission and after obtaining the consent of the European Parliament.
(2) The request of the Member States which wish to establish enhanced cooperation between themselves within the framework of the common foreign and security policy shall be addressed to the Council. It shall be forwarded to the High Representative of the Union for Foreign Affairs and Security Policy, who shall give an opinion on whether the enhanced cooperation proposed is consistent with the Union's common foreign and security policy, and to the Commission, which shall give its opinion in particular on whether the enhanced cooperation proposed is consistent with other Union policies. It shall also be forwarded to the European Parliament for information.
Authorisation to proceed with enhanced cooperation shall be granted by a decision of the Council acting unanimously.

Article 330. All members of the Council may participate in its deliberations, but only members of the Council representing the Member States participating in enhanced cooperation shall take part in the vote.
Unanimity shall be constituted by the votes of the representatives of the participating Member States only.
A qualified majority shall be defined in accordance with Article 238(3).

Article 331. (1) Any Member State which wishes to participate in enhanced cooperation in progress in one of the areas referred to in Article 329(1) shall notify its intention to the Council and the Commission.
The Commission shall, within four months of the date of receipt of the notification, confirm the participation of the Member State concerned. It shall note where necessary that the conditions of participation have been fulfilled and shall adopt any transitional measures necessary with regard to the application of the acts already adopted within the framework of enhanced cooperation.

However, if the Commission considers that the conditions of participation have not been fulfilled, it shall indicate the arrangements to be adopted to fulfil those conditions and shall set a deadline for re-examining the request. On the expiry of that deadline, it shall re-examine the request, in accordance with the procedure set out in the second subparagraph. If the Commission considers that the conditions of participation have still not been met, the Member State concerned may refer the matter to the Council, which shall decide on the request. The Council shall act in accordance with Article 330. It may also adopt the transitional measures referred to in the second subparagraph on a proposal from the Commission.

(2) Any Member State which wishes to participate in enhanced cooperation in progress in the framework of the common foreign and security policy shall notify its intention to the Council, the High Representative of the Union for Foreign Affairs and Security Policy and the Commission.

The Council shall confirm the participation of the Member State concerned, after consulting the High Representative of the Union for Foreign Affairs and Security Policy and after noting, where necessary, that the conditions of participation have been fulfilled. The Council, on a proposal from the High Representative, may also adopt any transitional measures necessary with regard to the application of the acts already adopted within the framework of enhanced cooperation. However, if the Council considers that the conditions of participation have not been fulfilled, it shall indicate the arrangements to be adopted to fulfil those conditions and shall set a deadline for re-examining the request for participation.

For the purposes of this paragraph, the Council shall act unanimously and in accordance with Article 330.

Article 332. Expenditure resulting from implementation of enhanced cooperation, other than administrative costs entailed for the institutions, shall be borne by the participating Member States, unless all members of the Council, acting unanimously after consulting the European Parliament, decide otherwise.

Article 333. (1) Where a provision of the Treaties which may be applied in the context of enhanced cooperation stipulates that the Council shall act unanimously, the Council, acting unanimously in accordance with the arrangements laid down in Article 330, may adopt a decision stipulating that it will act by a qualified majority.

(2) Where a provision of the Treaties which may be applied in the context of enhanced cooperation stipulates that the Council shall adopt acts under a special legislative procedure, the Council, acting unanimously in accordance with the arrangements laid down in Article 330, may adopt a decision stipulating that it will act under the ordinary legislative procedure. The Council shall act after consulting the European Parliament.

(3) Paragraphs 1 and 2 shall not apply to decisions having military or defence implications.

Article 334. The Council and the Commission shall ensure the consistency of activities undertaken in the context of enhanced cooperation and the consistency of such activities with the policies of the Union, and shall cooperate to that end.

Part Seven. General and Final Provisions

Article 335. In each of the Member States, the Union shall enjoy the most extensive legal capacity accorded to legal persons under their laws; it may, in particular, acquire or dispose of movable and immovable property and may be a party to legal proceedings. To this end, the Union shall be represented by the Commission. However, the Union shall be represented by each of the institutions, by virtue of their administrative autonomy, in matters relating to their respective operation.

Article 336. The European Parliament and the Council shall, acting by means of regulations in accordance with the ordinary legislative procedure and after consulting the other institutions concerned, lay down the Staff Regulations of Officials of the European Union and the Conditions of Employment of other servants of the Union.

Article 337. The Commission may, within the limits and under conditions laid down by the Council acting by a simple majority in accordance with the provisions of the Treaties, collect any information and carry out any checks required for the performance of the tasks entrusted to it.

Article 338. (1) Without prejudice to Article 5 of the Protocol on the Statute of the European System of Central Banks and of the European Central Bank, the European Parliament and the Council, acting in accordance with the ordinary legislative procedure, shall adopt measures for the production of statistics where necessary for the performance of the activities of the Union.
(2) The production of Union statistics shall conform to impartiality, reliability, objectivity, scientific independence, cost–effectiveness and statistical confidentiality; it shall not entail excessive burdens on economic operators.

Article 339. The members of the institutions of the Union, the members of committees, and the officials and other servants of the Union shall be required, even after their duties have ceased, not to disclose information of the kind covered by the obligation of professional secrecy, in particular information about undertakings, their business relations or their cost components.

Article 340. The contractual liability of the Union shall be governed by the law applicable to the contract in question.

In the case of non-contractual liability, the Union shall, in accordance with the general principles common to the laws of the Member States, make good any damage caused by its institutions or by its servants in the performance of their duties.

Notwithstanding the second paragraph, the European Central Bank shall, in accordance with the general principles common to the laws of the Member States, make good any damage caused by it or by its servants in the performance of their duties.

The personal liability of its servants towards the Union shall be governed by the provisions laid down in their Staff Regulations or in the Conditions of Employment applicable to them.

Article 341. The seat of the institutions of the Union shall be determined by common accord of the governments of the Member States.

Article 342. The rules governing the languages of the institutions of the Union shall, without prejudice to the provisions contained in the Statute of the Court of Justice of the European Union, be determined by the Council, acting unanimously by means of regulations.

Article 343. The Union shall enjoy in the territories of the Member States such privileges and immunities as are necessary for the performance of its tasks, under the conditions laid down in the Protocol of 8 April 1965 on the privileges and immunities of the European Union. The same shall apply to the European Central Bank and the European Investment Bank.

Article 344. Member States undertake not to submit a dispute concerning the interpretation or application of the Treaties to any method of settlement other than those provided for therein.

Article 345. The Treaties shall in no way prejudice the rules in Member States governing the system of property ownership.

Article 346. (1) The provisions of the Treaties shall not preclude the application of the following rules:
(a) no Member State shall be obliged to supply information the disclosure of which it considers contrary to the essential interests of its security;
(b) any Member State may take such measures as it considers necessary for the protection of the essential interests of its security which are connected with the production of or trade in arms, munitions and war material; such measures shall not adversely affect

the conditions of competition in the internal market regarding products which are not intended for specifically military purposes.

(2) The Council may, acting unanimously on a proposal from the Commission, make changes to the list, which it drew up on 15 April 1958, of the products to which the provisions of paragraph 1(b) apply.

Article 347. Member States shall consult each other with a view to taking together the steps needed to prevent the functioning of the internal market being affected by measures which a Member State may be called upon to take in the event of serious internal disturbances affecting the maintenance of law and order, in the event of war, serious international tension constituting a threat of war, or in order to carry out obligations it has accepted for the purpose of maintaining peace and international security.

Article 348. If measures taken in the circumstances referred to in Articles 346 and 347 have the effect of distorting the conditions of competition in the internal market, the Commission shall, together with the State concerned, examine how these measures can be adjusted to the rules laid down in the Treaties.

By way of derogation from the procedure laid down in Articles 258 and 259, the Commission or any Member State may bring the matter directly before the Court of Justice if it considers that another Member State is making improper use of the powers provided for in Articles 346 and 347. The Court of Justice shall give its ruling in camera.

Article 349. Taking account of the structural social and economic situation of Guadeloupe, French Guiana, Martinique, Réunion, Saint–Barthélemy, Saint–Martin, the Azores, Madeira and the Canary Islands, which is compounded by their remoteness, insularity, small size, difficult topography and climate, economic dependence on a few products, the permanence and combination of which severely restrain their development, the Council, on a proposal from the Commission and after consulting the European Parliament, shall adopt specific measures aimed, in particular, at laying down the conditions of application of the Treaties to those regions, including common policies. Where the specific measures in question are adopted by the Council in accordance with a special legislative procedure, it shall also act on a proposal from the Commission and after consulting the European Parliament.

The measures referred to in the first paragraph concern in particular areas such as customs and trade policies, fiscal policy, free zones, agriculture and fisheries policies, conditions for supply of raw materials and essential consumer goods, State aids and conditions of access to structural funds and to horizontal Union programmes.

The Council shall adopt the measures referred to in the first paragraph taking into account the special characteristics and constraints of the outermost regions without undermining the integrity and the coherence of the Union legal order, including the internal market and common policies.

Article 350. The provisions of the Treaties shall not preclude the existence or completion of regional unions between Belgium and Luxembourg, or between Belgium, Luxembourg and the Netherlands, to the extent that the objectives of these regional unions are not attained by application of the Treaties.

Article 351. The rights and obligations arising from agreements concluded before 1 January 1958 or, for acceding States, before the date of their accession, between one or more Member States on the one hand, and one or more third countries on the other, shall not be affected by the provisions of the Treaties.

To the extent that such agreements are not compatible with the Treaties, the Member State or States concerned shall take all appropriate steps to eliminate the incompatibilities established. Member States shall, where necessary, assist each other to this end and shall, where appropriate, adopt a common attitude.

In applying the agreements referred to in the first paragraph, Member States shall take into account the fact that the advantages accorded under the Treaties by each Member State form an integral part of the establishment of the Union and are thereby inseparably linked with the creation of common institutions, the conferring of powers upon them and the granting of the same advantages by all the other Member States.

Article 352. (1) If action by the Union should prove necessary, within the framework of the policies defined in the Treaties, to attain one of the objectives set out in the Treaties, and the Treaties have not provided the necessary powers, the Council, acting unanimously on a proposal from the Commission and after obtaining the consent of the European Parliament, shall adopt the appropriate measures. Where the measures in question are adopted by the Council in accordance with a special legislative procedure, it shall also act unanimously on a proposal from the Commission and after obtaining the consent of the European Parliament.

(2) Using the procedure for monitoring the subsidiarity principle referred to in Article 5 (3) of the Treaty on European Union, the Commission shall draw national Parliaments' attention to proposals based on this Article.

(3) Measures based on this Article shall not entail harmonisation of Member States' laws or regulations in cases where the Treaties exclude such harmonisation.

(4) This Article cannot serve as a basis for attaining objectives pertaining to the common foreign and security policy and any acts adopted pursuant to this Article shall respect the limits set out in Article 40, second paragraph, of the Treaty on European Union.

Article 353. Article 48(7) of the Treaty on European Union shall not apply to the following Articles:
- Article 311, third and fourth paragraphs,
- Article 312(2), first subparagraph,
- Article 352, and
- Article 354.

Article 354. For the purposes of Article 7 of the Treaty on European Union on the suspension of certain rights resulting from Union membership, the member of the European Council or of the Council representing the Member State in question shall not take part in the vote and the Member State in question shall not be counted in the calculation of the one third or four fifths of Member States referred to in paragraphs 1 and 2 of that Article. Abstentions by members present in person or represented shall not prevent the adoption of decisions referred to in paragraph 2 of that Article.

For the adoption of the decisions referred to in paragraphs 3 and 4 of Article 7 of the Treaty on European Union, a qualified majority shall be defined in accordance with Article 238(3)(b) of this Treaty.

Where, following a decision to suspend voting rights adopted pursuant to paragraph 3 of Article 7 of the Treaty on European Union, the Council acts by a qualified majority on the basis of a provision of the Treaties, that qualified majority shall be defined in accordance with Article 238(3)(b) of this Treaty, or, where the Council acts on a proposal from the Commission or from the High Representative of the Union for Foreign Affairs and Security Policy, in accordance with Article 238(3)(a).

For the purposes of Article 7 of the Treaty on European Union, the European Parliament shall act by a two–thirds majority of the votes cast, representing the majority of its component Members.

Article 355. In addition to the provisions of Article 52 of the Treaty on European Union relating to the territorial scope of the Treaties, the following provisions shall apply:

(1) The provisions of the Treaties shall apply to Guadeloupe, French Guiana, Martinique, Réunion, Saint-Barthélemy, Saint-Martin, the Azores, Madeira and the Canary Islands in accordance with Article 349.

(2) The special arrangements for association set out in Part Four shall apply to the overseas countries and territories listed in Annex II.

The Treaties shall not apply to those overseas countries and territories having special relations with the United Kingdom of Great Britain and Northern Ireland which are not included in the aforementioned list.

(3) The provisions of the Treaties shall apply to the European territories for whose external relations a Member State is responsible.

(4) The provisions of the Treaties shall apply to the Åland Islands in accordance with the provisions set out in Protocol 2 to the Act concerning the conditions of accession of the Republic of Austria, the Republic of Finland and the Kingdom of Sweden.

(5) Notwithstanding Article 52 of the Treaty on European Union and paragraphs 1 to 4 of this Article:

(a) the Treaties shall not apply to the Faeroe Islands;

(b) the Treaties shall not apply to the United Kingdom Sovereign Base Areas of Akrotiri and Dhekelia in Cyprus except to the extent necessary to ensure the implementation of the arrangements set out in the Protocol on the Sovereign Base Areas of the United Kingdom of Great Britain and Northern Ireland in Cyprus annexed to the Act concerning the conditions of accession of the Czech Republic, the Republic of Estonia, the Republic of Cyprus, the Republic of Latvia, the Republic of Lithuania, the Republic of Hungary, the Republic of Malta, the Republic of Poland, the Republic of Slovenia and the Slovak Republic to the European Union and in accordance with the terms of that Protocol;

(c) the Treaties shall apply to the Channel Islands and the Isle of Man only to the extent necessary to ensure the implementation of the arrangements for those islands set out in the Treaty concerning the accession of new Member States to the European Economic Community and to the European Atomic Energy Community signed on 22 January 1972.

(6) The European Council may, on the initiative of the Member State concerned, adopt a decision amending the status, with regard to the Union, of a Danish, French or Netherlands country or territory referred to in paragraphs 1 and 2. The European Council shall act unanimously after consulting the Commission.

Article 356. This Treaty is concluded for an unlimited period.

Article 357. This Treaty shall be ratified by the High Contracting Parties in accordance with their respective constitutional requirements. The Instruments of ratification shall be deposited with the Government of the Italian Republic.

This Treaty shall enter into force on the first day of the month following the deposit of the Instrument of ratification by the last signatory State to take this step. If, however, such deposit is made less than 15 days before the beginning of the following month, this Treaty shall not enter into force until the first day of the second month after the date of such deposit.

Article 358. The provisions of Article 55 of the Treaty on European Union shall apply to this Treaty.

IN WITNESS WHEREOF, the undersigned Plenipotentiaries have signed this Treaty.

Done at Rome this twenty-fifth day of March in the year one thousand nine hundred and fifty-seven.

[*List of signatories not reproduced*]

23 Protocols to the EU Treaties[5]

Protocol (No 1) on the Role of National Parliaments in the European Union

THE HIGH CONTRACTING PARTIES,
RECALLING that the way in which national Parliaments scrutinise their governments in relation to the activities of the Union is a matter for the particular constitutional organisation and practice of each Member State,
DESIRING to encourage greater involvement of national Parliaments in the activities of the European Union and to enhance their ability to express their views on draft legislative acts of the Union as well as on other matters which may be of particular interest to them,
HAVE AGREED UPON the following provisions, which shall be annexed to the Treaty on European Union, to the Treaty on the Functioning of the European Union and to the Treaty establishing the European Atomic Energy Community:

Title I. Information for National Parliaments

Article 1. Commission consultation documents (green and white papers and communications) shall be forwarded directly by the Commission to national Parliaments upon publication. The Commission shall also forward the annual legislative programme as well as any other instrument of legislative planning or policy to national Parliaments, at the same time as to the European Parliament and the Council.

Article 2. Draft legislative acts sent to the European Parliament and to the Council shall be forwarded to national Parliaments.
For the purposes of this Protocol, "draft legislative acts" shall mean proposals from the Commission, initiatives from a group of Member States, initiatives from the European Parliament, requests from the Court of Justice, recommendations from the European Central Bank and requests from the European Investment Bank, for the adoption of a legislative act.
Draft legislative acts originating from the Commission shall be forwarded to national Parliaments directly by the Commission, at the same time as to the European Parliament and the Council.
Draft legislative acts originating from the European Parliament shall be forwarded to national Parliaments directly by the European Parliament.

---

5 Protocol (No 1) On the role of National Parliaments in the European Union and Protocol (No 2) on the application of the principles of subsidiarity and proportionality, as published with the consolidated versions of the TEU and the TFEU in the Official Journal of the European Union on 26 October 2012. The remaining Protocols to the Treaties are omitted.

Draft legislative acts originating from a group of Member States, the Court of Justice, the European Central Bank or the European Investment Bank shall be forwarded to national Parliaments by the Council.

Article 3. National Parliaments may send to the Presidents of the European Parliament, the Council and the Commission a reasoned opinion on whether a draft legislative act complies with the principle of subsidiarity, in accordance with the procedure laid down in the Protocol on the application of the principles of subsidiarity and proportionality.
If the draft legislative act originates from a group of Member States, the President of the Council shall forward the reasoned opinion or opinions to the governments of those Member States.
If the draft legislative act originates from the Court of Justice, the European Central Bank or the European Investment Bank, the President of the Council shall forward the reasoned opinion or opinions to the institution or body concerned.

Article 4. An eight–week period shall elapse between a draft legislative act being made available to national Parliaments in the official languages of the Union and the date when it is placed on a provisional agenda for the Council for its adoption or for adoption of a position under a legislative procedure. Exceptions shall be possible in cases of urgency, the reasons for which shall be stated in the act or position of the Council. Save in urgent cases for which due reasons have been given, no agreement may be reached on a draft legislative act during those eight weeks. Save in urgent cases for which due reasons have been given, a ten–day period shall elapse between the placing of a draft legislative act on the provisional agenda for the Council and the adoption of a position.

Article 5. The agendas for and the outcome of meetings of the Council, including the minutes of meetings where the Council is deliberating on draft legislative acts, shall be forwarded directly to national Parliaments, at the same time as to Member States' governments.

Article 6. When the European Council intends to make use of the first or second subparagraphs of Article 48(7) of the Treaty on European Union, national Parliaments shall be informed of the initiative of the European Council at least six months before any decision is adopted.

Article 7. The Court of Auditors shall forward its annual report to national Parliaments, for information, at the same time as to the European Parliament and to the Council.

Article 8. Where the national Parliamentary system is not unicameral, Articles 1 to 7 shall apply to the component chambers.

Title II. Interparliamentary Cooperation

Article 9. The European Parliament and national Parliaments shall together determine the organisation and promotion of effective and regular interparliamentary cooperation within the Union.

Article 10. A conference of Parliamentary Committees for Union Affairs may submit any contribution it deems appropriate for the attention of the European Parliament, the Council and the Commission. That conference shall in addition promote the exchange of information and best practice between national Parliaments and the European Parliament, including their special committees. It may also organise interparliamentary conferences on specific topics, in particular to debate matters of common foreign and security policy, including common security and defence policy. Contributions from the conference shall not bind national Parliaments and shall not prejudge their positions.

Protocol (No 2) on the Application of the Principles of Subsidiarity and Proportionality

THE HIGH CONTRACTING PARTIES,
WISHING to ensure that decisions are taken as closely as possible to the citizens of the Union,
RESOLVED to establish the conditions for the application of the principles of subsidiarity and proportionality, as laid down in Article 5 of the Treaty on European Union, and to establish a system for monitoring the application of those principles,
HAVE AGREED UPON the following provisions, which shall be annexed to the Treaty on European Union and to the Treaty on the Functioning of the European Union:

Article 1. Each institution shall ensure constant respect for the principles of subsidiarity and proportionality, as laid down in Article 5 of the Treaty on European Union.

Article 2. Before proposing legislative acts, the Commission shall consult widely. Such consultations shall, where appropriate, take into account the regional and local dimension of the action envisaged. In cases of exceptional urgency, the Commission shall not conduct such consultations. It shall give reasons for its decision in its proposal.

Article 3. For the purposes of this Protocol, "draft legislative acts" shall mean proposals from the Commission, initiatives from a group of Member States, initiatives from the European Parliament, requests from the Court of Justice, recommendations from the European Central Bank and requests from the European Investment Bank, for the adoption of a legislative act.

Article 4. The Commission shall forward its draft legislative acts and its amended drafts to national Parliaments at the same time as to the Union legislator.

The European Parliament shall forward its draft legislative acts and its amended drafts to national Parliaments.

The Council shall forward draft legislative acts originating from a group of Member States, the Court of Justice, the European Central Bank or the European Investment Bank and amended drafts to national Parliaments.

Upon adoption, legislative resolutions of the European Parliament and positions of the Council shall be forwarded by them to national Parliaments.

Article 5. Draft legislative acts shall be justified with regard to the principles of subsidiarity and proportionality. Any draft legislative act should contain a detailed statement making it possible to appraise compliance with the principles of subsidiarity and proportionality. This statement should contain some assessment of the proposal's financial impact and, in the case of a directive, of its implications for the rules to be put in place by Member States, including, where necessary, the regional legislation. The reasons for concluding that a Union objective can be better achieved at Union level shall be substantiated by qualitative and, wherever possible, quantitative indicators. Draft legislative acts shall take account of the need for any burden, whether financial or administrative, falling upon the Union, national governments, regional or local authorities, economic operators and citizens, to be minimised and commensurate with the objective to be achieved.

Article 6. Any national Parliament or any chamber of a national Parliament may, within eight weeks from the date of transmission of a draft legislative act, in the official languages of the Union, send to the Presidents of the European Parliament, the Council and the Commission a reasoned opinion stating why it considers that the draft in question does not comply with the principle of subsidiarity. It will be for each national Parliament or each chamber of a national Parliament to consult, where appropriate, regional parliaments with legislative powers.

If the draft legislative act originates from a group of Member States, the President of the Council shall forward the opinion to the governments of those Member States.

If the draft legislative act originates from the Court of Justice, the European Central Bank or the European Investment Bank, the President of the Council shall forward the opinion to the institution or body concerned.

Article 7. (1) The European Parliament, the Council and the Commission, and, where appropriate, the group of Member States, the Court of Justice, the European Central Bank or the European Investment Bank, if the draft legislative act originates from them, shall take account of the reasoned opinions issued by national Parliaments or by a chamber of a national Parliament.

Each national Parliament shall have two votes, shared out on the basis of the national Parliamentary system. In the case of a bicameral Parliamentary system, each of the two chambers shall have one vote.

(2) Where reasoned opinions on a draft legislative act's non-compliance with the principle of subsidiarity represent at least one third of all the votes allocated to the national Parliaments in accordance with the second subparagraph of paragraph 1, the draft must be reviewed. This threshold shall be a quarter in the case of a draft legislative act submitted on the basis of Article 76 of the Treaty on the Functioning of the European Union on the area of freedom, security and justice.

After such review, the Commission or, where appropriate, the group of Member States, the European Parliament, the Court of Justice, the European Central Bank or the European Investment Bank, if the draft legislative act originates from them, may decide to maintain, amend or withdraw the draft. Reasons must be given for this decision.

(3) Furthermore, under the ordinary legislative procedure, where reasoned opinions on the non-compliance of a proposal for a legislative act with the principle of subsidiarity represent at least a simple majority of the votes allocated to the national Parliaments in accordance with the second subparagraph of paragraph 1, the proposal must be reviewed. After such review, the Commission may decide to maintain, amend or withdraw the proposal.

If it chooses to maintain the proposal, the Commission will have, in a reasoned opinion, to justify why it considers that the proposal complies with the principle of subsidiarity. This reasoned opinion, as well as the reasoned opinions of the national Parliaments, will have to be submitted to the Union legislator, for consideration in the procedure:

(a) before concluding the first reading, the legislator (the European Parliament and the Council) shall consider whether the legislative proposal is compatible with the principle of subsidiarity, taking particular account of the reasons expressed and shared by the majority of national Parliaments as well as the reasoned opinion of the Commission;

(b) if, by a majority of 55 % of the members of the Council or a majority of the votes cast in the European Parliament, the legislator is of the opinion that the proposal is not compatible with the principle of subsidiarity, the legislative proposal shall not be given further consideration.

Article 8. The Court of Justice of the European Union shall have jurisdiction in actions on grounds of infringement of the principle of subsidiarity by a legislative act, brought in accordance with the rules laid down in Article 263 of the Treaty on the Functioning of the European Union by Member States, or notified by them in accordance with their legal order on behalf of their national Parliament or a chamber thereof.

In accordance with the rules laid down in the said Article, the Committee of the Regions may also bring such actions against legislative acts for the adoption of which the Treaty on the Functioning of the European Union provides that it be consulted.

Article 9. The Commission shall submit each year to the European Council, the European Parliament, the Council and national Parliaments a report on the application of Article 5 of the Treaty on European Union. This annual report shall also be forwarded to the Economic and Social Committee and the Committee of the Regions.

24 Charter of Fundamental Rights of the European Union[6]

The peoples of Europe, in creating an ever closer union among them, are resolved to share a peaceful future based on common values.

Conscious of its spiritual and moral heritage, the Union is founded on the indivisible, universal values of human dignity, freedom, equality and solidarity; it is based on the principles of democracy and the rule of law. It places the individual at the heart of its activities, by establishing the citizenship of the Union and by creating an area of freedom, security and justice.

The Union contributes to the preservation and to the development of these common values while respecting the diversity of the cultures and traditions of the peoples of Europe as well as the national identities of the Member States and the organisation of their public authorities at national, regional and local levels; it seeks to promote balanced and sustainable development and ensures free movement of persons, services, goods and capital, and the freedom of establishment.

To this end, it is necessary to strengthen the protection of fundamental rights in the light of changes in society, social progress and scientific and technological developments by making those rights more visible in a Charter.

This Charter reaffirms, with due regard for the powers and tasks of the Union and for the principle of subsidiarity, the rights as they result, in particular, from the constitutional traditions and international obligations common to the Member States, the European Convention for the Protection of Human Rights and Fundamental Freedoms, the Social Charters adopted by the Union and by the Council of Europe and the case-law of the Court of Justice of the European Union and of the European Court of Human Rights. In this context the Charter will be interpreted by the courts of the Union and the Member States with due regard to the explanations prepared under the authority of the Praesidium of the Convention which drafted the Charter and updated under the responsibility of the Praesidium of the European Convention.

Enjoyment of these rights entails responsibilities and duties with regard to other persons, to the human community and to future generations.

The Union therefore recognises the rights, freedoms and principles set out hereafter.

Title I. Dignity

Article 1. Human dignity is inviolable. It must be respected and protected.

Article 2. (1) Everyone has the right to life.
(2) No one shall be condemned to the death penalty, or executed.

---

6 As published in the Official Journal oft he European Union on 26 October 2012 (2012/C 326/02).

Article 3. (1) Everyone has the right to respect for his or her physical and mental integrity.
(2) In the fields of medicine and biology, the following must be respected in particular:
(a) the free and informed consent of the person concerned, according to the procedures laid down by law;
(b) the prohibition of eugenic practices, in particular those aiming at the selection of persons;
(c) the prohibition on making the human body and its parts as such a source of financial gain;
(d) the prohibition of the reproductive cloning of human beings.

Article 4. No one shall be subjected to torture or to inhuman or degrading treatment or punishment.

Article 5. (1) No one shall be held in slavery or servitude.
(2) No one shall be required to perform forced or compulsory labour.
(3) Trafficking in human beings is prohibited.

Title II. Freedoms

Article 6. Everyone has the right to liberty and security of person.

Article 7. Everyone has the right to respect for his or her private and family life, home and communications.

Article 8. (1) Everyone has the right to the protection of personal data concerning him or her.
(2) Such data must be processed fairly for specified purposes and on the basis of the consent of the person concerned or some other legitimate basis laid down by law. Everyone has the right of access to data which has been collected concerning him or her, and the right to have it rectified.
(3) Compliance with these rules shall be subject to control by an independent authority.

Article 9. The right to marry and the right to found a family shall be guaranteed in accordance with the national laws governing the exercise of these rights.

Article 10. (1) Everyone has the right to freedom of thought, conscience and religion. This right includes freedom to change religion or belief and freedom, either alone or in

community with others and in public or in private, to manifest religion or belief, in worship, teaching, practice and observance.
(2) The right to conscientious objection is recognised, in accordance with the national laws governing the exercise of this right.

Article 11. (1) Everyone has the right to freedom of expression. This right shall include freedom to hold opinions and to receive and impart information and ideas without interference by public authority and regardless of frontiers.
(2) The freedom and pluralism of the media shall be respected.

Article 12. (1) Everyone has the right to freedom of peaceful assembly and to freedom of association at all levels, in particular in political, trade union and civic matters, which implies the right of everyone to form and to join trade unions for the protection of his or her interests.
(2) Political parties at Union level contribute to expressing the political will of the citizens of the Union.

Article 13. The arts and scientific research shall be free of constraint. Academic freedom shall be respected.

Article 14. (1) Everyone has the right to education and to have access to vocational and continuing training.
(2) This right includes the possibility to receive free compulsory education.
(3) The freedom to found educational establishments with due respect for democratic principles and the right of parents to ensure the education and teaching of their children in conformity with their religious, philosophical and pedagogical convictions shall be respected, in accordance with the national laws governing the exercise of such freedom and right.

Article 15. (1) Everyone has the right to engage in work and to pursue a freely chosen or accepted occupation.
(2) Every citizen of the Union has the freedom to seek employment, to work, to exercise the right of establishment and to provide services in any Member State.
(3) Nationals of third countries who are authorised to work in the territories of the Member States are entitled to working conditions equivalent to those of citizens of the Union.

Article 16. The freedom to conduct a business in accordance with Union law and national laws and practices is recognised.

Article 17. (1) Everyone has the right to own, use, dispose of and bequeath his or her lawfully acquired possessions. No one may be deprived of his or her possessions, except in the public interest and in the cases and under the conditions provided for by law, subject to fair compensation being paid in good time for their loss. The use of property may be regulated by law in so far as is necessary for the general interest.
(2) Intellectual property shall be protected.

Article 18. The right to asylum shall be guaranteed with due respect for the rules of the Geneva Convention of 28 July 1951 and the Protocol of 31 January 1967 relating to the status of refugees and in accordance with the Treaty on European Union and the Treaty on the Functioning of the European Union (hereinafter referred to as 'the Treaties').

Article 19. (1) Collective expulsions are prohibited.
(2) No one may be removed, expelled or extradited to a State where there is a serious risk that he or she would be subjected to the death penalty, torture or other inhuman or degrading treatment or punishment.

Title III. Equality

Article 20. Everyone is equal before the law.

Article 21. (1) Any discrimination based on any ground such as sex, race, colour, ethnic or social origin, genetic features, language, religion or belief, political or any other opinion, membership of a national minority, property, birth, disability, age or sexual orientation shall be prohibited.
(2) Within the scope of application of the Treaties and without prejudice to any of their specific provisions, any discrimination on grounds of nationality shall be prohibited.

Article 22. The Union shall respect cultural, religious and linguistic diversity.

Article 23. Equality between women and men must be ensured in all areas, including employment, work and pay.
The principle of equality shall not prevent the maintenance or adoption of measures providing for specific advantages in favour of the under-represented sex.

Article 24. (1) Children shall have the right to such protection and care as is necessary for their well-being. They may express their views freely. Such views shall be taken into consideration on matters which concern them in accordance with their age and maturity.

(2) In all actions relating to children, whether taken by public authorities or private institutions, the child's best interests must be a primary consideration.
(3) Every child shall have the right to maintain on a regular basis a personal relationship and direct contact with both his or her parents, unless that is contrary to his or her interests.

Article 25. The Union recognises and respects the rights of the elderly to lead a life of dignity and independence and to participate in social and cultural life.

Article 26. The Union recognises and respects the right of persons with disabilities to benefit from measures designed to ensure their independence, social and occupational integration and participation in the life of the community.

Title IV. Solidarity

Article 27. Workers or their representatives must, at the appropriate levels, be guaranteed information and consultation in good time in the cases and under the conditions provided for by Union law and national laws and practices.

Article 28. Workers and employers, or their respective organisations, have, in accordance with Union law and national laws and practices, the right to negotiate and conclude collective agreements at the appropriate levels and, in cases of conflicts of interest, to take collective action to defend their interests, including strike action.

Article 29. Everyone has the right of access to a free placement service.

Article 30. Every worker has the right to protection against unjustified dismissal, in accordance with Union law and national laws and practices.

Article 31. (1) Every worker has the right to working conditions which respect his or her health, safety and dignity.
(2) Every worker has the right to limitation of maximum working hours, to daily and weekly rest periods and to an annual period of paid leave.

Article 32. The employment of children is prohibited. The minimum age of admission to employment may not be lower than the minimum school-leaving age, without prejudice to such rules as may be more favourable to young people and except for limited derogations.

Young people admitted to work must have working conditions appropriate to their age and be protected against economic exploitation and any work likely to harm their safety, health or physical, mental, moral or social development or to interfere with their education.

Article 33. (1) The family shall enjoy legal, economic and social protection.
(2) To reconcile family and professional life, everyone shall have the right to protection from dismissal for a reason connected with maternity and the right to paid maternity leave and to parental leave following the birth or adoption of a child.

Article 34. (1) The Union recognises and respects the entitlement to social security benefits and social services providing protection in cases such as maternity, illness, industrial accidents, dependency or old age, and in the case of loss of employment, in accordance with the rules laid down by Union law and national laws and practices.
(2) Everyone residing and moving legally within the European Union is entitled to social security benefits and social advantages in accordance with Union law and national laws and practices.
(3) In order to combat social exclusion and poverty, the Union recognises and respects the right to social and housing assistance so as to ensure a decent existence for all those who lack sufficient resources, in accordance with the rules laid down by Union law and national laws and practices.

Article 35. Everyone has the right of access to preventive health care and the right to benefit from medical treatment under the conditions established by national laws and practices. A high level of human health protection shall be ensured in the definition and implementation of all the Union's policies and activities.

Article 36. The Union recognises and respects access to services of general economic interest as provided for in national laws and practices, in accordance with the Treaties, in order to promote the social and territorial cohesion of the Union.

Article 37. A high level of environmental protection and the improvement of the quality of the environment must be integrated into the policies of the Union and ensured in accordance with the principle of sustainable development.

Article 38. Union policies shall ensure a high level of consumer protection.

Title V. Citizens' Rights

Article 39. (1) Every citizen of the Union has the right to vote and to stand as a candidate at elections to the European Parliament in the Member State in which he or she resides, under the same conditions as nationals of that State.
(2) Members of the European Parliament shall be elected by direct universal suffrage in a free and secret ballot.

Article 40. Every citizen of the Union has the right to vote and to stand as a candidate at municipal elections in the Member State in which he or she resides under the same conditions as nationals of that State.

Article 41. (1) Every person has the right to have his or her affairs handled impartially, fairly and within a reasonable time by the institutions, bodies, offices and agencies of the Union.
(2) This right includes:
(a) the right of every person to be heard, before any individual measure which would affect him or her adversely is taken;
(b) the right of every person to have access to his or her file, while respecting the legitimate interests of confidentiality and of professional and business secrecy;
(c) the obligation of the administration to give reasons for its decisions.
(3) Every person has the right to have the Union make good any damage caused by its institutions or by its servants in the performance of their duties, in accordance with the general principles common to the laws of the Member States.
(4) Every person may write to the institutions of the Union in one of the languages of the Treaties and must have an answer in the same language.

Article 42. Any citizen of the Union, and any natural or legal person residing or having its registered office in a Member State, has a right of access to documents of the institutions, bodies, offices and agencies of the Union, whatever their medium.

Article 43. Any citizen of the Union and any natural or legal person residing or having its registered office in a Member State has the right to refer to the European Ombudsman cases of maladministration in the activities of the institutions, bodies, offices or agencies of the Union, with the exception of the Court of Justice of the European Union acting in its judicial role.

Article 44. Any citizen of the Union and any natural or legal person residing or having its registered office in a Member State has the right to petition the European Parliament.

Article 45. (1) Every citizen of the Union has the right to move and reside freely within the territory of the Member States.
(2) Freedom of movement and residence may be granted, in accordance with the Treaties, to nationals of third countries legally resident in the territory of a Member State.

Article 46. Every citizen of the Union shall, in the territory of a third country in which the Member State of which he or she is a national is not represented, be entitled to protection by the diplomatic or consular authorities of any Member State, on the same conditions as the nationals of that Member State.

Title VI. Justice

Article 47. Everyone whose rights and freedoms guaranteed by the law of the Union are violated has the right to an effective remedy before a tribunal in compliance with the conditions laid down in this Article.
Everyone is entitled to a fair and public hearing within a reasonable time by an independent and impartial tribunal previously established by law. Everyone shall have the possibility of being advised, defended and represented.
Legal aid shall be made available to those who lack sufficient resources in so far as such aid is necessary to ensure effective access to justice.

Article 48. (1) Everyone who has been charged shall be presumed innocent until proved guilty according to law.
(2) Respect for the rights of the defence of anyone who has been charged shall be guaranteed.

Article 49. (1) No one shall be held guilty of any criminal offence on account of any act or omission which did not constitute a criminal offence under national law or international law at the time when it was committed. Nor shall a heavier penalty be imposed than the one that was applicable at the time the criminal offence was committed. If, subsequent to the commission of a criminal offence, the law provides for a lighter penalty, that penalty shall be applicable.
(2) This Article shall not prejudice the trial and punishment of any person for any act or omission which, at the time when it was committed, was criminal according to the general principles recognised by the community of nations.
(3) The severity of penalties must not be disproportionate to the criminal offence.

Article 50. No one shall be liable to be tried or punished again in criminal proceedings for an offence for which he or she has already been finally acquitted or convicted within the Union in accordance with the law.

Title VII. General Provisions Governing the Interpretation and Application of the Charter

Article 51. (1) The provisions of this Charter are addressed to the institutions, bodies, offices and agencies of the Union with due regard for the principle of subsidiarity and to the Member States only when they are implementing Union law. They shall therefore respect the rights, observe the principles and promote the application thereof in accordance with their respective powers and respecting the limits of the powers of the Union as conferred on it in the Treaties.
(2) The Charter does not extend the field of application of Union law beyond the powers of the Union or establish any new power or task for the Union, or modify powers and tasks as defined in the Treaties.

Article 52. (1) Any limitation on the exercise of the rights and freedoms recognised by this Charter must be provided for by law and respect the essence of those rights and freedoms. Subject to the principle of proportionality, limitations may be made only if they are necessary and genuinely meet objectives of general interest recognised by the Union or the need to protect the rights and freedoms of others.
(2) Rights recognised by this Charter for which provision is made in the Treaties shall be exercised under the conditions and within the limits defined by those Treaties.
(3) In so far as this Charter contains rights which correspond to rights guaranteed by the Convention for the Protection of Human Rights and Fundamental Freedoms, the meaning and scope of those rights shall be the same as those laid down by the said Convention. This provision shall not prevent Union law providing more extensive protection.
(4) In so far as this Charter recognises fundamental rights as they result from the constitutional traditions common to the Member States, those rights shall be interpreted in harmony with those traditions.
(5) The provisions of this Charter which contain principles may be implemented by legislative and executive acts taken by institutions, bodies, offices and agencies of the Union, and by acts of Member States when they are implementing Union law, in the exercise of their respective powers. They shall be judicially cognisable only in the interpretation of such acts and in the ruling on their legality.
(6) Full account shall be taken of national laws and practices as specified in this Charter.
(7) The explanations drawn up as a way of providing guidance in the interpretation of this Charter shall be given due regard by the courts of the Union and of the Member States.

Article 53. Nothing in this Charter shall be interpreted as restricting or adversely affecting human rights and fundamental freedoms as recognised, in their respective fields of application, by Union law and international law and by international agreements to which the Union or all the Member States are party, including the European Convention for the Protection of Human Rights and Fundamental Freedoms, and by the Member States' constitutions.

Article 54. Nothing in this Charter shall be interpreted as implying any right to engage in any activity or to perform any act aimed at the destruction of any of the rights and freedoms recognised in this Charter or at their limitation to a greater extent than is provided for herein.

European Human Rights

25 European Convention for the Protection of Human Rights and Fundamental Freedoms[1]

The governments signatory hereto, being members of the Council of Europe, Considering the Universal Declaration of Human Rights proclaimed by the General Assembly of the United Nations on 10 December 1948;
Considering that this Declaration aims at securing the universal and effective recognition and observance of the Rights therein declared;
Considering that the aim of the Council of Europe is the achievement of greater unity between its members and that one of the methods by which that aim is to be pursued is the maintenance and further realisation of human rights and fundamental freedoms;
Reaffirming their profound belief in those fundamental freedoms which are the foundation of justice and peace in the world and are best maintained on the one hand by an effective political democracy and on the other by a common understanding and observance of the human rights upon which they depend;
Being resolved, as the governments of European countries which are likeminded and have a common heritage of political traditions, ideals, freedom and the rule of law, to take the first steps for the collective enforcement of certain of the rights stated in the Universal Declaration,
Have agreed as follows:

Article 1. The High Contracting Parties shall secure to everyone within their jurisdiction the rights and freedoms defined in Section I of this Convention.

Section I. Rights and freedoms

Article 2. (1) Everyone's right to life shall be protected by law. No one shall be deprived of his life intentionally save in the execution of a sentence of a court following his conviction of a crime for which this penalty is provided by law.
(2) Deprivation of life shall not be regarded as inflicted in contravention of this Article when it results from the use of force which is no more than abso-lutely necessary:
(a) in defence of any person from unlawful violence;
(b) in order to effect a lawful arrest or to prevent the escape of a person lawfully detained;
(c) in action lawfully taken for the purpose of quelling a riot or insurrection.

---

1   Rome, 40 November 1950, as last amended by Protocol 14 to the Convention (1 June 2014).

Article 3. No one shall be subjected to torture or to inhuman or degrading treatment or punishment.

Article 4. (1) No one shall be held in slavery or servitude.
(2) No one shall be required to perform forced or compulsory labour.
(3) For the purpose of this Article the term "forced or compulsory labour" shall not include:
(a) any work required to be done in the ordinary course of detention imposed according to the provisions of Article 5 of this Convention or during conditional release from such detention;
(b) any service of a military character or, in case of conscientious objectors in countries where they are recognised, service exacted instead of compulsory military service;
(c) any service exacted in case of an emergency or calamity threatening the life or well-being of the community;
(d) any work or service which forms part of normal civic obligations.

Article 5. (1) Everyone has the right to liberty and security of person. No one shall be deprived of his liberty save in the following cases and in accordance with a procedure prescribed by law:
(a) the lawful detention of a person after conviction by a competent court;
(b) the lawful arrest or detention of a person for non-compliance with the lawful order of a court or in order to secure the fulfilment of any obligation prescribed by law;
(c) the lawful arrest or detention of a person effected for the purpose of bringing him before the competent legal authority on reasonable suspicion of having committed an offence or when it is reasonably considered necessary to prevent his committing an offence or fleeing after having done so;
(d) the detention of a minor by lawful order for the purpose of educational supervision or his lawful detention for the purpose of bringing him before the competent legal authority;
(e) the lawful detention of persons for the prevention of the spreading of infectious diseases, of persons of un-sound mind, alcoholics or drug addicts or vagrants;
(f) the lawful arrest or detention of a person to prevent his effecting an unauthorised entry into the country or of a person against whom action is being taken with a view to deportation or extradition.
(2) Everyone who is arrested shall be informed promptly, in a language which he understands, of the reasons for his arrest and of any charge against him.
(3) Everyone arrested or detained in accordance with the provisions of paragraph (1) (c) of this Article shall be brought promptly before a judge or other officer authorised by law to exercise judicial power and shall be entitled to trial within a reasonable time or to release pending trial. Release may be conditioned by guarantees to appear for trial.

(4) Everyone who is deprived of his liberty by arrest or detention shall be entitled to take proceedings by which the lawfulness of his detention shall be decided speedily by a court and his release ordered if the detention is not lawful.

(5) Everyone who has been the victim of arrest or detention in contravention of the provisions of this Article shall have an enforceable right to compensation.

Article 6. (1) In the determination of his civil rights and obligations or of any criminal charge against him, everyone is entitled to a fair and public hearing within a reasonable time by an independent and impartial tribunal established by law. Judgment shall be pronounced publicly but the press and public may be excluded from all or part of the trial in the interests of morals, public order or national security in a democratic society, where the interests of juveniles or the protection of the private life of the parties so require, or to the extent strictly necessary in the opinion of the court in special circumstances where publicity would prejudice the interests of justice.

(2) Everyone charged with a criminal offence shall be presumed innocent until proved guilty according to law.

(3) Everyone charged with a criminal offence has the following minimum rights:

(a) to be informed promptly, in a language which he understands and in detail, of the nature and cause of the accusation against him;

(b) to have adequate time and facilities for the preparation of his defence;

(c) to defend himself in person or through legal assistance of his own choosing or, if he has not sufficient means to pay for legal assistance, to be given it free when the interests of justice so require;

(d) to examine or have examined witnesses against him and to obtain the attendance and examination of wit-nesses on his behalf under the same conditions as witnesses against him;

(e) to have the free assistance of an interpreter if he cannot understand or speak the language used in court.

Article 7. (1) No one shall be held guilty of any criminal offence on account of any act or omission which did not constitute a criminal offence under national or international law at the time when it was committed. Nor shall a heavier penalty be imposed than the one that was applicable at the time the criminal offence was committed.

(2) This Article shall not prejudice the trial and punishment of any person for any act or omission which, at the time when it was committed, was criminal according to the general principles of law recognised by civilised nations.

Article 8. (1) Everyone has the right to respect for his private and family life, his home and his correspondence.

(2) There shall be no interference by a public authority with the exercise of this right except such as is in accordance with the law and is necessary in a democratic society in the interests of national security, public safety or the economic well-being of the country, for the prevention of disorder or crime, for the protection of health or morals, or for the protection of the rights and freedoms of others.

Article 9. (1) Everyone has the right to freedom of thought, conscience and religion; this right includes freedom to change his religion or belief and freedom, either alone or in community with others and in public or private, to manifest his religion or belief, in worship, teaching, practice and observance.
(2) Freedom to manifest one's religion or beliefs shall be subject only to such limitations as are prescribed by law and are necessary in a democratic society in the interests of public safety, for the protection of public order, health or morals, or for the protection of the rights and freedoms of others.

Article 10. (1) Everyone has the right to freedom of expression. This right shall include freedom to hold opinions and to receive and impart information and ideas without interference by public authority and regardless of frontiers. This Article shall not prevent States from requiring the licensing of broadcasting, television or cinema enterprises.
(2) The exercise of these freedoms, since it carries with it duties and responsibilities, may be subject to such formalities, conditions, restrictions or penalties as are prescribed by law and are necessary in a democratic society, in the interests of national security, territorial integrity or public safety, for the prevention of disorder or crime, for the protection of health or morals, for the protection of the reputation or rights of others, for preventing the disclosure of information received in confidence, or for maintaining the authority and im-partiality of the judiciary.

Article 11. (1) Everyone has the right to freedom of peaceful assembly and to freedom of association with others, including the right to form and to join trade unions for the protection of his interests.
(2) No restrictions shall be placed on the exercise of these rights other than such as are prescribed by law and are necessary in a democratic society in the interests of national security or public safety, for the prevention of disorder or crime, for the protection of health or morals or for the protection of the rights and freedoms of others. This Article shall not prevent the imposition of lawful restrictions on the exercise of these rights by members of the armed forces, of the police or of the administration of the State.

Article 12. Men and women of marriageable age have the right to marry and to found a family, according to the national laws governing the exercise of this right.

Article 13. Everyone whose rights and freedoms as set forth in this Convention are violated shall have an effective remedy before a national authority notwithstanding that the violation has been committed by persons acting in an official capacity.

Article 14. The enjoyment of the rights and freedoms set forth in this Convention shall be secured without discrimination on any ground such as sex, race, colour, language, religion, political or other opinion, national or social origin, association with a national minority, property, birth or other status.

Article 15. (1) In time of war or other public emergency threatening the life of the nation any High Contracting Party may take measures derogating from its obligations under this Convention to the extent strictly required by the exigencies of the situation, provided that such measures are not inconsistent with its other obligations under international law.
(2) No derogation from Article 2, except in respect of deaths resulting from lawful acts of war, or from Articles 3, 4 § 1 and 7 shall be made under this provision.
(3) Any High Contracting Party availing itself of this right of derogation shall keep the Secretary General of the Council of Europe fully informed of the measures which it has taken and the reasons therefor. It shall also inform the Secretary General of the Council of Europe when such measures have ceased to operate and the provisions of the Convention are again being fully executed.

Article 16. Nothing in Articles 10, 11 and 14 shall be regarded as preventing the High Contracting Parties from imposing restrictions on the political activity of aliens.

Article 17. Nothing in this Convention may be interpreted as implying for any State, group or person any right to engage in any activity or perform any act aimed at the destruction of any of the rights and freedoms set forth herein or at their limitation to a greater extent than is provided for in the Convention.

Article 18. The restrictions permitted under this Convention to the said rights and freedoms shall not be applied for any purpose other than those for which they have been prescribed.

Section II. European Court of Human Rights

Article 19. To ensure the observance of the engagements undertaken by the High Contracting Parties in the Convention and the Protocols thereto, there shall be set up a European Court of Human Rights, hereinafter referred to as "the Court". It shall function on a permanent basis.

Article 20. The Court shall consist of a number of judges equal to that of the High Contracting Parties.

Article 21. (1) The judges shall be of high moral character and must either possess the qualifications required for appointment to high judicial office or be jurisconsults of recognised competence.
(2) The judges shall sit on the Court in their individual capacity.
(3) During their term of office the judges shall not engage in any activity which is incompatible with their independence, impartiality or with the demands of a full-time office; all questions arising from the application of this paragraph shall be decided by the Court.

Article 22. The judges shall be elected by the Parliamentary Assembly with respect to each High Contracting Party by a majority of votes cast from a list of three candidates nominated by the High Contracting Party.

Article 23. (1) The judges shall be elected for a period of nine years. They may not be re-elected.
(2) The terms of office of judges shall expire when they reach the age of 70.
(3) The judges shall hold office until replaced. They shall, however, continue to deal with such cases as they already have under consideration.
(4) No judge may be dismissed from office unless the other judges decide by a majority of two-thirds that that judge has ceased to fulfil the required conditions.

Article 24. (1) The Court shall have a Registry, the functions and organisation of which shall be laid down in the rules of the Court.
(2) When sitting in a single-judge formation, the Court shall be assisted by rapporteurs who shall function under the authority of the President of the Court. They shall form part of the Court's Registry.

Article 25. The plenary Court shall
(a) elect its President and one or two Vice-Presidents for a period of three years; they may be re-elected;
(b) set up Chambers, constituted for a fixed period of time;
(c) elect the Presidents of the Chambers of the Court; they may be re-elected;
(d) adopt the rules of the Court;
(e) elect the Registrar and one or more Deputy Registrars;
(f) make any request under Article 26 § 2.

Article 26. (1) To consider cases brought before it, the Court shall sit in a single-judge formation, in Committees of three judges, in Chambers of seven judges and in a Grand Chamber of seventeen judges. The Court's Chambers shall set up Committees for a fixed period of time.
(2) At the request of the plenary Court, the Committee of Ministers may, by a unanimous decision and for a fixed period, reduce to five the number of judges of the Chambers.
(3) When sitting as a single judge, a judge shall not examine any application against the High Contracting Party in respect of which that judge has been elected.
(4) There shall sit as an ex officio member of the Chamber and the Grand Chamber the judge elected in respect of the High Contracting Party concerned. If there is none or if that judge is unable to sit, a person chosen by the President of the Court from a list submitted in advance by that Party shall sit in the capacity of judge.
(5) The Grand Chamber shall also include the President of the Court, the Vice-Presidents, the Presidents of the Chambers and other judges chosen in accordance with the rules of the Court. When a case is referred to the Grand Chamber under Article 43, no judge from the Chamber which rendered the judgment shall sit in the Grand Chamber, with the exception of the President of the Chamber and the judge who sat in respect of the High Contracting Party concerned.

Article 27. (1) A single judge may declare inadmissible or strike out of the Court's list of cases an application submitted under Article 34, where such a decision can be taken without further examin-ation.
(2) The decision shall be final.
(3) If the single judge does not declare an application inadmissible or strike it out, that judge shall forward it to a Committee or to a Chamber for further examination.

Article 28. (1) In respect of an application sub-mitted under Article 34, a Committee may, by a unanimous vote,
(a) declare it inadmissible or strike it out of its list of cases, where such decision can be taken without further examination; or
(b) declare it admissible and render at the same time a judgment on the merits, if the underlying question in the case, concerning the interpretation or the application of the Convention or the Protocols thereto, is already the subject of well-established case-law of the Court.
(2) Decisions and judgments under paragraph (1) shall be final.
(3) If the judge elected in respect of the High Contracting Party concerned is not a member of the Committee, the Committee may at any stage of the proceedings invite that judge to take the place of one of the members of the Committee, having regard to all relevant factors, including whether that Party has contested the application of the pro-cedure under paragraph (1) (b).

Article 29. (1) If no decision is taken under Article 27 or 28, or no judgment rendered under Article 28, a Chamber shall decide on the admissibility and merits of individual applications submitted under Article 34. The decision on admissibility may be taken separately.
(2) A Chamber shall decide on the admissibility and merits of inter-State applications submitted under Article 33. The decision on admissibility shall be taken separately unless the Court, in exceptional cases, decides otherwise.

Article 30. Where a case pending before a Chamber raises a serious question affecting the interpretation of the Convention or the Protocols thereto, or where the resolution of a question before the Chamber might have a result inconsistent with a judgment previously delivered by the Court, the Chamber may, at any time before it has rendered its judgment, relinquish jurisdiction in favour of the Grand Chamber, unless one of the parties to the case objects.

Article 31. The Grand Chamber shall
(a) determine applications submitted either under Article 33 or Article 34 when a Chamber has relinquished jurisdiction under Article 30 or when the case has been referred to it under Art-icle 43;
(b) decide on issues referred to the Court by the Committee of Ministers in accordance with Article 46 § 4; and
(c) consider requests for advisory opinions submitted under Article 47.

Article 32. (1) The jurisdiction of the Court shall extend to all matters concerning the interpretation and application of the Convention and the Protocols thereto which are referred to it as provided in Articles 33, 34, 46 and 47.
(2) In the event of dispute as to whether the Court has jurisdiction, the Court shall decide.

Article 33. Any High Contracting Party may refer to the Court any alleged breach of the provisions of the Convention and the Protocols thereto by another High Contracting Party.

Article 34. The Court may receive applications from any person, non-governmental organisa-tion or group of individuals claiming to be the victim of a violation by one of the High Contracting Parties of the rights set forth in the Convention or the Protocols thereto. The High Contracting Parties undertake not to hinder in any way the effective exercise of this right.

Article 35. (1) The Court may only deal with the matter after all domestic remedies have been exhausted, according to the generally recognised rules of inter-national law, and within a period of six months from the date on which the final decision was taken.
(2) The Court shall not deal with any application submitted under Article 34 that
(a) is anonymous; or
(b) is substantially the same as a matter that has already been examined by the Court or has already been submitted to another procedure of international investigation or settlement and contains no relevant new infor-mation.
(3) The Court shall declare inadmissible any individual application submitted under Article 34 if it considers that:
(a) the application is incompatible with the provisions of the Convention or the Protocols thereto, manifestly ill-founded, or an abuse of the right of individual application; or
(b) the applicant has not suffered a significant disadvantage, unless respect for human rights as defined in the Convention and the Protocols thereto requires an examination of the application on the merits and provided that no case may be rejected on this ground which has not been duly considered by a domestic tribunal.
(4) The Court shall reject any application which it considers inadmis-sible under this Article. It may do so at any stage of the proceedings.

Article 36. (1) In all cases before a Chamber or the Grand Chamber, a High Contracting Party one of whose nationals is an applicant shall have the right to submit written com-ments and to take part in hearings.
(2) The President of the Court may, in the interest of the proper administration of justice, invite any High Contracting Party which is not a party to the proceedings or any person concerned who is not the applicant to submit written comments or take part in hearings.
(3) In all cases before a Chamber or the Grand Chamber, the Council of Europe Com-missioner for Human Rights may submit written comments and take part in hearings.

Article 37. (1) The Court may at any stage of the proceedings decide to strike an appli-cation out of its list of cases where the circumstances lead to the conclusion that
(a) the applicant does not intend to pursue his application; or
(b) the matter has been resolved; or
(c) for any other reason established by the Court, it is no longer justified to continue the examination of the application.
However, the Court shall continue the examination of the application if respect for human rights as defined in the Convention and the Protocols thereto so requires.
(2) The Court may decide to restore an application to its list of cases if it considers that the circumstances justify such a course.

Article 38. The Court shall examine the case together with the representatives of the parties and, if need be, undertake an investigation, for the effective conduct of which the High Contracting Parties concerned shall furnish all necessary facilities.

Article 39. (1) At any stage of the proceedings, the Court may place itself at the disposal of the parties concerned with a view to securing a friendly settlement of the matter on the basis of respect for human rights as defined in the Convention and the Protocols thereto.
(2) Proceedings conducted under para-graph 1 shall be confidential.
(3) If a friendly settlement is effected, the Court shall strike the case out of its list by means of a decision which shall be confined to a brief statement of the facts and of the solution reached.
(4) This decision shall be transmitted to the Committee of Ministers, which shall supervise the execution of the terms of the friendly settlement as set out in the decision.

Article 40. (1) Hearings shall be in public unless the Court in exceptional circumstances decides otherwise.
(2) Documents deposited with the Registrar shall be accessible to the public unless the President of the Court decides otherwise.

Article 41. If the Court finds that there has been a violation of the Convention or the Protocols thereto, and if the internal law of the High Contracting Party concerned allows only partial reparation to be made, the Court shall, if necessary, afford just satisfaction to the injured party.

Article 42. Judgments of Chambers shall become final in accordance with the provisions of Article 44 § 2.

Article 43. (1) Within a period of three months from the date of the judgment of the Chamber, any party to the case may, in exceptional cases, request that the case be referred to the Grand Chamber.
(2) A panel of five judges of the Grand Chamber shall accept the request if the case raises a serious question affecting the interpretation or application of the Convention or the Protocols thereto, or a serious issue of general importance.
(3) If the panel accepts the request, the Grand Chamber shall decide the case by means of a judgment.

Article 44. (1) The judgment of the Grand Chamber shall be final.
(2) The judgment of a Chamber shall become final
(a) when the parties declare that they will not request that the case be referred to the Grand Chamber; or

(b) three months after the date of the judgment, if reference of the case to the Grand Chamber has not been requested; or

(c) when the panel of the Grand Chamber rejects the request to refer under Article 43.

(3) The final judgment shall be pub-lished.

Article 45. (1) Reasons shall be given for judgments as well as for decisions declaring applications admissible or inadmissible.

(2) If a judgment does not represent, in whole or in part, the unanimous opinion of the judges, any judge shall be entitled to deliver a separate opinion.

Article 46. (1). The High Contracting Parties under-take to abide by the final judgment of the Court in any case to which they are parties.

(2) The final judgment of the Court shall be transmitted to the Committee of Ministers, which shall supervise its execution.

(3) If the Committee of Ministers considers that the supervision of the execution of a final judgment is hindered by a problem of interpretation of the judgment, it may refer the matter to the Court for a ruling on the question of

interpretation. A referral decision shall require a majority vote of two thirds of the representatives entitled to sit on the Committee.

(4) If the Committee of Ministers considers that a High Contracting Party refuses to abide by a final judgment in a case to which it is a party, it may, after serving formal notice on that Party and by decision adopted by a majority vote of two-thirds of the representatives entitled to sit on the Committee, refer to the Court the question whether that Party has failed to fulfil its obligation under paragraph (1).

(5) If the Court finds a violation of paragraph (1), it shall refer the case to the Committee of Ministers for consideration of the measures to be taken. If the Court finds no violation of paragraph (1), it shall refer the case to the Committee of Ministers, which shall close its examination of the case.

Article 47. (1) The Court may, at the request of the Committee of Ministers, give advisory opinions on legal questions concerning the interpretation of the Convention and the Protocols thereto.

(2) Such opinions shall not deal with any question relating to the content or scope of the rights or freedoms defined in Section I of the Convention and the Protocols thereto, or with any other question which the Court or the Committee of Ministers might have to consider in consequence of any such proceedings as could be instituted in accordance with the Convention.

(3) Decisions of the Committee of Ministers to request an advisory opinion of the Court shall require a majority vote of the representatives entitled to sit on the Committee.

Article 48. The Court shall decide whether a request for an advisory opinion submitted by the Committee of Ministers is within its competence as defined in Article 47.

Article 49. (1) Reasons shall be given for advisory opinions of the Court.
(2) If the advisory opinion does not represent, in whole or in part, the unanimous opinion of the judges, any judge shall be entitled to deliver a separate opinion.
(3) Advisory opinions of the Court shall be communicated to the Committee of Ministers.

Article 50. The expenditure on the Court shall be borne by the Council of Europe.

Article 51. The judges shall be entitled, during the exercise of their functions, to the privileges and immunities provided for in Article 40 of the Statute of the Council of Europe and in the agreements made thereunder.

Article 52. On receipt of a request from the Secretary General of the Council of Europe any High Contracting Party shall furnish an explanation of the manner in which its internal law ensures the effective implementation of any of the provisions of the Convention.

Article 53. Nothing in this Convention shall be construed as limiting or derogating from any of the human rights and fundamental freedoms which may be ensured under the laws of any High Contracting Party or under any other agreement to which it is a party.

Article 54. Nothing in this Convention shall prejudice the powers conferred on the Committee of Ministers by the Statute of the Council of Europe.

Article 55. The High Contracting Parties agree that, except by special agreement, they will not avail themselves of treaties, conventions or declarations in force between them for the purpose of submitting, by way of petition, a dispute arising out of the interpretation or application of this Convention to a means of settlement other than those provided for in this Convention.

Article 56. (1) Any State may at the time of its ratification or at any time thereafter declare by notification addressed to the Secretary General of the Council of Europe that the present Convention shall, subject to paragraph (4) of this Article, extend to all or any of the territories for whose international relations it is responsible.

(2) The Convention shall extend to the territory or territories named in the notification as from the thirtieth day after the receipt of this notification by the Secretary General of the Council of Europe.

(3) The provisions of this Convention shall be applied in such territories with due regard, however, to local requirements.

(4) Any State which has made a declaration in accordance with para-graph 1 of this Article may at any time thereafter declare on behalf of one or more of the territories to which the declaration relates that it accepts the competence of the Court to receive applications from individuals, non-governmental organisations or groups of individuals as provided by Article 34 of the Convention.

Article 57. (1) Any State may, when signing this Convention or when depositing its instrument of ratification, make a reservation in respect of any particular provision of the Convention to the extent that any law then in force in its territory is not in conformity with the provision. Reservations of a general character shall not be permitted under this Article.

(2) Any reservation made under this Article shall contain a brief statement of the law concerned.

Article 58. (1) A High Contracting Party may denounce the present Convention only after the expiry of five years from the date on which it became a party to it and after six months' notice contained in a notification addressed to the Secretary General of the Council of Europe, who shall inform the other High Contracting Parties.

(2) Such a denunciation shall not have the effect of releasing the High
Contracting Party concerned from its obligations under this Convention in respect of any act which, being capable of constituting a violation of such obligations, may have been performed by it before the date at which the denunciation became effective.

(3) Any High Contracting Party which shall cease to be a member of the Council of Europe shall cease to be a party to this Convention under the same conditions.

(4) The Convention may be denounced in accordance with the provisions of the preceding paragraphs in respect of any territory to which it has been declared to extend under the terms of Article 56.

Article 59. (1) This Convention shall be open to the signature of the members of the Council of Europe. It shall be ratified. Ratifications shall be deposited with the Secretary General of the Council of Europe.

(2) The European Union may accede to this Convention.

(3) The present Convention shall come into force after the deposit of ten instruments of ratification.

(4) As regards any signatory ratifying subsequently, the Convention shall come into force at the date of the deposit of its instrument of ratification.

(5) The Secretary General of the Council of Europe shall notify all the members of the Council of Europe of the entry into force of the Convention, the names of the High Contracting Parties who have ratified it, and the deposit of all instruments of ratification which may be effected subsequently.

26 PROTOCOLS TO THE ECHR[2]

Protocol No. 1 to the Convention for the Protection of Human Rights and Fundamental Freedoms. Paris, 20 March 1952.

The governments signatory hereto, being members of the Council of Europe,
Being resolved to take steps to ensure the collective enforcement of certain rights and freedoms other than those already included in Section I of the Convention for the Protection of Human Rights and Fundamental Freedoms signed at Rome on 4 November 1950 (hereinafter referred to as 'the Convention'),
Have agreed as follows:

Article 1. Every natural or legal person is entitled to the peaceful enjoyment of his possessions. No one shall be deprived of his possessions except in the public interest and subject to the conditions provided for by law and by the general principles of international law.
The preceding provisions shall not, however, in any way impair the right of a State to enforce such laws as it deems necessary to control the use of property in accordance with the general interest or to secure the payment of taxes or other contributions or penalties.

Article 2. No person shall be denied the right to education. In the exercise of any functions which it assumes in relation to education and to teaching, the State shall respect the right of parents to ensure such education and teaching in conformity with their own religious and philosophical convictions.

Article 3. The High Contracting Parties undertake to hold free elections at reasonable intervals by secret ballot, under conditions which will ensure the free expression of the opinion of the people in the choice of the legislature.

[Articles 4 – 6 are omitted.]

Protocol No. 4 to the Convention for the Protection of Human Rights and Fundamental Freedoms securing certain rights and freedoms other than those already included in the Convention and in the first Protocol thereto. Strasbourg, 16 September 1963.
[The Preamble is omitted.]

---

2 Selected Protocols and provisions: Protocol No. 1, articles 1-3; Protocol No. 4, articles 1-4; Protocol No. 6, articles 1 and 2; Protocol No. 7, articles 1-5; Protocol No. 12, article 1; Protocol No. 13, article 1; Protocol No. 15, articles 1-9; Protocol No. 16.

Article 1. No one shall be deprived of his liberty merely on the ground of inability to fulfil a contractual obligation.

Article 2. (1) Everyone lawfully within the territory of a State shall, within that territory, have the right to liberty of movement and freedom to choose his residence.
(2) Everyone shall be free to leave any country, including his own.
(3) No restrictions shall be placed on the exercise of these rights other than such as are in accordance with law and are necessary in a democratic society in the interests of national security or public safety, for the maintenance of ordre public, for the prevention of crime, for the protection of health or morals, or for the protection of the rights and freedoms of others.
(4) The rights set forth in paragraph (1) may also be subject, in particular areas, to restrictions imposed in accordance with law and justified by the public interest in a democratic society.

Article 3. (1) No one shall be expelled, by means either of an individual or of a collective measure, from the territory of the State of which he is a national.
(2) No one shall be deprived of the right to enter the territory of the state of which he is a national.

Article 4. Collective expulsion of aliens is prohibited.

[*Articles 5 – 7 are omitted.*]

Protocol No. 6 to the Convention for the Protection of Human Rights and Fundamental Freedoms concerning the abolition of the death penalty. Strasbourg, 28 April 1983.

[*The Preamble is omitted.*]

Article 1. The death penalty shall be abolished. No-one shall be condemned to such penalty or executed.

Article 2. A State may make provision in its law for the death penalty in respect of acts committed in time of war or of imminent threat of war; such penalty shall be applied only in the instances laid down in the law and in accordance with its provisions. The State shall communicate to the Secretary General of the Council of Europe the relevant provisions of that law.

[*Articles 3 – 9 are omitted.*]

Protocol No. 7 to the Convention for the Protection of Human Rights and Fundamental Freedoms. Strasbourg, 22 November 1984.
[*The Preamble is omitted.*]

Article 1. (1) An alien lawfully resident in the territory of a State shall not be expelled therefrom except in pursuance of a decision reached in accordance with law and shall be allowed:
(a) to submit reasons against his expulsion,
(b) to have his case reviewed, and
(c) to be represented for these purposes before the competent authority or a person or persons designated by that authority.
(2) An alien may be expelled before the exercise of his rights under paragraph (1)(a), (b) and (c) of this Article, when such expulsion is necessary in the interests of public order or is grounded on reasons of national security.

Article 2. (1) Everyone convicted of a criminal offence by a tribunal shall have the right to have his conviction or sentence reviewed by a higher tribunal. The exercise of this right, including the grounds on which it may be exercised, shall be governed by law.
(2) This right may be subject to exceptions in regard to offences of a minor character, as prescribed by law, or in cases in which the person concerned was tried in the first instance by the highest tribunal or was convicted following an appeal against acquittal.

Article 3. When a person has by a final decision been convicted of a criminal offence and when subsequently his conviction has been reversed, or he has been pardoned, on the ground that a new or newly discovered fact shows conclusively that there has been a miscarriage of justice, the
person who has suffered punishment as a result of such conviction shall be compensated according to the law or the practice of the State concerned, unless it is proved that the non-disclosure of the unknown fact in time is wholly or partly attributable to him.

Article 4. (1) No one shall be liable to be tried or punished again in criminal proceedings under the jurisdiction of the same State for an offence for which he has already been finally acquitted or convicted in accordance with the law and penal procedure of that State.
(2) The provisions of the preceding paragraph shall not prevent the reopening of the case in accordance with the law and penal procedure of the State concerned, if there is evidence of new or newly discovered facts, or if there has been a fundamental defect in the previous proceedings, which could affect the outcome of the case.
(3) No derogation from this Article shall be made under Article 15 of the Convention.

Article 5. Spouses shall enjoy equality of rights and responsibilities of a private law character between them, and in their relations with their children, as to marriage, during marriage and in the event of its dissolution. This Article shall not prevent States from taking such measures as are
necessary in the interests of the children.

[*Articles 6 – 10 are omitted.*]

Protocol No. 12 to the Convention for the Protection of Human Rights and Fundamental Freedoms. Rome, 4 November 2000.
[*The Preamble is omitted.*]

Article 1. (1) The enjoyment of any right set forth by law shall be secured without discrimination on any ground such as sex, race, colour, language, religion, political or other opinion, national or social origin, association with a national minority, property, birth or other status.
(2) No one shall be discriminated against by any public authority on any ground such as those mentioned in paragraph (1).

[*Articles 2 – 6 are omitted.*]

Protocol No. 13 to the Convention for the Protection of Human Rights and Fundamental Freedoms Concerning the abolition of the death penalty in all circumstances. Vilnius, 3 May 2002.
[*The Preamble is omitted.*]

Article 1. The death penalty shall be abolished. No one shall be condemned to such penalty or executed.

[*Articles 2 – 8 are omitted.*]

Protocol No. 15 amending the Convention on the Protection of Human Rights and Fundamental Freedoms. Strasbourg, 24 June 2013.[3]

---

3   Protocol No. 15 will enter into force upon ratification by all High Contracting Parties. On the copy date of the present volume (May 2019), two of the High Contracting Parties, Italy and Bosnia and Herzegovina, had not yet ratified the Protocol.

*The member States of the Council of Europe and the other High Contracting Parties to the Convention for the Protection of Human Rights and Fundamental Freedoms, signed at Rome on 4 November 1950 (hereinafter referred to as "the Convention"), signatory hereto,
Having regard to the declaration adopted at the High Level Conference on the Future of the European Court of Human Rights, held in Brighton on 19 and 20 April 2012, as well as the declarations adopted at the conferences held in Interlaken on 18 and 19 February 2010 and ??zmir on 26 and 27 April 2011;
Having regard to Opinion No. 283 (2013) adopted by the Parliamentary Assembly of the Council of Europe on 26 April 2013;
Considering the need to ensure that the European Court of Human Rights (hereinafter referred to as "the Court") can continue to play its pre-eminent role in protecting human rights in Europe,
Have agreed as follows:*

Article 1. At the end of the preamble to the Convention, a new recital shall be added, which shall read as follows:

> "Affirming that the High Contracting Parties, in accordance with the principle of subsidiarity, have the primary responsibility to secure the rights and freedoms defined in this Convention and the Protocols thereto, and that in doing so they enjoy a margin of appreciation, subject to the supervisory jurisdiction of the European Court of Human Rights established by this Convention,"

Article 2. (1) In Article 21 of the Convention, a new paragraph (2) shall be inserted, which shall read as follows:

> "Candidates shall be less than 65 years of age at the date by which the list of three candidates has been requested by the Parliamentary Assembly, further to Article 22."

(2) Paragraphs (2) and (3) of Article 21 of the Convention shall become paragraphs (3) and (4) of Article 21 respectively.
(3) Paragraph (2) of Article 23 of the Convention shall be deleted. Paragraphs (3) and (4) of Article 23 shall become paragraphs (2) and (3) of Article 23 respectively.

Article 3. In Article 30 of the Convention, the words "unless one of the parties to the case objects" shall be deleted.

Article 4. In Article 35, paragraph (1) of the Convention, the words "within a period of six months" shall be replaced by the words "within a period of four months".

Article 5. In Article 35, paragraph (3), sub-paragraph (b) of the Convention, the words "and provided that no case may be rejected on this ground which has not been duly considered by a domestic tribunal" shall be deleted.
Final and transitional provisions

Article 6. (1) This Protocol shall be open for signature by the High Contracting Parties to the Convention, which may express their consent to be bound by:
(a) signature without reservation as to ratification, acceptance or approval; or
(b) signature subject to ratification, acceptance or approval, followed by ratification, acceptance or approval.
(2) The instruments of ratification, acceptance or approval shall be deposited with the Secretary General of the Council of Europe.

Article 7. This Protocol shall enter into force on the first day of the month following the expiration of a period of three months after the date on which all High Contracting Parties to the Convention have expressed their consent to be bound by the Protocol, in accordance with the provisions of Article 6.

Article 8. (1) The amendments introduced by Article 2 of this Protocol shall apply only to candidates on lists submitted to the Parliamentary Assembly by the High Contracting Parties under Article 22 of the Convention after the entry into force of this Protocol.
(2) The amendment introduced by Article 3 of this Protocol shall not apply to any pending case in which one of the parties has objected, prior to the date of entry into force of this Protocol, to a proposal by a Chamber of the Court to relinquish jurisdiction in favour of the Grand Chamber.
(3) Article 4 of this Protocol shall enter into force following the expiration of a period of six months after the date of entry into force of this Protocol. Article 4 of this Protocol shall not apply to applications in respect of which the final decision within the meaning of Article 35, paragraph (1) of the Convention was taken prior to the date of entry into force of Article 4 of this Protocol.
(4) All other provisions of this Protocol shall apply from its date of entry into force, in accordance with the provisions of Article 7.

Article 9. The Secretary General of the Council of Europe shall notify the member States of the Council of Europe and the other High Contracting Parties to the Convention of:
(a) any signature;
(b) the deposit of any instrument of ratification, acceptance or approval;
(c) the date of entry into force of this Protocol in accordance with Article 7; and
(d) any other act, notification or communication relating to this Protocol.

Protocol No. 16 to the Convention on the Protection of Human Rights and Fundamental Freedoms. Strasbourg, 2 October 2013.

The member States of the Council of Europe and other High Contracting Parties to the Convention for the Protection of Human Rights and Fundamental Freedoms, signed at Rome on 4 November 1950 (hereinafter referred to as "the Convention"), signatories hereto,

Having regard to the provisions of the Convention and, in particular, Article 19 establishing the European Court of Human Rights (hereinafter referred to as "the Court");

Considering that the extension of the Court's competence to give advisory opinions will further enhance the interaction between the Court and national authorities and thereby reinforce implementation of the Convention, in accordance with the principle of subsidiarity;

Having regard to Opinion No. 285 (2013) adopted by the Parliamentary Assembly of the Council of Europe on 28 June 2013,

Have agreed as follows:

Article 1. (1) Highest courts and tribunals of a High Contracting Party, as specified in accordance with Article 10, may request the Court to give advisory opinions on questions of principle relating to the interpretation or application of the rights and freedoms defined in the Convention or the protocols thereto.

(2) The requesting court or tribunal may seek an advisory opinion only in the context of a case pending before it.

(3) The requesting court or tribunal shall give reasons for its request and shall provide the relevant legal and factual background of the pending case.

Article 2. (1) A panel of five judges of the Grand Chamber shall decide whether to accept the request for an advisory opinion, having regard to Article 1. The panel shall give reasons for any refusal to accept the request.

(2) If the panel accepts the request, the Grand Chamber shall deliver the advisory opinion.

(3) The panel and the Grand Chamber, as referred to in the preceding paragraphs, shall include ex officio the judge elected in respect of the High Contracting Party to which the requesting court or tribunal pertains. If there is none or if that judge is unable to sit, a person chosen by the President of the Court from a list submitted in advance by that Party shall sit in the capacity of judge.

Article 3. The Council of Europe Commissioner for Human Rights and the High Contracting Party to which the requesting court or tribunal pertains shall have the right to submit written comments and take part in any hearing. The President of the Court may, in the interest of the proper administration of justice, invite any other High Contracting Party or person also to submit written comments or take part in any hearing.

Article 4. (1) Reasons shall be given for advisory opinions.
(2) If the advisory opinion does not represent, in whole or in part, the unanimous opinion of the judges, any judge shall be entitled to deliver a separate opinion.
(3) Advisory opinions shall be communicated to the requesting court or tribunal and to the High Contracting Party to which that court or tribunal pertains.
(4) Advisory opinions shall be published.

Article 5. Advisory opinions shall not be binding.

Article 6. As between the High Contracting Parties the provisions of Articles 1 to 5 of this Protocol shall be regarded as additional articles to the Convention, and all the provisions of the Convention shall apply accordingly.

Article 7. (1) This Protocol shall be open for signature by the High Contracting Parties to the Convention, which may express their consent to be bound by:
(a) signature without reservation as to ratification, acceptance or approval; or
(b) signature subject to ratification, acceptance or approval, followed by ratification, acceptance or approval.
(2) The instruments of ratification, acceptance or approval shall be deposited with the Secretary General of the Council of Europe.

Article 8. (1) This Protocol shall enter into force on the first day of the month following the expiration of a period of three months after the date on which ten High Contracting Parties to the Convention have expressed their consent to be bound by the Protocol in accordance with the provisions of Article 7.
(2) In respect of any High Contracting Party to the Convention which subsequently expresses its consent to be bound by it, the Protocol shall enter into force on the first day of the month following the expiration of a period of three months after the date of the expression of its consent to be bound by the Protocol in accordance with the provisions of Article 7.

Article 9. No reservation may be made under Article 57 of the Convention in respect of the provisions of this Protocol.

Article 10. Each High Contracting Party to the Convention shall, at the time of signature or when depositing its instrument of ratification, acceptance or approval, by means of a declaration addressed to the Secretary General of the Council of Europe, indicate the courts or tribunals that it designates for the purposes of Article 1, paragraph (1), of this Protocol. This declaration may be modified at any later date and in the same manner.

Article 11. The Secretary General of the Council of Europe shall notify the member States of the Council of Europe and the other High Contracting Parties to the Convention of:
(a) any signature;
(b) the deposit of any instrument of ratification, acceptance or approval;
(c) any date of entry into force of this Protocol in accordance with Article 8;
(d) any declaration made in accordance with Article 10; and
(e) any other act, notification or communication relating to this Protocol.

In witness whereof the undersigned, being duly authorised thereto, have signed this Protocol.

Done at Strasbourg, this 2nd day of October 2013, in English and French, both texts being equally authentic, in a single copy which shall be deposited in the archives of the Council of Europe. The Secretary General of the Council of Europe shall transmit certified copies to each member State of the Council of Europe and to the other High Contracting Parties to the Convention.